"…useful for ideas about at-home jobs as well as job leads."
— *Good Housekeeping*

"…excellent reference book."
— *Parents* Magazine

"…if you want a job at home, get *The Work at Home Sourcebook.*"
— *Woman's Day*

"Lynie Arden is sending office workers home."
— *USA Today*

"The perfect prelude to a telecommuting job search...a comprehensive classic."
— *Home Office Computing* — *American Reference Books Annual*

"…a neat package…"
— *The Salt Lake Tribune*

"…don't have a clue about how to get started? Check out *The Work at Home Sourcebook.*"
— *Working Mother* Magazine

"…[this] book shows you how to move your work home."
— *Knight-Ridder*

"…an excellent reference to getting a job that lets you work at home…"
— *The Secretary* Magazine

"…eye-opening, I'd even say inspiring…"
— *Whole Earth Review*

"…one of the best books on the market on this subject…"
— *Small Press Reviews*

"I recommend it most enthusiastically; compliments to author Lynie Arden for a job well done."
— R.H. Hoffman, WNWK TV

"Arden has done her homework—literally and figuratively."
— *Spokane Chronicle*

The Work at Home Sourcebook

Tenth Edition

Lynie Arden

Live Oak Publications
Lakeville, Minnesota

ISBN: 978-0-911781-20-5

Cover image:
Young couple sitting on sofa, using laptops © Nyul. Image from istockphotos.com
Work From Home © Bonnie Jacobs. Image from istockphotos.com

The Work-at Home-Sourcebook, 10th Edition
By Lynie Arden

Live Oak Publications
An Imprint of Finney Company
8075 215th Street West
Lakeville, Minnesota 55044
www.finneyco.com

Printed in the United States of America

TABLE OF CONTENTS

1. How to Go to Work From Your Home *1*

2. Home Business Opportunities *10*

3. Markets for Handcrafts *134*

4. Telecommuting and Other Employee Options................*152*

5. Learning at Home to Work at Home *180*

6. Getting a Home-based Job, Step-by-Step........................*189*

7. Opportunities in the Arts..*196*

8. Opportunities in Computers *217*

9. Opportunities in Miscellaneous *244*

10. Opportunities in Office Support Positions....................*263*

11. Opportunities in Sales..*308*

12. Opportunities Working With People.............................*341*

HOW TO GO TO WORK FROM YOUR HOME

Personnel manager Pat Mahy wasn't looking for a job at home, but when Escrow Overload asked her to give it a try, she said okay.

"Starting out, I had my doubts. I couldn't imagine being without the stimulation of other people at work. It had some appeal, though. I figured my time might be better spent if I wasn't wasting it commuting. Well, I was thrilled within a week!"

Pat is one of the 65 million Americans who currently work at home, a number that is growing by a whopping 600,000 per year. Some government studies have indicated that as much as 75% of the work done in this country will be moved home by 2010.

Not everyone would be happy working at home, of course, and many people are simply not interested in moving their work home. Still, more and more people are having the same experience as Pat Mahy, who says "I'm still finding more hidden benefits to working at home the longer I do it."

Using This Book

If you want to try working at home, this book is a good place to start. It won't teach you how to start a home business from scratch, nor will it duplicate certain other work-at-home topics that are well covered in other books. As far as we know, though, nowhere else can you find as many specific opportunities for working at home assembled into one neat package.

A Wide Range of Possibilities

You'll quickly notice that there are a variety of work styles represented in this book. Once you leave the confines of the traditional nine-to-five centralized work mode, a colorful rainbow of employment options appear. There is freelancing, independent contracting, working on commission, salaried positions, and various combinations of these and other ways of working. You can get paid by the hour, by the piece, by the sale, by the project, or by the year.

You'll want to consider your needs carefully. Do you need the security of a salary? If so, freelancing is not for you. Have you always wished you could get paid for what you produce because you do it faster and better than almost everybody else? Then you may be able to boost your income by opting for piece rates. Alternately, you might want to be able to depend on a set salary, yet have lots of opportunities for earning more than the base rate by earning commissions, bonuses, or other incentives. Telemarketing and market research positions, for example, often offer this type of compensation package.

One other point needs to be made about salaries. In comparing the salaries (and other forms of compensation) offered for working at home to those of conventional employment, be sure to take into consideration the many savings you'll enjoy by working at home. The money you'll save on clothing, commuting, parking, lunches, and other items may make it worthwhile for you to take a home-based job that, on the surface at least, offers less money than you would make going into an office every day.

Opportunities Everywhere

You'll find over 1,000 companies in this book that have work-at-home arrangements, but it's important to keep in mind that these listings represent only a small sample of the work-at-home opportunities actually available today. This book will be most valuable to you if you use it as an idea generator.

Suppose, for example, that in skimming through the company listings you notice there are a number of medical billing jobs at home. You had a job doing the billing for a GP for several years and feel confident you could do the work, but for one reason or another none of the specific jobs in the listings are exactly right for your situation.

By all means don't be discouraged. Study the job listings carefully, noting the names of the companies, their pay structure, how many home workers they employ and other pertinent information. Then go talk to hospitals, clinics, and doctors in your town. They may never have considered hiring home workers before but if you can explain how other medical groups have organized their home work programs—and the benefits they are getting from their programs—you'll have a good chance at getting exactly the work you want.

Some of the benefits you'll want to mention are the following (and they're not limited to medical groups):

Increased Productivity

A 20% increase in productivity is average, with some employers reporting substantially more than that. Some dedicated telecommuters have reported up to an 80% increase over their office-bound counterparts.

Lower Turnover

Once settled into a home-based job, would you give it up? Turnover among home-working employees is so low, some companies have waiting lists up to a year long for new applicants.

Near Zero Absenteeism

Flexiplace usually means flexitime, too. Work schedules can be manipulated to accommodate child-care needs, fevers and sniffles, and yes, an occasional case of playing hooky on a beautiful spring day. As long as the work gets done within the overall time limits of the job, everyone's happy.

Improved Recruiting

In areas with low unemployment, flexiplace is often used as an added inducement to potential employees. This is especially true for fields like computer programming where demand for highly qualified workers often exceeds supply. Several years ago, Continental Illinois Bank had a problem finding qualified secretaries in the Chicago area. They reasoned that many competent women were at home with children and were therefore unable to participate in the job market. The bank started Project HomeWork to solve the problem.

Lower Costs

Many companies start homework programs when they run out of room for expansion and don't want to tie up additional capital in office space. Insurance, utilities, training, maintenance and other costs often go down when workers go home.

Home Work and the Law

There are two areas of the law that directly affect home workers; labor laws and zoning ordinances.

Labor Laws

Only a handful of states have labor laws specifically regarding working at home. In each case, their purpose is to govern "industrial home work" (work which would normally be done in a factory such as product assembly). Industrial homework is usually low skilled, low pay work in which there has been a history of worker exploitation. The purpose of the state labor laws is to ensure worker safety and ensure that minimum wage requirements are met. States without labor laws specifically relating to homework fall under the jurisdiction of the U.S. Dept. of Labor and its Fair Labor Standards Act of 1938 (FLSA).

The FLSA initially prohibited seven industries from using home workers. In 1938, this was a good idea since sweatshop conditions were the established norm. In December, 1984, after years of see-sawing through the courts, the ban on knitted outerwear was lifted. The remaining prohibited industries were: gloves and mittens, belts and buckles, jewelry, women's apparel, embroidery, and handkerchiefs.

Senator Orrin Hatch introduced the Freedom of the Workplace bill (S.665) soon after the ban on knitted outerwear was lifted. It calls for the complete reversal of the FLSA restrictions on homework. As written, workers' rights would be protected by the same certification process that is required for home knitters.

Congresswoman Olympia Snowe of Maine introduced a similar bill, the Home Employment Enterprise Act (HR2815) in the House of Representatives. It was virtually the House twin of Hatch's bill. Congresswoman Snowe told the House, "Cottage industries play a vital role in the economy of the state of Maine, large parts of New England, and other areas of the nation. The independent nature of homework and the unavailability of alternative employment opportunities make working at home ideal. It is time to safeguard the freedom to choose to work at home."

Before either bill came up for a vote, prohibitions on industrial homework in five of the six industries were lifted by the U.S. Dept. of Labor, effective January 9, 1989. New, tougher enforcement requirements went into effect at the same time.

Ann McLaughlin, Secretary of Labor, said "Workforce flexibility is a critical element of our effort to create jobs, enhance the quality of work life for American workers and improve our competitive edge in world markets. The changing workforce demographics demand that we provide employment opportunities that allow workers the freedom to choose flexible alternatives including the ability to work in one's own home. Women, for example, have entered the workforce by the millions; homework adds a measure of worker flexibility and economic freedom.

"At a time when flexibility is an operational imperative to our competitive advantage, government should enhance, not impede, workers' choices," McLaughlin added.

There is only one industry the FLSA still prohibits from using home workers: women's apparel. This omission was apparently an attempt on behalf of the DOL to avoid direct confrontation with its most active opponent in this action, The International Ladies Garment Workers Union. Aside from the prohibition mentioned here, there are no other occupations covered by labor laws. Furthermore, these laws only pertain to employees, not independent contractors, independent business people, or otherwise self-employed workers.

Zoning

Before working at home in any capacity, you should find out what your local zoning ordinance has to say about it. If you live in a rural area, chances are good that you have nothing to worry about. In populated areas, however, there are often specific provisions in the zoning laws pertaining to home occupations.

Zoning laws tend to focus on the impact of a given activity. Sometimes called "nuisance laws," they are designed to protect neighborhoods from disruptive noise, traffic, odors, etc.

Chicago is an extreme example. Until recently, within the city limits, it was illegal to use electrical equipment in a home occupation. That meant no calculators, no typewriters, no computers. The laws were outdated in Chicago and are still too often outdated elsewhere around the country. It took public pressure to get the city council in Chicago to adopt a new ordinance that would be more accommodating to homework, and it is possible for you to initiate zoning changes in your city, too.

Zoning boards are made up of your neighbors and local business people, and it is likely they are unaware of problems caused by outdated zoning ordinances. If you are frustrated by your city's zoning code, get to know these people, attend some meetings, and propose that the laws be changed.

Independent Contractor Status and Tax Savings

More often than not, home workers are paid as independent contractors. In essence, this means you are totally responsible for your own work. While different government agencies don't necessarily agree on the definition of independent contractor, generally speaking, there are two major factors affecting how home workers are classified. They are the "degree of control which the employer exercises over the manner in which the work is performed," and "opportunities for profit and loss."

It should be noted that no government agency will take you on your word that you are an independent contractor. Even if you have a written contract with a company declaring that you both agree to an employer/independent contractor relationship, the legitimacy of that relationship must be proven.

The issue here is not whether being an employee is better or worse than being an independent contractor. There are advantages and disadvantages in every situation. Rather, the issue is whether the term "independent contractor" is being applied consistently and correctly. If you meet all I.R.S. criteria for independent contractor status, you'll be responsible for your own taxes, most notably Social Security tax, which is renamed "Self-Employment Tax" for this purpose.

Business expenses will help you at tax time, so you need to keep records right from the start of any and all expenditures. Business expenses generally fall into two categories: direct and indirect.

Direct expenses are those that occur in the day-to-day operation of your business. Costs for office supplies, phone service, advertising, bookkeeping, equipment, books, trade publications and seminars related to your work, and insurance are all examples of direct, fully deductible expenses.

You shouldn't forget the more subtle types of deductions, either. Entertainment in the course of your work, whether in your own home or not, is ordinarily deductible (at least a certain percentage of it anyway) if you discuss or conduct business while you're entertaining and keep a record of what went on and with whom.

The same thing is true for vacations. You can generally write off a portion of your vacation expenses if you spend some time along the way looking for new business. Remember, the government expects you to try to expand your business.

Indirect expenses are those that are a part of your usual domestic bills— utilities, rent or mortgage payments, maintenance and housecleaning, property insurance, etc. Indirect expenses come under the heading of the Home Office Deduction.

The Home Office Deduction is the most common and significant way for home workers to reduce their federal tax. In order to claim the deduction, you must show that your homework space is used regularly and exclusively as your principal place of business and meeting place. (If you are a salaried employee, you may also be eligible if you can prove that your employer requires you to keep a home office as a condition of employment. In this case, you should consult an expert to determine if you meet the requirements.)

Home office expenses are deductible at the rate of whatever percentage of square footage your workspace takes up. If your home is 1,000 square feet and you use 200 square feet exclusively for workspace, you can normally deduct 20% of those receipts. A word of caution: if you use your workspace for any other purpose than work, you cannot deduct any of these expenses. Therefore, working on the kitchen table is a bad idea unless you really don't have any choice.

At last count, there were some 23 possible deductions for a home office. To make sure you don't miss any, get a copy of I.R.S. Publication 587, "Business Use of the Home." It is available free from any I.R.S. office and is updated annually.

Making the Most of Working at Home

If you persevere in your efforts to land a home job, in time you're likely to succeed. Your home work space is where you will be spending a large portion of your life—in fact, you will most likely spend more time there than any other place. The consideration you give to its design could have a tremendous impact on the success of your homework experience.

Wouldn't it be wonderful to have a work place all your own, some private space free from distractions? A beautiful office maybe, with a separate entrance, big windows facing out onto a garden, with elegant furniture and the latest equipment modern technology has to offer. Fortunately, dreaming is free.

You may have to start out on the kitchen table or in a corner of the living room. Millions have started the same way and that's okay—for a while. To make the most out of working at home, though, you'll need to begin planning ways to make your working space more comfortable, efficient and permanent.

Five elements directly affect mental attitude and productivity in every workspace: light, sound, furniture, air quality, and color.

Proper lighting is essential to the good health of any worker. It has been conclusively demonstrated that improper or inadequate light has varying degrees of negative effects on people. At the very least, it can cause significant decreases in productivity. Some people have more serious reactions, including long-term bouts with depression.

Adequate overall lighting is not necessarily optimal lighting. Care should be taken to reduce glare from both direct and indirect sources. Whether light is reflected from a bright window or from a computer monitor, glare can cause eyestrain and headaches. You can usually solve glare problems by moving your furniture around, changing the type and strength of your light bulbs, or installing screens over windows and monitors.

Sound doesn't usually have the same impact on the work place as light, but it is an important factor to consider. Noise can come from traffic, children and lawnmowers outside and appliances, children, pets, and your own work equipment inside, causing distraction and lower productivity. You can install sound absorbing material to reduce noise or you can attempt to mask the noise with neutral sounds (white noise) or with music. Most electronics stores sell white noise generators.

The right furniture can also make a difference in your work performance and satisfaction. The type of work surface you need depends on the type of work you're doing, but in any case it doesn't have to be fancy or expensive. What is important is that the surface be large enough to suit the task, that the height is right for you, and that it is sturdy enough to hold your equipment without wobbling.

A good chair is definitely worth the investment. It should provide ample back support, thereby reducing fatigue and backaches. Features such as adjustable back tension, an easily adjusted height mechanism and rollers will make your life easier, too. If you work with a keyboard, even for short periods of time, don't get a chair with armrests. Armrests can prevent you from getting close enough to the edge, with resulting aches and pains in your back, neck and shoulders.

Air quality and temperature can also have a major impact on your physical comfort. Ideally, you want fresh, clean air no warmer than 75 degrees or cooler than 68 degrees. Indoor pollution can be caused by lack of ventilation, especially with highly weatherized homes. Pollution sources include carpets, upholstery, stoves, aerosols and cleaning fluids, to name only a few. In addition, there are few jobs that don't involve their own polluting substances. Correction fluid, hobby and craft supplies, paint, glue, and lint are examples.

The best way to clean up your indoor air is with ventilation. Plants help, too. Certain common houseplants, such as Spider Plants, gobble up indoor toxins. Electric air filters can help, too. They cost more than plants, but require less care. Negative ion generators are especially helpful in the presence of electronic equipment such as computers.

Color is the final factor, which you should consider. It can set the overall tone of your workspace and make it a place you want to be—or a place you'd rather avoid.

White and very light colors aren't stimulating, but do reflect the most light, making a space appear larger than it is. Blacks, browns, and grays make a space appear smaller than it is, absorbing light and creating feelings of fatigue. Blues and greens are relaxing, feel cool, and reduce blood pressure. Reds, oranges, and yellows are bright, stimulating, cheerful, and warm. With too strong a contrast, however, they can cause irritability and increased blood pressure.

Carefully choosing the color scheme and other aspects of your workspace can make a big difference in your productivity as well as how you feel about your work. It's usually not necessary to spend a lot of money to make your work place pleasant; just use some imagination and take the time to think through how you can make the most of the space that's available to you.

HOME BUSINESS OPPORTUNITIES

——AUTOMOTIVE——

Automotive services, particularly in the after-market, have always comprised a huge industry. That hasn't changed. What has changed is the need to have all automotive services performed at centralized locations. More and more opportunities are opening up to home-based entrepreneurs, mostly through mobile services.

In this section you will find a variety of opportunities to make a good income taking care of cars. Auto detailing, one of the most popular business opportunities, is now a $2.5 billion industry. Its popularity among new entrepreneurs is based on the assumption that anyone can clean a car, even if this is the ultimate car wash. And it's true. Furthermore, it's a business that can be started for under $1,000 and profits can go into six figures annually!

The next step up from detailing is restoration. Restoration services include paint chip repair; paintless dent repair; and the repair and recoloring of vinyl, leather, and plastic parts.

A long, long time ago we were able to get our car oil changed at our friendly neighborhood service station. The word "service" was changed to "gas" and quick lube shops took over the oil and lube responsibilities. Today, you don't even have to leave home to get an oil change. Mobile services will come to you, wherever you are, so all you have to do is make a phone call. This business is more expensive to get into because there is the need for a properly outfitted van, but there is a tremendous opportunity for repeat business which is very appealing.

And finally, glass repair is still growing fast, saving customers time and money over the replacement alternative.

AIRBAG TECHNOLOGY, INC.

9675 SE 36th Street, Suite 100 Mercer Island, WA 98040

www.airbagservice.com

(425) 391-9664

Franchise: Yes.

Description: Mobile airbag replacement and repair servicing the body shop and automotive collision industry.

Requirements: You should have some mechanical experience or aptitude at the least. The standard franchise fee is $25,000. You will also need about $35,000 for van, tools, computer, etc.

Provisions: The fee covers an exclusive territory, three weeks technical training course, proprietary software, live technical support, established business system, national and local marketing and advertising support.

AMSOIL, INC.

925 Tower Ave., Superior, WI 54880

www.amsoil.com

(800) 777-8491

Franchise: No.

Description: AMSOIL manufactures synthetic lubricants and automotive performance products for a wide range of applications including cars, RVs, trucks, ATVs, boats, snowmobiles, and other equipment. This is an opportunity for a dealership.

Requirements: There are no inventory requirements or capital investment in office or warehouse space. The start-up costs range from $50 to $250.

Provisions: Strong support network and company support, marketing and promo materials, and leads. No territory restrictions.

APPEARANCE PLUS, INC.

170 E. Hillsboro Blvd., Deerfield Beach, FL 33441

www.appearance-plus.com

(800) 408-5020 or (954) 596-2112

Franchise: No.

Description: Auto detailing, mobile washing, and waxing of cars, boats, aircraft and RVs.

Requirements: Start as low as $2,000 or go as high as $25,000.

Provisions: Products, equipment, marketing material, the right to use the name as an authorized dealer, ongoing company support, and full training program at the corporate office.

Profit Potential: $50,000 to $100,000 per year.

AUTO APPRAISAL NETWORK

17845 Sky Park Circle, Suite F, Irvine, CA 92614

www.autoappraisalnetwork.com

(800) 454-1313

Franchise: Yes.

Description: Vehicle appraisal service.

Requirements: Total investment ranges from $19,700 to $74,200. The ongoing royal fee is a flat rate of $75-95 per appraisal. Industry experience is required.

Provisions: Training at company headquarters for a week followed by unlimited corporate support in the field. Company provides national media exposure and co-op advertising opportunities, local marketing support, laptop, and digital camera.

Comments: "If you join us, you will not only be actively involved in the Classic, Collector, Custom Car, Show Car, and Street Rod hobby, you will also be recognized and accepted as an expert who makes significant contributions to the profession!"

AUTOPLUS WINDOW STICKERS

12750 Yacht Club Cir., Ft. Myers, FL 33919

www.autoplusnet.com

(800) 825-4838

Franchise: No.

Description: Produce window stickers for used car sales and provide window sticker service to new and used car dealerships.

Requirements: The new introductory software package is $195 and the standard distributor package is $995. For another $1,000, they'll throw in a digital camera and Palm Pilot or handheld computer in the Express package.

Provisions: Distributors get training, technical support, software, tools, and supplies.

CHIPS AWAY

1536 Saw Mill Run Blvd., Pittsburgh, PA 15210

www.chipsaway.com

(800) 837-CHIP

Franchise: No.

Description: A mobile service that provides scratch, scuff, and paint chip repair quickly and easily. Since the Patent Pending process only adheres to primer paint, no masking is necessary. Paint colors are easily and exactly matched for a flawless finish. Send for video if you're interested in this opportunity.

Requirements: The system starts at $6,995 and can go as high as $14,000. Financing is available for up to 48 months.

Provisions: The fee buys complete training and all tools, equipment, and supplies necessary to start the business.

Profit Potential: It is possible to make a six-figure income.

DETAIL PLUS

P.O. Box 20755, Portland, OR 97294

www.detailplus.com

(800) 284-0123

Franchise: No.

Description: Complete turnkey setup for auto detailing and car appearance. All phases of auto detailing and cosmetic car care including windshield repair, paint touch-up, paintless dent repair, 24K gold plating, and vinyl and leather repair.

Requirements: Each service system is sold separately from $500 to $5,000. With start-up expenses, costs will be much higher depending on the size of the workshop.

Provisions: Full development help, installation of equipment, plus management and technical training on-site.

Profit Potential: "Unlimited."

FIBRENEW

Box 33, Site 16, RR8, Calgary, AB, Canada T2J 2T9

www.fibrenew.com

(603) 278-7818

Franchise: Yes.

Description: A service that specializes in repairing plastics and leather in the aviation, automobile, commercial marine, and residential markets.

Requirements: The total investment ranges between $30,000 and $50,000. Must also have a good vehicle because this is a mobile service.

Provisions: The cost covers airfare to Canada, 18 nights accommodations, training, and complete product, equipment, and office package. Ongoing support.

FITZGERALD'S

221 North American St., Stockton, CA 95202

www.fitzgeraldsrestoration.com

(800) 441-3326

Franchise: No.

Description: Automotive interior restoration including the repair and recoloring of vinyl, leather, velour, and plastic parts on the side of vehicles. The typical job takes less then an hour and the work is done on-site right out of the licensee's vehicle.

Requirements: $500 for one subject and $3,000 for complete package of all four subjects (vinyl, leather, velour, and plastic).

Provisions: All licensees receive all of the necessary equipment and chemicals, plus marketing help and sales leads. Five days of training is followed up by a bi-monthly newsletter and unlimited consultation.

Profit Potential: Approximately $1,000 per week or more.

Comments: Fitzgerald's has over 1,500 home-based licensees.

GLASS MECHANIX, INC.

    4881 W. Hacienda Ave., #6 Las Vegas, NV 89118
    www.glassmechanix.com
    (800) 826-8523

Franchise: No.

Description: Windshield repair service.

Requirements: $1,900; financing is available.

Provisions: The fee covers training, machines, and enough materials to repair 500 windshields.

Profit Potential: A windshield takes about 15 minutes to repair, and the average charge is $35. The cost is about 50 cents, so it is possible to earn up to $300 a day in this business.

Comments: This company was started in a two-bedroom condominium in 1982 and now has over 3,000 licensees.

GLASS TECHNOLOGY, INC.

    434 Turner Drive, Durango, CO 81301
    www.gtglass.com
    (800) 441-4527

Franchise: No.

Description: Windshield repair.

Requirements: Total cost ranges from $1,500 to $5,000.

Provisions: Glass Technology offers a complete windshield repair business including everything needed to get started: equipment, supplies, training, and ongoing support. Training covers not only the technical aspects of the business, but business management as well.

Profit Potential: Profit per repair is about $34 for 15 minutes of work. Performing nine repairs per day would yield $80,000 per year.

Comments: This can be a good business if you take advantage of the market by approaching insurance companies, fleet accounts, and car dealers. How to get these accounts is included in the training.

GLAS-WELD SYSTEMS

20578 Empire Blvd., Bend, OR 97701

www.glasweld.com

(800) 321-2597 or (541) 388-1156

Franchise: No.

Description: Glass repair service.

Requirements: $1,695 to $3,300.

Provisions: The investment includes equipment and enough materials to make 125 repairs and earn over $4,000 in revenue. A set of six training tapes is also included. Training topics include business start-up, generating sales, expansion, customer relations, advertising and promotion, and time management. Video training and field training are available options.

Profit Potential: Up to $75,000 a year. Glas-Weld currently has over 2,000 licensees.

HI-TECH INDUSTRIES

236 S. Rainbow Blvd., #151, Las Vegas, NV 89145

www.hi-techind.com

(702) 878-4948

Franchise: No.

Description: Recycle antifreeze for the industries such as auto, construction, fleet, farm, mining, logging, government, etc. All services are performed on customer's site.

Requirements: Areas available starting at $9,850. Financing is available.

Provisions: You get all the equipment, supplies, chemicals, ad proofs, support, training needed to perform the service plus an assigned marketing area.

Profit Potential: Up to $150,000 a year.

LIQUID RESINS INTERNATIONAL

4295 N. Holly Rd., Olney, IL 62450

www.liquidresins.com

(800) 458-2098

Franchise: No.

Description: Glass repair is one of the fastest growing parts of the automotive industry. Most mobile windshield repair technicians travel from one business location to another, show samples of the work that can be done and request permission to inspect the business vehicles on a regular basis.Upon finding breaks in the windshield, a repair is quickly performed and the bill is sent to the owner's insurance company, which in turn normally pays for the total cost of the repair.

Requirements: $500 for Mobile Repair Kit and training, which varies in price depending on the method you choose.

Provisions: The entrepreneur receives a complete repair kit with all the tools necessary to perform repairs on any type of break or crack. There are enough resins in the kit to provide the purchaser with $8,000 to $12,000 income. The average price per repair, across the country, is $40. The purchaser can have his/her choice of manual, video, classroom or on-the-job training, which is priced separately.

Profit Potential: Three repairs per day at $40 each equals $31,200 per year; nine repairs per day at $40 each equals $93,600 per year.

LOCATIONLUBE

> P.O. Box 700, E. Sandwich, MA 02537
> www.locationlube.com
> (508) 888-5000

Franchise: No.

Description: Mobile oil change van, servicing vehicles at customer's location.

Requirements: The total investment is $11,500. Financing is available with $1,000 to $5,000 down.

Provisions: Equipment and training.

MATCO TOOLS

> 4403 Allen Rd., Stow, OH 44224
> www.matcotools.com
> (888) 696-2826

Franchise: Yes.

Description: Distributor of professional hand tools and equipment. This company has been in business since 1979 and is well known for its quality mechanics' tools and service equipment from toolboxes to shop equipment. There are now over 1,200 franchisees.

Requirements: The total investment ranges from $60,000 to $152,000 with financing available through the franchisor. The franchisor also has financing available for accounts receivable.

Provisions: Extensive training, equipment, and inventory.

NATIONAL DETAIL SYSTEMS

> 2510-G N. Las Posas Rd., #450, Camarillo, CA 93010
> www.nationaldetail.com
> (800) 356-9485 or (805) 384-9349

Franchise: No.

Description: Mobile auto detailing service.

Requirements: No experience is necessary. The package starts at $2,400.

Provisions: All dealers are given complete instructions from start to finish through our exclusive step-by-step training and operations manuals, full-color 90-minute videotape and companion audiocassette training tapes. You can work part-time with extremely flexible business hours. Included is an initial supply of products enough to complete 30 to 40 vehicles. You will also receive upscale promotional material and camera-ready artwork for business cards, gift certificates, referral cards, business forms, brochures, yellow page and newspaper ads, direct mail coupons and much more.

Profit Potential: The company says that you will earn approximately $30 to $60 per hour. Your typical cost of cleaning/polishing products to complete an average detail is only $3.50. You should be able to generate approximately $3,000 worth of business from your initial order of supplies. National Detail currently has over 900 licensees.

NOVUS

> 10425 Hampshire Ave., Minneapolis, MN 55438
> www.novusglass.com
> (800) 944-6811

Franchise: Yes.

Description: NOVUS offers a windshield repair and scratch removal business.

Requirements: The franchise fee starts at $10,000, plus there are additional costs for training, equipment, supplies, and materials that add up to around $35,000.

POP-A-LOCK, a division of Systems Forward

> 1018 Harding St., #101, Lafayette, LA 70503
> www.popalock.com
> (337) 233-6211

Franchise: Yes.

Description: Mobile locksmithing and roadside assistance services. This can be run as an absentee ownership business (40% are absentee owners). One sure sign of a good franchise opportunity is the number of franchisees that own more than one unit.

Requirements: Total investment starts at about $125,000. There is third party financing available. General business experience and marketing experience needed.

Provisions: Training starts with one week at company headquarters, followed by one to two weeks at the franchisee's location. Also provides one to two weeks of training for tech/employees. There is also ongoing support plus a marketing package that includes ad slicks, regional advertising, a mentor program, tech support, national accounts, DVDs, and PR support.

Comments: About 75% of Pop-A-Lock franchisees own more than one unit—an exceptionally high number!

Close up: Pop-A-Lock

Sooner or later, every driver locks the keys in the car or gets stuck at the side of the road with a flat tire. When it happens to you, who ya gonna call? 1-888-POP-OPEN is the national dispatch number for Pop-a-Lock, a home-based franchise that is also the world's largest door unlocking and roadside emergency service. "We cover 2,500 cities in 36 states and service about 100 million customers," reports Pop-a-Lock CEO, Don Marks.

Pop-A-Lock was founded by two former law enforcement officers in Lafayette, Louisiana, in 1991. They had been opening locked car doors as a public service the old-fashioned way for years. But when vehicle locking and latching systems started to get sophisticated, they found the common methods like "Slim Jims" didn't work anymore. Worse, they were likely to damage the car. Still, the officers thought they had a good idea for a business and proceeded to do exhaustive vehicle research and invested in specialized tools that would work with the new locking technologies. The result was Pop-A-Lock, a service that caught on quickly.

The service is operated 24 hours a day, 7 days a week. Marks says, "Day or night, when a customer calls the toll-free number, the call is routed automatically to the local franchise operator who then dispatches a technician to the customer's location. In almost all cases, we reach customers within half an hour. We can unlock a car in a matter of seconds or maybe a few minutes depending on the car. Or we'll fix a flat tire, give a jump-start if the battery is dead, or bring you gas. We are fast and we never close. And there's really no competition. The only alternative is to call a towing company or wait until the next day to call a locksmith."

The majority of Pop-A-Lock calls coming directly from the general public. But Marks says a significant percentage of business comes from referral services, from mall security to bars. It is also the largest service provider for road clubs like Geiko, AAA, and Allstate. "When your car is in trouble and you call GM, for example, you think it's GM. It's really not. The call has been routed through to us."

Pop-A-Lock is looking for new franchisees coast-to-coast (and in other countries). "We really want to get to 90% of all the metro markets because we have a lot of referral customers who need us in all states. But, this could fit into the smallest market because the road clubs and national accounts need our services even in small communities. We have franchisees from very sophisticated business people to small town car door unlockers. We are just as interested in the small guys as we are in the big guys. That's why we are the largest provider to road clubs and the largest service of this kind anywhere in the world."

SNAP-ON TOOLS

2801 80th St., P.O. Box 1410, Kenosha, WI 53141

www.snapon.com

(800) 776-3344

Franchise: Yes.

Description: Professional tools and equipment sales to mechanics at their place of business.

Requirements: The franchise fee is only $5,000, but you will need at least another $10,000 for inventory and that could go much higher to be properly outfitted. The franchisor does, however, make financing available for inventory, accounts receivable, and even payroll. The monthly royalty fee is $50.

Provisions: Training, inventory, and exclusive territory.

ULTRA BOND

2458 I-70 Business Loop B-1, Grand Junction, CO 81501

www.ultrabond.com

(800) 347-2820

Franchise: No.

Description: Glass repair service.

Requirements: The combination repair kit costs $1,750. To buy exclusive rights to a protected territory, the initial cost is $3,250, plus a $100 monthly supply order is required.

Provisions: Your investment covers all equipment and supplies, two days of training in California, a training video, monthly newsletter, business start-up assistance, and ongoing support.

Profit Potential: Over $50 an hour.

——BUSINESS SERVICES——

Business services include any business whose customers are business owners and/or managers. This area covers quite a range, and so this section will describe opportunities in advertising, payroll services, business consulting, bookkeeping and accounting, tax preparation, management training, financial management, various office support services, business products, pre-employment screening, and an assortment of miscellaneous services that cater to niche markets.

As you can see by viewing these services as a group, an incredible number of dollars is being spent by businesses. There are 20 million companies that require bookkeeping, accounting, and tax preparation services. These businesses also spend $150+ billion annually on business products such as office supplies, furniture, printing, and business forms. That amount alone comprises over 3% of the GNP. Advertising takes a minimum 5% of any company's budget. The cooperative direct mail industry, although its growth has slowed somewhat with the advent of the Internet, still stands at $20 billion a year business. Corporations, more concerned than ever about how productivity is affecting the bottom line, spend $30 billion on management training each year.

Clearly, there is a lot of money to be made in business services. This is not, however, safe ground for amateurs. It is quite different from dealing with the public. Whereas a consumer may be willing to take a chance on an unknown product or an unfamiliar company, a business owner will not be so willing to take chances when it may affect the health of the business. Business owners are also more knowledgeable than the general public about the products and services they need. They trust only those who understand their business needs and who are willing to take the time to nurture a lasting business relationship. This takes time, but those with patience will be rewarded.

Those most likely to succeed in business services have assertive personalities and business experience. They are used to dealing with business owners and have some contacts within the business community. Working from a home office need not be a hindrance, but it is especially important to project a professional image.

10 TIL 2

7476 E. 29th Ave., #13, Denver, CO 80238

www.tentiltwo.com

(303) 909-3868

Franchise: Yes.

Description: Part-time employment staffing services.

Requirements: The franchise fee is $25,000. Ongoing royalty fee is 5%.

Provisions: One week of training at company headquarters followed by on-site support for grand opening and ongoing field support. Provides co-op advertising programs, regional marketing, and prepared ad slicks.

ACCU-RATE

2805 Rocky Ridge Dr., El Paso, TX 79904

www.increaseyourincome.com

(915) 757-7819

Franchise: No.

Description: Accu-Rate reviews hospital bills and identifies billing errors for corporations, unions, schools, and local government agencies. Most hospital bills are inaccurate and/or have hidden fees that would rival the overcharges of the Defense Department. Clients pay a percentage of the savings only after savings have been recovered.

Requirements: There are two levels; $995 and $4,995. Must have a computer with MS Office, printer, fax, and answering machine.

Provisions: Three days of training, training manual, list of prospective clients, daily update of organizations requiring Accu-Rate services, telephone support, and promotional material.

ACCUTRAK INVENTORY SPECIALISTS

1818C Hwy. 17 N., #320 Surfside Beach, SC 29575

www.accutrakinventory.com

(843) 293-8274

Franchise: Yes.

Description: AccuTrak Inventory Specialists is an inventory auditing and consulting franchise that conducts inventories and offers inventory control and loss prevention consulting. Franchisees help businesses of all sizes to control inventory, reduce shrink, improve employee performance, identify additional profit opportunities, and protect their bottom line.

Requirements: The franchise fee is $22,500 and total start-up costs will range from $30,000 to $50,000. There is an ongoing royalty fee of 7%.

Provisions: Specialized inventory software, in-depth training for one week at corporate headquarters, an additional week at the franchisee's location, continued support, and immediate income.

ACTION INTERNATIONAL
> 5670 Wynn Rd., #C, Las Vegas, NV 89118
> www.action-international.com
> (888) 483-2828

Franchise: Yes.

Description: Franchisees act as business coaches and mentors. They work with employees and owners of small to medium-sized businesses, to find the right balance between company performance and personal lifestyle.

Requirements: The franchise fee starts at $25,000 and the total start-up costs are around $60,000. Third party financing is available. The ongoing royalty is a flat $1,500 per month. A solid background in business and marketing skills are also necessary.

Provisions: The 10-day training program is provided at company headquarters or arrangements can be made for on-site training at the franchisee's location.

AIR BROOK LIMOUSINE
> P.O. Box 123, Rochelle Park, NJ 07662
> www.airbrook.com
> (800) 800-1990 or (201) 587-8385

Franchise: Yes.

Description: Limousine service to transport business owners and managers between office and airport.

Requirements: The franchise fee ranges from $7,500 to $12,500. A refundable deposit of $2,000 is required for start-up. Royalties range from 35% to 40%.

Provisions: The fee buys a 10-year franchise license and training. Financing is available from the company with no interest.

Comments: This company has been around since 1969 and has over 125 franchise operators.

ALTERNATIVE BOARD
> 11031 Sheridan Blvd., Westminster, CO 80020
> www.thealternativeboard.com
> (800) 727-0126

Franchise: Yes.

Description: Peer advisory boards and business coaching facilitated by franchisees. This is a membership organization for CEOs, presidents and business owners, who meet once a month to discuss ways of improving their businesses. Each group is made up of no more than 12 members whose businesses are not in competition with one another. Some franchisees use TAB to complement an existing consulting practice.

Requirements: Total investment starts at $55,000.

Provisions: The training provided by this organization is as intense as it gets. Initial training at company headquarters is 6 days, but it is followed by 4 weeks of training at the franchisee's location. Also provides comprehensive marketing support.

AMERICAN INSTITUTE

American Institute Bldg., First Floor, 7326 S.W. 48th Street, Miami, FL 33155

www.hiddenmoney.com

(800) US-AUDIT

Franchise: No.

Description: Business services including utility bill auditing. This business teaches you how to audit electric bills, catch overcharges, and save your clients money. It can even be run like a mail-order business. All you need is a telephone answering machine and calculator.

Requirements: Fees range from $100.

Provisions: Complete training to set up a home business immediately.

Profit Potential: $80,000 from home.

AT-HOME PROFESSIONS

2001 Lowe Street, Fort Collins, CO 80525

www.at-homeprofessions.edu

(800) 359-3455

Franchise: No.

Description: At-Home Professions is a unique institution established in 1981. It develops and provides career education specifically for the types of jobs that are commonly performed at home. At-Home Professions offers accredited training in Professional Medical Transcription. The school's training methods utilize at-home study and can be completed at the student's own pace.

Requirements: Applicants must be a high school graduate, hold a GED, or pass an admissions test. Tuition can be paid as-you-go with no interest. The school is approved for military education benefits as well as SLM Financing.

Provisions: In addition to providing quality training programs and course materials, this organization also includes great follow-up services. At-Home Professions provides their graduates with personal counseling in job-search techniques as well as continuing on-the-job support. At-Home Professions is accredited by the Distance Education and Training Council (DETC) in Washington, DC.

BANKS, BENTLEY & CROSS

    5015 Birch St., #121, Newport Beach, CA 92660

    (949) 786-0161

Franchise: No.

Description: This professional business debt management service provides business arbitration, debt negotiation, and other financial consultation services for businesses.

Requirements: $995.

Provisions: Complete business plan, training, turnkey marketing program, and consultation.

Profit Potential: Six figures annually.

BEVINCO BAR SYSTEMS LTD.

    510-505 Consumers Rd., Toronto, ON, Canada M2J 4V8

    www.bevinco.com

    (888) 238-4626

Franchise: Yes.

Description: Liquor inventory control service involving weekly on-site audits of liquor use. The service is computerized and well received by bar and restaurant owners because they can save a lot of money. This is a very lucrative business that is the largest of its kind in the world.

Requirements: Start-up costs will be about $40,000 and there is an ongoing fee of $12 per audit performed.

Provisions: The heart of the program is the proprietary software program. In addition, there are two weeks of hands-on training, ongoing toll-free support from a Master franchisee in your area, and a protected territory that has at least 250 licensed establishments.

BILTMORE FRANCHISE CONSULTING

    P.O. Box 10164, Scottsdale, AZ 85271

    www.biltmorefranchise.com

    (888) 428-7711

Franchise: Yes.

Description: Help business owners and managers prepare to sell franchises.

Requirements: The franchise fee is $38,000, with free financing available.

Provisions: National lead-sharing program, good profit margins, and demand in a field that is not overly competitive.

BOOKKEEPING EXPRESS

6862 Elm St., #800, McLean, VA 22101

www.bookkeepingexpress.com

(703) 766-5757

Franchise: Yes.

Description: This is the only bookkeeping franchise company focusing solely on bookkeeping services nationwide.

Requirements: Franchise fee is $30,000 with minimal additional start-up expenses.

Provisions: Full training and certification program, local and national marketing campaign, and local PR.

BUSINESS ROUND TABLE

37 Chandler Crescent, Moncton, NB, Canada E1E 3W6

www.businessroundtable.org

(506) 857-8177

Franchise: Yes.

Description: Mentoring groups for small businesses, dedicated to helping entrepreneurs succeed in their businesses and personal lives. Groups of 10 to 12 members meet once a month to discuss business problems and opportunities, then work together to solve problems and build more successful businesses. Franchisees in Canada and now in the United States act as facilitators and teachers for group members.

Requirements: Total start-up only $20,000.

Provisions: Training is provided at the franchisee's location (only) for two 2 weeks followed by ongoing support.

BUTLER LEARNING SYSTEMS

1325 West Dorothy Lane, Dayton, OH 45409

(937) 298-7462

Franchise: Yes.

Description: This company produces and publishes management training programs in the areas of human resources development and sales marketing.

Requirements: There are no franchise fees, but there is a contractual agreement that states the consultants will market and use the Butler products in the way they were intended to be used. The materials are then purchased wholesale, and the consultants make a profit from the markup.

Provisions: Complete training is provided.

THE CLIENT TOUCH/CARDSENDERS
> 47 Oxbow Creek, Laguna Hills, CA 92653
> www.cardsenders.com
> (877) 832-1424

Franchise: No.

Description: Provide personalized mailing services for businesses and professionals in your community. Help businesses create good will and loyalty by sending highly creative greeting cards to their customers and employees, plus provide greeting card services to friends and family. Part-time or full-time opportunity.

Requirements: Home-Study License, for complete business package is $6,995.

Provisions: License package includes comprehensive written reference materials, greeting card presentation portfolio, proprietary system, software, marketing materials, toll-free telephone and Web-based support, plus available training classes.

Close up: The Client Touch/CardSenders

In today's high-tech atmosphere, it is even more important for businesses to keep in personal touch with their customers. Sending personalized greeting cards is an inexpensive, reliable means of doing just that. Amidst the hastily written e-mails and impersonal faxes, it's a greeting card that stands out.

Jo Adamczyk of Louisville, Kentucky, was working for a large corporation and searching for her own business. She spent about a year researching the various home-based businesses that were available. When she found CardSenders, she immediately fell in love with the concept.

"This was the most positive, uplifting thing out there," Jo says. "I had to believe in what I was going to do. What I do is help companies foster loyalty by using greeting cards. Loyalty is so important in business. It is much cheaper to keep a customer than to get one. If you can get customers to perceive that they are wanted and their satisfaction is number one, then they will stay with you. I do that with thank-you notes, anniversary, and birthday cards." Jo mostly sends birthday cards, not just to customers but to employees as well. "With employees, it boosts morale and productivity. I also send a lot of holiday cards—but not just for traditional holidays. When is the last time you received a card for Ground Hog's Day? It gets your attention and makes you smile—and makes a lasting impression!"

Jo says her business practically started itself. "I did everything I was told to do in training. It was not a hard thing to sell. I got my first customer when

I presented the concept to our insurance agent. I told my agent what I did and he said, 'Gee, I have to do that.' It's not like you have to sell something like screws or even an insurance policy. People understand the value of this intuitively. A lot of companies are already doing it for themselves so, for them, I don't even have to explain the concept. I just point out why I am less expensive and more efficient."

There are two elements that make the system work: the great selection of cards and the mailing software. Signatures and business logos are actually reproduced inside the cards, often using handwritten samples from the sender. The result looks amazingly real.

The software is used to address and maintain customer lists. Jo says she can take small or big customers and give them the same cost effectiveness. "The value is so great, my customers love it."

CEO FOCUS

9465 Counselors Row, #200, Indianapolis, IN 46240

www.ceofocus.com

(317) 805-4924

Franchise: Yes.

Description: Peer groups for small-business owners. Franchisees assist CEOs and company owners with the difficulties of running a business by providing a forum for owners to discuss key business issues.

Requirements: $25,000 franchise fee.

Provisions: Complete training manuals/video, all marketing templates needed to run the business, seminar materials and "playbook" for driving membership, mailing list for the 5,000-10,000 companies in your market, and everything necessary to launch your groups.

Comments: "Peer groups are *hot*. Ten years ago, very few businesses owners knew what a CEO group was. Today, it is common knowledge. Market awareness has greatly expanded the market for CEO peer group services."

CFO TODAY

545 E. Tennessee St., Tallahassee, FL 32308

www.ledgerplus.com

(888) 643-1348

Franchise: Yes.

Description: Professional accounting, tax, and financial services for small businesses. CFO Today is the first accounting organization to specifically

address the needs of businesses with revenues of less than $1 million a year.
Requirements: Franchise fee is $24,000. General business experience plus knowledge of accounting and income tax preparation required.
Provisions: All the tools and the marketing system needed to build your business rapidly.

CLIENT CONNECTION, INC.

1780 S. Bellaire St., Suite 608, Denver, CO 80222
www.clientconnectioninc.com
(800) 331-4097

Franchise: No.
Description: Greeting card mailing service that provides professionals with customized greeting cards to their current and prospective client base to help them build repeat and referral business.
Requirements: $8,995.
Provisions: Comprehensive training, airfare, and accommodations in Denver, six months of mentoring, office supplies, sales presentation videos, and six months of software tech support.

COST CONTAINMENT SOLUTIONS, INC.

9921 Fringe Tree Ct., Louisville, KY 40241
www.costcontain.com
(800) 872-3709

Franchise: No.
Description: Business-to-business expense reduction service for the small to mid market in most industries.
Requirements: Laptop computer, proficiency in MS Office, plus a licensing fee. Total start-up costs are around $30,000.
Provisions: Initial and ongoing training, access to system and trademark, Web site listing, ongoing support, and joint advertising opportunities.

CRESTCOM, INT'L, INC.

6900 E. Belleview Ave., Greenwood Village, CO 80111
www.crestcom.com
(303) 267-8200

Franchise: Yes.
Description: Franchisees provide training for management, sales, and office personnel.
Requirements: General business experience and marketing expertise is necessary. The franchise fee starts at $39,500 and there is financing available.

Provisions: Training is provided at company headquarters.

Comments: Absentee ownership is allowed.

CYBERTARY

1217 Pleasant Grove Blvd., #100, Roseville, CA 95678

www.cybertary.com

(916) 781-7799

Franchise: Yes.

Description: Virtual office assistant services including database creation and support, desktop publishing (newsletters, etc.), document/OCR scanning, editing and formatting, accounting and bookkeeping, graphics, etc.

Requirements: Franchise fee of $19,000 plus ongoing royalty fee of $400 per month.

Provisions: Training plus ongoing marketing support, personal coaching, inter-company referrals, and national accounts.

EMPIRE BUSINESS BROKERS, INC.

928 French Rd., Buffalo, NY 14227

www.empirebb.com

(716) 240-2544

Franchise: Yes.

Description: Selling of existing businesses for the owners and also representing franchisers in the sale of their franchises. Franchise development and financial brokerage services are also offered.

Requirements: $15,000 franchise fee included in a total start-up investment of $20,000.

Provisions: You get five days of training, ongoing support, free home page, and access to over 4,000 listings of businesses for sale.

Profit Potential: Six figures.

ENTREPRENEUR'S SOURCE

900 Main St. S., Bldg. 2, Southbury, CT 06488

www.theesource.com

(800) 289-0086

Franchise: Yes.

Description: This is a franchise consulting firm that's been around for 20 years. The clients are people who are looking for a franchise opportunity. Franchisees match them up with the best franchise for them. The clients pay nothing for the service. The profit is paid by the franchisor when a successful match is completed.

Requirements: The franchisee fee is $45,000 and there is no financing offered.
Provisions: Training starts with a week at company headquarters and there is plenty of ongoing training and support.
Profit Potential: Not available.
Comments: 100% of franchisees are owner/operators.

eSHIPPING

> 173 English Landing Dr., #210, Kansas City, MO 64152
> www.eshipping.com
> (816) 505-0198

Franchise: Yes
Description: Shipping and logistics services.
Requirements: Franchise fee is $22,500 plus ongoing royalty fee is 35%.
Provisions: Complete training.

EXPENSE REDUCTION CONSULTING, INC.

> 6920 Annapolis Ct., Parkland, FL 33067
> www.ercinc.com
> (954) 255-2511

Franchise: No.
Description: Providing expense-reduction consulting services to businesses.
Requirements: The start-up investment is about $16,000 and the company offers financing.
Provisions: Training is conducted at corporation headquarters and at the operator's location. Also provided are advertising and marketing training and support, newsletters, technical support, operations manuals, phone support, and sales leads.

eYARDSALE.COM

> 10700 Montgomery Rd., #300, Cincinnati, OH 45242
> www.eyardsale.com
> (800) 291-0771

Franchise: Yes.
Description: eBay consignment selling services.
Requirements: The company provides financing for the franchise fee, which is only $3,000. You only need an additional $1,000 for start-up expenses. The ongoing royalty is 6%.
Provisions: Five days of training is available at headquarters, followed by sales boot camps, and ongoing support. Also provides purchasing cooperatives, ad slicks, and national media exposure.

FILTAFRY

> 5401 S. Kirkman Rd., #310, Orlando, FL 32819
> www.filtafry.com
> (407) 926-0255

Franchise: Yes.

Description: FiltaFry provides a mobile on-site service for the micro-filtration of cooking oil, the vacuum based cleaning of deep fryers, and full fryer management. Customers include restaurants of all kinds. The service is welcomed because it saves money, improves food quality, and reduces health and safety risks.

Requirements: General business experience is only required for those who want multi-unit franchises. The franchise fee is $15,000. There is financing available, but only for the start-up costs.

Provisions: Training is thorough and extensive. Two weeks are spent at company headquarters and 2-3 weeks are at the franchisee's location.

Comments: This a fairly new franchise that has grown to 28 franchisees in just two years.

GREEN AND CHRISTMAS CONCEPTS

> 3960 S. Higuera St., San Luis Obispo, CA 93401
> www.green-concepts.com and www.christmasconcepts.com
> (805) 782-0128

Franchise: Yes.

Description: Learn to lease living plants or Christmas decorations to banks, hotels, restaurants, offices and more.

Requirements: $7500. No royalties or residuals. No experience needed, just a desire to be self employed.

Provisions: 3 large manuals, 10 hours of DVD training, free Web site, free seminar aboard an upcoming east or west coast cruise ship, ongoing monthly newsletters, exclusive members Web site area to share questions and answers from all 800 members, photo club to share photos of before and afters with members, unlimited phone, fax and e-mail support forever. Leather Portfolio with 50 glossy 8x10s to impress clients, aprons and caps for staff, ongoing training forever at no additional cost.

Profit Potential: Many members are in the $15,000 per month range for the plant rental business and many Christmas members make over $100,000 in less than 2 months per year.

THE GROWTH COACH

10700 Montgomery Rd., #300, Cincinnati, OH 45242

www.thegrowthcoach.com

(888) 292-7992

Franchise: Yes.

Description: Provides business coaching and mentoring for small business owners and self-employed individuals. Coaching can be arranged on a regular basis or for special projects only.

Requirements: The franchise fee is $17,500 and there is financing available. for that. The additional start-up costs are low at only $3,000. General business experience is required.

Provisions: Initial training is conducted at company headquarters. After that, it is ongoing over the phone whenever necessary. There is plenty of marketing support including tools, ad slicks, and strategies.

INTERQUEST DETECTION CANINES

21900 Tomball Parkway, Houston, TX 77070

www.interquestfranchise.com

(281) 320-1231

Franchise: Yes.

Description: With this franchise, you would use highly trained dogs to detect drugs and other contraband (such as weapons) in public schools, private schools, and businesses. Other services to offer include providing trained dogs to police departments and offering security consulting and drug testing programs.

Requirements: The investment required is about $50,000.

Provisions: This is a comprehensive offering with everything you need to start and run a successful business.

INXPRESS

6770 S. 900 East, #102, Midvale, UT 84047

www.inxpressusa.com

(801) 262-2038

Franchise: Yes.

Description: Discounted shipping services.

Requirements: Total start-up costs are just over $30,000.

Provisions: A complete proven business system.

KUSTOM CARDS INTERNATIONAL, INC.
1018 E. Willow Grove Ave., Wyndmoor, PA 19038

www.kustomcards.com

(800) 207-1678

Franchise: No.

Description: Kustom Cards designs and manufactures photographic business cards and magnets.

Requirements: The cost of getting into this dealership ranges from $50 to $350. Readers of this book receive a 50% discount.

Provisions: The fee buys a complete sales manual with samples, order forms, and ongoing phone support.

LEADERSHIP MANAGEMENT, INC.
4567 Lake Shore Dr., Waco, TX 76710

www.lmi-bus.com

(800) 568-1241

Franchise: Yes.

Description: This company has been providing management training and consulting since 1965.

Requirements: The franchise fee is $30,000 and there is financing available. There is very little additional capital needed for start-up.

Provisions: All the necessary materials and training.

Comments: LMI programs are distributed in 23 languages and 60 countries.

LITTLE BLACK BOOK FOR EVERY BUSY WOMAN
P.O. Box 21466, Charleston, SC 29413

www.everybusywoman.com

(843) 958-8600

Franchise: Yes.

Description: Word-of-mouth directory for women that includes hundreds of women-recommended businesses in cities across the country plus helpful hints, tips, and advice from busy women in all stages of life.

Requirements: Start-up costs vary, ranging from $12,000 to $22,000.

Provisions: Training, support, brand identity, production and design services, software, and marketing package.

MR. PLANT
1106 2nd St., Encinitas, CA 92024

www.mrplant.com

(800) 974-0488

Franchise: Yes.

Description: Franchisees sell, rent, or lease foliage for interior landscaping. Ongoing maintenance is also provided to customers.

Requirements: The franchise fee is $14,950 and there is financing available for that. Start-up costs amount to another $4,000.

Provisions: In addition to the training program at company headquarters, franchisees receive a home study course. Marketing support includes yellow pages advertising, co-op advertising opportunities, and ad slicks. Cooperative purchasing is available, but not required.

PADGETT BUSINESS SERVICES

160 Hawthorne Pk., Athens, GA 30606

www.smallbizpros.com

(800) 723-4388

Franchise: Yes.

Description: Provides payroll services, financial consulting, and tax services to small businesses.

Requirements: The franchise fee is $25,000 and arrangements can be made for third party financing. Start-up costs require an additional $25,000. Experience in finance is definitely necessary.

Provisions: Training starts with 10 days at company headquarters and continues at the franchisee's location for at least 6 days. There are also annual conventions and seminars to keep franchisees up-to-date, particularly in regards to changes in tax codes.

Comments: Padgett has been in business for over 35 years and has over 400 franchisees.

PLAN AHEAD EVENTS

2121 Vista Pkwy, West Palm Beach, FL 33411

www.planaheadevents.com

(866) 257-6025

Franchise: Yes.

Description: A full-service event management company, serving clientele worldwide. Franchisees also come up with creative solutions for meetings, conventions, trade shows, special events, and incentive travel, bringing enthusiasm, experience and insight to every occasion, whether it be a corporate party, meeting, conference, wedding, grand opening, or evening gala.

Requirements: Total investment is around $25,000. No experience is necessary, but creativity is helpful.

Provisions: This is a turnkey franchise with a two-week training program, plus all the hardware/software needed to run your business.

PMA FRANCHISE SYSTEMS
> 1950 Spectrum Cir, #B-310, Marietta, GA 30067
> www.pmafranchise.com
> (800) 466-7822

Franchise: Yes.

Description: Since 1985, Personalized Management Associates (PMA) has been placing employees in a variety of positions in the retail, restaurant and service industries, including store/branch, mid-management, technical, corporate, and executive levels.

Requirements: The franchise fee is $30,000; financing is available from the company.

Provisions: Provides "live training" so you can experience the recruiting life before opening your office. Cash flow is possible within 60 days.

Comments: "PMA is the only executive search franchise in the United States franchising in the hospitality, restaurant, and retail management industries. We have the lowest initial total investment of *all* staffing industry franchise opportunities."

PRIORITY MANAGEMENT SYSTEMS
> 180, 13200 Delf Place, Richmond, BC, Canada V6V 2A2
> www.prioritymanagement.com
> (800) 672-6768

Franchise: No.

Description: Priority Management has designed a program to help corporate employees develop personal effectiveness skills. Specifically, employees are taught to manage time and projects, cope with stress, run meetings, delegate tasks, and communicate effectively. The purpose is to teach busy professionals to be able to control personal business lives while simultaneously reducing stress.

Requirements: Business operators are required to be educated, experienced, and highly motivated. The total investment required for this opportunity is under $100.

Provisions: Training starts with an intensive two-week session at company headquarters. Follow-up support is offered in several different ways.

Comments: This business is for experienced professionals who need to polish their skills. This is a lucrative market, but only heavy hitters survive.

PROFORMA, INC.

8800 E. Pleasant Valley Rd., Cleveland, OH 44131

www.proforma.com

(800) 825-1525 or (216) 741-0400

Franchise: Yes.

Description: Sales of business products including forms, commercial printing, and computer and office supplies.

Requirements: The franchise fee is $14,900. You will need $5,000 for living expenses while you get started. The royalty is 8% and the advertising royalty is 1%.Marketing or executive management experience is required.

Provisions: The fee buys marketing systems, license agreement, ongoing support, trademarks, vendor relations, and lines of credit.

Profit Potential: Not available, but this is a huge industry.

Comments: This is a highly rated company with about 385 franchise operators.

RECRUITERS PROFESSIONAL NETWORK

8 Grenada Circle, Nashua, NH 03062

www.RecProNet.com

(888) 598-6633

Franchise: No.

Description: RPN trains individuals to become physician and healthcare professional recruiters and consultants.

Requirements: The cost ranges from $315 to $515.

Provisions: The one-time fee buys the manual and unlimited training via telephone.

REFERRAL INSTITUTE

151 Virginia Ave., Attleboro Falls, MA 02763

www.referralinstitute.com

(508) 809-9789

Franchise: Yes.

Description: Referral training, coaching, and consulting. The Referral Institute is an international franchised referral training and consulting company with locations in 13 countries.

Requirements: The total investment is around $20,000.

Provisions: A total 128 hours of training is available at company headquarters. A marketing plan and marketing support is provided.

Comments: "At the Referral Institute, we'll teach you how to make all your business relationships become more valuable to you and your business. As a result, you'll not only enjoy an increased quality of life because your business is flourishing, but you will also gain lifelong relationships."

RENAISSANCE EXECUTIVE FORUMS, INC.
7855 Ivanhoe Ave., #300, La Jolla, CA 92037
www.executiveforums.com
(858) 551-6600

Franchise: Yes.

Description: Business consulting service.

Requirements: The ideal candidate for this franchise is a retired executive who has plenty of knowledge and experience to offer to clients. There is an orientation process, which weeds out unqualified contenders. For those who make the cut, the investment starts at $45,000 with a hefty ongoing royalty fee of 20%.

Provisions: Franchisees are considered "partners." Extensive training is provided in all the key areas needed for success: marketing, presentation techniques, facilitation skills and coaching. The initial training is followed by an advanced certification program. The complete business start-up package also includes an operations manual, all necessary stationery and office supplies, mail and phone sales support, press release kit, customized business plan, protected market, and field support. In addition, the corporate office will do all the invoicing and billing.

SANDLER SYSTEMS
10411 Stephenson Rd., Stephenson, MD 21153
www.sandler.com
(410) 653-1993

Franchise: Yes.

Description: Franchisees offer corporate training programs designed to help client companies boost productivity and generate more profits.

Requirements: The franchise fee is $30,000 with limited financing available.

Provisions: Complete training and follow-up support is provided.

SAVE IT NOW!
9100 Keystone Crossing, #750, Indianapolis, IN 46240
www.saveitnow.com
(317) 208-4836

Franchise: Yes.

Description: Franchisees offer business clients profit-building solutions to reduce purchase costs, gain control of spending, and increase staff productivity.

Requirements: Investment starts at $75,000.

Provisions: Initial training runs 12 days at company headquarters than another 6+ days (or more as needed) at franchisee's location. Also, 7 days of advanced training are available and Web training as needed.

SHOCK PR

P.O. Box 3174, Bourne, MA 02532

http://shockpr.com

(508) 743-9993

Franchise: Yes.

Description: Custom PR services for small firms who are ready to launch, and medium-size, more established firms who want to become better known in the industry.

Requirements: The franchise fee is $10,000 and the ongoing royalty fee is 5%.

Provisions: A quick-start, turnkey operation, a support network of other professionals, and national branding.

SUPER COUPS COOPERATIVE DIRECT MAIL

The Mail House, 180 Bodwell St., Avon, MA 02322

www.supercoups.com

(800) 626-2620

Franchise: Yes.

Description: Franchisees sell ad space in their mailings to local and national businesses. They also design and write copy for the ads, but with extensive help from Super Coups.

Requirements: The franchise fee is $31,000.

Provisions: Complete training as well as exceptional follow-up support is provided.

TIME PLUS, INC.

500 Colonial Center Pkwy., #650, Roswell, GA 30076

www.timeplus.com

(888) 720-7587

Franchise: No.

Description: Services for human resources departments including payroll, timekeeping, and other recordkeeping systems.

Requirements: Minimum $15,000 for start-up. Financing is available.

Provisions: Training in operations and marketing is provided in classroom session at corporate headquarters and on-site. An operations manual, training video, and online training is provided as well. Ongoing support is extensive, covering every possible scenario that might come up. Sales leads are also provided.

USA FOR HEALTHCLAIMS, INC.
   39 E. Kings Hwy., Audubon, NJ 08106
   www.usaforhealthclaims.com
   (866) 793-5583

Franchise: No.

Description: Licensing program enables individuals to process medical claims electronically through a central clearinghouse. The company currently has over 1,500 licensees.

Requirements: $4,990 plus a PC.

Provisions: Fee buys software, manuals, marketing manuals, brochures, training class, ongoing technical support and all updates.

Profit Potential: Unlimited.

WIRTH BUSINESS CREDIT
   4200 Dahlberg Dr., #100, Minneapolis, MN 55422
   www.wirthbusinesscredit.com
   (800) 567-6600

Franchise: Yes.

Description: A unique financing company specializing in equipment leasing for small to mid-sized businesses.

Requirements: The franchise fee is $35,000. There are no ongoing royalties.

Provisions: Offers complete initial and ongoing training.

WORLDWIDE EXPRESS
   2501 Cedar Springs Rd., #450, Dallas, TX 75201
   www.wwex.com
   (800) 758-SHIP

Franchise: Yes.

Description: Be an authorized Worldwide Express reseller.

Requirements: The average total investment starts at about $40,000. You will also need a computer, fax and phone lines, fax machine, voicemail, and e-mail.

Provisions: Your revenue stream will come from the difference between what you charge your customer and what you pay Worldwide. Obviously, this is a repeat business in which the bulk of your efforts will be in obtaining clients. Once they sign up, you will continue to get a percentage of what they spend on Worldwide services. Franchise territories are protected so other franchisees cannot sell in your zip codes. Complete training, software, weekly updates, marketing advice, and ongoing support is provided.

———HOME AND COMMERCIAL——— PROPERTY IMPROVEMENTS

Home improvement may be the single biggest industry represented in this book. Product sales alone top $160 billion each year and there doesn't appear to be a slowdown in sight. Put those products together with services and you have a whopping number of opportunities. The main reason for the size of this industry in past years was the growing number of homeowners. Today, the reason is a little different—people can't afford to buy or sell in the current market, but they still want the biggest investment of their lives to grow in beauty and in value.

To most of us, property improvement means remodeling. And there are indeed remodeling opportunities in this chapter. But there is much more to the property improvement industry than paint and carpentry. Included in this chapter's assortment of businesses are services that you may have thought of, such as carpet dyeing and repair, decorating services, floor coverings, handyman services, drapery cleaning, and lawn care.

There are also a few that you may not have considered. Water and gas leak detection provides a unique and valuable service. Porcelain refinishing is a popular alternative to bathroom fixture replacement for hotels, schools, interior decorators, and landlords. And businesses such as Foliage Design Systems offer unique services such as installing and maintaining interior landscaping.

Generally, the businesses in this chapter are very straightforward with no fancy image or special skills required. Down-to-earth working people who want the advantages of owning a business, such as greater income potential and freedom, will find some good possibilities here. Most of these businesses can also be run part-time, which is helpful if you are looking for something with flexibility.

ARCHADECK

2112 W. Laburnum Ave., #100, Richmond, VA 23727
www.archadeck.com
(800) 789-3325

Franchise: Yes.

Description: Franchisees work with homeowners and builders to design and construct decks and gazebos. This is a very fast-growing company with over 80 franchise units added since 1985.

Requirements: The franchise fee is $28,000. Financing for half the franchise fee is available.

Provisions: Training and support.

AVANTE WINDOW FASHIONS
23052 Alicia Parkway #H202, Mission Viejo, CA 92692
www.startablindbiz.com
(949) 768-6695

Franchise: No.
Description: Low cost, shop-at-home window fashions—a $5 billion dollar industry. Owned by BBN, America's largest covering buying group.
Requirements: $199.
Provisions: Training materials, DVD's and samples are included.
Profit Potential: $500-$4,500 a month, part-time.
Comments: Perfect part-time income.

BATHCREST
2425 S. Progress Dr., Salt Lake City, UT 84119
www.bathcrest.com
(800) 826-6790 or (801) 972-1110

Franchise: No.
Description: Bathcrest is in the porcelain refinishing business.
Requirements: The start-up cost is around $25,000 for training, the costs of attending training sessions, a complete equipment package, printed materials and enough products to return $20,000 in gross sales.
Comments: This is a family business that has been around since 1974. They have substantial experience to offer.

BIRTHFLOWERS.COM
161 Swint Ave., Milledgeville, GA 31061
http://birthflowers.com
(478) 452-0008

Franchise: Yes.
Description: Landscape design, installation and maintenance. This is a design/build landscaping franchise that uses a patent pending system for color all year with flowers that includes a two-year guarantee on the life of installed plants.
Requirements: The total investment starts at $10,000. There is in-house financing available for the franchise fee portion, which is $7,000. There is an annual $1,500 minimum royalty is paid against a royalty of 5.5% of total retail sales. You only pay for books and lodging during the intensive hands-on week-long training trial that ends with a written test.
Provisions: After the initial training, there are quarterly visits to your business to offer suggestions for improvement and help with promotion.

Support is available 24/7 to assist you in your business development. You are provided a professional business coach your first 2 years of operation.

Comments: "Selling horticultural therapy (the spiritual and physical enjoyment of owning a flower garden) is the primary thrust of our landscaping contractors."

BUDGET BLINDS, INC.

    1927 N. Glassell St., Orange, CA 92865

    www.budgetblinds.com

    (800) 420-5374

Franchise: Yes.

Description: Budget Blinds is the nation's largest window-coverings franchise.

Requirements: The total investment is $64,950, including the franchise fee of $25,000. You will also need a fax machine, computer, and a cargo or minivan. The van can be owned or leased.

Provisions: The investment includes an operations manual, start-up supplies, personal Web site, two weeks of corporate training including the cost of the hotel, and an exclusive territory.

CARPET NETWORK

    109 Gaither Drive Suite 302, Mount Laurel, NJ 08054

    (800) 428-1067

Franchise: Yes.

Description: Carpet Network is a top-ranked mobile floor and window-covering retail model specializing in the residential market but with the ability to cater to Main Street businesses as well as commercial and builder markets. Each franchisee has a unique, custom Unicell vehicle, carrying a vast array of over 5,000 products to accommodate customers' requests for commercial carpets, traditional and exotic hardwood, laminate, vinyl, ceramic, window treatments, and area rugs.

Requirements: No experience required. The investment range is $50,585–$72,385 (franchise fee $29,500 plus start-up $15,000).

Provisions: Offers in-home training prior to attending "Carpet Network College"—a 6-day training session held at company headquarters. There is follow-up with post-training, ongoing Webinars, and annual conventions.

CLEAN & HAPPY WINDOWS

10019 Des Moines Memorial Dr, Seattle, WA 98168

www.cleanhappy.com

(866) 762-7617

Franchise: Yes.

Description: Franchises clean windows, gutters, roofs, screens and awnings in buildings with four or fewer stories.

Requirements: There is no franchise fee. Ongoing royalties are 7%.

Provisions: A full week of training is provided at company headquarters and there is ongoing support both online and in the field. The company provides an online scheduling service.

Comments: You won't find a cheaper franchise than this one. You can get started with as little as $100.

COLOR-CROWN CORPORATION

928 Sligh Avenue, Seffner, FL 33584

www.stardek.com

(800) 282-1599

Franchise: No.

Description: Color-Crown manufactures STARDEK products and has been in the concrete coating business since 1972. The products are used in the decorative concrete coating business.

Requirements: The only requirement is that you attend a free two-day training program. There is no franchise fee or minimum purchase required.

Provisions: "Unlike many companies that ask you to invest in them first only for you to find out it is not what they really told you or you just don't like it, we actually invest in you when you attend our free training class."

CONCRETE TECHNOLOGY, INC.

8770 133rd Ave. N., Largo, FL 33773

www.flycti.com

(800) 447-6573

Franchise: No.

Description: Company manufactures state-of-the-art concrete resurfacing product sold to a network of dealers and distributors worldwide.

Requirements: Exclusive territories are available through an initial inventory purchase of at least $10,000.

Provisions: 100% product inventory along with marketing materials, etc. to offer a turnkey operation.

Profit Potential: Average crew dealer has the opportunity to make $100,000 annually.

CRACK TEAM, THE

> 1850 Craigshire Plaza, #201, St. Louis, MO 63146
> www.thecrackteam.com
> (314) 426-0900

Franchise: Yes.

Description: The Crack Team has been repairing foundation cracks since 1985. Using the company's epoxy injection system, franchisees waterproof foundation wall cracks for customers that include homeowners, contractors, remodelers, and realtors.

Requirements: The total investment starts at about $65,000.

Provisions: This is a turnkey business system including all training, tools, and support necessary to start and operate a successful business.

CREATIVE COLORS INTERNATIONAL, INC.

> 5550 W. 175th St., Tinley Park, IL 60477
> www.creativecolorsintl.com
> (800) 933-2656

Franchise: Yes.

Description: The CCI franchise system specializes in providing services for the repair, coloring, cleaning, and restoration of leather, vinyl, cloth, velour, plastics, and other upholstery surfaces and related services on a mobile basis primarily to commercial customers.

Requirements: The franchise fee is $19,500 and you will need $8,000 for supplies. The total investment, including minivan, is around $50,000. Financing is available for supplies up to $8,000.

Provisions: Two weeks of training at headquarters, one week in franchisee's territory, and ongoing support through newsletters, seminars, and an advisory council.

Profit Potential: This business can be expanded into all markets that have a need for repairing and re-dyeing of leather, vinyl, velour, plastics, etc.

CRITTER CONTROL

> 9435 E. Cherry Bend Rd., Traverse City, MI 49684
> www.crittercontrol.com
> (231) 947-2400

Franchise: Yes.

Description: This is an interesting company that started out as a chimney cleaning service. So often animals were part of the debris stuck in the chimneys, that animal removal was offered as a service—not only from chimneys but attacks, decks, and other areas. Customers include both businesses and homeowners and also cities that do not have their own animal control agencies. Services have been expanded to include damage repair and pest management (such as screening vents or closing entry holes).

Requirements: This is a low-cost opportunity. Total start-up can be under $10,000 including the $3,000 franchise fee. Experience is the main requirement. General business, marketing, and animal or wildlife control knowledge are all necessary.

Comments: The company has been around since 1983 and now has 90 franchisees.

DECOR & YOU, INC.

900 Main St. South, Bldg. #2, Southbury, CT 06488
www.decorandyou.com
(203) 264-3500

Franchise: Yes.

Description: Interior decorating.

Requirements: The total investment starts at approximately $28,000.

Provisions: The investment buys training at company headquarters, which covers all aspects of the decorating business from design to accounting. You also get ongoing support.

DECORATING DEN

19100 Montgomery Ave., Montgomery Village, MD 20866
www.decoratingden.com
(800) 686-6393 or (301) 272-1500

Franchise: Yes.

Description: Decorating Den is a shop-at-home decorating service. The franchisee goes by appointment to a customer's home in a "ColorVan" containing over 5,000 samples of fabrics, wall coverings, carpets, draperies, furniture, and accessories. There is no charge for the decorating service because the profit comes from the difference between the wholesale and retail prices on the products sold to the customer. There are over 1,100 franchises operating throughout the US, Canada, United Kingdom, Japan, Europe, and Australia.

Requirements: The franchise fee is $24,900. An additional $5,000 to $15,000 working capital is needed. Some business and decorating experience is preferred.

Provisions: The franchise fee covers complete training which takes about six months, national advertising, promotional materials, business and record keeping systems, access to quality products at wholesale discounted prices, a selection of product samples, and all the necessary paperwork down to printed checks and business cards.

DR. VINYL & ASSOCIATES, LTD.

821 NW Commerce St., Lee's Summit, MO 64086

www.drvinyl.com

(800) 531-6600

Franchise: Yes.

Description: Dr. Vinyl franchisees repair vinyl, cloth, leather, strip molding, windshields, and plastic for car dealerships, restaurants, and doctors' offices.

Requirements: The franchise fee starts at $32,500 and you will need a van, new or used.

Provisions: The fee includes $5,000 worth of inventory, training, and ongoing support.

DURA-OAK CABINET REFACING PRODUCTS

863 Texas Ave., Shreveport, LA 71101

www.dura-oak.com

(800) 228-7702

Franchise: No.

Description: Refacing existing cabinets, saving the homeowner about half the cost of a complete kitchen remodel.

Requirements: $10,000 investment with no royalty fee, no inventory, and no show room necessary. Financing is available.

Provisions: Exclusive territory, never ending sales training that includes videos and personal training, marketing tools, technical support, TV and radio ads, and manuals.

FLOOR COVERINGS INTERNATIONAL

5182 Old Dixie Hwy., Forest Park, GA 30050

www.floorcoveringsintl.com

(800) 955-4324

Franchise: Yes.

Description: Mobile floor covering retailer offering convenient shop-at-home service to today's time-starved consumers.

Requirements: The franchise fee is $16,000 with total start-up costs ranging from $30,000 to $40,000; royalties are 5%; and the ad fund is 2%.

Provisions: Comprehensive training program, regional workshops, monthly newsletter, national accounts, national advertising, toll-free help line, marketing manual and materials, operations manual, annual convention, and buying group discounts.

FOLIAGE DESIGN SYSTEMS

496 35th St., Orlando, FL 32811

www.foliagedesign.com

(800) 933-7351 or (407) 245-7776

Franchise: Yes.

Description: Interior foliage design, sales, and or maintenance.

Requirements: The franchise fee depends on a market analysis performed by the company, but it ranges from $25,000 to $100,000 with additional costs amounting to about $15,000. The royalty is 4% of gross.

Provisions: Each franchise receives a protected territory, two weeks of training in Florida, operating manuals, operation systems, a computerized management information system to minimize administrative chores, leads from national advertising, and toll-free support. Plant materials can be obtained from over 200,000 sq. ft. of company-owned greenhouses. Training covers tested and proven methods of record keeping, order writing, marketing, filing, collections, and accounting, as well as the care, design, and use of foliage in commercial and residential spaces.

Comments: This company has been in business since 1971 and has won numerous nationally recognized awards.

HOME FIXOLOGY

11100 S.W. 93rd Court Rd., #10-120, Ocala, FL 34481

http://homefixology.com

(352) 237-1008

Franchise: Yes.

Description: Handyman home repair franchise.

Requirements: The total start-up investment starts at about $65,000. That includes the franchise fee, which starts at $20,000. Company financing is available for the franchise fee only.

Provisions: Complete training, purchasing cooperatives, and marketing/ advertising programs.

HOME REMEDIES

1539 Hewlett Ave., Hewlett, NY 11557

www.hrnbiz.com

(516) 374-8504

Franchise: No.

Description: Home-improvement referral network. The HRN business fills an important niche in the home improvement marketplace. HRNs locate, screen, and refer home improvement contractors ranging from painters, plumbers, and electricians to architects, general contractors, and handymen. Contractors referred by an HRN pay a pre-negotiated commission for any work secured, which means the service is free to homeowners.

Requirements: Start-up investment ranges from $1,999 to $6,500.

Provisions: Provides training and a complete turnkey business system.

IDEA VISION

> 1814 Big Oak Ln., Kissimmee, FL 34746
> www.ideavisn.com
> (407) 343-5020

Franchise: No.

Description: A business opportunity for helping people visualize their building, landscaping, home improvement and decorating ideas.

Requirements: $12,500 start-up costs. Must participate in an evaluation class before acceptance.

Provisions: Imaging software, imaging portfolio, complete training, and technical support.

JET-BLACK SEALCOATING & REPAIR

> 25 W. Cliff Rd., #103, Burnsville, MN 55337
> www.Jet-Black.com
> (888) 538-2525 or (952) 890-8343

Franchise: Yes.

Description: Asphalt/blacktop seal coating, hot rubber crack filling, oil spot treatment, patchwork, grass edging and striping.

Requirements: $39,500 includes the franchise fee.

Provisions: You get a complete business package including a trailer, equipment, uniforms, office supplies, a week of corporate training, and grand opening advertising.

KITCHEN SOLVERS

> 401 Jay St., La Crosse, WI 54601
> www.kitchensolvers.com
> (800) 845-6779

Franchise: Yes.

Description: Kitchen Solvers has been in business since 1984 and now has 138 franchises throughout the US and Canada. The company specializes in custom cabinet refacing for the kitchen. Other services offered include pre-built and custom cabinetry, laminate, solid surface, and stone countertops, kitchen planning and design, kitchen accessories, bathtub and surround wall

shower liners, glueless laminate flooring, and storage organizing systems.
Requirements: The franchise fee for an owner operator franchise is $25,000, plus the standard supplies package, which is $7,995.
Provisions: Comprehensive supplies package, exclusive territory, two weeks of extensive training in the areas of installation, marketing, administration, software and design, product/supplier knowledge, pricing, and ongoing corporate support.

KITCHEN TUNE-UP, INC.

813 Circle Dr., Aberdeen, SD 57401

www.kitchentuneup.com

(800) 333-6385 or (605) 225-4049

Franchise: Yes.
Description: Kitchen Tune-Up offers consumers a new way to renew, repair and remodel their kitchens. They offer "Kitchen Solutions for any Budget" with wood restorations, cabinet recoating, cabinet refacing and a brand line of custom cabinetry.
Requirements: The franchise fee is $25,000 and additional start-up expenses amount to about $9,000.
Provisions: The fee buys a protected territory, national supplier discounts, ongoing support, monthly newsletters, and regional and national conventions.

KOTT KOATINGS

27161 Burbank St., Foothill Ranch, CA 92610

www.thebathtubpeople.com

(949) 770-5055

Franchise: No.
Description: Porcelain and fiberglass refinishing.
Requirements: The franchise fee is $17,500. There is financing available from the company for the franchise fee, equipment, and inventory.
Provisions: A dealer package includes 5 days of training at company headquarters, a complete custom "factory on wheels" trailer unit with generator, a complete equipment package of all necessary tools and supplies, a protected territory, and manuals.

LANGENWALTER INDUSTRIES, INC.

1111 S. Richfield Rd., Placentia, CA 92670

www.langdye.com

(800) 422-4370

Franchise: Yes.

Description: Franchisees do carpet color correction work for apartment, hotels, and commercial properties, saving the owners up to 85% on carpet replacement costs.

Requirements: Must have management experience and $30,000 liquid capital. This company is on the SBA approved list for financing.

Provisions: Fee includes five days of intensive training, operations manual, marketing package, complete equipment package, technical assistance, and ongoing support.

LAWN DOCTOR

> 142 State Rte 34, Holmdel, NJ 07733
> www.lawndoctorfranchise.com
> (866) 529-6362

Franchise: Yes.

Description: Lawn Doctor is the nation's leading lawn service and lawn care company; specializing in lawn care services, tree and shrub care, weed control, and pest control.

Requirements: $75,000 liquidity.

Provisions: Includes three weeks of training, start-up marketing program, all equipment and van layouts necessary, and proprietary software.

Profit Potential: See Item 19 of the company's FDD.

MAINTENANCE MADE SIMPLE

> 9820 E. Dreyfus Ave., Scottsdale, AZ 85260
> www.m2simple.com
> (866) 778-6283

Franchise: Yes.

Description: Handyman and home maintenance services.

Requirements: Total costs including franchise fee runs around $35,000. There is financing available from third party sources. No experience is necessary.

Provisions: Training is provided at company headquarters and continues at franchisee's location. There is very strong marketing support including national and regional media, co-op advertising, an inbound and outbound call center, national accounts program, and catalog of marketing collateral.

MIRACLE METHOD

> 4239 N. Nevada Ave., #115, Colorado Springs, CO 80907
> www.miraclemethod.com
> (800) 444-8827 or (719) 594-9196

Franchise: Yes.

Description: Since 1979 Miracle Method has provided expert refinishing of bathroom and kitchen tubs, tile, counters, sinks, and cabinets. Their process saves customers up to 70% versus the cost of replacement.

Requirements: The franchise fee is $30,000 with estimated start-up costs of $5,000 for equipment. Negotiable financing is available.

Provisions: Franchisees get proprietary bonding agent, access to hi-tech coatings, specific territory, initial 10-day training and ongoing training, customized advertising program, toll-free support, and free start-up package.

Profit Potential: 20–25% pre-tax profit.

Comments: The majority of Miracle Method franchises start at home. As their business and number of employees grow, they eventually open up showrooms and shops.

MR. ELECTRIC

1020 N. University Parks Dr., Waco, TX 76707

www.mrelectric.com

(800) 805-0575

Franchise: Yes.

Description: Provides residential and light commercial electrical service and repair.

Requirements: Total start-up costs start at $65,000. Only the franchise fee of $19,500 can be financed. Experience in the field of electrical repair is needed.

Provisions: Training is provided both at company headquarters and on-site. Ongoing support is provided via the Internet, toll-free phone line, meetings, and newsletters.

Comments: This company is owned by Dwyer, Inc., which owns other home maintenance franchise companies including Mr. Rooter, Mr. Appliance, Glass Doctor, and Rainbow Int'l.

NATIONWIDE CARPET BROKERS

P.O. Box 1472, Dalton, GA 30720

(800) 322-7299

Franchise: No.

Description: This is a national floor covering and decorating business that offers agents major mill purchasing. You could elect to set up your car or van with the Nationwide logo and be ready to call on your in-home or in-office shoppers. Presently about 20% of Nationwide agencies are full-time businesses with the rest on a part-time basis.

Requirements: Minimum investment is $4,900 in areas where there are no other agents.

Provisions: For the minimum investment you would receive a complete collection of samples, training in your area, technical support, an 800 number for free quotes and inventory availability, video tape training, cards, invoices, letterheads, and basic forms to start your business.

Profit Potential: $30,000 and up depending on the person.

PARKER INTERIOR PLANTSCAPE, INC.

1325 Terrill Rd., Scotch Plains, NJ 07076

www.parkerplants.com

(908) 322-5552

Franchise: Yes.

Description: Part I is the installation of plants, trees, flowers, silks, Christmas decorations, containers, etc. to offices, malls, atriums, etc. Part II is the continual care and maintenance of these plants and products on location.

Requirements: $35,000.

Provisions: Training from the largest, most successful, privately owned interior plantscaping company in the USYou will be taught all the secrets, operations, sources, etc.

Profit Potential: First year, after costs and salaries, $20,000; second year $40,000; third year $60,000, etc. "It is almost like a pyramid. Each time you get an account, you should keep the monthly billing coming in. Each new account just adds to the last."

POSIGRIP

825 Gate park Drive #3 Daytona, FL 32114

www.posigrip.com

(800) 662-9299

Franchise: No.

Description: Safety product for floors tubs and showers.

Requirements: $10,000.

Provisions: Includes on-site training, manual, and video.

Profit Potential: Over $100,000 per year.

Comments: Over 1,400 operators in all 50 states and 38 countries.

PUROSYSTEMS, INC.

6001 Hiatus Rd., Taramac, FL 33321

www.puroclean.com

(800) 247-9047

Franchise: Yes.

Description: Provides property restoration and reconstruction due to water, fire, and smoke damage.

Requirements: The total investment is around $50,000 with half of that going to the franchise fee.

Provisions: A total of 3 weeks of training is provided, divided between company headquarters and the franchisee's site.

SCREEN MACHINE

> 4173 First St., Livermore, CA 94557
> www.screen-machine.com
> (877) 505-1985

Franchise: Yes.

Description: A mobile service business specializing in the custom fabrication, replacement, and repair of window and door screens as well as other related services.

Requirements: The franchise fee is $25,000. An equipment and supplies package costs at least $11,350 and general business expenses are $5,500 minimum. The total initial investment ranges from $45,000 to $70,000.

Provisions: Your investment buys training in marketing strategies, advertising techniques, business management, basic accounting methods, operational procedures, and "hands-on" technical instruction on how to custom fabricate screens and perform screen repair and related work. Also provided are advertising materials, audiovisual training, ongoing support, and all of the materials, supplies, and equipment necessary for the basic operation of the business. A custom-built mobile workshop with a generator and power miter box saw are all part of the equipment package.

SPRING-GREEN LAWN CARE

> 11909 Spaulding School Dr., Plainfield, IL 60544
> www.spring-green.com
> (800) 435-4051

Franchise: Yes.

Description: Franchisees offer to residential and commercial customers regular lawn fertilization, weed control, lawn aeration, and pruning and feeding of trees and shrubs.

Requirements: The franchise fee is $21,900 and the total investment ranges from $80,000 to $90,000.

Provisions: You get an exclusive territory and complete training, computer hardware and software, equipment and vehicle.

STARSCAPES INTERNATIONAL

427 W. Chilton St., Chandler, AZ 85224

www.starscapes.com

(602) 926-1982

Franchise: No.

Description: Licensees produce glow-in-the-dark ceiling murals of astronomically correct skyscapes. Clients include individuals, hotels, motels, resorts, etc.

Requirements: The complete start-up package is under $300.

Profit Potential: Up to $1,500 per day.

SURFACE DOCTOR

4239 North Nevada Ave, #115, Colorado Springs, CO 80907

www.surfacedoctor.com

(800) 735-5055

Franchise: Yes.

Description: Surface restoration and refinishing service for tile, counter tops, bathtubs, sinks, metal appliances and more. Surface Doctor's technology allows bathrooms and kitchens to be transformed without the chaos and expense of conventional remodeling methods.

Requirements: Franchise fee is $15,00; start-up costs range from $7,800 to $11,780; royalties are $175 per month; and the ad fund is $25 per month.

Provisions: Comprehensive training program, marketing manuals and materials, operations manual, toll-free Help Line, annual convention, newsletter, ongoing training, and research and development.

USE-WHAT-YOU-HAVE INTERIORS

109 East 73rd St., New York, NY 10021

www.redecorate.com

(212) 288-8888

Franchise: No.

Description: Pioneer of one-day redecorating consultations.

Requirements: Talent and passion for interior design. Investment of $3,000 for training materials, certification dinner and other expenses.

Provisions: Weeklong decorator training program for novices and professionals and membership in the Interior Refiners Network. Also offers training completely online for those who can't make it to New York. Trainees learn everything they need to know to have a home-based decorating consultation business plus certification in network.

LON WALTENBERGER TRAINING SERVICES
5410 Mt. Tahoma Dr. S.E., Olympia, WA 98503
www.lonwaltenberger.com
(360) 456-1949
Franchise: No.
Description: Repair/refinish porcelain, gel coat and acrylic bathtubs; sinks; counters (Formica-type and cultured marble); ceramic tiles; spas; ranges and hoods; refrigerators; and dishwashers. Use only primer that requires no acid etching or sanding for savings in labor and durability.
Requirements: The training fee is $295 and you will need about $2,000 for equipment and supplies. "You will repay your total investment with your first 10 jobs."
Provisions: The $295 buys a 14-hour video program plus two manuals with advertising examples, forms, prices, inventory of equipment, and all the information you will need to successfully manage your business. The company president insists that you should shop your hometown sources and manufacturers for all supplies. Technical support is available.
Profit Potential: Profit margin for this industry is high.

WEED MAN
11 Grand Marshall Dr., Scarborough, ON, Canada M1B 5N6
www.weed-man.com
(416) 269-5754
Franchise: Yes.
Description: Franchisees provide lawn management services to home owners.
Requirements: The total start-up investment is around $50,000 including the franchise fee. The company provides help with third party financing for start-up costs, the franchise fee, and equipment. General business experience is also required.
Provisions: Training is provided at company headquarters, at the franchisee's site, and other locations. Particular attention is paid to safety and security precautions.
Comments: Franchisees operate throughout Canada and the US.

——RESIDENTIAL AND COMMERCIAL——
CLEANING AND MAINTENANCE

Residential and commercial cleaning businesses are the essence of service businesses. No products are exchanged, and no special skills are required. The basic purpose is to save customers time.

Home cleaning services is a $200 million a year industry, and it is growing all the time. "In John Naisbitt's best seller, Megatrends, maid services was listed among the six growth industries," says Frank Flack, chief executive officer of Molly Maid, the fastest growing international maid service. "Most American households are two-income families. There are 70 million women in the work force—more than half of them have some form of domestic help. Juggling a career and family can take some doing. A working woman is likely to exchange money for time—something she has precious little of. She can save five or six hours a week to do things that are more gratifying than cleaning windows or dusting under the bed."

There are dozens of maid services, and more are entering the field every day. Most can be operated from home. Although they are not the least expensive home-based opportunities to get into, the potential return on investment is excellent. A well-run maid service, utilizing the team cleaning method, can expect to gross over $100,000 by the second year.

Also targeting the residential customer are carpet cleaning, chimney sweeps, and window washing services.

Other businesses in this chapter cater to commercial customers. Office cleaning, janitorial services, mobile power washing, and restaurant cleaning are among these opportunities. Commercial cleaning businesses tend to require bigger investments and more commitment of time and effort. On the plus side, commercial customers are often repeat customers with long-term contracts that offer extra security.

One of the fastest growing services in this category is window cleaning and window coverings such as shutters and blinds. According to the National Home Builders Association, there are 110 million single family homes in the US. More and more of these are being built with open floor plans with an average of 25-35 windows per home. That's almost 4 billion windows and coverings someone has to clean. You don't need a calculator to figure out that there is a lot of profit to be made!

AMERICAN LEAK DETECTION

888 Research Drive, Suite 100, Palm Springs, CA 92262
www.americanleakdetection.com
(800) 755-6697

Franchise: Yes.

Description: Franchisees use electronic instruments and tools to find and repair water, gas, and sewer leaks in both commercial and residential buildings.

Requirements: The franchise fee is $57,500 and up. You also need a work vehicle and tools.

Provisions: Complete training, both business and technical, is provided.

BLIND DOCTORS TRAINING ACADEMY

269 Market Place Blvd. Suite 342, Cartersville, GA 30121

www.blindsshadesandshutters.com

(770) 975-9009

Franchise: No.

Description: Cleaning, repairing, selling, and installing blinds, shades, and shutters to residential and commercial customers. The cleaning equipment employs a specialized mobile pressure washing system and is safe for all types—vinyl, metal, fabric, or wood. It's easy to transport and anyone can use it easily—even petite women.

Requirements: There are two programs to choose from when starting the blind cleaning and repair business. The cost for the "Starter Plan" is $2,990 and the most popular program is "Plan A" for $9,990. There are also have two additional programs for cleaning, repairing, selling and installing of blinds, shades and shutters that cost $14,990 and $17,990 respectively. "We recommend starting with "Plan A" and then moving on to selling and installing when the business is able to pay for the expansion." There are no geographic restrictions or other special requirements.

Provisions: This is turnkey business opportunity that has all the benefits of a franchise without ongoing fees, territorial restrictions and contracts. The fees include everything: the equipment, a how-to operational manual including all the forms needed to run the business, a hiring and training manual, how-to video training tapes on cleaning and repairing blinds, shades and shutters, marketing and advertising materials on CD-ROM and hard copy for easy cost effective printing, a complete bookkeeping package, and a source for purchasing blinds and repair parts at wholesale cost. Also offered is unlimited consulting time and ongoing company support for one full year.

Comments: "Service two accounts each morning—working from 7 a.m. to 11 a.m.—and gross between $400 and $650 each morning Monday through Friday. The average blind takes 90 seconds to clean with our equipment."

BEARCOM BUILDING SERVICES

7022 South 400 West, Midvale, UT 84047

www.bearcomservices.com

(888) 569-9533

Franchise: Yes.

Description: The Laser Chem advanced carpet dry cleaning system thoroughly cleans carpet, dries quickly, and does not re-soil. "This new system has revolutionized the carpet cleaning industry."

Requirements: The franchise fee is $9,900 and you'll need another $3,000 for start-up.

Provisions: Month to month support via newsletter, toll-free technical assistance, and benefits of in-house research and development.

CEILTECH

> 825 Gate Park Drive, #3, Daytona Beach, FL 32114
> www.ceiltechinc.com
> (800) 662-9299

Franchise: No.

Description: Ceiling cleaning service.

Requirements: Start-up costs are about $13,000 and there are leasing plans available.

Provisions: The system includes all necessary equipment, supplies, and accessories to generate over $4,000 in gross income. Also included are marketing materials and a training manual.

Profit Potential: You can net in excess of $150 per hour.

CHEM-DRY CARPET, DRAPERY AND UPHOLSTERY CLEANING

> 1530 North 1000 West, Logan, UT 84321
> www.chemdry.com
> (877) 307-8233

Franchise: Yes.

Description: Chem-Dry franchises clean carpet, drapery, upholstery and most fabrics with a patented, heated carbonating system. Chem-Dry specializes in the hard-to-remove stains and has four patents with several more pending.

Requirements: The franchise fee is $11,950. There is a financing plan available with $5,950 down payment with a full purchase price of $18,950 (including equipment, supplies, etc.). The remaining $15,000 is financed over 56 months at 0% interest.

Provisions: Your fee will get you all of the equipment, solutions, paperwork, and training needed to start the business. Plus you can expect the constant support of the parent company, a technical department to help with any questions, newsletters, etc.

Provisions: The investment covers everything necessary to start a full-time business.

CLEAN & HAPPY WINDOWS

10019 Des Moines Memorial Dr., Seattle, WA 98168

www.cleanhappy.com

(866) 762-7617

Franchise: Yes.

Description: Franchises clean windows, gutters, roofs, screens, and awnings. Customers include home owners and businesses with buildings no taller than four stories.

Requirements: This is a very inexpensive franchise opportunity. There is no franchise fee and it can be started for $100. Business and marketing experience is the basic requirement. Must be comfortable working several stories up.

Provisions: Training is available and an online scheduling service is provided.

Comments: About half the franchisees are absentee owners.

CLEANNET USA

9861 Broken Land Pkwy., #208, Columbia, MD 21046

www.cleannetusa.com

(800) 735-8838

Franchise: Yes.

Description: Provides a variety of professional cleaning services for commercial, retail and industrial facilities.

Requirements: This is an excellent opportunity that can be started for under $4,000. Financing is available.

Provisions: The amount of training is impressive considering the low cost. One to four weeks is provided at company headquarters and/or the franchisee's location.

Comments: This company has experienced tremendous growth over the past five years. There are now over 2,600 franchisees.

COVERALL CLEANING CONCEPT

500 West Cypress Creek Rd., Suite 580, Ft. Lauderdale, FL 33309

www.coverall.com

(800) 537-3371

Franchise: Yes.

Description: Commercial cleaning services. These services include hard floor care, carpet cleaning, restroom sanitation, lawn maintenance, and painting. Coverall also offers pest control by Orkin.

Requirements: The franchise fee ranges from $6,000 to $32,200.

Provisions: Coverall offers a turnkey program that goes from start-up through expansion. It includes complete training in the latest technology, innovative cleaning techniques, business management, and safety procedures. The fee includes an equipment package, an initial customer base, and participation in volume buying. There are financing options available as well as national membership opportunities.

THE DALE GROUP

23052 Alicia Pkwy., #H-202, Mission Viejo, CA 92692

www.myblindbiz.com

(888) 922-5463

Franchise: No.

Description: Mobile mini-blind wash and wax; on-site sales of blinds, drapes or shutters; and high tech window tinting.

Requirements: The cost is $3,000 and there is financing available.

Provisions: The investment covers all needed tools and equipment, working samples, proven marketing plan, advertising plan, and free ongoing support.

DR. GLASS

3573 Nyland Way, Lafayette, CO 80206

www.docglass.com

(888) 282-3535

Franchise: No.

Description: Window washing service. This particular company has started more than 200 business operators across the country. It's a great part-time business with a proven system and very low start-up cost.

Requirements: The total cost is $2,660 with a down payment of $500 and the balance financed in-house.

Provisions: Turnkey system includes equipment to start a small scale residential window cleaning business. The system includes manuals, videos, template, marketing and advertising materials, e-mail bulletin board access, and all business materials.

HEAVEN'S BEST CARPET & UPHOLSTERY CLEANING

P.O. Box 607, Rexburg, ID 83440

www.heavensbest.com

(800) 359-2095 or (208) 359-1106

Franchise: Yes.

Description: An alternative to the traditional wet saturation carpet cleaning offering the advantages of modern, low moisture cleaning. "Our operators receive professional training. These factors with a low flat rate royalty fee ensure success."

Requirements: The franchise fee is very low at only $2,900 and the royalty is $80 a month. Additional start-up expenses amount to $13,000.

Provisions: Complete equipment and training package, exclusive territory, and enough initial supplies to re-coop $10,000.

JANI-KING INTERNATIONAL, INC.

16885 Dallas Pkwy., Addison, TX 75001

www.janiking.com

(800) 552-5264 or (214) 991-0900

Franchise: Yes.

Description: Jani-King is the world's largest janitorial franchise. Operators perform light office cleaning and janitorial services for commercial and industrial buildings on a long-term contract basis.

Requirements: The franchise fee starts at $8,500, but can go as high as $32,000. Financing is available.

Provisions: All franchisees receive training, business forms, and ongoing support.

JANITIZE AMERICA, INC.

15449 Middlebelt, Livonia, MI 48154

www.jantize.com

(800) 968-9182

Franchise: Yes.

Description: Commercial cleaning service.

Requirements: The franchise fee ranges starts at $3,500 and the initial start-up package (computer system, equipment, supplies, etc.) is another $6,000. You can lower that cost by using the company's computer service instead which reduces the cost by $2,500. Monthly royalties are 8% of gross sales and the advertising fee is 1% of gross.

Provisions: In addition to the provisions stated above, Janitize provides all business forms, a supply of uniforms, and ongoing support.

JAN-PRO

383 Strand Industrial Dr., Little River, SC 29566

www.jan-pro.com

(800) 668-1001

Franchise: Yes.

Description: This is a commercial cleaning franchise with over 2,800 franchisees throughout the United States and Canada.

Requirements: It is possible to start this business for under $1,000. The company even provides financing for that. The royalty is hefty though at 8%. Management skills are also needed.

Provisions: Training is provided for up to four weeks, first at company headquarters then at the franchisee's location. There is a lot of ongoing support, too.

MAID BRIGADE

4 Concourse Pkwy., #200, Atlanta, GA 30328
www.maidbrigade.com
(800) 722-6243

Franchise: Yes.

Description: Supervised team-cleaning services for single-family homes.

Requirements: The franchise fee is $19,500. Operating expenses will require an additional $15,000+. The royalty is 3.5% to 6.9%. A business background is preferred.

Provisions: The fee buys the right to use the name, a one-week training class, operations manual, and a start-up kit that includes janitorial supplies, printed materials, training videos, and marketing materials.

THE MAIDS INTERNATIONAL

4820 Dodge St., Omaha, NE 68132
www.maids.com
(800) 843-6243

Franchise: Yes.

Description: Computerized residential cleaning service.

Requirements: The franchise fee is $16,900. Another $25,000 will be needed for operating capital including leases for cars and computers, labor and advertising. The royalty ranges from 5% to 7% and the advertising royalty is 2%.

Provisions: The fee buys the use of the company name, the exclusive system, pre-training, corporate training, post-training, and a complete equipment and advertising package. Financing is available only for expanding territories.

MAID SERVICES OF AMERICA

475 East Main St., Suite 151, Cartersville, GA 30121
www.maidservicesofamerica.com
(770) 387-2455 or (800) 289-8642

Franchise: No.

Description: Maid service and property maintenance.

Requirements: Business plans with unlimited consulting and support start at $2,495 and go up to $9,995. Start-up costs are an additional $2,500.

Provisions: One-week training at company headquarters; management software; 8-page Web site that includes hosting, maintenance, and regular updates; professional logo design; 10,000 4-color flyers for door to door distribution; direct mail campaign to 10,000 qualified homes; training manuals, business forms and training dvd's.

Profit Potential: Average gross sales are over $100,000 in first year with approximately 25% profit margin.

Comments: Maid Services of America is the second oldest maid service chain in the United States with hundreds of independently owned and operated offices across the country. Established in 1977. "Our success has been built on the quality of service and support we provide. In over 30 years there has never been a single negative report filed against the company with the BBB. Recently expanded offering mobile blind cleaning service opportunities."

MOLLY MAID, INC.
3948 Ranchero Dr., Ann Arbor, MI 48108
www.mollymaid.com
(800) 665-5962

Franchise: Yes.

Description: Regularly scheduled cleaning services with weekday business hours. This is an affordable investment in an exploding industry. Repeat cash business. "Award winning technology."

Requirements: No experience is necessary, but a business background is considered a plus. The franchise fee of $9,900 is included in the total investment of $35,000 to $70,000. The additional working capital is needed for leased cars, insurance, and bonding of the employees. The royalty decreases from 6% to 3% as sales increase. The advertising royalty is 2%.

Provisions: The fee buys exclusive rights to the territory, equipment and supplies, training, and start-up business documents.

Profit Potential: Not available, however, franchisees said that they were earning well into the six figures and grew so fast it was hard to keep the business at home.

Comments: This is the largest maid service franchise with over 400 operators and 16 years of experience. The company believes in projecting a quality image and it works.

NATIONAL PRO CLEAN CORPORATION

445 C East Cheyenne Mtn Blvd #105, Colorado Springs, CO 80918
www.nationalproclean.com
(800) 796-4680

Franchise: No.

Description: Complete program to establish cleaning contractors in janitorial, maid service, carpet cleaning, construction cleanup or restroom sanitation services.

Requirements: The program costs $300; optional equipment costs range from $500 to $3,000, and optional telemarketing service costs an additional $200 to $400.

Provisions: Complete setup program, home study course, and ongoing consulting. The program includes four training manuals, seven hours of instructional audiotapes, all necessary forms, advertising and bid materials, marketing flyers, certification test and diploma, and free follow-up consulting.

Profit Potential: Usually $40,000 part-time and up to $100,000 full-time within 3-5 years.

Comments: "Exclusive training program includes our best selling JanBid Estimating Software. No royalties or commissions are ever charged to our clients. You keep 100% of your earnings. See free article on our Web site to learn all the basics of starting your own cleaning service provided by a 38-year industry veteran."

OMEGASONICS

330 E. Easy Street, Suite A, Simi Valley, CA 93065
www.omegasonics.com
(800) 669-8227

Franchise: No.

Description: Omegasonics gives entrepreneurs and existing cleaning businesses the opportunity to expand into the ultrasonic blind cleaning service and sales market.

Requirements: Total costs range from $9,500 to $18,950. There is financing available.

Provisions: The company provides equipment, initial set of cleaning supplies, training manual, training video, two days of hands-on training at the factory, toll-free support line, annual convention and conference.

PROFESSIONAL CARPET SYSTEMS

4211-C Atlantic Ave., Raleigh, NC 27604

www.procarpetsys.com

(800) 925-5055

Franchise: Yes.

Description: Professional Carpet Systems is a leader in on-site carpet redyeing and a total carpet maintenance service. PCS services include carpet cleaning and repair, water/flood damage restoration, smoke removal, guaranteed odor control, and more.

Requirements: Franchise fee is $14,950; start-up costs range from $18,000 to $50,000; and the royalties are 4-6% with rebates. Financial assistance is provided.

Provisions: Comprehensive training program, annual convention, newsletter, toll-free Help Line, and ongoing research and development. Training consists of two weeks in Raleigh, NC (five days extended available), two days on-site, and 11 two-day training sessions held every year for additional training, most with industry certification available. In addition to this, there are periodic workshops and an annual convention.

Comments: "Professional Carpet Systems is the leader in on-site carpet redyeing, servicing thousands of apartment complexes, hotels, and motels worldwide. Complete carpet service is a niche that is not being filled in the market place by anyone else. Because service and replacement is offered, this business is very recession resistant. This is a business for someone who wants to build a company, not for the absentee owner—direct involvement is vital."

SERVICEMASTER

3839 Forest Hill Irene Rd., Memphis, TN 38125

www.ownafranchise.com

(800) 255-9687

Franchise: Yes.

Description: Professional residential and commercial cleaning and lawn-care services with more than two million customers worldwide.

Requirements: The franchise fee ranges from $16,900 to $43,000 depending on the type of franchise. You will need up to $10,000 for training, equipment, and supplies. The royalty is 10% and the advertising is 1%.

Provisions: The fee buys one week of training at headquarters and ongoing support. Financing is offered for up to 65% of total investment.

Comments: This is a franchise that everyone knows. It has been around since 1947 and now has over 4,200 franchise operators.

SERVPRO

575 Airport Blvd., Gallatin, TX 37066

www.servpro.com

(800) 826-9586

Franchise: Yes.

Description: Full-service residential and commercial cleaning business that also specializes in fire restoration.

Requirements: The franchise fee is $26,000 with an equal amount needed for start-up.

Provisions: Complete training and technical support are provided. Financing is available.

Comments: This is one of the oldest services businesses in the industry with over 1,000 franchisees.

STEAMATIC, INC.

3333 Quorum Drive, Ste. 280 Fort Worth, TX 76137

www.steamatic.com

(800) 544-1303

Franchise: Yes.

Description: Steamatic provides cleaning and disaster recovery services worldwide that includes the cleaning of residential and commercial air duct/coil systems, carpets, furniture, drapery and the restoration of homes/buildings and their contents following fire, smoke, water or mold damage. Other services include wood restoration, hard surface cleaning, corrosion control and deodorization. No other franchise in the cleaning and restoration industry offers this range of services. Steamatic is aggressively looking to grow worldwide and operates in over 400 franchise territories in the U.S. and 27 countries.

Requirements: Sales and marketing background helpful. No previous cleaning experience necessary. Start-up costs range from $25,000 to $80,000. Financing is available.

Provisions: Initial training at company headquarters for three weeks (2 weeks in class training, 1 week on the job/hands on training). Training covers sales/marketing and operations training. IICRC certification for carpet cleaning, water and fire/smoke damage.

SWISHER HYGIENE

6849 Fairview Rd., Charlotte, NC 28210

www.swisheronline.com

(800) 444-4138

Franchise: Yes.

Description: Commercial restroom cleaning and sanitation. Products and services provided to 35,000 customers every week. "We are one of the top 50 franchise in North America."

Requirements: Franchise fees start at $35,000 plus another $26,000 is required for start-up expenses.

Provisions: Full initial and ongoing training, and access to an extremely successful business.

WINDOW GANG

> 1509 Ann St., Beaufort, NC 28516
> www.windowgang.com
> (252) 726-4314

Franchise: Yes.

Description: Window, gutter, blind, and pressure cleaning service.

Requirements: The franchise fee starts at $5,000 plus a minimum $9,000 for equipment. You will also need a truck.

Provisions: A complete business package and ongoing training in cleaning procedures, equipment operation, maintenance procedures, sales and marketing techniques, and cleaning solutions and application tips. Also provides telemarketing leads, group business and health insurance, national advertising, and initial credit line for supplies.

——COMPUTER AND—— TECHNICAL SERVICES

After 20 or so years of computers making their way into the workplace, it is rare to find a business without one. This chapter is comprised mostly of businesses that either service computer equipment or are based specifically on the services a computer (or other technology) can provide.

There are several opportunities in the computer training industry. In some cases, training services alone provides the income, but usually these businesses also sell hardware and software. That can make a big difference in the bottom line, but obviously it also involves sales (which can be done by your employees).

There are a lot of opportunities related to the Internet. You will find businesses here that offer Web design, Web hosting, domain names, e-commerce solutions, and other services to help people make the most of their Web experience.

Anyone who has tried to set up a new computer or figure out what to do when one crashed can appreciate a little on-site help. Companies like Geeks

On Call come to the rescue with house calls, an idea whose time has definitely come. There are several newcomers to this field, which is growing hotter by the day. The best part is, you don't have to know a thing about computers yourself. Most of these businesses hire skilled college students to handle the actual service calls.

AIS MEDIA, INC.

> 115 Perimeter Center Terrace, #540, Atlanta, GA 30346
> www.aisprivatelabel.com
> (800) 784-0919

Franchise: No.
Description: Services include Web site design, Web hosting, domain registration, e-mail services, custom database development, programming, search engine registration, credit card merchant accounts and other e-commerce services.
Requirements: Start-up costs total $10,000.
Provisions: Training is provided via the Internet and over the phone. Advertising and marketing support is provided including sales leads.
Profit potential: Six figure income possible.
Comments: Can be run part-time.

CM IT SOLUTIONS

> 537 Woodward Dr., #D, Austin, TX 78704
> www.cmit.biz
> (800) 710-2648

Franchise: Yes.
Description: Computer services and training for businesses.
Requirements: Start-up costs range from $55,000 to $100,000 and there is no financing available. Business and marketing skills are also needed.
Provisions: There is a two-week training session at company headquarters followed by ongoing support via Internet and toll-free phone line.

COMPUCHILD USA

> 602 Main Street, Suite 2, Rochester, IN 46975
> www.compuchild.com
> (800) 619-5437

Franchise: No.
Description: Educational and entertaining classes in computer education designed to give preschoolers a head start in the computerized world. This is

the largest preschool computer education system in the world. It has grown tremendously since its inception in 1994.

Requirements: The investment is $12,500 with no financing available.

Provisions: Intensive training is provided in all aspects of the business at the licensee's location. There is also plenty of follow-up support.

COMPUTER MEDICS OF AMERICA

2260 N. Green Forest Drive, Palmer, Alaska 99645

www.computermedicsofamerica.com

(907) 694-0371

Franchise: Yes.

Description: Mobile repair service for all kinds of PCs, laptops, and networks. Customers include both individuals at home and businesses.

Requirements: Franchise owners are all required to have computer repair experience. The franchise fee is based on the population of the county/counties that they will cover. It can range from $5,000-$20,000. After the franchise fee, the initial costs for getting started are typically from $1,000-$5,000.

Provisions: Training is conducted at company headquarters and ongoing support is provided primarily over the Internet.

Profit Potential: Full-time operators are making $6,000-$12,000 a month. It is a franchise model that can be operated full or part-time. Company does not charge any royalty or administrative fees to our franchise owners.

COMPUTER TROUBLESHOOTERS

755 Commerce Drive, Suite 605, Decatur, GA 30030

www.comptroub.com

(404) 477-1300

Franchise: Yes.

Description: Provide computer services and support to business owners and home office owners.

Requirements: The initial franchise fee is $19,500 with an ongoing royalty fee of $220 per month. In addition, you should have computer skills in hardware, Internet, networking, software or training.

Provisions: Proven business plan and marketing campaigns, training, worldwide network of support, and regularly updated utility CDs.

Comments: Computer Troubleshooters is highly ranked by both Entrepreneur Magazine and Franchise Business Review, and currently has over 475 locations in 26 countries.

CONCERTO NETWORKS

501 W. Broadway, #800, San Diego, CA 92101

www.concertonetworks.com

(866) 482-6623

Franchise: Yes.

Description: Franchisees provide mobile, on-site small office and residential computer and network solutions.

Requirements: The most important requirement is experience with computer repairs. The total cost of start-up is about $35,000. The ongoing royalty is very high at 14%.

Provisions: The company provides strong training and support. Part of the royalty pays for regional and national advertising designed to drum up business for franchisees.

E-BACKUPS

11756 Borman Dr., St. Louis, MO 63146

www.e-backups.net

(800) 749-2737

Franchise: No.

Description: Computer backup service.

Requirements: Start-up costs $199.

Provisions: Provides training, technical support, advertising, and sales leads.

Comments: "You can create your own brand without having to host the data yourself."

EXPETEC TECHNOLOGY SERVICES

12 2nd Ave. SW, Aberdeen, SD 57401

www.expetec.com

(605) 225-0054

Franchise: Yes.

Description: Provides mobile on-site, high-level technology services to commercial, small business, and consumer customers. Services include computer maintenance, consulting, computer upgrades, repairs, networking, Web hosting, Web design, and other business technology services.

Requirements: Although the investment is hefty at $62,000 to $83,200, the company has a program for those with qualifying credit so it is possible to start with as little as $5,000.

Provisions: The cost covers three weeks of training in a state-of-the-art training center, testing and diagnostic equipment, a business system, and a service vehicle called the TAV (Technical Assault Vehicle) which is equipped with a built-in custom networked repair center.

FRIENDLY COMPUTERS

3145 N. Rainbow Blvd., Las Vegas, NV 89108

www.friendlycomputers.com/franchise

(800) 656-3115

Franchise: Yes.

Description: Computer sales, repair, and support for businesses and consumers. Services cover the entire range from helping beginners set up their first computer to installing networks and providing e-commerce solutions to large corporations.

Requirements: This is one of the better deals among franchises of this type. A franchise operation can be started for under $15,000. Business experience is required.

Provisions: Training start with one week at the company's site, followed by one week at the franchisee's site. Ongoing support is provided in a number of ways including the Internet, toll-free phone line, newsletters, and cooperative purchasing and advertising programs.

GEEKS ON CALL AMERICA

814 Kempsville Rd, #106, Norfolk, VA 23502

www.geekchoice.com

(888) 667-4577

Franchise: Yes.

Description: Providing computer support on-site including repairs, networking, and training.

Requirements: $20,000 franchise fee plus at least another $28,000 for start-up. The royalty fee varies.

Provisions: Extensive training is provided with special emphasis on helping you build a business from the ground up. The company provides a comprehensive marketing plan, which is customized for your territory. State-of-the-art support system includes marketing research databases, prospect databases, telephone and central dispatching systems.

JUST THE FAX, a division of Fulcrum Financial Enterprises Inc.

711 Medford Center, #153, Medford, OR 97504

www.justthefax-bizop.com

(541) 734-9260

Franchise: No.

Description: A unique service that helps restaurants acquire customers and business people with their "where to go to lunch today" decision, by faxing Lunch Specials from local restaurants to businesses daily.

71

Requirements: A computer with a modem and phone line. One-time license fee: $850–$1,385 depending on choice of purchase plans. No experience necessary.

Provisions: The license fee includes two manuals: a 130-page business and marketing manual plus a Web site marketing manual, rights to use the Just The Fax trademarked name and all copyrighted materials (provided on CD), consulting, resale rights, referral agreement, and a guarantee of satisfaction.

Profit Potential: $1,200 to $3,600 per month.

Comments: Dave and Jaimi Helbert, the creators of Just The Fax, have licensed over 210 people to operate Just the Fax businesses in their own towns and cities throughout the US and Canada.

Close up: Just The Fax

"I must be an entrepreneur at heart because I'm always on the lookout for an additional source of income," says Dawn Harrington, of upstate New York. "Just The Fax really fit the bill. It must be the best sideline business there is."

Dawn is one of millions of people who work as full-time employees and run sideline businesses out of their homes. As an administrative assistant for a university, she thought at first that she wanted to leave her job, then realized all she really wanted was to supplement the family income.

Dawn's first attempt to go into business failed before it got started because she paid for an unscrupulous business opportunity that never delivered what it promised. She was more careful, downright leery, when she decided to try again.

"I figured I was already out $6,000 and I had a $3,000 computer just sitting there in my house. I was determined to find something that would work." Dawn found Just The Fax right here in *The Work-at-Home Sourcebook*. This time she was more careful about checking out the company.

"After seeing the preliminary package, it just didn't seem like it could lose," Dawn says. "Actually, it seemed like fun."

The Just The Fax business concept is simple. You fax daily lunch specials from local area restaurants to businesses where workers will likely go out to lunch on weekdays. It works because it's an inexpensive way for the restaurants to advertise and because it targets the customers they're after—the people who want to go out to eat.

Best of all, it takes only an hour a day to operate the business. Even in a small population area, the earnings are $1,200 a month with virtually no overhead. Larger areas can bring in up to $7,200 a month with very little extra time needed.

Dawn says if it can work where she lives, it can work anywhere. "This is a small area with a sluggish economy. But it was so easy to get started, it was surprising. I followed instructions and started sending letters copied verbatim from the manual. That was in December. By February 3rd I was up and running with enough restaurants to earn $1,000 a month."

Could you ask for a better part-time business? "I don't think so," says Dawn. "I can work full-time, and I don't have to take any extra time away from my kids. I do it after they're in bed. And the fringe benefits aren't bad either. I love to eat, and I've picked up a lot of recipes and cooking tips, too."

NERD FORCE
97 New Dorp Plaza, Staten Island, NY 10306
www.nerdforce.com
(800) 979-6373

Franchise: Yes.

Description: Tech support services available to customers seven days a week. Franchisees provide service to individuals as well as small and medium-sized businesses, both on-site and remotely with branded IT managed services.

Requirements: The franchise fee is $14,000 with a weekly royalty that's a flat $100. No technical experience is necessary.

Provisions: Complete training and support, fully developed marketing material and programs, plus a 24/7 call center that offers customer service, sales, and dispatch services to all franchisees.

REMOTE BACKUP SYSTEMS
319 Poplar View Lane West Suite 1, Collierville, TN 38017
www.remote-backup.com
(901) 850-9920

Franchise: Yes.

Description: This is an interesting concept that makes you wonder why someone didn't think of it sooner. Operators provide remote computer backup services for businesses and anyone else who uses a computer a lot.

Requirements: Packages available from $798, but can go higher if you don't already have the necessary computer setup. Free evaluation is offered.

Provisions: Advertising and marketing plans, phone support, technical support, and sales leads.

RESCUECOM

2560 Burnet Ave., Syracuse, NY 13206

www.rescuecom.net

(800) 737-2837

Franchise: Yes.

Description: Computer consulting and repair service.

Requirements: Must qualify by being a top-notch computer professional such as a tech pro, computer executive, or computer company owner. The investment is low. The franchise fee starts at just $2,500 with financing available.

Provisions: Complete business training and support.

SOFT-TEMPS WORLDWIDE

1280 NE Business Park Place, Jensen Beach, FL 34957

http://stworldlink.com

(800) 221-2880

Franchise: Yes.

Description: Provide on-site computer services to local small to midsize businesses using a database of skilled consultants.

Requirements: This is an excellent value at only $1,900 for start-up including franchise fee. The 4% royalty includes 1% for advertising.

Provisions: Web site, full-time technical and corporate support, and a huge amount of marketing materials (brochures, videos, CD-ROM master, etc.). Minimum market area granted is 25,000 population per franchisee.

THRIFTY IMPRESSIONS

1046 E. Walker St., Blackfoot, ID 83221

www.thriftyimpressions.com

(208) 782-0349

Franchise: No.

Description: Computerized signs and banners for businesses and consumers.

Requirements: Total start-up is about $2,000.

Provisions: Training is provided in classroom session at company headquarters, plus ongoing training is available in a manual, video, and online. There is ongoing support for advertising and marketing strategies, plus technical support online or on the phone. Sales leads are provided.

WSI INTERNET
>5915 Airport Rd., #300, Toronto, ON, Canada L4V 1T1
>www.wsicorporate.com
>(905) 678-7588

Franchise: Yes.

Description: This company formerly known as Worldsites provides Internet services to small and medium-sized businesses.

Requirements: The bulk of the investment required is the $40,000 franchise fee.

Provisions: Training is available at company headquarters. There is ongoing support.

Comments: This company has grown quickly over the past five years. There are now over 500 franchisees throughout Canada and the US.

———REAL ESTATE AND——— FINANCIAL SERVICES

Real estate is a business commonly based in a home office. Although there are no real estate businesses per se listed in this chapter, there are a variety of businesses closely associated with the industry. Home inspection services, for instance, are employed by real estate brokers and homebuyers to carefully check out buildings for hidden problems. Lindal Cedar Homes franchisees do more than sell homes, they offer personalized design services and sometimes act as contractors too. Income property owners need to check out new tenants before renting, and for them, the National Tenant Network offers computerized tenant screening services.

Closely related to the real estate industry are financial services. There are several companies that focus on different ways to reduce costs and get refunds for customers that have been overbilled.

All of these businesses require a higher level of expertise and business acumen. If you consider buying one of these businesses, you should have a strong interest in the business and be able to deal effectively with people and project yourself professionally.

AMERICAN ELITE HOMES, INC.
P.O. Box 1160, Kannapolis, NC 28082
www.aehi.com
(800) 792-3443 ext. 567

Franchise: No.

Description: Market a full line of panelized homes and commercial buildings.

Requirements: There is no charge to become a representative, however, you are required to purchase or sell a house to get started. The initial down payment is $5,000.

Provisions: Model home to sell, live in, or use as office. Also books, manual, literature, blueprints, and complete construction information.

Profit Potential: $5,000 to $50,000 per sale.

AMERISPEC HOME INSPECTION SERVICE
889 Ridge Lake Blvd., Memphis, TN 38120
www.amerispecfranchise.com
(800) 426-2270

Franchise: Yes.

Description: Amerispec is the number one home inspection company in North America. Business owners conduct a 400+ item home inspection and provide a computer-generated report for homebuyers and sellers.

Requirements: The franchise fee ranges from $19,900 to $29,900 with additional start-up costs estimated at $5,000.

Provisions: Amerispec has a network of customer services, marketing, and trainers. You receive extensive marketing and technical training plus ongoing training and support.

COST CONTAINMENT SOLUTIONS, INC.
9921 Fringe Tree Ct., Louisville, KY 40241
www.costcontain.com
(800) 872-3709

Franchise: No.

Description: Business to business contingency-based expense reduction service.

Requirements: The initial licensing investment is $29,900. You will also need a notebook computer.

Provisions: This is a turnkey expense reduction system that includes operations manuals, software templates, supplier networks, initial and ongoing training and support.

DEBT ZERO

14 Hughes St., #B205, Irvine, CA 92618

www.debtzerollc.com

(949) 625-2565

Franchise: No.

Description: Debt settlement services.

Requirements: Start-up costs are under $3,000.

Provisions: Continuous training and support. 24/7 access to customer service reps. Free software with lead tracking. Leads provided.

DISABILITY ASSOCIATES

4610 S Ulster St., Denver, CO 80237

www.ssahelp.com

(303) 766-1111

Franchise: No.

Description: A Disability Advocate, also known as a Disability Consultant, Disability Specialist or Non-attorney Representative, is a specially trained individual who assists others who are applying for Social Security disability benefits. This service was created by Congress and the Social Security Administration and can be verified via the Federal Code of Regulations.

Requirements: Start-up costs range from $1,000 to $5,000.

Provisions: Training is provided at the licensee's location and also via manual, video, Internet, and phone. There is ample marketing support including sales leads. Software is also provided.

Profit Potential: Up to $5300 per successful case.

Comments: The company has 1,500 licensees.

HOME STAGING RESOURCE

1611-A S. Melrose Dr., #316, Vista, CA 92081

www.homestagingresource.com

(888) 563-9271

Franchise: No.

Description: Home staging service for people who are trying to sell their homes for the best price possible.

Requirements: Start-up costs $945.

Provisions: Provides classes, certification, advertising, sales leads, and ongoing support.

THE HOMETEAM INSPECTION SERVICE, INC.
575 Chamber Dr., Milford, OH 45150
www.hmteam.com
(800) 598-5297

Franchise: Yes.

Description: Home inspections using the "team" concept, using multiple people on inspections which cuts the inspection time in half and gives a better inspection.

Requirements: The franchise cost ranges from $11,900 to $29,900 depending on population size of territory. Additional start-up costs are approximately $8,000.

Provisions: Designated franchise area; an extensive 14 days of training which includes marketing, technical knowledge, and business procedures; and continuous ongoing support.

Profit Potential: Average $100,000 annually.

HOUSEMASTER OF AMERICA, INC.
421 W. Union Ave., Bound Brook, NJ 08805
www.housemaster.com
(800) 526-3939

Franchise: Yes.

Description: HouseMaster has developed a complete system for doing business in the home inspection industry. It is not necessary to know anything about housing, engineering, real estate, or law to take advantage of this opportunity.

Requirements: The franchise fee range from $12,000 to $29,000. Other first year costs range between $10,000 and $18,000.

Provisions: The fee buys training, customized data base software, and ongoing support.

The real estate market has seen better days. Everybody's affected, but none more so than those who make their living in the industry. Should you consider starting a business in the real estate sector at this time?

The answer is yes—if you're careful about where you invest your money and energy. For example, HouseMaster, the oldest home inspection franchise company in the country, is still a very good choice. For the 400 HouseMaster franchisees operating throughout the US and Canada, business has never been better. Marianne Murphy, VP Marketing and Development for HouseMaster reports that the real estate slump has actually been a boon for her company.

The key to thriving in tough economic times is to stick with a company that has been around a while and understands the opportunities that lurk behind every gray cloud. Murphy says, "We're quite busy because we've been through many, many market changes and we know how to work in any climate."

It's all about positioning and adapting. For example, if it's a seller's market, the buyers need home inspections. If it's a buyer's market, the sellers need home inspections. Right now, it's a buyer's market. How can you make that work for you? How about helping sellers prepare their homes in accordance with "staging." It's a huge business and you don't even need formal training or a license. And the business can be started with very little, if any, money.

Another technique that works in this market is to focus on pre-sale services. The US market is glutted with listings and anything that can help sellers stay one step ahead of the pack is valuable. Again, using HouseMaster as an example, franchisees use "pre-inspections" as a lead generating tool for real estate agents. The sellers get home inspections early on so the agent can say, "I've got a home inspection on this house, call me." It works.

If you're nervous about the future, stick with a company you can depend on to help get you started right. This is where franchising comes in. One of the beauties of being part of a franchise is that you're not out there alone trying to figure out what the heck is going to happen. A good franchise organization has the big picture and the resources to put the most profitable plans into action. They can do the expensive forecasting for you, and react before changes (good or bad) actually happen.

HUNTING LEASE NETWORK

11516 Nicholas St., Omaha, NE 68154

www.nationalhuntingleases.com

(800) 346-2650

Franchise: Yes.

Description: Land leasing for hunting and fishing. The Hunting Lease Network connects landowners and sportsmen from all across the country.

Requirements: The initial franchise fee is $15,000 and the estimated initial investment required ranges from $23,500 to $39,000 (includes franchise fee).

Provisions: Most territories are half a state in size, so there are plenty of counties to find landowners in your area. Free three-day training in Omaha, start-up kit to get you going right away, on-site support, Web-based training, continuing education, accounting services, telephone support, and annual conferences.

THE INTERFACE GROUP LTD.

2182 Dupont Drive, # 221, Irvine, CA 92612

www.interfacefinancial.com

(800) 387-0860

Franchise: Yes.

Description: Franchisees provide short-term working capital for small businesses through an innovative invoice-discounting program.

Requirements: The initial franchise fee is $30,000; working capital required is $100,000+. Home-based-franchisees need phone, fax, computer and a car.

Provisions: The fee covers all documentation, operations manuals, newsletters, full training program, and extensive ongoing support.

Comments: "We provide 30+ years of experience, extensive training, and hand holding. Franchisees have the opportunity to be part of a 130-unit team and part of a trillion dollar world wide market place. This is a lifestyle business."

INTERNATIONAL HOMES OF CEDAR, INC.

P.O. Box 886, Woodinville, WA 98072

www.ihoc.com

(800) 767-7674

Franchise: No.

Description: IHC produces custom pre-cut homes and commercial building packages featuring solidly engineered timber walls to provide superior energy efficiency, structural strength, reduced maintenance, and ease of construction.

Requirements: Purchase of model home.

Provisions: IHC provides training and technical support.

INTERNATIONAL MERGERS AND ACQUISITIONS

4300 N. Miller Rd., #230, Scottsdale, AZ 85251

www.ima-world.com

(480) 990-3899

Franchise: Yes.

Description: Providing consulting and financing assistance to public and private companies with mergers, acquisitions and funding.

Requirements: This is a high level business that requires a solid background in management. Ideal candidates are former high-level executives from major national and international corporations, but other experts with hands-on experience would be considered if proven to be capable of working in the international business environment. The total investment required is $25,000 with no ongoing royalty fee.

Provisions: Upon completion of training, you will become part of a worldwide network of consultants with all the support that that implies.

LINDAL CEDAR HOMES, INC.

P.O. Box 24426, Seattle, WA 98124

www.lindal.com

(800) 221-6063

Franchise: No.

Description: Lindal Cedar Homes is the world's largest manufacturer of cedar homes.

Requirements: The cost of a dealership is $5,000.

Provisions: Comprehensive training and a comprehensive cooperative advertising program.

NATIONAL PROPERTY INSPECTIONS

11620 Arbor St., Suite 100, Omaha, NE 68144

www.npiweb.com

(800) 333-9807

Franchise: Yes.

Description: Residential and commercial property inspections.

Requirements: The total investment, including franchise fee, is $21,800 with partial financing available.

Provisions: The fee includes two weeks of comprehensive training in Omaha, in-field training, ongoing and responsive technical and marketing support, computer system that produces on-site reports, warranty program and award-winning National Relocation Referral Program.

NATIONAL TENANT NETWORK, INC.

P.O. Box 1664, Lake Grove, OR 97035

www.ntnnet.com

(503) 635-1118

Franchise: Yes.

Description: This is a unique computerized tenant tracking and screening system for residential and commercial tenants.

Requirements: The franchise fee is $45,000. An additional investment of $20,000 is required for a marketing and feasibility study and for equipment.

Provisions: The franchise investment covers the cost of two fully programmed access terminals, modems, and telecommunications software as well as training and marketing assistance.

PROVENTURE BUSINESS GROUP, INC.

P.O. Box 338, Needham Heights, MA 02194

(781) 444-8278

Franchise: Yes.

Description: In this business, the franchisee would perform two functions: business brokering and franchise consulting.

Requirements: A solid background in top-level management and/or business ownership is required. The total investment for start-up is about $35,000 of which $10,000 is the franchise fee. The monthly royalty is 6%.

Provisions: Training, software, leads, and marketing support.

SIERRA JUDGMENT RECOVERY

P.O. Box 5040, Saint Marys, GA 31558

www.recoverycourse.com

(912) 882-8190

Franchise: No.

Description: Judgment recovery services.

Requirements: Start-up costs $165.

Provisions: Provides training and follow-up support via Internet and phone.

STAGING DIVA

177 Bellefair Ave., Toronto, ON, Canada M4L 3V1

www.stagingdiva.com

(416) 691-6615

Franchise: No.

Description: Home staging service.

Requirements: Get started for under $1,000.

Provisions: Provides training, sales leads, and ongoing support.

ZAIO.COM
> Suite 200, 1013 17th Avenue SW, Calgary, AB, Canada T2T 0A7
> www.zaio.com
> (877) 318-0537

Franchise: Yes.

Description: ZAIO.COM is in the process of photographing each and every property in cities across the country. The company has named this process "GeoPic." The database will be continuously maintained and updated as properties change. Franchisees earn fees in their exclusive geographic areas in a variety of ways. The digital images are accessed exclusively over the Internet by real estate, mortgage, and insurance industries, police, fire and ambulance dispatching, and portals and media outlets.

Requirements: Must live in an available territory of at least 5,000 population. The total investment of $17,000 minimum includes the franchise fee. There is an ongoing royalty of 6%. Financing is available.

Provisions: Proprietary software, access to the database, and training in business and marketing techniques.

———PERSONAL SERVICES———

These days, it seems there are not enough hours in the day to do everything that needs to be done. The result is a lot of busy working people are demanding all kinds of services. Some services are designed to make more quality time available while others help enhance the quality of life.

Through these businesses, customers can have their meals delivered to their door at dinnertime, have their pets and plants tended to while on vacation, find sitters for their children temporarily or nannies permanently, and find all kinds of help through personal referral services. They can also find potential mates, have someone else shop for them while they work, have their clothing custom-made, have their dry cleaning picked up while they're at work, or have custom-made gift baskets sent to their kids in college. There's something here for everyone, customers and entrepreneurs alike.

One of the fastest growing services is elder care. Not only are we living longer, we are living healthier, more independent lives. Elder care services generally do not include medical treatments or supervision of any kind. Rather, it focuses on the routine chores of daily living. By offering these services, seniors can continue to live in their own homes without having to work too hard at maintaining their independent lifestyles.

A CARD-IN-THE-YARD

> 3245 Ramblewood Rd. Ellicott City, MD 21042
> www.acardintheyard.com
> (410) 480-9200

Franchise: No.

Description: This is a unique and fun business that will literally turn heads and stop traffic. Just as the name implies, it involves producing a variety of whimsical yard sign designs, which can be personalized for virtually any occasion. The signs are removable and re-usable after each use. Each setup includes 6-foot-high fun signs, a yard-full of props and decorations which customers rent from you to announce special occasions.

Requirements: $499 business package. Must have van, suv, or truck to transport signs. Some small equipment/tools needed to produce signs.

Provisions: The complete business system includes a business manual, 5 to-scale patterns, 50 sample ads, sample coupons and flyers, wholesale sources, recordkeeping forms and tips, and all the necessary instructions to make the business work. Ongoing support is available by phone or e-mail.

Comments: "This is ideal for stay-at-home moms or empty-nesters."

AEGIN PLACE

> 2521 N. Main St., Las Cruces, NM 88001
> www.aeginplace.com
> (866) 659-1834

Franchise: Yes.

Description: Live-in nonmedical care for seniors. Franchisees match qualified companions with older adults for long-term home assignments at an affordable price. The insured live-in companions can assist older adults in maintaining a self-sufficient status in their own home. The goal of the program is to facilitate older adults with daily activities on a live-in basis as an alternative to an assisted living center, boarding home or nursing home placement.

Requirements: Total start-up costs start at $46,000 with ongoing royalties of 3%.

Provisions: Training and ongoing support. Marketing support includes regional advertising, lead generation, and initial materials.

CANDY BOUQUET
423 East 3rd St., Little Rock, AR 72201
www.candybouquet.com
(877) CANDY-01

Franchise: Yes.

Description: Candy bouquets are floral-like creations crafted from gourmet chocolates and candies. They are customized into one-of-a-kind gifts that won't wilt, fade, or die.

Requirements: Approximate initial start-up costs range from $7,500 to $45,000.

Provisions: Exclusive territory, operations manual, trademarked name and logo, business training, marketing training, Candy Bouquet design training, discounts from suppliers, new design updates, online catalog, newsletters, and continuing support. There are no royalties.

COMFORT KEEPERS
6640 Poe Ave., #200, Dayton, OH 45414
www.comfortkeepers.com
(800) 387-2415

Franchise: Yes.

Description: Care for seniors in their own homes. This service includes only assistance in the daily tasks of living and does not include any medical care. The franchisee is a manager, not a caregiver.

Requirements: The franchise fee is just under $20,000 with an equal amount needed for start-up. There is an ongoing royalty ranging from 3-5%.

Provisions: Complete training and ongoing support.

COMPANION CONNECTION SENIOR CARE
304 Park Ave. S., 11th Fl., New York, NY 10010
www.companionconnectionseniorcare.com
(800) 270-6949

Franchise: No.

Description: Provides live-in or live-out non-medical home care to seniors and infirm or disabled individuals.

Requirements: Start-up costs total $10,000 and there is financing available.

Provisions: Provides a business manual and video plus training at headquarters. Marketing support includes sales leads and Web site.

CHRISTMAS CONCEPTS

> 3960 S. Higuera St., San Luis Obispo, CA 93401
> www.christmasconcepts.com
> (805) 782-0128

Franchise: No.

Description: Rent Christmas decorations commercially to banks, hotels, restaurants, retirement homes, car dealerships, and malls.

Requirements: The start-up cost ranges from $350 to $1,800, including licensing fee and there is financing available from the company.

Provisions: Complete training is provided at company headquarters and on-site. The licensee also receives a training manual, portfolio, and video. There is plenty of ongoing support as well as advertising and marketing materials and the company will even help get accounts.

CHRISTMAS DECOR

> P.O. Box 5946, Lubbock, TX 79408
> www.christmasdecor.net
> (800) 687-9551

Franchise: Yes.

Description: Provide decorating services for holidays and other special events. Customers are both residential and commercial.

Requirements: The total investment is under $20,000. Half of that can be financed.

Provisions: Training is provided and there is plenty of ongoing support. Profits can be raised by participating in the company's cooperative purchasing program but it is not a requirement.

Close up: Christmas Decor

There are lots of great businesses that operate full steam in the warm months, but then in winter they're forced to lay off workers and hope for an early spring. But one person's off-season is another person's peak season. Just ask any of the 375 Christmas Decor business owners. Blake Smith was one of those warm-weather business owners looking for a cure for the off-season blues. One year, he started putting up Christmas lights for his landscaping customers in Lubbock, Texas. This solution has worked wonders for his bottom line.

Christmas Decor's marketing director, Brandon Stephens, says, "Our founder had a great idea. It took five years, but he developed a pretty nice system that allowed him (and his crew) to work in the off-season when nobody else could." Being able to operate 12 months out of the year as opposed to 9 or 10 months makes a huge difference even to a successful business. During those initial five years, the company grew from $250,000 to a $1.3 million in sales. "Of that $1.3 million," Stephens points out, "about $300,000 was Christmas Decor work, *but* it accounted for 50% of the total profit. Today, Christmas Decor has over 40,000 customers in 48 states and Canada."

As a franchise, Christmas Decor tends to attract green industry business owners. "Probably 85-90% of our franchisees are small businesses doing lawn care, landscaping, pest control, or irrigation. They already have the labor force, the trucks, trailers, and tools. And they have a customer base that they can leverage through cross-selling, which helps them get started a lot faster," says Stephens.

How much are homeowners willing to pay for this service? On average (nationally) a Christmas Decor installation runs about $1,380. "Each display is custom to the property," says Stephens. "Our typical customer is going to get some roof lighting and a few windows, some shrubs, and a couple of trees. And there may be some stake lighting around the walkways and driveway." The crews start installing in mid-October, sometimes even earlier. They return to take down the lights in January and finish up by early February—just in time to get ready for spring.

CLUTTERBUSTERS

    15521 Grinnell Terrace, Derwood, MD 20855

    www.clutterbusters.com

    (301) 309-9614

Franchise: Yes.

Description: Professional organizers develop customized systems for clients so they can find needed items in a minimal amount of time. They also help the client decide what should be done with their items, educate the client on organizational techniques, and develop strategies and install systems so the client can maintain the organized space.

Requirements: The franchise fee is $25,000; there is third-party financing available.

Provisions: Training takes place at company headquarters and at the franchisee's location. Marketing support includes co-op advertising, ad slicks, regional advertising, proprietary software, Web site lead generation, and individual Web page.

DRY CLEANING TO-YOUR-DOOR

1121 N.W. Bayshore Dr., Waldport, OR 97394
www.dctyd.com
(800) 318-1800

Franchise: Yes.

Description: Franchisees pick up dry cleaning from customers' homes and drop it off the next day, for free. A cleaning bill is presented to the customer at the end of every month.

Requirements: Total investment of $40,000. You will also need a van.

Provisions: Training and support, racks, logos and paint for the van, uniforms, heavy-duty laundry bags, hangers, computer calling board and routing database, Web site, new customer kits, and more.

ENTREES ON TRAYS, INC.

3 Lombardy Terrace, Fort Worth, TX 76132
www.entreesontrays.com
(817) 735-8558

Franchise: No.

Description: A dinner delivery service operated without labor or inventory. You would work with 20-50 local restaurants within a six-mile radius, acting as a home delivery service, not a caterer. The business is run from home from 5:00 to 9:00 p.m.

Requirements: The one-time license agreement fee is $8,750.

Provisions: You will receive two days of training, working hands-on in Fort Worth. Also included with your fee is all equipment and materials necessary to initiate business (except radios negotiated on a local basis).

Profit Potential: See below.

Comments: This is a great business idea that has been perfected by this company. Entrees on Trays has delivered 100,000 dinners amounting to over $1 million annually in the Fort Worth metroplex while 11 out of 11 competing companies have gone out of business.

GRAVE GROOMERS

13055 Riverdale Dr. N.W., #500-220, Minneapolis, MN 55448
www.gravegroomers.com
(888) 828-7805

Franchise: No.

Description: Licensees provide complete cemetery care and maintenance. Services include beautification, cleaning, grass cutting, laying flowers and wreaths, restoring broken/damaged markers and monuments, stone leveling, planting, and more.

Requirements: Total start-up costs are under $5,000.

Provisions: Exclusive territories. Business can be run part-time. Company offers training at the licensee's location.

GRISWOLD SPECIAL CARE

> 717 Bethlehem Pike, #300, Erdenheim, PA 19073
> www.griswoldspecialcare.com
> (215) 402-0200

Franchise: Yes.

Description: Home care for seniors who need help with daily tasks. This does not include medical care. People being cared for may be disabled, bed- or wheelchair-bound, recovering from illness or surgery, or just needing to give a respite to family members.

Requirements: Franchisees in this business need to be caring people in addition to having management skills. The cost is low, starting at $6,000 and there is no franchise fee. There is partial financing available.

Provisions: Training and proprietary software.

GROCERY LADY

> 20600 Hansen Rd., Maple Heights, OH 44137
> www.thegrocerylady.com
> (216) 510-4132

Franchise: No.

Description: Grocery shopping and delivery service. Customers can place their orders directly through the Web site (no software is needed). The orders come to you (the licensee) by e-mail or they call you on the telephone. You confirm the order, arrange for payment, shop and deliver the items, and get paid for the groceries and your fee.

Requirements: Only $30.

Provisions: Training by Internet and phone. Provides sales leads and phone support.

HAWKEYE'S HOME SITTERS

> 14920-95 A St., Edmonton, AB, Canada T5E 4A6
> www.homesitter.com
> (888) 247-2787

Franchise: Yes.

Description: An expanded home-sitting service that includes everything from security checks to lawn maintenance.

Requirements: You must be adaptable, willing to be of service, and be extremely reliable. The cost is based upon population and starts at $4,000.

Provisions: You receive a comprehensive start-up package, a proven business system, continuous support, and the benefits of national and regional advertising campaigns.

HOMEWATCH INTERNATIONAL, INC.

2865 South Colorado Blvd., Denver, CO 80222
www.homewatchcaregivers.com
(800) 777-9770

Franchise: Yes.

Description: Full-service house-sitting by trained, bonded, and insured adults for people who are away from home on business or vacation; companion sitting (non-medical); and handyman services.

Requirements: The fee ranges from $15,500 to $19,500 for a franchise, plus additional costs of approximately $7,500. You must be able to afford the franchise, be a compassionate people-oriented person, and have the desire to succeed in business.

Provisions: The fee buys a geographic area with a population of 200,000, five days of training including software training, logo, manual, bond/insurance for one year, exclusive area, ongoing support, and advertising materials. You will also get a grand opening at your location. Financing is available, but only when buying multiple territories.

Comments: This is a good part-time business for retired or semi-retired people.

INNERACTIVE INC.

11949 Jefferson Blvd, #105, Culver City, CA 90230
www.aura.net
(800) 578-5810

Franchise: No.

Description: Aura Video Systems and Aura Shop. This business is for health- and wellness-oriented entrepreneurs. The system is used to check your clients' emotional and energetic state and also provide energy balancing products.

Requirements: The investment starts at $8,995.

Provisions: The complete video system plus Aura Shop Products, training, and support.

JUNE WEDDING, INC.

19375 Pine Glade, Guerneville, CA 95446

www.junewedding.com

(415) 279-7423

Franchise: No.

Description: Be a wedding, event, and/or party consultant.

Requirements: Start-up costs amount to about $5,000.

Provisions: The investment includes a three-month home study course, manual, forms, certification, and ongoing technical support. To find out more, check out the Web site. Any inquiries by mail must be accompanied by $15 and letter of request.

PARAMOUNT HOME BEAUTY

100 N. Main St., Chagrin Falls, OH 44022

www.paramounthomebeauty.com

(440) 893-0920

Franchise: Yes.

Description: Mobile salon and spa services for medically restricted individuals.

Requirements: Total investment of $44,000 includes a $14,000 franchise fee.

Provisions: Training is provided at company headquarters for five days after which the franchisee can opt for an additional five days at their location. Ongoing support includes marketing and advertising, both national and regional.

PARTY PERSONNEL

11720 Hadley, Overland Park, KS 66210

www.partypersonnelkc.com

(913) 451-0218

Franchise: Yes.

Description: Hospitality and entertainment staffing. A Party Personnel franchise provides temporary, skilled, uniformed, reliable banquet servers and bartenders to hotels, country clubs, sport teams, sporting events, upscale caterers, and private homes for parties, weddings, banquets, picnics, and corporate events, primarily in major metropolitan markets. Clients include hotels, country clubs, event planners, caterers, restaurants, and individuals who enjoy entertaining at home.

Requirements: The franchise fee is $15,000. Additional start-up costs are at least $5,000.

Provisions: Initial training takes place at company headquarters, lasting two weeks. The franchisee also receives another two weeks of training every year at their location.

PRESSED4TIME

8 Clock Tower Pl., #110, Maynard, MA 01754
www.pressed4time.com
(800) 423-8711

Franchise: Yes.

Description: Franchisees provide pick-up and drop-off services to local businesses, delivering items to local dry cleaners. They also collect clothing, shoes, handbags, and luggage for repairs.

Requirements: This franchise costs about $20,000 to start. Marketing skills are also needed.

Provisions: Training is provided at headquarters and at the franchisee's location. Marketing support includes ad slicks and other marketing materials plus a public relations program designed to bring in new customers.

PUUR SPA MOBILE DAY SPA

P.O. Box 9575, San Diego, CA 92169
www.puurspa.com
(888) 267-1858

Franchise: No.

Description: Mobile day spa featuring massage, body treatments, anti-aging, facials, eyelash extensions, detox, and more.

Requirements: Start-up costs are under $2,500.

Provisions: Training and support.

QUIETBEAUTY MOBILE SPA

P.O. Box 93, Victorville, CA 92393
www.quietbeautymobilespa.com
(888) 247-4311

Franchise: No.

Description: Spa services and products are provided to people in their homes, particularly through "spa parties."

Requirements: Start-up costs are about $1,000.

Provisions: Training provided at licensee's location and over the Internet.

SAFETY MATTERS

478 Barberry Road, Highland Park, IL 60035

www.safetymatters.com

(800) 972-3306

Franchise: Yes.

Description: This is a baby-proofing service.

Requirements: About $35,000 including franchise fee. The royalty is 5%.

Provisions: Training and inventory, plus continuous support.

SEEKING SITTERS

3411 E. 21st St., Tulsa, OK 74114

www.seekingsitters.com

(918) 749-3588

Franchise: Yes.

Description: Babysitter referral service. Franchisees provide an efficient and low-cost babysitter background screening process that is unique in this industry.

Requirements: The franchisee fee starts at $18,500.

Provisions: All background checks are performed through Seeking Sitters in-house investigation company, which has been in business since 1978. In addition, the online management program provides contact to the national office for support 24 hours a day, 7 days a week.

SITTERS UNLIMITED

2351 Sunset Blvd., Suite 170, PMB 120, Rocklin, CA 95765

www.sittersunlimited.com

(800) 328-1191

Franchise: Yes.

Description: A coast-to-coast sitting service for children, the elderly, homes, and pets, on both a temporary and permanent basis. In addition to quality in-home care, traveling families can rely on hotel and convention care services.

Requirements: The franchise fee for an exclusive territory is $13,000.

Provisions: The fee includes five days of corporate training, ongoing training and support, and one month's free supply of required materials. Literature, business cards, and all required forms are designed for you. No purchase of products except an answering machine and forms is necessary.

Comments: The company has been in business since 1979.

SUPER MOMMIES FITNESS

5503 Tiara Ct., Arlington, TX 76017
www.supermommiesbusiness.com
(817) 719-1019

Franchise: No.

Description: Pre and post-natal fitness programs.

Requirements: Can start for well under $2,000.

Provisions: Training program includes everything you need to hit the ground running.

Comments: "You can earn your investment back in your very first month-long class."

TOTAL NUTRITION TECHNOLOGY

8416 Wren Creek Dr., Charlotte, NC 28269
www.tntgetfit.com
(704) 549-9550

Franchise: No.

Description: TNT specializes in helping individuals attain their health goals through common sense and practical lifestyle changes. There are no gimmicks, supplements, or prepackaged foods. The program promotes fat loss and lean tissue preservation by combining healthy low-fat eating with an active lifestyle.

Requirements: Start-up costs are under $3,000.

Provisions: Training is provided at company headquarters, followed by on-site training at the licensee's location. Plenty of ongoing support including advertising and marketing.

VISITING ANGELS

28 W. Eagle Rd., #201, Havertown, PA 19083
www.livingassistance.com
(800) 365-4189

Franchise: Yes.

Description: Franchisees provide living assistance services to homebound customers. Services include hygiene assistance, meal preparation, light housekeeping, errands, shopping, and companionship. No medical services are provided.

Requirements: The total cost including franchise fee is around $22,000. The royalty fee is low, from 2.9% down to 2%.

Provisions: The initial training at headquarters is followed by five regional training meetings each year. Marketing support includes ads in national media, Internet marketing, and a public relations program.

———CHILDREN———

Kids represent huge opportunities for business owners of all kinds. Four million babies are born every year in the United States and most families are dual-income households. That combination has created $60 billion in annual revenues for the childcare industry. As the number of children increases, so does the competition to get into the best schools. Parents are feeling the pressure to help their kids get a competitive edge and a growing number are willing to pay for supplemental education services. And more than ever, parents are looking for enrichment programs for their kids—the kind that will help them become the next Einstein, Meryl Streep, or Bobby Fisher.

ACTOR'S GARAGE

152 Ryder Rd., Manhasset, NY 11030

www.theactorsgarage.com

(516) 627-7211

Franchise: Yes.

Description: Children's acting school conducted through after-school and weekend programs.

Requirements: The franchise fee is $24,000. An addition $5,000 is needed to cover start-up costs.

Provisions: The company provides regional advertising, training, and field operations support.

CHILDREN'S TECHNOLOGY WORKSHOP

109 Vanderhoof Ave., Toronto, ON, Canada M4G 2H7

www.ctworkshop.com

(866) 704-2267

Franchise: Yes.

Description: Children's enrichment programs in technology, engineering, and science. Focus is on engineering and robotics, video game creation, graphic design and digital art, animation, and digital video production.

Requirements: Start-up costs run about $50,000. There is third-party financing available.

Provisions: Comprehensive training, ongoing support, and marketing.

COMPUTER EXPLORERS

> 12715 Telge Road, Cypress, TX 77429
>
> www.computerexplorers.com
>
> (888) 280-2053

Franchise: Yes.

Description: The Computer Explorers franchise began in 1988. It now reaches more than 30,000 children per week at nearly 2,000 locations in the United States and internationally. In a Computer Explorers franchise, franchisees become an extension of partner schools, providing a turnkey program—software, curriculum, educators—to teach computer skills.

Requirements: Investment ranges from $62,950 to $73,250.

Provisions: Three weeks pre-training, two weeks at corporate headquarters, and eight weeks post-training.

COMPUTERTOTS

> 12715 Telge Rd., Cypress, TX 77429
>
> www.computertots.com
>
> (888) 638-8722

Franchise: Yes.

Description: Computertots is a computer enrichment program offered through day-care centers and private preschools to children ages three to six. In addition to a complete computer system and an extensive software library of the latest educational software, Computertots uses alternate keyboards, light pens, graphic tablets, and computer-controlled robots to introduce computers to children in a fun way.

Requirements: The franchise fee starts at $15,000 with an additional need for at least $13,000 to get started.

Provisions: The fee includes an exclusive territory, a collection of computer software programs, eight monthly curriculum packages, some hardware, master copies of printed materials, and complete training in every aspect of the business.

DRAMA KIDS INT'L, INC.

> 525-K East Market Street #250 Leesburg, VA 20176
>
> www.dramakids.com
>
> (866) 809-1055

Franchise: Yes.

Description: This is the world's largest and most popular after-school children's drama program, serving age groups 3 to 18 via a wide range of offerings that are held in locations convenient for students and parents. The business can be run out of a home-based office with weekly classes held throughout communities in schools, community centers, etc. The specialized curriculum combines with customized teaching techniques to ensure that each student—regardless of age, ability, or personality—receives quality instruction, fast-paced fun, and well-deserved recognition.

Requirements: The investment ranges from $17,000 to $35,000, including franchise fee. There is an ongoing royalty fee of 10%. No acting or teaching experience is required.

Provisions: Extensive training, marketing assistance, ongoing support, regular seminars, newsletters, and Internet connections are provided.

ENCOURAGYM ACTIVE LEARNING PROGRAMS

6125 Golden Eagle Dr., Zionsville, IN 46077
www.encouragym.com
(317) 334-1966

Franchise: No.
Description: Children's gym, art, sports programs, and birthday parties.
Requirements: Start-up costs are $200.
Provisions: Provides training, technical support, advertising, and sales leads. Will train your staff.

GYM ROMPERS

193 W. Oakridge Park, Metairie, LA 70005
www.gymrompers.com
(504) 833-2155

Franchise: No.
Description: This is a parent-child interactive music and movement program for young children, 3 months to 4 years. The purpose is to develop learning skills through fun play activities and to help develop sensory-motor skills. Over forty pieces of specially chosen play equipment are utilized to enhance a child's normally developing gross motor skills, basic coordination and sensory-motor learning.

Requirements: It is possible to start with only $500, but the investment can be higher depending on the goals of the licensed operator.

Provisions: Training is provided at company headquarters in Louisiana with follow-up support available over the phone and the Internet.

HIGH TOUCH HIGH TECH

P.O. Box 8495, Asheville, NC 28814
www.sciencemadefun.net
(800) 444-4968

Franchise: Yes.

Description: Franchisees provide 90-minute, hands-on interactive science programs at schools from pre-school to high school. The programs cover the physical, natural, environmental, and mathematical sciences and meet the National Board of Education Student Science Performance Standards. Additional income comes from "Sizzlin Science" birthday parties. Franchisees run the business, but usually don't provide the actual programs at the schools. They hire educators who are required to have four-year teaching degrees from accredited colleges or universities, as well as certificates in teaching science.

Requirements: Franchise fee of $35,000 plus $6,000 to $8,000 start-up costs.

Provisions: Provides training, customized marketing plan, individualized business plan, and ongoing support.

Comments: "With more than 2 million children participating in our programs annually, High Touch High Tech has emerged as the leader in innovative science programming."

HO MATH & CHESS LEARNING CENTRE

#4, 2265 W. 41st, Vancouver, BC, Canada V6M 2A3
www.mathandchess.com
(604) 263-4321

Franchise: Yes.

Description: Math and chess learning program for children. Ho Math and Chess invented the world's first math and chess integrated workbook (patent pending) and unique, effective chess training set for children as young as four years old.

Requirements: The only expense is the franchise fee, which is a very low $2,100. There are no royalty fees.

Provisions: The investment covers complete training at company headquarters and ongoing participation in co-op advertising programs.

Your parents were right—education really is the key to success. These days, education is big business. It wasn't long ago that supplemental education programs were only for rich kids whose parents wanted to guarantee placement in the best schools. Today, it's a $25 billion industry serving kids in all economic sectors from preschool to college. What changed? There are a lot of different reasons for the growing interest in different kinds of learning programs. But mostly, it's tougher than ever to get into college. The No Child Left Behind Act is another contributor. This controversial piece of legislation requires schools to provide tutoring services if their programs don't meet performance standards for two consecutive years.

Businesses are springing up everywhere with learning programs that offer everything from personalized home work help to enrichment programs. The types of businesses that can be home-based fall into three main categories:

1. Online tutoring. This is a hot new area that is especially popular among high school and middle school students. K-12 programs are also common and preschool is an up-and-coming area as more states mandate preschool for all children. Currently, online tutoring is a $115 million market and it's growing. The smartest business owners sell the service to schools, rather than directly to parents. With the guaranteed volume of business, they can hire qualified tutors and spend their time managing the business (from home). The highest demand for tutoring is in math and reading, but interest in science tutoring is on the rise.

2. In-home tutoring. This concept is more flexible than the standard training center type of tutoring service. It's also more convenient and affordable, which means the potential market is much larger. Some concepts focus on certain subject areas, learning skills, and self-esteem. Others work closely with teachers, focusing only on material introduced in class and helping with home work assignments. Either way, this is very personalized, one-on-one tutoring designed to meet the student's personality and individual needs.

3. After-school programs. Some of these programs are enrichment programs while others are strictly academic. All of them provide a much-needed solution to the problem of latchkey kids. Many of these programs are conducted on school grounds, but some enrichment programs require special facilities. For example, an ordinary classroom will do for an abacus class or mock courtroom. But the culinary arts must be taught in a kitchen and certain science and engineering classes require more lab facilities than some schools have. Again, business owners spend most of their time in their home offices while hired teachers work with the kids.

99

HOME TUTORING
>   P.O. Box 536, Meadow Vista, CA 95722
>   www.hometutoring.com
>   (888) 368-8867

Franchise: No.

Description: A home tutoring service.

Requirements: An interest in furthering the education of children is the most important prerequisite, but you don't need to be a teacher to run this business. You do not need to tutor, for your network of teachers can tutor your students. With the complete and step-by-step manual, anyone can run this business. This business has very little start-up and overhead costs. If you already have a computer and home office, then all you need are business licenses, stationery, advertising expense, miscellaneous office supplies, and perhaps another phone line and insurance. The investment is small, only $495.

Provisions: Training is provided both at the company's location and the licensee's. You will receive a complete business package including an operations manual, software, and ongoing support via phone and on the Internet.

Profit Potential: The sky truly is the limit, as there are no "exclusive territories" to limit your growth.

KINDERDANCE INTERNATIONAL, INC.
>   1333 Gateway Drive # 1003, Melbourne Beach, FL 32901
>   www.kinderdance.com
>   (800) 554-2334

Franchise: Yes.

Description: Kinderdance is a program for children ages 2 to 12 that is designed to develop motor and cognitive skills through dance and movement. Ballet, tap, acrobatics, and modern dance are blended with numbers, colors, and shapes in the basic program.

Requirements: You must have a desire to work with young children or to manage a team of instructors. Total costs range from $14,950 to $46,100 including franchise fee. KD offers up to 50% financing of the franchise fee.

Provisions: The fee buys training, an operations manual, printed materials including promotional materials and forms, props, dance wear, cassette and videotapes, and file cabinet.

Comment: This company has an excellent reputation and the opportunity is ideal for someone who loves children, has an educational background, and enjoys dance.

KINDERMUSIK INTERNATIONAL

P.O. Box 26575, Greensboro, NC 27415

www.kindermusik.com

(336) 273-3363

Franchise: Yes.

Description: Kindermusik is a unique, highly creative, music and movement learning experience for children 18 months to 7 years of age. Professional curricula workshops are designed to acquaint participants with the principles of the Kindermusik curricula and prepare them to teach the program.

Requirements: $125 to $200.

LITTLE SCIENTISTS

14 Selden St., Woodbridge, CT 06525

www.Little-Scientists.com

(800)FACT-FUN

Franchise: Yes.

Description: Children's science educational "hands-on" franchise.

Requirements: The fee is $20,000. No science education background is needed.

Provisions: Training, protected territory, and enough supplies for 40 children.

MCGRUFF SAFE KIDS

15500 Wayzata Blvd., #812, Wayzata, MN 55391

www.mcgruff-safe-kids.com

(888) 209-4218

Franchise: Yes.

Description: Computerized children's identification system.

Requirements: The franchise fee is $30,000 and there is financing available. Business experience is also required.

Provisions: Training and ongoing support.

NANNY POPPINZ

1404 S. New Road, Waco, TX 76711

www.nannypoppinz.com

(254) 757-1445

Franchise: Yes.

Description: Nanny placement services. The services are customized to meet the needs of clients, so in addition to long-term nanny and temporary babysitter referrals, franchisees can also offer referrals for newborn specialists, other childcare situations and domestic as well as other professional services.

Requirements: $35,000 for the franchise fee and an additional $30,000 for start-up costs.

Provisions: Franchisees receive use of Nanny Poppinz™ name, marks and logos, Web-based software, marketing and advertising programs, and extensive training and ongoing support.

PEE WEE WORKOUT

34976 Aspenwood Ln., Willoughby, OH 44094
www.peeweeworkout.com
(800) 356-6261

Franchise: Yes.
Description: Aerobic fitness program for children.
Requirements: The franchise fee is $2,500 and start-up costs are another $300.
Provisions: Programs, training, and start-up materials.

PRE-FIT FRANCHISES, INC.

10926 S. Western Ave., Chicago, IL 60643
www.pre-fit.com
(773) 233-7771

Franchise: Yes.
Description: A home-based mobile preschool fitness program of sports, exercise, and health classes designed for two to six year olds.
Requirements: The franchise fee is $8,500; additional start-up costs are $1,250 to $3,500.
Provisions: Your fee buys uniforms, initial and continuous training program, lesson plans, workout routines, marketing tools, bookkeeping materials, class equipment, exclusive territory, and toll-free support.

SAFETY MATTERS

478 Barberry Road, Highland Park, IL 60035
www.safetymatters.com
(800) 9SAFE06

Franchise: Yes.
Description: This is a baby-proofing service.
Requirements: About $35,000 including franchise fee. The royalty is 5%.
Provisions: Training and inventory, plus continuous support.

SITTERS UNLIMITED

2351 Sunset Blvd., Suite 170, PMB 120, Rocklin, CA 95765
www.sittersunlimited.com
(800) 328-1191

Franchise: Yes.

Description: A coast-to-coast sitting service for children, the elderly, homes, and pets, on both a temporary and permanent basis. In addition to quality in-home care, traveling families can rely on hotel and convention care services.
Requirements: The franchise fee for an exclusive territory is $13,000.
Provisions: The fee includes five days of corporate training, ongoing training and support, and one month's free supply of required materials. Literature, business cards, and all required forms are designed for you. No purchasing of products except an answering machine and forms is necessary.
Profit Potential: Not available.
Comments: The company has been in business since 1979.

STRETCH-N-GROW
P.O. Box 7955, Seminole, FL 33775
www.stretch-n-grow.com
(727) 596-7614
Franchise: Yes.
Description: Fitness classes for children are taught at childcare and recreation centers, elementary schools, YMCA and YWCA centers, Mothers' Day Out programs and Head Start facilities. Franchisees offer other programs, too, including after-school programs, birthday parties and sports camps. All are designed to help children stay fit and healthy.
Requirements: The investment totals around $20,000. The royalty is a flat $150 per month. A strong desire to work with children is a prerequisite.
Provisions: Training is provided in Florida and followed up on the Internet and on the phone. Marketing support includes ads in day-care center publications.

TOP SECRET SCIENCE CORP.
10 Tower Office Park, #310, Woburn, MA 01801
www.topsecretscience.com
(781) 935-9925
Franchise: No.
Description: If you've ever lamented the state of American education, this business is for you. It's a fantastic hands-on approach to teaching science and math to children. You'll be offering programs that are exciting, magical and fun and designed to get kids to discover and explore the world around them. Kids get to interact with lots of weird experiments and state-of-the-art high-tech equipment.
Requirements: In addition to having an interest in education, you should enjoy children and be a highly motivated businessperson. The start-up costs

are low at only $2,500 and there is financing available from the company to make it even easier to get started.

Provisions: Training is provided in person and online, plus you'll have a manual and video to refer to. Follow-up support continues via phone and the Internet. Sales leads are also provided.

PETS

Americans also love their pets. Today, a majority of US households have at least one pet cat or dog. There are over 160 million pet cats and dogs, not to mention countless birds, fish, reptiles, and other miscellaneous critters in this country. We spend billions on our pets, and it seems nothing is too good for our furry friends. We don't just buy dog food anymore; we buy scientifically formulated diets. Since what goes in must come out, there are opportunities at both ends of the pet care spectrum. You'll see what that means when you read about Pet Butler and Doody Calls.

AT-HEEL LEARNING CENTERS

10205 Canoe Branch Rd., Castalian Springs, TN 37031
(615) 374-2141

Description: Dog training and boarding.
Requirements: Start-up costs average $60,000.
Provisions: This is a turnkey business system.

AUSSIE PET MOBILE

34189 Pacific Coast Hwy., #203, Dana Point, CA 92629
www.aussiepetmobile.com
(949) 234-0680

Franchise: Yes.
Description: This is a cute idea that makes a lot of sense. In this franchise, you would offer a convenient, affordable, reliable and efficient service to pet owners by operating a mobile pet grooming service. You will use environmentally friendly products and bring a highly organized professional approach to mobile grooming.
Requirements: Must love animals, work well with people, and have at least $60,000 to invest.
Provisions: The investment covers the cost of training, the mobile grooming unit, which includes a heated hydrobath, regional and national advertising support, a national toll-free number with dispatch service, and full support.

BARK BUSTERS

250 W. Lehow Ave. Englewood, CO 80110

www.barkbusters.com

(303) 471-4935

Franchise: Yes.

Description: This is a non-aggressive dog training service performed in the dog owner's home. The unique dog behavior correction concept originated in Australia in 1989, the brainchild of world-renowned grand master dog trainers, Sylvia and Danny Wilson. Bark Busters' mission is to promote clear communication between owners and their dogs, using simple, effective, and natural pet training methods that appeal to the canine psyche.

Requirements: Must love animals, be willing to learn new techniques, and also work well with pet owners. The total investment is around $70,000.

Provisions: Complete training and support.

Comments: "The market for dog training services is enormous. Dog owners are willing to pay for effective, quality services, not only for their own benefit, but also out of respect for their neighbors. A dog behaving badly is socially unacceptable. This demand creates a unique recession-resistant industry that will continue to grow each year. The pet industry is the 7th largest industry in the United States (bigger than jewelry, candy, toys, or hardware industries). Americans spend over $42 billion on their pets each year, with projected spending at over $52 billion by 2010. There are 70 million dogs in the US today (and most need training!) Bark Busters is positioned as the industry leader, with *no* direct competitors of similar scale."

CRITTER CONTROL, INC.

9435 E. Cherry Bend Rd., Traverse City, MI 49684

www.crittercontrol.com

(231) 947-2400

Franchise: Yes.

Description: Founded in 1983, Critter Control pioneered an entirely new category in the animal control and wildlife removal business. It is now the nation's leading wildlife control company and a nationally recognized animal control brand. Franchisees provide animal control and animal removal services to homeowners, property management companies, industrial and commercial clients, municipalities, and Fortune 500 companies.

Requirements: The total investment can start as low as $11,000.

Provisions: Training is provided at company headquarters. There is plenty of follow-up support. Provides complete marketing package and national and regional advertising.

DOODY CALLS

> 114 4th Street SE, Suite A, Charlottesville, VA 22902
> www.doodycalls.com
> (800) 366-3922

Franchise: Yes.

Description: Pet waste removal service.

Requirements: The franchise fee is $24,500.

Provisions: As a new franchisee, you'll receive 30 hours of training on how to deliver the service, plus all of the systems and procedures to attract and establish a lucrative client base.

FETCH! PET CARE, INC.

> 2101 Los Angeles Ave., Berkeley, CA 94707
> www.fetchpetcare.com
> (866) 338-2463

Franchise: Yes.

Description: Pet-sitting and dog-walking services.

Requirements: The franchise fee is $12,000 and the total investment is about $20,000.

Provisions: This is a turnkey business system that starts with the industry's most comprehensive training curriculum. An all-encompassing, five-day home office or tele-training program is followed by in-depth interaction with the Fetch! Pet Care franchise operations team to get your business launched and running successfully.

PET BUTLER

> 2611 Westgrove, Carrollton, TX 75006
> www.petbutler.com
> (800) PET-BUTLER (738-2885)

Franchise: Yes.

Description: World's biggest and best pet waste cleanup and removal service.

Requirements: Investment range is $20,000 to $100,000.

Provisions: Provides 5 days of training at national headquarters.

Profit Potential: One territory can generate $500,000 per year gross; $200,000 per year net.

Comments: "130 franchises in 27 states launched in the first 30 months! Amazing software, national call center, billing/collections center, graphic design, routing, training, customer service and support second to none."

Close up: Pet Butler

Pet Butler is the first coast-to-coast pet waste removal service for homes and multi-family communities. The concept is unique. Founder and CEO, Matt Boswell, says, "It really grabs someone's attention that someone would 1) scoop poop for money and 2) that they really can make money at it." Boswell says no one actually goes looking for a pet clean-up business. "They run across it by accident. First they laugh at the idea and then they are intrigued by it and finally they are almost enamored by it. Once they realize how lucrative it can be and how much demand there is, they love the idea."

The demand for the service is definitely there. There are over 70 million pet dogs in the United States, each "going" an average 23 times a week. "That really fills a yard up fast," says Boswell. "Not to mention it is hazardous to the environment. While taking away the hassle of cleaning up after pets around the yard, we also give pet owners time to enjoy their pets, their yard, and their family."

Most customers use the service twice a week, but it can be any frequency—three times a week, every other week, or maybe just monthly. There are also one-time spring cleanups and additional services to plump up the bottomline. "With the additional services the average once-a-week customer will pay approximately $80 a month." Not bad for a service that only takes a few minutes per visit. "Most people think we're in the yard 30 minutes plus, but my guys average 5-7 minutes easily. We drive 5 minutes, then scoop 5 minutes and so on. If we had houses back to back we could do 120 houses in a day, but half the time is drive time," says Boswell.

Pet Butler business owners hire technicians to do the "field work." That leaves only one task: get customers—and that's easy. "At corporate headquarters, we handle the phone calls and every bit of billing forever. When a potential customer calls in, we answer all the questions. We quote prices, we tell them what day their route is on, when they'll be cleaned, and their technician's name. Then we put it all into our ARF software, which puts the customer on the technician's route in real time. Each technician has a Blackberry in the field so they can see their routes in real time."

The demand for the service is there, the only obstacle to overcome is awareness. Not many people know this industry exists so it's all about marketing. There are no big government regulations; you don't have to buy big equipment or have a big retail office, and you don't invest in inventory. But you do have to get the word out. "That's why we train our franchisees in every area of marketing. We are extremely serious about our marketing," states Boswell. "The pet industry is exploding. Home services are exploding. With this combination, you can't go wrong."

PETS ARE INN

> 5100 Edina Industrial Blvd., #206, Minneapolis, MN 55439
> www.petsareinn.com
> (866) 343-0086 or (952) 944-8298

Franchise: Yes.

Description: Perform pet lodging service in private homes—not the owners', but a network of hosts that you, the franchisee, develop. You provide the pick-up and delivery of the animals. Is a unique alternative to the usual boarding and kennels.

Requirements: The minimum start-up cost is $20,000.

Provisions: This is a turnkey opportunity that includes all marketing, promoting, and operating systems for this specialized service. Included is proprietary software that makes the service dependable, efficient, and easy to manage. The company's master insurance plan makes it possible for all franchisees to obtain Liability Insurance. Follow-up support is provided through e-mail and a toll-free phone number.

PET-TENDERS

> P.O. Box 23622, San Diego, CA 92193
> www.pet-tenders.com
> (619) 283-3033

Franchise: No.

Description: In-home pet/house-sitting service that cares for pets in the comfort of their own home.

Requirements: The total investment is between $10,500 and $13,900. The royalty fee is 5% of gross sales per month and the advertising fee is 2%. Must love animals.

Provisions: The costs include the franchise fee (for which you are given an exclusive territory), training, and a complete operation and training manual for your business. The training package includes up to five days of lectures, hands-on training, telephone techniques, voice training, and on-the-job training with a working pet-sitter.

Profit Potential: Varies on area and hard work.

TATTOO A PET, INC.
    6571 S.W. 20th Ct., Fort Lauderdale, FL 33317
    www.tattoo-a-pet.com
    (800) 828-8667
Franchise: No.
Description: Pet protection and recovery service. This is the world's largest network of pet protection registration and recovery utilizing a permanent painless identification on a pet.
Requirements: $250-$285.
Provisions: Training provided at company headquarters. Company provides sales leads, does advertising and marketing, and gives ongoing support.

——PHOTO AND VIDEO SERVICES——

Of the opportunities described in this chapter, few actually involve traditional, still-shot photography. The Visual Image is perfect for anyone who loves children and animals. It caters to the proud parents of preschoolers and devoted pet owners by providing keepsake portraits.

Some other businesses here are in the booming video/DVD market. Each services a different and unique function. MDM International trains business operators to record weddings and other special events in a modernized version of standard photography services. And for Spielberg wannabes, Home Video Studio will have you producing videos in your own home.

As technology changes, opportunities automatically open up. There are still plenty of 8mm home movies and videotapes that need to be transferred to DVDs before they deteriorate to the point of uselessness.

These opportunities offer some interesting possibilities for people interested in photography or video. It is a market that is sure to continue growing and changing.

AMERICAN ENTERTAINMENT DISTRIBUTORS
    2514 Hollywood Blvd., #200, Hollywood, FL 33020
    (954) 929-6860
Franchise: No.
Description: DVD rentals through automated machines located in located in all kinds of retail establishments, apartment buildings, and office buildings.
Requirements: Cost of start-up runs around $40,000.
Provisions: This is a turnkey business with all the training, support, and

supplies provided. The company provides basic installation and maintenance. Ongoing technical support is provided over the phone toll-free and via the Internet.

CREATIVE PHOTO CONCEPTS

18027 Hwy. 99, #D, Lynnwood, WA 98037

www.creative-photo.com

(800) 833-5655

Franchise: No.

Description: Photo glazing system.

Requirements: Total start-up is $5,000.

Provisions: Extensive training in the classroom and at your location plus through manual, video, and online. There is also plenty of help along the way with technical support, advertising advice, sales leads, etc.

EAGLESHOTZ

6834 Grand Marina Cir., Gainesville, GA 30506

www.eagleshotz.com

(888) 553-2453

Franchise: Yes.

Description: Event photography specializing in corporate, charity, and celebrity golf events.

Requirements: The only investment required is the franchisee fee, which is $34,000.

Provisions: The fee covers everything needed to start this business: All necessary equipment to begin providing services, access to operational systems, training programs for the franchisee and the franchisee's staff, ongoing support, and advertising and marketing programs to assist in gathering leads.

FACES N CUPS, INC.

6130 W. Flamingo Road, #455, Las Vegas, NV 89103

www.facesncups.com

(702) 365-6847

Franchise: No.

Description: This is a photo imaging system used to transfer photos to mugs, shirts, mouse pads, plates, puzzles, and a variety of small products.

Requirements: $9,950.

Provisions: Fee buys complete video imaging system, training and installation at your site, ongoing technical support (365 days a year), monthly newsletter, and marketing assistance.

HOME VIDEO STUDIO, INC.

8148 Raven Rock Dr., Indianapolis, IN 46236

www.homevideostudio.com

(800) 464-8220

Franchise: No.

Description: Producing videos from your own home video studio. Products and services include: photo videos, duplication, editing, tape repair, international conversion, audio tape duplication, format conversion, home movie transfer, video prints, and full service video tape production.

Requirements: The full cost of start-up is about $89,900. The company does offer financing.

Provisions: Training is extensive and offered both at the company's location and your own. There is plenty of handholding available after start-up.

IDENT-A-KID Services of America, Inc.

2810 Scherer Dr., Ste 100, St. Petersburg, FL 33716

www.ident-a-kid.com

(800) 890-1000

Franchise: Yes.

Description: There are nearly one million children reported lost, missing, or separated from their parents each year. The personal experience of a close friend inspired the company founder, Robert King, to start this company in 1986. The business involves producing identification cards for children that are sold en masse through schools.

Requirements: The cost of the franchise is $29,500, including exclusive territory, equipment, inventory, and comprehensive training.

Provisions: Equipment package includes a laptop computer, desktop computer, digital card printer, wide format forms printer, digital photography equipment (camera, fingerprint scanner, lighting, backdrop, etc.), and miscellaneous office equipment. Four custom software packages are also included enabling quick and easy processing of ID cards and forms. Inventory includes 10,000 marketing pieces, components to produce 8,400 ID cards, and various marketing supplies. This inventory is designed to provide you with enough initial income to pay for the entire cost of the franchise. Training includes a comprehensive operations manual, an audio CD, two video CDs, two weeks of phone pre-training, and three days of on-site field training. The on-site training is preformed in your territory, both performing the program at a local school and marketing to other schools in your community.

Close up: IDENT-A-KID

IDENT-A-KID, a franchise based in Florida, provides credit-card-sized ID cards for parents to carry; the card contains the photograph, fingerprint, weight, measurements, and other identifying information about their child. The cards sell for six to ten dollars, depending on quantity. Since the service is primarily offered through schools, those quantities can run into the thousands.

Not only does IDENT-A-KID provide a much-needed service, but it offers the kind of flexibility necessary to have a fulfilling family life as well. Before starting her franchise 14 years ago, Joyce Johnston of Greensboro, North Carolina, worked as a supervisor for a mortgage corporation. At that time, as a single parent, getting home after six each night made her very unhappy. Now her schedule is hers to make as she sees fit.

"I work when I want to," she says. "I don't work on Monday, I reserve Fridays for computer work, and when the kids come home from school I'm done. With children you can't beat that." Joyce takes the photos and gathers all the necessary data at the schools, then returns home to produce the cards, a process that takes about four days. To further reduce her time away from home, she recently hired somebody to go out and do the photo shoot.

As a parent, Joyce felt comfortable in the school and daycare environment. Her first order of business was to line up appointments to make her presentations. She has yet to be turned down and her business grew so fast she was working to capacity right away. She now services over 100 schools. "I do the schools during the school year and save the daycares for summer."

You might think that cutting down on hours means cutting down on income. But Joyce says, "You can't even compare incomes. My business went over $100,000 this year. I could never go back to working for someone else."

LIL' ANGELS

> 4041 Hatcher Cir., Memphis, TN 38118
> www.lilangelsphoto.com
> (901) 682-9566

Franchise: Yes.

Description: Provides professional "dress-up" photography services in day-care centers and preschools.

Requirements: The total investment, including franchise fee and professional studio equipment, comes to $39,000. Sales experience is also needed.

Provisions: Training is provided at headquarters and on-site. Marketing support includes special opportunities and meetings so that franchisees can network and build on multi-location accounts.

LUKSA INDUSTRIES, INC.
3150 Innisdale Rd., Mississauga, ON, Canada L5N 7T3
www.luksa.com
(905) 785-9018

Franchise: No.

Description: Aerial photography from a tripod extending up to 60 feet. The operator can view and select each photo on the ground console. The system has over 100 applications.

Requirements: Minimum start-up is $5,450.

Provisions: Equipment package consisting of a custom telescoping tripod and remote control robotics plus business training at the company's location.

MDM INTERNATIONAL MULTI MEDIA
7949 Woodley Ave., #215A, Van Nuys, CA 91406
www.webmdm.com
(888) 663-6932

Franchise: No.

Description: Digital video and photography production and services.

Requirements: $8,900.

Provisions: This is a turnkey business designed to launch your own wedding and event photography, videography, and DJ services. It includes a comprehensive training and marketing package for quick start-up without a huge learning curve. There is free phone support for the first year with additional years of phone support available for $350 per year. The initial (and intensive) training session lasts from four to six days and covers all aspects of photography, videography, editing, and mobile disc jockey services.

OPEN2VIEW.COM
865 Tahoe Blvd., #214, Incline Village, NV 89451
www.open2view.com
(866) 231-0662

Franchise: Yes.

Description: Real estate digital photography services.

Requirements: The franchise fee starts at $10,000.

Provisions: Everything needed to start a hands-on owner-operated business.

VIDEOMASTERS

2200 Dunbarton Drive, Suite D, Chesapeake, VA 23325

www.vdsvideo.com

(800) 836-9461

Franchise: No.

Description: Videotaping service.

Requirements: $25,900 for a turnkey system.

Provisions: The price includes a complete equipment package based on the Amiga computer, training, marketing materials, and ongoing support.

Profit Potential: Over $100,000 annually.

THE VISUAL IMAGE, INC.

100 E. Bockman Way, Sparta, TN 38583

www.thevisualimageinc.com

(931) 826-2800

Franchise: Yes.

Description: If you always wanted to be a photographer, you'll probably enjoy this franchise, which will get you the warm-and-fuzzy business of photographing kids and pets. You'll take portraits of young children by working through preschools and portraits of pets will be taken in their owners' homes.

Requirements: Obviously, you should love working with children and animals. You don't need to have any experience as a photographer. The start-up cost is $35,000 including the franchise fee. Financing is available. No experience is required.

Provisions: Training in starting and operating this business as well as photographic skills and techniques. The investment covers the price of all necessary equipment and supplies for a portable studio.

ZAIO.COM

Suite 200, 1013 - 17th Avenue SW, Calgary, AB, Canada T2T 0A7

www.zaio.com

(877) 318-0537

Franchise: Yes.

Description: ZAIO.COM is in the process of photographing each and every property in cities across the country. The company has named this process "GeoPic." The database will be continuously maintained and updated as properties change. Franchisees earn fees in their exclusive geographic areas in a variety of ways. The digital images are accessed exclusively over the

Internet by real estate, mortgage and insurance industries, police, fire and ambulance dispatching, and portals and media outlets.

Requirements: Must live in an available territory of at least 5,000 population. The total investment of $17,000 minimum includes the franchise fee. There is an ongoing royalty of 6%. Financing is available.

Provisions: Proprietary software, access to the database, and training in business and marketing techniques.

———PUBLISHING———

There has been an opportunity explosion in the publishing industry that has not been seen since Guttenberg invented the printing press. Technology has made it possible for anyone, anywhere, interested in any subject, to become a publisher with a minimal amount of money and experience. This is an industry where home-based business operators can buy into a low-cost business opportunity and expect to make it big. There are actual cases of business owners who started at home and built publishing empires worth millions of dollars. Without a doubt, the opportunities in this chapter offer the greatest potential of any of this book. Fees start as low as $149 and top out at only $20,000. Some require experience, but most do not.

The actual involvement in the business of publishing ranges from simply signing up advertisers, to snapping some pictures and writing editorials, to performing every task necessary to publish a complete book.

Probably the best way to choose a publishing business is to decide what subject you are most interested in. If you like children's books, then you might want to take a closer look at Hefty Publishing. If you love bingo, Bingo Bugle would be a better choice for you. Java junkies, look at Coffee News. Other opportunities presented in this chapter cover real estate, television, fashion, entertainment, shopping, travel, and wedding information. Plus there are unique opportunities to publish specialty items such as maps, church directories, and coupon books.

BINGO BUGLE NEWSPAPER

K & O Publishing, Inc., P.O. Box 527, Vashon, WA 98070
www.bingobugle.com
(800) 327-6437

Franchise: Yes.

Description: Monthly publication for bingo players. Franchisee is responsible for sales, publishing, and distribution.

Requirements: $1,500 to $5,000 plus cost of telephone, camera, automobile, typewriter and/or computer if franchisee doesn't own one.

Provisions: A two-day training session is provided to franchisees, along with manuals and start-up materials. A monthly package is provided each month that includes camera-ready copy, clip art, industry news, etc. Other support is given as needed.

COFFEE NEWS USA

P.O. Box 8444, Bangor, ME 04402

www.coffeenewsusa.com

(207) 941-0860

Franchise: Yes.

Description: Coffee News is a weekly restaurant publication printed locally by franchisees and delivered free of charge to all restaurants and the hospitality industry. Franchisees sell industry exclusive advertising space to local businesses to generate an income.

Requirements: This is one of the lowest investment franchises you can get. Franchises sell for $5,500 each plus a one time training fee of $2,500. Royalty fees are phased in over time and start at $75/week for the first franchise after three months and $20/week for each additional franchise after 9 months under the agreement.

Provisions: The Coffee News franchise system provides all content, templates for business cards and rate sheets, a three-day training program, online chat group worldwide, a newsletter, advertising resources to help sell advertising, a free Web page, and mentor support. Training is provided and there is an ongoing mentoring program. Marketing materials are also supplied.

Profit Potential: No income estimates are given as readership per franchise can vary based on population, and franchisees are free to set their own rates. Recent company-owned franchises have produced a net income per franchise of between $25,000-$30,000 per year.

Comments: This is such a great franchise that 94% of franchisees own more than one unit. The average franchisee owns three franchises and the most franchises owned by any one franchisee is 22 franchises.

Close up: Coffee News

Coffee News is a weekly publication delivered free of charge to restaurants, coffee shops, hotels, hospital cafeterias, and any other place where people are sitting around waiting to be served. "It fills that time void," says Bill Buckley, President of Coffee News USA, "after the food is ordered and there is 10 or 15 minutes with nothing to do but wait." Coffee News sure beats reading the back of sugar packets. The content, which franchisees receive from the company each week, is filled only with good news. "It's a quick read," says Buckley, "a bit like Weekly Reader with all the fun and entertaining things in it, but for adults."

There is also a space for local happenings, but the rest is reserved for 32 original ads. That's where the money comes from. "It's a soft sell that goes over easy with local businesses because it's cheap, effective, and exclusive. "We only allow one of each type of business to buy a space," explains Buckley.

Coffee News appeals to people who want to get out of the Dilbert world, work fewer hours, but still make good money. The entire operation—selling ads, collecting money, designing ads, printing, and distribution—takes about 10 hours a week. "Our business model projects an annual income of approximately $25,000-$30,000 per franchise unit. Our average publisher owns three units. For someone who wants to make $75,000-$90,000 working from home, this is a pretty good deal," says Buckley.

It costs $7,500 for the first franchise unit. That includes a $2,500 training and mentoring fee. Each additional unit is only $5,000. To make it easy to get up to the break-even point, the weekly royalty is waived for the first three months. "That's their start-up period. Starting with the 4th month, there is a $75 a week (flat) fee on the first franchise. A second franchise would only be another $20 a week—and that doesn't start for 9 months. So the maximum fee if you own two franchises is only $95 a week. For that, you're going to own a pretty good home-based business," asserts Buckley.

CREATE-A-BOOK, INC.
77 N. Magneto Dr., Pueblo West, CO 81007
www.hefty.com
(719) 647-1161
Franchise: No.
Description: Producing personalized children's books. This company

originated the concept 20 years ago. Today they offer 40 titles.

Requirements: Packages start under $500.

Provisions: You'll receive an online manual, software, and online support. There is phone support, technical support, and some sales leads are provided.

Profit potential: Over $10 per book. Books can be made in ten minutes or less using a computer.

DISCIPLE'S DIRECTORY, INC.

      P.O. Box 100, Wilmington, MA 01887

      www.disciplesdirectory.com

      (800) 696-2344

Franchise: No.

Description: Publish award-winning local Christian business and ministry guides (Christian Yellow Pages).

Requirements: $6,000 plus sales experience.

Provisions: Investment covers complete training, all materials needed to start a business, three days of onsite training, sample directories from other areas, and marketing materials.

FIESTA CARTOON MAPS

      942 N. Orlando, Mesa, AZ 85205

      www.fiesta-cartoon-maps.com

      (800) 541-4963

Franchise: No.

Description: Dealers sell cartoon maps of area, usually as a fundraising project for local organizations. Licensees can grow as large as desired. Maps are updated each year resulting in an annual money making venture.

Requirements: The one-time fee for a territory large enough for a 100 ad map is $6,495. Additional territories are $1,500 each. No experience is necessary.

Provisions: The fee covers hotel and round-trip airfare to Phoenix for three days of training, operations manual, sales manual, 100 maps for samples, invoices, business cards, reference letters, in-house production, ongoing support, and promotional materials.

Profit Potential: Net profit for a 100-ad map is $30,000.

Comments: This can be run part-time or as an absentee ownership. Part of the training course is devoted to hiring, training, and managing sales teams.

GRAFFITTI GRAPHICS

>3 Micasa Pl., Victoria, BC, Canada V9B 1S3
>www.puzzlemachine.com
>(350) 384-5555

Franchise: No.

Description: Producing custom jigsaw puzzles. There are three main markets: personal gift giving, commercial advertising (more fun than a pen), and fundraising. This is a high profit margin business which reportedly does especially well during slow economic times.

Requirements: Total start-up costs run around $9,000.

Provisions: You'll learn to use the machine with a manual and a video. Other support, such as marketing, is provided over the Internet and by phone. Some sales leads are provided.

HOMES & LAND PUBLISHING CORP.

>1600 Capital Cir. S.W., Tallahassee, FL 32310
>www.homesandland.com
>(850) 574-2111

Franchise: Yes.

Description: Homes & Land is the largest publisher of community real estate magazines in the United States with over 275 communities now being serviced by franchisees. The pictorial magazines are published either in black and white or in color, and each contains property listings of real estate companies. Franchisees sell advertising space to real estate brokers and distribute the magazines throughout the community.

Requirements: The franchise offering is $25,000. Royalties vary. Aside from the franchise fee, about $25,000 will be needed to cover initial printing costs and operating expenses. It is common for franchisees to own more than one franchise, and the company expects that all franchisees will operate on a full-time basis. No experience is required.

Provisions: The fee pays for training, field assistance for obtaining initial sales, sixty distribution racks, business cards, invoices, copy folders, stationery, and rate sheets. Training is a one-week orientation at company headquarters covering production, sales, and financial management. An operations manual and sales aids are provided at this time. Franchisees can start as soon as training is completed.

THE HOMESTEADER

Knox Trail Office Bldg., 2352 Main St., Concord, MA 01742
www.publishingopportunity.com
(800) 941-9907

Franchise: No.

Description: Publish a local newspaper for new homeowners. This is a good opportunity for anyone with a sales, publishing, or business background.

Requirements: Franchise fee is $5,000; other costs vary from $3,000 to $17,000.

Provisions: Fee covers exclusive territory, training, support, and monthly editorial packages to use in local publication. Training and editorial supplied. The successful publisher will focus on advertising sales. Papers distributed by direct mail and drop-off locations. Can use company Web site.

Profit Potential: Sole proprietors can earn $5,000-$10,000 per month per edition. Multiple-edition owners can achieve printing and sales efficiencies for greater potential profit.

Comments: Company offers a six-month trial period, where fees are not paid in full until the local publisher has had the opportunity to try the business and see if it is a good fit.

SPECTRUM UNLIMITED

2261 Market St., Ste 276, San Francisco, CA 94114
www.clientbirthday.com
(415) 647-1070

Franchise: No.

Description: Computer software for IBM compatible systems that creates beautiful history-packed birthday or anniversary greetings telling what happened on the day you were born or got married. The cards highlight the events that occurred on any date back to the year 1880.

Requirements: The best program is "News of the Past Professional." One time cost of $200.

Provisions: The fee includes News of the Past software and 200 greeting forms. You also get ongoing support via fax, Internet, and telephone.

Profit Potential: You pay no royalties so your cost is only the price of a sheet of printer paper and printer ink.

Comments: "We offer a 30 day unconditional money-back guarantee."

——TRAVEL——

Computers have made it possible for the first time for travel agencies to be run from home. You will find several companies here that can get you set up in your own agency or work as an associate. These are not mass market ticket sellers—Travelocity, Orbitz, and Expedia make that kind of business unprofitable.

Being a travel agent is one of those occupations that straddles the line between business ownership and employment. There are several opportunities for travel agents listed in the Job Bank. They are there because no investment is required in those instances.

Specialty travel is gaining in popularity. Wheelchair Getaways and Outdoor Connection are two good examples of prepackaged travel and tours that cater to travelers with specific interests and needs.

ALL ABOUT HONEYMOONS

7887 E. Belleview, #540, Englewood, CO 80111
www.allabouthoneymoons.com
(888) 845-4488

Franchise: Yes.
Description: Travel agency specializing in honeymoons/destination weddings.
Requirements: The franchisee fee is $9,500; there is in-house financing available.
Provisions: Initial training starts at headquarters and continues on-site at franchisee's request. Self-paced Internet classes are also available. The company provides comprehensive marketing program and advertising campaigns, offline and online.

CRUISE PLANNERS

3300 University Dr., #602, Coral Springs, FL 33065
www.cruiseagents.com
(888) 582-2150

Franchise: Yes.
Description: This is an exclusively home-based travel agency franchise specializing in cruise packages.
Requirements: The franchise fee is under $10,000. Other start-up expenses could add up to anther $8,000.
Provisions: Training is provided in Florida and follow-up support is available online or with a toll-free phone line. Marketing support includes national and regional advertising campaigns.

CRUISEONE

1415 Cypress Creek Road, #205, Ft. Lauderdale, FL 33309
www.cruiseone.com/franchise
(954) 958-3700

Franchise: Yes.

Description: Travel agency specializing in cruises.

Requirements: The franchise fee is $10,000. Fees are based on experience. Travel industry experience is recommended, but not required, as CruiseOne Franchise Owners come from all walks of life and all industries.

Provisions: Training is conducted at headquarters for eight days. Ongoing support includes Internet, toll-free phone line, newsletters, and regular meetings.

Profit Potential: The sky is the limit! Highest commissions in the travel industry.

Comments: "Our concept was to take a typical travel agency, keep all the benefits and availability, but reduce the overhead and allow the members to build a business that is home-based. To ensure high returns, we focused on the most profitable niche in travel. That's why we specialize in cruising exclusively—it's the most lucrative piece of the travel industry. The future of cruising looks good, too. From now until 2010, the cruise lines are bringing into the marketplace approximately 20 new ships. There's a lot of growth in the industry. We will do $145 million in sales this year." A proud member of the International Franchise Association, Cruise Line International Association, Better Business Bureau, VetFran initiative and others, CruiseOne consistently ranks in *Entrepreneur Magazine*'s "Top 500", *The Franchise Times*' "Top 200" and *Franchise Market Magazine*'s "Top 100 Home Based Companies."

CRUISES INC.

1415 Cypress Creek Road, #205, Ft. Lauderdale, FL 33309
www.sellcruises.com
(954) 958-3700

Franchise: No.

Description: A travel service dealing exclusively with cruise packages.

Requirements: One-time registration fee starting at $49, depending on level of experience in the travel industry.

Provisions: Complete training is provided at company headquarters or online if you prefer. Ongoing support is available in a variety of ways. Sales leads are provided.

Profit Potential: Cruises Inc. offers access to the top cruise lines and because of the company's buying power, agents enjoy the highest possible commissions.

Comments: "Cruises Inc. offers the convenience of working from home, the cruise industry's highest agent commissions, leading technologies, travel benefits, no monthly fees, complete back office processing, turnkey marketing programs, lead generation, continuing education at no additional cost, toll-free ongoing support and more."

OUTDOOR CONNECTION
424 Neosho, Burlington, KS 66839
www.outdoor-connection.com
(620) 364-5500

Franchise: Yes.

Description: Market fishing and hunting trips to corporations and individuals in their area.

Requirements: The franchise fee is $9,500 and there is financing available for half. The total additional start-up costs range from $900 to $5,900.

Provisions: You get master catalogs with complete information on the 100+ lodges you will represent, corporate banners for trade shows, training at the corporate office, daily corporate support and guidance.

WHEELCHAIR GETAWAYS, INC.
P.O. Box 605, Versailles, KY 40383
www.wheelchair-getaways.com
(800) 536-5518

Franchise: Yes.

Description: Wheelchair Getaways, Inc. provides wheelchair accessible van rentals for people with disabilities. One can rent full-sized vans and minivans on a daily, weekly, or monthly basis.

Requirements: There is a one-time franchise fee of $17,500. There is a cost of $550 per van for national advertising and a royalty fee of $550 per van per year.

Provisions: You get national advertising, ongoing support, name recognition, training, national insurance plan, and leasing program for vans.

——MISCELLANEOUS——

Many changes in consumers' needs have taken place in recent years, and home-based businesses have proven flexible enough to meet those needs. New businesses are started all the time to fill market niches that never even existed before. In this chapter you will find an assortment of business opportunities, most of which defy classification. If you are looking for something just a little different, this chapter is for you.

ALOETTE COSMETICS

4900 Highlands Pkwy., Smyrna, GA 30082
www.aloette.com
(800) ALOETTE

Franchise: Yes.

Description: Aloette is the only cosmetics franchise opportunity that does not require a storefront.

Requirements: The franchise fee is $20,000. Financing is available.

Provisions: Training in sales and management skills is provided along with manuals and videos, an accounting manual and journals.

Comments: The profit potential is tremendous for those who follow through with the training.

AMERICAN MOBILE SOUND

1213 State St., Suite J, Santa Barbara, CA 93101
www.amsdj4u.com
(805) 899-4000

Franchise: Yes.

Description: Mobile entertainment business providing DJs and MCs for weddings, school dances, reunions, or any event that needs great music.

Requirements: The franchise fee ranges from $6,000 to $15,000, marketing materials cost $2,400, and system with music is $6,000.

Provisions: Full training in Santa Barbara and marketing training on-site.

COMPLETE MUSIC, INC.

7877 L St., Omaha, NE 68127
www.cmusic.com
(800) 843-3866

Franchise: Yes.

Description: Music disc jockeys provide the entertainment for parties and celebrations of all kinds. About 70% of the time, they are used for wedding receptions. The disc jockeys bring everything, including stereo sound and light equipment as well as a music tape library. The tape collection is the largest music disc jockey collection in the country, with over 30,000 selections in all categories. The entire system packs easily into a compact car.

Requirements: The entire initial investment is $26,500 in most markets.

Provisions: Start-up package, 14 days of training, and ongoing support.

Profit Potential: 33% net.

Comments: This is the nation's largest DJ entertainment service with 129 franchisees now in operation.

THE DENTIST'S CHOICE

774 Mays Blvd., #10-297, Incline Village, NV 89451

www.thedentistschoice.com

(800) 757-1300

Franchise: Yes.

Description: Franchisees primarily repair, rebuild and maintain all models of dental drills. Other services include rethreading and burring tools, replacing fiber optics, and selling new handpieces to dentists.

Requirements: The total investment for start-up is around $30,000. Marketing skills are necessary.

Provisions: Training and ongoing support is provided. Marketing support is exceptional and includes an extensive marketing manual.

ELIZA J

Box 99, Harwich, MA 02645

www.elizaj.com

(508) 430-0037

Franchise: Yes.

Description: Upscale portable restrooms for outdoor events.

Requirements: Total investment starts at $36,000.

Provisions: A turnkey operation with easy start-up and a large and identifiable customer base.

GUMBALL GOURMET

1460 Commerce Wy., Idaho Falls, ID 83403

www.gumballgourmet.com

(866) 486-2255

Franchise: Yes.

Description: Gumball machine kiosks.

Requirements: Total investment including franchise fee is around $25,000. Some background in business is required.

Provisions: Training, support, toll-free phone line, kiosk signs, and Internet marketing.

HANDPIECE EXPRESS
    1615 Hill Road #7, Novato, CA 94947
    www.handpieceexpress.com
    (800) 895-7111

Franchise: No.

Description: Home-based business providing rapid repair service to dentists.

Requirements: $32,500, some technical ability, sales and marketing ability, and hard work. Financing is available.

Provisions: Investment covers one week of initial training, manuals, videos, software package, toll-free support for one year, specialized tools, and inventory.

Profit Potential: Expect loyal clientele with repeat business. Other areas of revenue include additional services provided and selling new and used equipment

Comments: Nice business-to-business niche that is somewhat recession-proof in the healthcare field.

HAYES HANDPIECE
    5375 Avenida Encinas, Carlsbad, CA 92008
    www.hayeshandpiece.com
    (760) 602-0521

Franchise: Yes.

Description: Franchisees offer dental handpiece repair with free pick-up and delivery service and 24-hour turnaround. They also occasionally sell new handpieces, but they specialize in selling rebuilt, used handpieces.

Requirements: Total start-up expenses including the franchise fee run around $50,000. The franchisor also wants to see business and marketing experience and especially sales skills.

Provisions: Training is provided at headquarters and the franchisee's location. Marketing support includes co-op advertising, ad slicks, regional and national advertising, and a call center.

Profit Potential: Since dentists typically need to repair 5-15 handpieces a year, there is tremendous opportunity for repeat business.

I9 SPORTS

> 1463 Oakfield Dr., #135, Brandon, FL 33511
> www.i9sports.com
> (813) 662-6773

Franchise: Yes.

Description: Franchisees operate local amateur sports leagues, tournaments, clinics and special events in two dozen sports, including baseball, soccer, golf and bowling. Additional profit comes from selling sponsorships, sporting goods, and customized uniforms.

Requirements: Start-up costs start at about $25,000. A background in business is required along with marketing skills.

Provisions: Training is provided at headquarters and the franchisee's location plus refresher training is available at any time. This business is highly dependent on good marketing and therefore, the marketing support is excellent. It includes co-op advertising programs, ad slicks, national and regional advertising, and ongoing guidance with sales and PR. Also provided are administrative services, billing and commission payment support; and visits from field support.

LE GOURMET GIFT BASKET, INC.

> 723 Anderson St., Castle Rock, CO 80104
> www.legift.com
> (800) 934-4386

Franchise: Yes.

Description: Providing elegant and affordable gourmet gift baskets for any occasion including birthdays, weddings, showers and for corporate clients. The baskets can be custom-made for any occasion or theme and shipped worldwide.

Requirements: There are three programs ranging in price from $3,500 to $8,500. This is a one-time fee; there are no royalties or additional fees.

Provisions: Training in person or by videotape. Also provides equipment, inventory, negotiated vendor deals, and referrals.

MAGIC RICE, INC.

> P.O. Box 592457, Orlando, FL 32859
> www.magicrice.com
> (407) 438-6650

Franchise: No.

Description: Personalized rice jewelry for necklaces, bracelets, key chains, and earrings.

Requirements: The cost ranges between $300 and $1,000.
Provisions: Supplies and instructions. The markup is very high—nearly 800%.

MARTY WOLF GAME COMPANY

2120 Highland Ave., Las Vegas, NV 89101
www.gamblersjunkyard.com
(702) 385-2963

Franchise: No.
Description: Own and operate a charity gambling casino for fundraising activities. It can be started in your garage part-time.
Requirements: The total investment for the complete party business package ranges from $220 to $5,000. There is financing available. You will also need a garage or storage area to store equipment.
Provisions: The investment covers all the tables, equipment and supplies required to stage a Las Vegas Style Gambling Party. A complete gambling casino accommodates 100 charity party gamblers. It also includes a five-day, casino dealer workshop in Las Vegas where you will learn and qualify to deal Blackjack, Craps, and Roulette; learn and qualify to training your own party dealers. There is ongoing support and training in how and where to find clients.

MICRO-REALITY MICRO-MILE

1500 S.W. 7th St., Atlantic, IA 50022
www.microreality.com
(712) 243-9035

Franchise: No.
Description: Portable drag racing.
Requirements: Start-up costs $25,000.
Provisions: Financing is available. Training is provided at company headquarters. Sales leads and ongoing support provided.

MINI-GOLF, INC.

202 Bridge St., Jessup, PA 18434
www.minigolfinc.com
(570) 489-8623

Franchise: No.
Description: Portable, prefabricated miniature golf courses that can be used indoors or outdoor. Courses are easy to set up, move and store. The courses can be rented for a wide variety of events from parties to fund raisers.
Requirements: $5,900.

Provisions: You get a portable, prefabricated miniature golf course with all the necessary accessories, and operators manual with ideas and promotions, and continuous support.

P & 1 INFLATABLES, INC.
P.O. Box1200, New Lenox, IL 60451
www.jumbousa.com
(888) 586-7464

Franchise: No.
Description: Inflatable amusement devices used in party rental business.
Requirements: Start-up costs are about $3,000 depending upon size and design of unit purchase.
Provisions: Cost includes products, manuals, and toll-free support.

PALM BEACH SPECIALTY COFFEE
3965 Investment Ln., #A-8, West Palm Beach, FL 33404
www.palmbeachcoffee.com
(561) 881-0803

Franchise: No.
Description: Espresso machine sales.
Requirements: Start-up costs total $12,000.
Provisions: Training is provided at headquarters and the franchisee's location. There is also a complete manual. Marketing support includes sales leads.

PATTY-CAKES INTERNATIONAL, INC.
1726 W. Third St., Montgomery, AL 36106
www.patty-cakes.com
(334) 272-2826

Franchise: Yes.
Description: Make the actual impression of a child's hand and foot and cast them in bronze. The bronzed impressions are then mounted on a variety of wall plaques to make a lasting keepsake.
Requirements: $7,900 for franchise and equipment fee.
Comments: In addition to franchise opportunities, also available are consultant opportunities, which are by far the most popular. Consultants pay a one-time fee and do not have to pay renewals or monthly royalties like a franchise. The investment for a consultant is $499 and is available in most states. Supplies are included with the start-up kit, as well as a training DVD and plenty of support from the home office. Experience in sales is a plus but not a requirement. Consultants average close to a 50% profit on each sale.

PERSONAL TOUCH PRODUCTS, INC.

2187 Vista Court, La Verne, CA 91750
www.PersonalTouchProducts.com
(877) 593-1249 or (909) 596-1166

Franchise: No.

Description: Utilizing your computer and the unique supplies offered by this company, you can create a wide variety of unique personalized gift items including framed keepsakes, jewelry boxes, mouse pads, ceramic plates, address books, key chains, clocks, calendars, etc. Among the special features offered by this company is the "Gifts on Art Business Software," which includes a database containing of over 100,000 first names origins, plus an extensive collection of personalize-able poetry. The software is easy to personalize, just print first names and poetry on any one of their 100+ specialty art backgrounds. The entire process takes about two minutes to create a gift. Both English and Spanish versions are available.

Requirements: The start-up investment is low at only $850. You will need a computer, but no technical experience is required.

Provisions: The system includes personalization software, a first names database, a poetry database, master books, specialty art backgrounds, instructions, order forms, brochures, training, and support. Enough starting inventory is supplied to recover your initial investment several times over.

PROFITABLE HOBBIES

517 S. Commerce Rd., Orem, UT 84058
www.profitablehobbies.com
(800) 624-7415

Franchise: No.

Description: Custom engraving system using micro-sandblasting and airbrush.

Requirements: Start-up costs range from $1,000 to $14,000.

Provisions: Provides training, marketing, and equipment.

PUZZLE MACHINE

3 Micassa Pl., Victoria BC, Canada V9B 1S3
www.puzzlemachine.com
(250) 384-5555

Franchise: No.

Description: A work-at-home business opportunity, creating high quality personalized and custom jigsaw puzzles from photocopies, photographs, or ink jet prints. The equipment is primarily aimed at the gift-giving and fundraising markets.

Provisions: Jigsaw puzzles are made for less than $3 and can be sold from $10 to $85 each.

SPACE WALK/INFLATABLE ZOO

450 31st St., Kenner, LA 70065

www.herecomesfun.com

(504) 464-5851

Franchise: No.

Description: Provide inflatable rides for private party rentals and corporate events. Space Walk was the original inflatable amusement ride and it's been around for 25 years now.

Requirements: $3,000-$5,000 start-up costs.

Provisions: Training is provided at company headquarters in all aspects of operating this business. Advertising and marketing strategies are provided along with sales leads. Ongoing support is available by phone, Internet, meetings, and newsletters.

SPORTSLIFE ENTERPRISES, INC.

1455 Old Bridge Rd., Suite 204, Woodbridge, VA 22192

www.sportslife.com

(800) 909-5433

Franchise: No.

Description: Dealers market sporting goods to schools, leagues, and businesses.

Requirements: Initial investment is $495 and there is a $30 ongoing fee each month.

Provisions: Price includes manual, directories, catalogs, monthly newsletters, and free business consulting.

STORK NEWS OF AMERICA, INC.

1305 Hope Mills Rd., Suite A, Fayetteville, NC 28304

www.storknews.com

(910) 426-1357

Franchise: Yes.

Description: Stork News is a newborn announcement service primarily providing outdoor display signs. Other products include announcement cards, newborn clothing for christening, and party supplies.

Requirements: The franchise fee starts at $5,000. Additional tools, advertising expenses, operating capital, equipment, and inventory can cost as much as $5,000.

Provisions: The fee buys a complete start-up package including introductory advertising materials, administrative supplies, and enough equipment and supplies to get started. Protected territory. This franchisor has an exclusive partnership with Babies R Us.

TEAM DOUBLE CLICK

W10530 Airport Road, Lodi, WI 53555
www.teamdoubleclick.com
(608) 592-3050

Franchise: No.

Description: Team Double Click is a virtual staffing agency with over 1,300 home-based workers in their database. The company now has an affiliate program that is custom-made for staffing firms looking to expand into the cutting-edge world of virtual staffing.

Requirements: The affiliate fee is a one-time fee of $1,500.

Provisions: The system is turnkey and includes two weeks training via phone and instant messenger plus ongoing support. Under the agreement, Team Double Click receives 25% of the affiliate's net profit. Provides 100% funding of client receivables and payroll for all virtual staffing contractors.

UNCO INDUSTRIES, INC.

7802 Old Spring Street, Racine, WI 53406
www.vermiculture.com
(800) 728-2415

Franchise: No.

Description: The business concerns raising night crawlers and producing organic fertilizer. The company has been in business for 17 years.

Requirements: You will need a small spare room, a portion of your garage, or a corner of your basement. You will need to spend two hours every two weeks per kit. Start-up costs $3,900 and includes complete training. Financing is available.

Provisions: Everything is supplied, including step-by-step training.

VENDX

3808 E. 109th N., Idaho Falls, ID 83401

www.vendx.com

(800) 527-8363

Franchise: No.

Description: Bulk candy/nut vending of nationally advertised products such as M&Ms, Skittles, etc.

Requirements: Start-up costs amount to about $7,000.

Provisions: You will be advised on which candies sell best and where to purchase your products. You will be provided with proven management tools. You will receive a sample route recordkeeping system, bi-monthly newsletter, product and vending information, operations manual, support materials, and ongoing support. Financial assistance is available.

Profit Potential: On most products, you will receive 64-84% gross profit.

MARKETS FOR HANDCRAFTS

This chapter is for serious artisans and handcrafters who want to spend more time producing their products than selling them. The traditional route for many crafters is to rent booth space at craft fairs, where they end up feeling more like retail clerks than artists. When going the craft fair route, it is often necessary to travel around in order to find enough events to keep busy. Plus, craft fairs tend to be very seasonal, leaving little opportunity for sales in the winter months. If you would rather be in your home studio doing the work that you love, this is the chapter for you.

The listings in this chapter include shops, galleries, and mail-order catalogs that will consider buying your handcrafts. While these buyers are willing to give new artisans a chance, they have no patience for hobbyists. You must deal with them on a professional level, making them believe you mean business.

There are also quite a few manufacturers' representatives and wholesalers listed. These are agents who deal regularly with numerous buyers, from small shops to huge chain stores. They work on a percentage commission, so you have to build that percentage into your pricing. You should only consider using a rep if you can produce your crafts in quantity. They are not in the business of dealing with one-of-a-kind items.

To approach any buyer, follow the instructions exactly. Start with a letter of introduction, preferably typed on letterhead. Always supply a self-addressed envelope. Keep the information brief and concise. Describe what you have to offer, stressing the quality of the work and materials used.

Include a price list. Keep in mind that a shop that buys outright will generally split 50/50, while you can expect another 10% if it is a consignment sale. Don't price yourself out of the market, but make sure you can make a healthy profit. It is an acceptable practice to set minimum orders, but keep them small, maybe a half dozen for example.

Send the best quality photos or slides of your work that you possibly can. You don't have to hire a professional photographer. Set up one or two items on a plain contrasting background such as a sheet or drapes. Keep the focus close enough to show the detail of your work. Remember, this is the first, and possibly only, impression that a potential buyer will have. Never send samples unless asked. Label the back of every photo with your name and address.

Contact more than one shop at a time. By doing business with several at once, you can be assured of making it through seasonal fluctuations and other lean times. Give plenty of time for them to respond. Rather than contacting the same shops repeatedly, go on to some others if you need more business. But do be patient. It is not unusual for several months to pass before you get a response from a buyer. Do not call them in the meantime. If they are interested, you will hear from them when they are ready.

Finally, make sure that you are capable of handling the volume of business each shop requires. It's very disappointing for everyone when an item is selling well, but the crafter can't, or won't, produce enough.

AMERICAN CRAFTS GALLERY
13010 Larchmere, Cleveland, OH 44120
Items Wanted: Contemporary fiber arts are accepted on consignment.
Payment: Pays 50/50 split.
Instructions: Submit slides (only) and prices you want. Include SASE.

AMERICRAFT CRAFT BROKERS
Stillwaters, 210 Lockes Village Rd., Wendell, MA 01379
Items Wanted: This wholesale rep handles handcrafts of all kinds, home accessories, pottery, and personalized items.
Payment: Sells items wholesale and takes a standard commission.
Instructions: Submit your bio and contact information, product description, catalog sheet or brochure or photo, wholesale price list, and sample.

AMISH ACRES
1600 West Market Street, Nappanee, IN 46550
www.amishacres.com
Items Wanted: This is a nonprofit organization that represents over 200 crafters. Visit the Web site and browse the wholesale catalog to get a good view of the types of products handled here.
Payment: Takes items on consignment paying 60% to the crafter. Provides

a detailed report of sales activity with payment on the 15th of each month. **Instructions:** Submit product description with brochure or photo and wholesale price.

ANNE MENAKER GORDON & CO.

2300 N. Stemmons Fwy, Dallas, TX 75258

Items Wanted: Giftwares, fine jewelry (prefers silver), and fashion accessories.
Payment: Sells items wholesale to stores in the Midwest and takes a commission.
Instructions: Send slides, documentation, and wholesale price list. Be sure to include information on quantity available of any given item as this is a manufacturer's rep.

THE APPLE TREE

54 East Street Road, West Chester, PA 19382

Contact: Jill Butler.
Items Wanted: Giftwares of all kinds, home and bath accessories, garden products, gifts for babies and children, pet products, books and stationary, and general collectibles. Looking for new and deferent items of good quality in the country or traditional style.
Payment: Buys outright.
Instructions: Submit product description, catalog or brochure or photo, wholesale price, and sample. Also indicate if there are any stores in this local area carrying your products.

ARTIQUE, INC.

259 Godwin Avenue, Midland Park, NJ 07432

Items Wanted: Good quality items based on Early American designs. Also, items that can be customized. Only interested in items that can be reordered. No precious metal items. No extremely fragile items or paper items.
Payment: Purchase with terms; credit references can be furnished.
Instructions: Send photos and price list. Later, samples may be requested. If necessary, would like craftsperson to use UPS.

ARTISANS GALLERY

P.O. Box 256, Mentone, AL 35984

www.folkartisans.com

Items Wanted: Folk art, weather vanes, quilts, paintings, carvings, etc. Visit the online catalog to see the type of products carried.
Payment: Purchases outright for sale in both the print catalog and online store.
Instructions: Send product description, photo, and price sheet to either Matt Lippa or Elizabeth Schaaf.

ARTISTS' PARLOR

126 Laurens Street, NW, Aiken, SC 29801

Items Wanted: Pottery, wood, jewelry, whimsical, but not country. Animal images are good.

Payment: Purchase outright.

Instructions: Any information is helpful; all will be returned.

ARTS & ARTISANS, LTD.

108 S. Michigan Ave., Chicago, IL 60603

www.artsartisans.com

Items Wanted: Blown glass in all forms, jewelry, wood, ceramic, frames, clocks, dolls, boxes—all media.

Payment: Purchase; net 30.

Instructions: Send photos, slides and prices (wholesale). Your background would also be helpful. This is a group of 4 galleries in downtown Chicago.

ARTWORKS PARK CITY

461 Main St., Park City, UT 84060

www.artworksparkcity.com

Items Wanted: Sophisticated, whimsical, contemporary crafts with an emphasis on hot glass, clay, and jewelry. There are over 200 artists represented here.

Payment: Mainly consignment 60/40; or purchase 50%.

Instructions: Send photos, prices, and information about the artist.

AVITA, INC.

138 Cedar St., Corning, NY 14830

Items Wanted: All types of decorative glass items for nationwide distribution.

Payment: Pays wholesale minus commission 30 days after sale.

Instructions: Send photos or slides along with wholesale price list and description of artist's work.

BARBARA SCHWARTZ ACCESSORIES

392 Fifth Ave. Lobby, New York, NY 10018

Items Wanted: High-end gift items and silver jewelry.

Payment: This wholesale rep takes a standard commission on items sold.

Instructions: Send slides, brochures, résumé, and price list.

BRASS SMITH HOUSE

1000 Technology Park Dr Ste 408 Billerica, MA 01821

Items Wanted: Interesting and unique crafts that would be appropriate for gift giving. Items are sold wholesale to department stores and smaller shops nationwide.

Payment: Pays wholesale minus standard commission.

Instructions: Send slides or photos, brochures, and price list. Indicate quantities available and delivery schedule.

BROOKLYN WOMEN'S EXCHANGE, INC.

55 Pierrepont St., Brooklyn, NY 11201

www.brooklyn-womens-exchange.org

Items Wanted: Hand-knitted sweaters, handmade toys, dolls, clothing for children.

Payment: Consignment 70/30 (this is a nonprofit group).

Instructions: Send photos and prices to be reviewed by consignor committee. This is a nonprofit organization staffed by volunteers continuing operation since 1854.

BUYLINK CORPORATION

future

222 3rd Ave. SE. Suite 8, Cedar Rapids, IA 52401

www.buylink.com

Items Wanted: This company was one of the pioneers of wholesaling online. Here you can put your catalog online for the 20,000+ store owners and other wholesale buyers to see.

Payment: Arrangement arrangements are made between the buyers and vendors (you).

Instructions: Visit the Web site and click on "Vendor" for instructions and/or contact Dave Stoddard. The cost of participating is $49.95 a month.

CAMBRIDGE SALES

451 East 58th, Suite 2145, Denver, CO 80216

Items Wanted: Country style crafts of the highest quality. Items are sold wholesale throughout the Western region of the US.

Payment: Pays cash less standard commission.

Instructions: Send photos or slides, price list, brochures, and samples if possible.

CARNEGIE ART CENTER
109 South Palouse, Walla Walla, WA 99362
www.carnegieart.com

Items Wanted: Handcrafted art items including pottery, jewelry, weavings, glass paperweights, vases, wooden toys, fabric toys, etc.

Payment: Consignment preferred; 60% of retail price goes to the artist.

Instructions: Send photos or slides, artist's catalog, résumé, and personal statement if available. "The Center is a nonprofit art gallery with a gift shop. Art classes for children and adults are offered."

COLDWATER CREEK HOME
5 Coldwater Creek Drive, Sandpoint, ID 83864
www.coldwater-creek.com

Items Wanted: This high-end mail-order catalog offers a variety of products, but is only looking for handcrafted home decor items and furniture. Will not consider any item that uses animal by-products (feathers, bones, etc.).

Payment: Buys outright at wholesale prices.

Instructions: Visit the Web site and look in the Home & Gifts section to get a good understanding of the kind of items carried. Then submit a letter of introduction to the merchandising department that includes your experience with other catalogs, how long in business, production capabilities, color photos or catalog, and whole price list. Do not send samples unless requested.

COLLAGE GALLERY
Attn: Delisa, 1345 18th St., San Francisco, CA 94107

Items Wanted: Contemporary crafts, bowls, clocks, jewelry, mirrors, picture frames, candleholders, and furniture.

Payment: Consignment; 50/50.

Instructions: Send photos or slides with price list. "Functional crafts sell really well."

CORVALLIS ARTS CENTER,
LINN-BENTON COUNCIL FOR THE ARTS
700 SW Madison, Corvallis, OR 97333
www.artcentric.org

Items Wanted: Jewelry, fine crafts, mostly functional.

Payment: On consignment: 60% to artists by the 20th of the month.

Instructions: Send photos or samples. Items are "juried" by a panel of several people so it often takes at least a full week to make a decision. Contact Alice Hall or Hester Coucke.

DAFA SALES ~~Stationary~~ *(handwritten)*

2100 N. Stemmons Freeway, #1733, Dallas, TX 75207

www.dafasales.com

Items Wanted: Gift items of any material, particularly that could be sold as souvenirs through mass distribution. Think college bookstores and you get the idea. Distributes mainly in the South.

Payment: Pays wholesale prices less standard commission.

Instructions: Send photos, slides, and/or samples. Make sure you only offer items that can be produced in quantity within reasonable time period. Include brochures, wholesale prices, etc.

DAVLINS

2060 Southdale Center, Edina, MN 55435

Items Wanted: Quality, unique wood gifts (some furniture), no country.

Payment: Consignment, monthly; net 30.

Instructions: Send photos, slides, or brochures. Contact Dave Loonet.

DELAWARE CENTER FOR THE CONTEMPORARY ARTS

200 S Madison St., Wilmington, DE 19801

Items Wanted: Contemporary crafts in any media.

Instructions: Submit letter of inquiry, résumé, and up to 20 slides with a corresponding slide sheet describing the work in detail. Be sure to include an SASE if you want your slides returned. This opportunity is open to Delaware residents only.

ESPECIAL DAY

9A Trolley Square, Wilmington, DE 19806

Items Wanted: Creative, useful gifts, jewelry cards made in the USA- "in this economy the more practical items are best."

Payment: Net 30 days.

Instructions: Send all information to the attention of Elizabeth Clayton.

ETOYS

12200 Olympic Blvd., Los Angeles, CA 90064

www.etoys.com

Items Wanted: Toys and gifts for children of all ages. This is probably the most successful online toy store.

Payment: Buys outright with purchase order; pays within 30 days.

Instructions: Visit the Web site first and get familiar with the extensive product line. Send your product description, photo, sample, and wholesale price to the merchandising department, attention "Product Submissions." If samples are too large for UPS shipment, send all other information and indicate the size.

ETCO, INC.
6100 4th S., Seattle, WA 98108

Items Wanted: This is a manufacturer's rep that handles handcrafts, pottery, sculpture, and hand-blown glass.

Payment: Works on standard commission agreement.

Instructions: Submit product description, photo, and/or catalog or brochure along with wholesale price list.

EZIBA
87 Marshall St North Adams, MA 01247

Items Wanted: This is a mail-order catalog that buys handcrafted items of all kinds, especially unique, hard to find products. "We buy handcrafted objects from around the world."

Payment: Pays within 30 days.

Instructions: Submit product information in the form of printed color catalogs, photographs, and price sheets. Do not send samples unless requested. Send information to the attention of the merchandising committee.

FRANZEN ENTERPRISES
222 Merchandise Mart Plaza, Chicago, IL 60654

Items Wanted: This is a manufacturer's rep for country crafts, folk art, and Victorian items.

Payment: Works on standard commission agreement.

Instructions: Submit photos and/or samples along with wholesale price list.

GALERIA EL DORADO
1054 Ashford Ave., Condado, PR 0090

Items Wanted: High-end sculptures in glass, wood, metal or ceramic.

Payment: Consignment with end of month inventory/payment.

Instructions: Prefer color pictures returnable upon selection. "We are an art and decor gallery, specializing in fine pieces of art, sculpture and porcelain. We are located on Main Avenue with both tourist and local trade."

GALLERY OF THE SANDIAS
Box 311, Sandia Park, NM 87047

Items Wanted: Most crafts (interested in proven crafts), also discontinued items and slight irregulars.

Payment: COD or check within 7 days of receipt.

Instructions: Send photos or slides.

GALLERY/SHOP AT WESLEYAN POTTERS
350 S. Main St., Middletown, CT 06457

www.wesleyanpotters.com

Contact: Maureen LoPresti.

Items Wanted: Fine, contemporary American handcrafts in all media except clay. Items are juried first. No country.

Payment: All work, after jurying, is on consignment at 37%; payment made every 60 days.

Instructions: Invitation to submit work for jurying is made after viewing photos and price list. Send SASE for return of photos. "We are primarily a craft education center, nonprofit, run as a cooperative. Most of our members are potters so we have more than enough clay work from them to sell."

GRASSROOTS HANDCRAFTS
93 East Main Street, Newark, DE 19711

www.grassrootshandcrafts.com

Contact: Marilyn Dickey.

Items Wanted: This is a very successful chain of four retail stores that has been in business for over 26 years and won numerous awards. They specialize in quality handcrafted contemporary gift items including American handthrown pottery, sterling silver jewelry, candles, ironware, fine wood items, etc. Visit Web site for complete picture of their product line.

Payment: Buys outright.

Instructions: Submit photos and/or samples along with wholesale price list.

H.O.M.E., INC.
Route 1, Orland, ME 04472

Items Wanted: H.O.M.E. stands for Homeworkers Organized for More Employment. It is a nonprofit co-operative founded in 1970 for the purpose of marketing handcrafted products from this economically depressed area. H.O.M.E. operates a country store, many types of craft and trade workshops, a child-care center, the Learning Center for adult education, a sawmill, a shingle mill, a woodlot, and two hospitality houses. It also publishes a quarterly newspaper (*This Time*) and a crafts catalog, and builds homes for otherwise homeless neighbors. Currently has 3,500 members. Anyone living in the area is encouraged to participate.

HUSTED GALLERY & ART FRAMES *Try first*

9776 Holman Road, NW, #111, Seattle, WA 98117

Items Wanted: Fine American made crafts: wood, glass, jewelry, pottery, Christmas.

Payment: Consignment 50/50 paid monthly or sooner if large sales accumulate.

Instructions: Send sample or photo with SASE for return. "We attract upper middle class repeat customers in this well-established north Seattle business. We dare in our sixteenth year doing custom picture framing and showing original artwork as well as gifts, cards and crafts."

J. MARCO GALLERIES

758 Medina Road, Medina, OH 44256

www.jmarco.com

Items Wanted: This is a mail-order catalog that also has an online showroom. Interested in jewelry, gifts, apparel, and home decor items.

Payment: Buys outright.

Instructions: Submit catalog or photo with wholesale price list and contact information. Send to the attention of Christa Ondrey.

JULIE HALL

1807 Ross Ave # 175, Dallas, TX 75201

Items Wanted: Jewelry, accessories, novelties, and especially textiles for distribution throughout the South.

Payment: Works on commission.

Instructions: Send photos and/or samples (samples preferred), brochures, wholesale price list, and contact information.

KAH-NEE-TAH GALLERY

4210 W. Highway 61, Lutsen, MN 55612

www.kahneetah.com

Items Wanted: This gallery carries only quality original work from Minnesota and regional artists and craftspersons. Items include pottery, jewelry, baskets, carvings, metal work, weaving, and local photography.

Payment: Consignment and outright purchase.

Instructions: Prefers to see work in person, but if not, send slides with résumé and price range.

KENNEDY BROTHERS MARKETPLACE

11 W. Main St., Vergennes, VT 05491

Items Wanted: Leather, stoneware, glass, wood and other crafts.

Payment: Pays for consignments on the 10th of each month.

Instructions: Send photos and/or samples to Edwin Grant.

LOOSE ENDS

2065 Madrona Ave., SE, Salem, OR 97302

www.looseends.com

Items Wanted: This mail-order catalog carries "organic" products for home and garden. Is looking for country and rustic gifts, garden and outdoor items, floral, baskets, ceramics and pots, handmade paper and stationary, etc.

Payment: Buys outright; pays within 30 days.

Instructions: Send sample, product description, and wholesale price to Product Development.

LOVE OF COUNTRY

137 Ault Rd., Urbana, OH 43078

www.loveofcountry.net

Items Wanted: Collector bears and dolls only.

Payment: Buys outright usually on net 30 days.

Instructions: Send photos. "I no longer buy and sell crafts—only dolls and sometimes bears."

MANSFIELD ART CENTER

700 Marion Ave., Mansfield, OH 44903

www.mansfieldartcenter.org

Items Wanted: The Gallery Shop carries work of original design in all of the art mediums ie, jewelry, glass, fiber, ceramics, wood, paintings, metal, etc. "We do not carry work made from kits!"

Payment: Both wholesale and consignment. Net 30 on wholesale; 60/40 on consignment.

Instructions: Photos and slides accepted as well as wholesale catalogs and price sheets. The gallery shop within the art center is open all year. Contact co-buyers Judy Cole and Judy Bemiller.

MARTY WASSERBERG & ASSOCIATES

P.O. Box 367, New Vernon, NJ 07976

Items Wanted: This wholesale rep deals in many different type of items including home decor items, nature and wood crafts, florals, and pottery.

Payment: Pays cash on sale minus commission.

Instructions: Send samples, brochure or catalog, wholesale price list, and any other supporting information.

MIKE FEINBERG CO.

1736 Penn Ave., Pittsburg, PA 15222

www.mikefeinbergcompany.com

Items Wanted: This rep deals in many different type of items, but is particularly interested in party supplies. Will also look at toys, novelties, and get-well items.

Payment: Pays cash on sale minus commission.

Instructions: Send samples, brochure or catalog, wholesale price list, and any other supporting information.

MILES KIMBALL

41 W. 8th Avenue, Oshkosh, WI 54906

www.mileskimball.com

Items Wanted: This well-established mail-order catalog carries a wide variety of gifts, home accessories, seasonal items, and garden products.

Payment: Buys with purchase order and pays within 30 days.

Instructions: Submit printed product information, wholesale prices, and photo. Send to the merchandising division. Do not send samples unless requested.

MOONSTONE GALLERY

4070 Burton Dr., Cambria, CA 93428

www.moonstones.com

Items Wanted: This gallery carries truly unique items such as kinetic art, kaleidoscopes, moonstone jewelry, holographic glass sculptures, waterfalls, and wood jewelry boxes. Over 200 artists are represented here and the competition is stiff, but if you have something you think will make the grade, they are willing to take a look.

Payment: Both outright purchase and consignment.

Instructions: Send photos, brochures, résumé, etc.

MOSSY CREEK POTTERY

Attn: Jeanne Davis, 483 S Immonen Rd., Lincoln City, OR 97367

www.mossycreekpottery.com

(503) 996-2415

Items Wanted: Handmade pottery. No commercial molds, please! All styles, glazes and price ranges considered.

Payment: Cash upon delivery (50% of retail price) of approved items or 60% of retail paid 1st of every month for consignment items.

Instructions: Send photos or slides; bring samples in person. Phone contact is best initially. Oregon, Washington, potters only. "We require exclusive sales rights within 20 mile radius. Willing to work with young or new potters or potters establishing market for new or different items."

NAPERVILLE FINE ART CENTER & GALLERY

508 N. Center St., Naperville, IL 60563

Items Wanted: This is a wonderful nonprofit gallery open to all kinds of arts and crafts. Items can be any style or material as long as the design is unique, original, and made with quality.

Payment: Consignment 60/40.

Instructions: Send photos, prices, and lead time needed.

NORTHFIELD ARTS GUILD

Attn: Ellie Lundblad, Executive Director
304 Division St., Northfield, MN 55057
www.northfieldartsguild.org

Items Wanted: High quality original handcrafted items—more fine arts, less "crafts."

Payment: Consignment: 60 artist/40 shop. Wholesale: 30 days.

Instructions: Send photos, slides, and/or samples. "Our shop is part of a center for the arts that includes a gallery, recital room, dance school, and classrooms. We'd appreciate having information about the artists represented in the shop since many of our customers like this 'personal' touch."

NORTHWEST IMAGES

6100 4th Ave. South, Room 363, Seattle, WA 98108

Items Wanted: Any gift items with a country theme. Only takes on items that can be produced in sufficient quantity for distribution through drug stores, department stores, and other mass merchandising outlets in the Northwest.

Payment: Pays wholesale prices less commission.

Instructions: Send samples, catalog, letter of introduction, and wholesale and retail price lists.

NOVICA WHOLESALE

11835 W. Olympic Blvd. Suite 750E
East Tower, Los Angeles, CA 90064
www.novica.com/wholesale

Items Wanted: NOVICA is one of the world's leading wholesalers of handcrafted products with offices around the world and online. They handle hundreds of unique jewelry, accessories, and home decor collections. Over 100,000 buyers come to the Web site to buy wholesale for their stores.

Payment: Web site order management system tracks all incoming order. Orders and payments are all processed through NOVICA.

Instructions: Visit the Web site and take the "Seller Tour" for instructions.

OCTAGON CENTER FOR THE ARTS

3.
>427 Douglas, Ames, IA 50010
>www.octagonarts.org

Items Wanted: Pottery, jewelry, stationery, fiber, children's items, books, wood, metal, sculpture, art.

Payment: Consignment 50/50 paid 15th of the month when items have sold.

Instructions: Contact Alissa Hansen to set up an appointment. Otherwise send letter with photos, slides, etc. "We also buy things outright, but we prefer consignment. We specialize in Iowa handcrafted art and art that coincides with our exhibit in the gallery."

THE ONLINE GIFT SHOW

>www.giftswholesale.com

Items Wanted: This online wholesale business is where 5,000 gift shops, gift basket makers, florists, and other retail businesses come to order their inventory wholesale online. For $19.95 per month, you can present your products and make them available for buyers and reps to view and order without having to have your own Web site.

Payment: Arrangements are made between you and the individual buyers.

Instructions: Visit the Web site for more information.

POOPSIE'S

>107 S. Main St., Galena, IL 61036
>www.poopsies.com

Contact: Susan Landes.

Items Wanted: Eccentric, unusual, and fun crafts of all kinds ranging in price from $5 to $2,000. Always looking for the original, innovative, and delightful. Carries only contemporary quality products.

Payment: Some outright purchase; some consignment.

Instructions: Send photos or slides along with descriptions, prices, and any helpful information about the artist such as how and where products are currently being marketed.

THE POTTER, ETC.

Box 305,331 Main St., Jerome, AZ 86331

Items Wanted: The shop inventory includes pottery, baskets, jewelry, clothing, candles, books, cards, handwovens, dried floral arrangements, and wall sprays. "We carry only handcrafted items."

Payment: Prefers wholesale purchase, but consignment considered on very high-end items.

Instructions: Send brochures. "We are interested in high quality crafts. No crocheted or knitted items."

PRAIRIE HOUSE

3013 Lindberg Blvd., Springfield, IL 62704

www.prairiefireglass.com

Items Wanted: Fine contemporary crafts, no country crafts or perishable items. The gallery has been in business for over 30 years and now represents the work of over 300 American artists.

Payment: Prefers purchase, but will consider consignment as long as quality is there.

Instructions: Prefers slides, but photos are acceptable. Include as much documentation as possible, such as brochures and show history.

PRINTS & PATCHES

38 Main St., Stowe, VT 05672

Items Wanted: Fabric-related handmade items that are one-of-a-kind or repeated design of products welcome.

Payment: Consignment: 2/3 goes to artisan.

Instructions: Send samples.

PUTTIN' ON THE DOG

5140 Shadow Path Lane, Lilburn, GA 30047

Items Wanted: Canine motif gifts, accessories, and collectibles. This includes art, gifts, apparel, jewelry, etc. Items should be available for at least 15 different breeds and must be breed specific.

Payment: Pays outright.

Instructions: Send information package including product description, dog breeds available, your bio and contact information, wholesale price, availability and delivery time, and photos. Samples are accepted but will not be returned.

THE QUILT RACQUE

37 Terrace St., Dallas, PA 18612

Items Wanted: Quilted wallhangings, table runners, placemats, coasters, pillows, and quilts for babies.

Payment: Prefers consignment with 2/3 to maker, 1/3 to shop. Will consider purchase if on approval basis for minimum two months.

Instructions: Photos would be best. "I prefer handquilted items but good machine quilted articles are acceptable, if price can be kept moderate. People want handcrafted look but the price will always get compared to the 'imports.' It's a constant education to the public, i.e. quality, handmade one of a kind, etc. My shop is not a fabric shop with supplies, etc. It is a one of a kind finished product, antique and new quilts, linens, and lace and—no imported linens or quilts!"

SAMCO

5105 Tollview Dr., #180, Rolling Meadows, IL 60008

Items Wanted: Quality giftwares for distribution in the Midwest.

Payment: Wholesale less 15%.

Instructions: Send samples, catalog, price list, etc.

THE SASSY CAT

4. 88 N. Main St., Chagrin Falls, OH 44022 Crosstitch

Items Wanted: One-of-a-kind works in wood, fabric, or other materials. Handmade toys and home decorations are especially popular.

Payment: Consignment.

Instructions: Bring in samples.

SASSY SOUTH

Atlanta Apparel Mart, Atlanta, GA 30303

www.sassysouth.com

Items Wanted: Unique hand crafted jewelry for wholesale distribution.

Payment: Works on standard commission.

Instructions: Send photos or slides, brochures, résumé, and wholesale price list.

SEVENTEENTH COLONY HOUSE

3991 Main St., Hilliard, OH 43026

Items Wanted: Handcarved Santas, Noah's Arks, Uncle Sams, decoys, etc., and woven throws, placemats, jewelry, country stoneware.

Payment: COD or AmEx.

Instructions: Send photos and sizes. "We look for any items that are collectible or can be used in the home."

SHOW OF HANDS

> 210 Clayton St, Denver, CO 80206
>
> http://showofhandsdenver.com

Items Wanted: Fine American contemporary craft. No country. No wearables except accessories.

Payment: Purchase/ consignment.

Instructions: Send slides and SASE with description, dimensions, and prices. Slides are viewed the second Tuesday of each month except December.

STATEMENTS UNLIMITED

> 17526 Aurora N., Seattle, WA 98133

Items Wanted: Traditional crafts to be sold in gift and interior design shops throughout the Northwest. Specializes in the Victorian theme.

Payment: Works on standard commission.

Instructions: Send samples and plenty of documentation to prove you can produce the quality and quantity required by a wholesaler.

SUSI'S GALLERY FOR CHILDREN

> 348 Huron Ave., Cambridge, MA 02138
>
> www.susigallery.com

Items Wanted: Whimsical, colorful, jewelry, furniture, clothing, mobiles, and picture frames.

Payment: Consignment 50/50.

Instructions: Send photos or slides. Contact Susi Cooper. "I'm looking for something that appeals to the child in all of us."

TOTAL ACCESSORIES

> 250 Spring St., NW, Atlanta, GA 30303

Items Wanted: This wholesaler deals mostly with textiles, but will also consider unique jewelry.

Payment: Pays wholesale prices less commission.

Instructions: Send photos first, then samples if requested. Include price list and thorough description.

VILLAGE WEAVERS

> 418 Villita, San Antonio, TX 78205
>
> www.villageweavers.com

Items Wanted: Handwoven items.

Payment: Consignment. "After item sells, we pay on the first day of the following month."

Instructions: Contact Romayne Mertens to discuss. "Village Weavers is located in a tourist area along the San Antonio river. Our customers are from everywhere."

WENDY GORDON GLASS STUDIO, INC., & CRAFT GALLERY

P.O. Box 878, Stevensville, MD 21666

http://wendygordonstudio.com

Items Wanted: Some whimsical and nautical themes in glass, wood, ceramics, fiber, jewelry. (Not limited to described themes though.) No country. Priced at $2 to $2,000.

Payment: Consignment, 70% to artist; purchase 50/50.

Instructions: Send photos and prices. Would like to know delivery time as well. The Craft Gallery is on Kent Island in Chesapeake Bay. It also has a working stained glass studio established in 1980.

WHOLESALE CRAFTS, INC.

2783 Martin Rd #125, Dublin, OH 43017

www.wholesalecrafts.com

Items Wanted: This online wholesaling company is looking for serious handcrafters only. You must have a proven and successful track record supplying at least two retail locations before being considered. No work from kits, patterns, molds, etc. Only quality handcrafts will be considered.

Instructions: Visit the Web site for more information.

WOODSTOCK GALLERY, INC.

904 Green Bay Rd., Winnetka, IL 60093

Items Wanted: Contemporary fine crafts that are also functional. Materials include glass, ceramics, wood, jewelry, metal and fabric.

Payment: Some purchases and some consignment.

Instructions: Send slides, artist documentation, and wholesale price list.

YVETTE FRY

54 W 39th St. # 5, New York, NY 10016

www.yvettefry.com

Items Wanted: This nationwide rep is always on the lookout for new handcrafted items such as silver jewelry and accessories.

Payment: Works on 15% commission.

Instructions: Send photos, description, letter from artist, and prices.

TELECOMMUTING AND OTHER EMPLOYEE OPTIONS

If you are like most people, you think that if you want a job working at home, you will have to give up your present job and start from scratch, and look for a new job that could be done at home. The fact is, however, that for 19 million Americans, taking their work home at least one day a week is routine. These home workers are commonly referred to as "telecommuters."

Telecommuting is an often-misused term. It means transporting work to the worker rather than the worker to the workplace. This can be accomplished in a number of ways, but most often it involves the use electronic communications—phones, fax machines, the Internet, and e-mail.

In this book, telecommuting will be defined as an option open to employees who are currently working for a company and have an express need to take their work home. A temporary need might be illness, temporary disability, pregnancy, or the need to take care of family members. Some workers desire to move home in order to work more productively on long projects, cut down on commuting, or spend more time with family.

Some telecommuting is done temporarily, some is part-time, and some is permanent. It is becoming a very common option in the corporate world with as many as 500 corporations reporting some kind of work-at-home option available to employees on an informal basis. A few of those have formal programs with the rules for working at home laid out in very specific detail.

If you are already working and you want to work at home, look in your own backyard first. Many employees have the opportunity to work at home and just don't know it. Before looking elsewhere for a new job that can be done at home, why not start by discussing with your manager the possibility of moving your present job home? You might be surprised by the answer.

The listings in this section should be considered as examples of successful telecommuting programs only. None of them are open to inquiries from anyone who is not currently an employee.

152

———MOVING YOUR WORK HOME———

If you are currently employed, moving your present job from its current location to your home is an option that you should explore before looking for a new employer.

Large corporations are most likely to accept the telecommuting arrangement. Of the several hundred major corporations in the United States that have home workers on the payroll, most prefer to hire home-based workers from within. As a rule, they want to develop confidence in their employees before allowing them to take their work home. Therefore, the very first thing to do is make sure you are known for being a valuable and trustworthy employee.

Next, develop a plan of action. Define the job tasks, which are feasible for home-based work. Don't ignore problems that could arise later and undermine your position. Consider all of the possible problems and devise a "worst case" scenario and alternative solutions for dealing with each of them. That way, you will be prepared and can confidently assure your company there will be no unpleasant surprises.

Be prepared to "sell" your home office idea to your employer, focusing on the ways moving your work home will benefit the company. Remember, your employer is in business to make a profit, and while s/he probably prefers happy employees, the bottom line is ultimately the highest priority. You can take comfort in the fact that the benefits employers gain from work-at-home arrangements are well documented. If you want to refer to some success stories, see the company profiles scattered throughout this book. In addition, the following information is likely to grab your employer's attention.

The number one benefit to employers is increased productivity. The best-documented cases are from Blue Cross/Blue Shield of South Carolina, which reported productivity gains of 50%, and from Control Data Corp., which showed gains of 35%. Employees at home tend to work at their individual peak hours, don't get paid for long lunch hours and time spent at the water cooler, and often continue to work while feeling slightly under the weather rather than take time off.

The second greatest benefit to employers is the cost savings from not spending money on additional office space, utilities, parking space, etc. This is especially helpful for growing companies and also for home-based businesses that need to expand while limiting the costs of doing so. Some companies have even sent employees home and rented out the unoccupied space to compatible firms. As a direct result of its home work program, Pacific Bell closed three offices in one year, saving $40,000 in rent alone.

Another advantage to employers is a far lower turnover rate among employees allowed to work at home. In some industries, rapid turnover is a serious problem. The insurance industry, for instance, has a turnover rate between 30% and 45%. As you would expect, recruiting and training costs are very high in such industries.

Even governments have come to view telecommuting as a viable solution to some of society's most pressing problems-air pollution, traffic congestion, and energy consumption. It has been estimated that a 20% reduction in commuting nationwide could save 110,000 barrels of gasoline a day! For these reasons, several states—led by California, Washington, and North Dakota—have formally endorsed telecommuting. California even offers tax incentives to companies that will send some of its employees home to work.

All of this should give you ample ammunition to convince your manager(s) to let you try working at home. It's usually best not to try for an immediate move to full-time home work though. Start slowly, asking to take your work home a couple of times in the afternoon, and then proposing a two-day project. While you're testing the waters, make sure you check in by phone to see if anything has come up at the office that you need to take care of. After a few months of occasionally working at home, you'll be ready to go to your manager and point out that you get more accomplished when you're not distracted by office routines and don't have to waste valuable time commuting. Remember, you're not asking for favors. You are simply offering what every employer wants—a motivated, efficient worker interested in increasing productivity.

———COMPANIES WITH——— TELECOMMUTING PROGRAMS

ADC TELECOMMUNICATIONS, INC.
Minnesota

ADC makes telecommuting an option for employees as the need arises. An employee need only get the okay from their supervisor.

AETNA LIFE & CASUALTY
Connecticut

Aetna has a formal program that includes over 2,000 employees. Among the telecommuters are claims representatives, sales consultants, claims processors, and account consultants.

AIR PRODUCTS & CHEMICALS, INC.
Pennsylvania
This is a very large company with over 10,000 employees, some of which are telecommuters. There is no formal arrangement and telecommuting is allowed on an individual basis as needed.

ALLERGAN, INC.
California
Allergan is a well-known manufacturer of eye care products. For the last decade, company programmers have been working at home due to lack of space at company headquarters. The policy has saved the company considerable money (from not having to expand) and given employees freedom and flexibility.

ALLSTATE INSURANCE COMPANY
Illinois
Allstate's telecommuting program originally started as an option for disabled employees, all of whom were programmers. The first was a systems programmer who was injured in a car accident. Then came some entries placed by Lift, Inc. Now, Allstate is open to the telecommuting option for any current employee with a job suitable to be taken home on an alternating schedule.

AMERICAN EXPRESS TRAVEL RELATED SERVICES COMPANY, INC.
New York
Over 50 travel counselors are offered telecommuting as an incentive program to top performers only.

AMERICAN INSTITUTES FOR RESEARCH
California
Ten researchers and analysts telecommute; each has made individual arrangements to do so.

AMERITECH CORPORATION
Illinois
Most of Ameritech's 250 telecommuters are in sales or customer service.

AMF BOWLING PRODUCTS GROUP, INC.
New York

Office-based employees are provided with computers and Internet access for after-hours telecommuting. Most telecommuting is done by those working in IT positions.

AMTRAK
Washington, DC

Amtrak's Customer Relations Group has increased its productivity and employee morale by implementing telecommuting on a small scale. Nine writers in the group work at home on a rotating schedule, with one writer working one day at home, then the next taking one day, and so on.

ANASAZI, INC.
Arizona

Programmers, engineers, and other high level technical personnel work at home. The company is very careful who is selected for telecommuting. Only persons who have proven that they are self-managing, have some experience working at home, and have proper technical equipment can participate. Employee status remains intact.

ANDREWS GLASS COMPANY, INC.
New Jersey

Glass lamp work and tool work on laboratory glass products is dispensed as an option for extra income for after-hours work for established employees only.

APOLLO GROUP, INC.
Arizona

Apollo Group is the corporation that owns University of Phoenix. About 100 employees in various positions ranging from enrollment representatives to financial aid coordinators work from home.

APPLE COMPUTER, INC.
California

Telecommuting at Apple is a natural. All employees receive a Mac for their home use and are part of the company's electronic network automatically. Couple that with the company's liberal attitude toward its employees in general and you have a lot of people working at home whenever it seems appropriate.

ARIZONA, DEPARTMENT OF ADMINISTRATION
Arizona

The state of Arizona began telecommuting in 1990. Now over 800 employees work at home.

ARTHUR ANDERSEN & COMPANY
Illinois

A small percentage of this "Big 8" accounting firm's 64,000 employees work at home. They are mostly in management positions, although the arrangement is open to all employees. The company's telecommuting program launched in 1998 formally and is considered to be just one of several flexible work options.

ARTHUR D. LITTLE, INC.
Massachusetts

Telecommuting is an informal option offered to staff members. Most telecommuting is done by information systems consultants. Equipment is provided as necessary.

AT&T
California

AT&T, like most of the "Baby Bells," is not only a participant in the telecommuting trend, but a leader as well. The company took a giant step forward when it launched "Telecommuting Day" back in 1994.

Telecommuting is so commonplace within the company that it is hard to estimate how many employees take advantage of the option at any given time. However, it is estimated that as many as 29% of the total workforce are indeed telecommuters. That's tens of thousands! The policy is so liberal that even newly hired employees can arrange to telecommute right from the start if that is the custom of the group they will be working with.

In addition, AT&T helps set up telecommuting programs for other companies in the Southern California area.

BALTIMORE EVENING SUN
Maryland

The work-at-home option, used by writers of all kinds, is available to any employee with the necessary equipment.

BANCTEC
California

Software engineers are allowed flexible scheduling with the telecommuting option.

BANKERS TRUST COMPANY
New York

Bankers Trust conducted its initial telecommuting pilot program with the help of Electronic Services Unlimited. Twenty employees worked at home for six months on a part-time basis only. The usual time spent at home working was two days a week unless the particular project allowed for longer periods of time. Employees were supplied with PCs networked into the mainframe in Manhattan. The work was originally done in the local mode using and transferring floppies. Now it utilizes the Internet. The pilot was successful so the program has been expanded to include more people.

BATTERYMARCH FINANCIAL MANAGEMENT COMPANY
Massachusetts

Batterymarch is an international investment-counseling firm with $12 billion worth of funds, mostly corporate pensions, to manage. Operation requires a 24-hour vigilance in order to keep up with world markets. Most employees, 30 out of 35, have terminals at home connected to the company's mainframe. Twenty professional brokers are also online with their own PCs. If a broker has a problem with the system, he/she can call one of the others at home for help. Throughout the night, the company's "Phantom Program" monitors the system automatically and transmits wake-up calls if something goes wrong.

"We've been using this system for over 10 years. Since starting the work-at-home routine, our productivity has increased tremendously. The owner had a vision that at some time everyone would work at home unless they absolutely could not."

BELL ATLANTIC
Pennsylvania

Bell Atlantic has over 1,500 full-time telecommuters and many other employees who telecommute from time to time. Most are claims representatives and consultants.

BELL COMMUNICATIONS
New Jersey

Experienced employees in the Research Department can make arrangements with their managers to take their work home on a project-by-project basis. There have been some full-time telecommuters, but the situation is not the rule.

BELL SOUTH
Arizona

Bell South conducted an experimental two-year telecommuting program before making it a company-wide policy. Telecommuters are all regular employees of Bell South and include both high-tech and low-tech personnel, mostly middle managers and marketers.

BENEFICIAL CORPORATION
New Jersey

Data processors and the top brass share the telecommuting option at Beneficial.

BEST WESTERN HOTELS INTERNATIONAL
Arizona

This is an interesting project where the home workers telecommute from their home in prison. Women prisoners in the Arizona State Prison handle telephone reservations for the hotel chain. They are provided with PCs, Internet access, extra phone lines, and complete training.

BLUE CROSS/BLUE SHIELD OF MARYLAND
Maryland

This particular branch of Blue Cross/Blue Shield allows experienced employees to work at home as word processors. They are part-time employees with part-time benefits.

BLUE CROSS/BLUE SHIELD OF THE NATIONAL CAPITOL AREA
Washington, DC

This program was fashioned after the similar program at Blue Cross/Blue Shield of South Carolina's data entry program. Basically, word processors enter data from insurance claims directly into the company's mainframe. The main difference is that here, all home-based workers are former employees. Each worker has a quota of at least 400 claims per day. PC terminals with modems are leased to the home workers. The company pays so much per claim on a biweekly basis.

BOOKMINDERS, INC.
Pennsylvania

This is a unique company that provides bookkeeping services to more than 200 small companies. It operates with a virtual staff meaning everyone works from home. Each time an employee is hired, a technician is dispatched to the worker's home office to do the necessary installations including software and phone lines.

BORG-WARNER CHEMICAL COMPANY
West Virginia

Sales personnel are equipped with PCs at home, which are networked to the company's mainframe. Telecommunications capabilities include e-mail. Sales people can now do analysis and forecasting without going into the office. Other professionals on staff are similarly equipped and can work at home as the need arises.

BRISTOL-MYERS SQUIBB COMPANY
New York

Working Mother Magazine named this corporation one of the best companies in America for working mothers three years running. Among the many flexible work options for women in this company is telecommuting. The option is available to the 44,000 employees company-wide.

BRONNER MANUFACTURING AND TOOL COMPANY
New Jersey

Work to take home is assigned only to regular in-house employees that wish to earn extra money at home. Work involves milling, turning, deburring, drilling, and lathe work. Pays piece rates.

BROWN WILLIAMSON TOBACCO COMPANY
Kentucky

Systems programmers work on a contract basis and divide their time between home and office. Only programmers that were previously employed in-house are chosen.

CALIFORNIA STATE DEPARTMENT OF GENERAL SERVICES
California

After two years of planning, The California State Telecommuting Project was finally conducted. State workers from 14 different state agencies volunteered to participate. That included anyone who thought his/her job could be done at home. About 200 participated in the pilot program with job titles ranging from clerk typists to managers. Locations included the greater Los Angeles area, San Francisco, and Sacramento.

Telecommuters were outfitted with PCs and ergonomically correct furniture. An electronic bulletin board replaced the "water cooler" as the center of internal communications. All workers were required to return to the office of origin at least once a week.

160

Jack Nilles, sometimes known as the "father of telecommuting," wrote the 150-page "Plan For Success" and was been selected to direct the project. David Fleming, who initiated the idea, hoped the experiment would serve as an example of successful telecommuting and thereby open up telecommuting opportunities elsewhere in government and private industry. To that end, many aspects are being monitored and evaluated to conclude how much fuel is saved, effects on traffic flow, possible effects on air quality, etc.

Fleming was gratified by the success of the program and the state has implemented and hugely expanded the program.

CHATAS GLASS COMPANY
New Jersey

Glassblowing and grinding of laboratory glassware can be done as a secondary income opportunity by established employees. Only part-time work is allowed at home. Pick-up and delivery of supplies and finished work is provided. This is handwork, so no machinery is needed. Pays piece rates.

CHILTON CREDIT REPORTING
Massachusetts

In-house employees must be thoroughly experienced before moving work home. About 14 workers have taken advantage of the option. They proof computer sheets and analyze the "decisions" made by the computers. Pays piece rates equaling approximately the same as in-house workers doing similar work.

CIGNA CORPORATION
Pennsylvania

Several hundred employees telecommute including underwriters, claims representatives, and accountants.

CITIBANK
New York

Citibank offers telecommuting as an option to regular employees on an informal basis as the need arises. Employees most often work at home during temporarily disability or pregnancy.

COLORADO DEPARTMENT OF PERSONNEL
Colorado

About 60 employees in a wide variety of positions telecommute in a formal program.

COLORADO NATIONAL BANK
Colorado

This major Colorado bank started telecommuting by conducting a pilot telecommuting program within the MIS department only. The purpose of the project was to determine whether telecommuting could help cut costs as it has in so many other organizations. The telecommuters wrote systems documentation four days a week. The workers provided their own PCs. Colorado National subsequently expanded the program to include other employees at the end of the pilot phase.

THE COMPUCARE COMPANY
Virginia

Several high level employees have found working at home necessary for various personal reasons.

CURTIS 1000
Connecticut

Company offers home work arrangement as option to in-house employees with proven need. For example, one disabled worker does hand inserting and other mail processing work at home.

DATA GENERAL CORPORATION
Massachusetts

Data General manufactures, designs, and sells business systems. One product is the "Comprehensive Electronic Office" system, which includes e-mail, spreadsheet analysis and more. Working at home is an option to in-house employees on a departmental level. Those taking advantage of the option are most often programmers, engineers, and word processors involved in software development.

The telecommuting employee's department is responsible for providing necessary equipment, generally a PC and modem which will be networked into the company mainframe. This is usually older equipment that has already been costed out. "Working at home has proven to be a convenient and useful tool. The key benefits are convenience and being close to family."

DECORATED PRODUCTS COMPANY
Massachusetts

Eight employees here make extra money by taking extra work home. They inspect nameplates manufactured at the plant. They are required to pick up and deliver the work themselves. Pays piece rates.

DENVER, CITY AND COUNTY
Colorado

In an effort to combat air pollution in the Denver area, the city and county offers telecommuting wherever feasible. There are now about 150 employees including data entry operators, engineers, and supervisors working at home on a regular basis.

DETROIT FREE PRESS
Michigan

Reporters, columnists, and editors telecommute. PCs are supplied. Work is transmitted to the company mainframe via the Internet. Examples of telecommuters include one-person bureaus in Los Angeles and Toronto, and a columnist who lives 40 minutes away from the office and has no reason to commute anyway for that type of work. Telecommuting was implemented as a company policy in 1984. Detroit Free Press also has several home-based freelance photographers who work on an assignment basis. Currently there are about 20 home workers in total. All telecommuters are staff members and are paid the same salary and benefits they could receive if they were in-house. Freelancers are paid by the job.

DIGITAL EQUIPMENT CORPORATION
Massachusetts

Digital, like Apple, has a very progressive attitude about its employees. Most of the technical workers have computers in their home offices and are allowed to work at home at their own discretion. Informally, the number of telecommuters (who work at home only part of the time) may run into the thousands.

EASTMAN KODAK COMPANY
New York

About 25 sales representatives work from home with full benefits.

EQUITABLE LIFE ASSURANCE
New Jersey

Telecommuting started here with several programmers and managers participating in the company's telecommuting program. Work involved database development, technical support, troubleshooting, budgeting, project monitoring and progress reporting. All equipment was supplied. Home terminals were connected to the large mainframe IMS. There was also a generous allowance for furniture. Employees were salaried with employee status intact. After final review of pilot, Equitable decided to expand telecommuting option to other departments.

Close up: Equitable Life Assurance

Success is a word that is rapidly becoming synonymous with telecommuting pilot programs. Equitable Life Assurance is no exception.

In 1992, Equitable relocated some of its departments from corporate headquarters in midtown Manhattan to Secaucus, New Jersey. For most employees involved, this was merely a matter of traveling in a different direction; some even lived in New Jersey and it meant less traveling. But, for those who lived on Long Island, travel time would double and it was feared that would be too much for some.

It was clear that something had to be done to avoid the costs of replacing valuable personnel. Telecommuting was offered to key people as an incentive to stay with Equitable. Six people, programmers, analysts, and one administrative assistant, were encouraged to stay home two or three days a week. They were each given all necessary equipment, a $400 furniture allowance, and retained their salary levels and employment status.

Telecommuting project coordinator, Jack Tyniec, credits Electronic Services Unlimited with providing the necessary training and guidance. ESU worked closely with Equitable's legal department, personnel manager, and prospective telecommuting managers to avoid problems in advance.

"We had no idea how many things could just creep out of the woodwork. ESU helped us spell out the issues and deal with them in advance—things like local zoning restrictions, labor laws, insurance liability both for company provided medical coverage and Workmen's Compensation, and even seemingly innocent wordings in our company personnel policy."

Phrases like "work to be performed in company office," found in standard employment contracts, may not have been intended to restrict working at home, but that is the legal effect, Tyniec points out. To rectify that situation, a supplementary contract was drawn up to specifically allow work at home.

The first formal review of the Equitable telecommuting program indicated that all was going well. The telecommuters loved it, Tyniec says, and their managers were equally enthusiastic. "Not only have we kept good people, but productivity has increased as well. We've measured productivity in terms of quality, not quantity, from a managerial point of view. The managers were unanimously in favor of continuing the program. The consensus is that these people (telecommuters) were good anyway, but now they're even better."

Telecommuting has since been formally integrated into Equitable's overall personnel policy. "It will spread now of its own accord," says Tyniec.

"Our personnel manager gave a presentation to other company PMs at their urging. It seems that somebody has to slay the dragons first, but once that's been done and it's been clearly demonstrated that it works, others will follow. At least for corporations, someone has to champion the effort to get telecommuting started."

FEDERAL RESERVE BANK
Georgia

Federal Reserve Bank offers a work-at-home option to its regular professional staff. First started as an experiment in the early 1980s with more than 65 employees in the research department participating, working at home is now an option incorporated into departmental policy for anyone who performs tasks such as writing or editing either full-time or part-time. Computers, when used, are usually laptops owned by the employees. "Reports of our home work program have been greatly exaggerated by the media. When they (employees) can work better at home, they do. It's a simple as that."

FIRST NATIONAL BANK OF CHICAGO
Illinois

This company has a formal home-based work program intended especially for data processing and other non-technical personnel. Program guidelines are designed to ensure success. "It basically uses a foundation of trust and it's up to the managers to make it work. There is support from top management in the company." There are no number goals or monitoring of employees. Working at home is considered a career option, which managers can use as a possible solution to employees' problems as they arise. "We've had some good experiences. In the case of some clerical, there has been a 30% increase in productivity." Any necessary equipment is paid for by the business unit budget. This is a program for experienced current employees only.

FT. COLLINS
Colorado

Working at home is a citywide option open to all city employees. If work can be done at home, it will be permitted. Several hundred city employees are currently working at home in Ft. Collins. Any necessary equipment, furniture, or supplies will be provided. Employees retain full status, pay, and benefits.

GANNETT
Virginia

Newspaper reporters and editors who are currently employed by Gannett can work at home with manager approval.

GE PLASTICS
West Virginia

Although the bulk of GE Plastics' 100 telecommuters are sales and sales support staff, anyone here may telecommute as long as there is manager approval. Most employees have their own computers at home, but the company will sometimes supply the necessary equipment for telecommuting.

GEICO DIRECT
Washington, DC

GEICO is a leading direct auto insurer with huge databases. Systems programmers and other IT employees are given the telecommuting option complete with salary and full benefits.

GENERAL TELEPHONE
California

GTE first experimented with telecommuting during the '84 Summer Olympics as part of a citywide call for people to reduce commuting as much as possible. The pilot program involved technical and programming personnel and systems analysts. All were provided with PCs, modems, printers, and pagers and all were kept on straight salary. The experiment was considered a complete success and now GTE is broadening the scope of telecommuting across departmental lines. Planners of the program feel management skills should improve after telecommuting employees are trained in self-management skills and managers learn to gauge productivity rather than count heads. GTE is also participating in telecommuting as part of the Southern California Association of Governments' plan to reduce traffic congestion and pollution. "We think telecommuting over a period of time will have a substantial impact on traffic in Southern California. There is a lot of potential here."

GEORGIA POWER
Georgia

Like many government entities endorsing telecommuting, Georgia Power has done so in response to environmental problems, in this case smog in the Atlanta area. Workers across the board are encouraged to work at home, particularly on official smog alert days. Those telecommuting on a regular basis—and there are over 250 of them—have a budget of up to $9,000 to cover the expenses of a computer and other home office necessities.

GTE
California

Over 400 employees including administrative staff and marketing representatives telecommute in GTE's formal telecommuting program.

HARRIS TRUST AND SAVINGS BANK
Illinois

Harris Trust has an informal agreement that allows certain experienced employees to work at home on laptops to complete paperwork. There are about 40 telecommuters here.

HARTFORD INSURANCE GROUP
Connecticut

Hartford first conducted a telecommuting pilot project in 1995 with guidelines developed by a special committee. Employees, all volunteers, were required to have a good performance record with the company, be highly productive, not be working on "sensitive projects," and have a manager's approval. Each worked four days a week at home and one day a week at the office. Hartford supplied computer equipment networked to the company's mainframe plus extra phone lines. Employee status and salary remained unchanged.

Although some problems were reported early on, telecommuting has since been integrated into Hartford's overall personnel policy. There are currently about 4,000 employees working at home. Each has been supplied with appropriate equipment, furniture, and office supplies.

HEWLETT PACKARD LABORATORIES
California

Working at home as an option is offered department-wide. Home workers (over 3,000) are usually programmers, hardware and software engineers, applications engineers, research scientists, speechwriters, and managers. Most work at home part of the time during the week; some do so in addition to in-house work. Equipment is provided as necessary. Individuals are responsible for their own phone bills, but can avoid toll charges by calling the company mainframe and requesting a callback—made at company expense.

HOLT, RINEHART, & WINSTON
New York

In-house copy editors and proofreaders can get permission to work at home if they have a need for any personal reason. Employees must have editor's approval.

HOMEQUITY, INC.
Connecticut

Telecommuters do programming, evaluating, systems analysis, and software development. Homequity is a leading relocation service company. Its primary business consists of finding new housing for transferred corporate employees. Phase One of the telecommuting pilot project lasted about four months and gave the company a chance to evaluate cost savings and productivity. The initial findings were excellent and Phase Two, "continuation and expansion," is now in progress. Most of the participants in Phase One were computer personnel, but many other employees now work at home on laptops. "Telecommuting only makes sense because the future of this business is in computers."

HONEYWELL, INC.
Minnesota

Working at home is an informal option for Honeywell employees on a departmental level. One example of its use involves handicapped phone operators. The operators have dedicated phone lines in their homes which route long distance calls on weekend and nights. Calls are relayed from Honeywell employees on the road with cell phones. Home-based operators patch through the calls, using a network. Pays salary plus benefits.

HOUSEHOLD INTERNATIONAL
Illinois

This financial services company has several dozen telecommuters, mostly working in customer service.

THE H.W. WILSON COMPANY
New York

Like Information Access Company (see below), this company is in the abstracting and indexing field. Although the number is smaller than its competitor, H.W. Wilson's indexers also work at home utilizing the company's electronic network and Federal Express.

IBM
New York
Home-based work is a company option for IBM employees only. IBM has provided over 8,000 PCs for its employees to use at home, either part-time during regular business hours or after hours. Working at home is allowed during regular hours on a project basis as a convenience to employees. Company recently participated in a formal two-year telecommuting experiment conducted by The Center for Futures Research at U.S.C.

INDUSTRIAL INDEMNITY INSURANCE
California
Approximately 125 insurance auditors in the company have been outfitted with computers, printers, and auditing software at the expense of the company. The purpose was to reduce commuting time to and from the office and to increase overall productivity. Both goals have been achieved.

INFORMATION ACCESS COMPANY
California
This company collects information from magazines and trade journals to maintain databases, including Magazine Index, Management Contents, and Trade and Industry Index; all of which are found in most libraries. At one time, Information Access had a fairly large home work operation with over 150 home-based indexers. Upon moving the operation to California, however, the home work program was scaled back severely. Now home-based indexers work only on weekly or monthly publications so deadlines can be met comfortably.

Workers come in once or twice a week to get supplies, materials, and any special instructions and to meet with their supervisor. Company provides Macs and special software. Workers are full-time employees with benefits and promotional opportunities equal to those of their in-house counterparts. Home indexers are used because they are more productive and have fewer errors.

INTUIT
California
Customer service reps work at home for this major software developer.

JET PROPULSION LABORATORY
California

Telecommuting is an employee option to be used only for health reasons.

LAFAYETTE VENETIAN BLIND
Indiana

About 40 sales representatives work at home on a full-time basis.

LANIER BUSINESS PRODUCTS, INC
Georgia

Lanier makes "Telestaf," a product used in telecommuting, which was used in American Express' initial homebound training program. It includes features such as voicemail and is transcription-facilitated. Within Lanier, home work is allowed as a necessary option. Usually home workers are word processors and administrative assistants working at home part-time as the need arises.

LENCO ELECTRONIC, INC.
Illinois

Lenco is an electronic manufacturing company. Experienced employees perform a small part of the job at home, connecting and soldering wires onto transformers.

LOS ANGELES COUNTY
California

In 1989, Los Angeles County joined a small but growing number of government entities that have decided to combat the problems associated with heavy work-related traffic with a telecommuting program. About 150 county employees started working at home as part of the initial pilot program. As many as 2,000 of the county's 17,000 employees could be telecommuting within the next 5 years. All departments have been instructed to identify and select potential telecommuters within their employee pools.

MARINE MIDLAND BANK
New York

Regular employees of Marine Midland have the option of working at home as the need arises. The option is most often taken by professionals on staff in cases of temporary disability or pregnancy. The company is planning to develop more definitive guidelines for telecommuting in the future after current reorganization is completed.

MCDONALD DOUGLAS
California

At one time (before the company went through reorganization) there were 200 full-time telecommuters, plus another 2,000 employees that worked at home part of the time. These were mostly consultants, project managers, sales and marketing personnel, programmers, and engineers. Home work is not quite as prevalent now, but it is still an available option on an informal basis. Any experienced worker whose job can be done at home can request permission from the manager in charge of their department.

MEGAHERTZ CORPORATION
Utah

It only makes sense that a company that designs and manufactures communications products for mobile computer operators would have telecommuters. About three dozen sales representatives and their managers work from home.

MELLON BANK
Pennsylvania

Mellon Bank has made computers available to its IT employees and other personnel for several years. Mostly the PCs are used at home for after-hours work, but some employees, programmers in particular, can work at home full-time on a project-by-project basis. Working at home is also used as a perk to boost the morale of management level employees.

MERRILL LYNCH
New York

This leading financial services provider has been endorsing telecommuting for seven years now. Currently there are about 2,500 employees working at home.

The company does not offer telecommuting frivolously. Investing in home office equipment is just the beginning of the process. Home offices are inspected for safety and ergonomics at the outset and employees are thoroughly trained in all aspects of working at home including technical as well as psychological ones.

In addition, each is expected to attend the "Telework Simulation Lab" for six full days before beginning any work at home. Think of this as a sensory deprivation experience. The participant has access to a computer, phone/fax, and that's it!

METROPOLITAN LIFE INSURANCE COMPANY
New York

Metropolitan has several handicapped computer programmers trained by Lift, Inc. (see listing) Agents are also home-based. Necessary equipment and phone lines are provided. All home workers are paid full benefits.

METROPOLITAN WATER DISTRICT OF SOUTHERN CALIFORNIA
California

This is one of several southern California government agencies that began a formal telecommuting program as a way to ease traffic congestion and air pollution. Most of the 50 telecommuters are IT professionals.

MONSANTO AGRICULTURAL GROUP
Missouri

About 25 employees, mostly involved in IT, telecommute under informal arrangements.

MONTGOMERY WARD & COMPANY. INC.
Illinois

Montgomery Ward uses home-based workers to handle mail opening and other jobs involved in the direct mail operation for insurance companies and other financial service clients. Only current employees or people referred by employees are considered. All are local residents.

MULTILINK INCORPORATED
Massachusetts

MultiLink is in the teleconferencing business, so telecommuting comes naturally. About a dozen employees involved in setting up teleconferences do so from home.

NEW YORK LIFE INSURANCE COMPANY
New York

About two dozen home workers are insurance claims processors and contract programmers. Equipment is provided as necessary. Employees retain in-house status and benefits.

NORTEL NETWORKS
North Carolina

This company is another natural candidate for telecommuting since it produces telecommunications equipment. The HomeBase program has been successfully operating since 1994. Telecommuting is huge and growing at a steady clip here with 250 more employees heading home each month and a total of over 5,000 already there. The company not only pays to outfit home offices for its full-time telecommuters, it even has several office modules available on display to choose from—and that includes furniture.

NORTH CAROLINA NATIONAL BANK
North Carolina

Telecommuting is being offered on a limited basis, along with other work options, as part of this company's personnel policy. The purpose of offering options is to answer some of the family issues raised in an employee survey. Currently, three employees are taking advantage of the telecommuting option by dividing their work equally between home and office.

NORTHWESTERN BELL INFORMATION TECHNOLOGIES
Nebraska

Northwestern Bell conducted a two-year telecommuting experiment involving middle managers, marketing personnel, and data processing personnel. The guidelines for the program were developed by the Center for Futures Research at USC. After conclusion of the experiment, telecommuting was evaluated and integrated into the company's permanent overall policy.

ORTHO PHARMACEUTICAL CORPORATION
New Jersey

Although telecommuting started small here with just a handful of computer programmers and data processors, it is an option that is being offered to any employee who deems it appropriate. Supervisors have reported increased productivity; therefore many more employees will likely be working at home in the future with management's blessing.

PACIFIC BELL
California

Engineers, marketing planners, project managers, forecasters, programmers, analysts, and some technicians and service reps work for Pacific Bell at home. Currently Pacific Bell has over 200 telecommuters in both Northern California and Southern California. Though not all positions require computers, PCs are supplied as necessary. Pagers and extra phone lines are also provided as necessary.

Close up: Pacific Bell

Pacific Bell has a work-at-home program that, after only five months, was hailed as a complete success. While most telecommuting programs to date have been designed specifically for data processing personnel only, from the start Pac Bell wanted to prove that any job could be done at home. And they have done just that.

Seventy-five employees went home in the program's first year, and 100 more are expected to make the move shortly. All are volunteers and no restrictions have been placed on job titles. The range of job classifications is broad—everything from marketing personnel to engineers.

Computers are used only by those who needed them before moving their work home. Second phone lines and pagers are the most added equipment. Geographically, the home workers are spread out all over the state of California.

Being closer to clients was the first noticeable benefit. "This made us much more effective in servicing our clients," says Leslie Crawford, Marketing Manager for the Pacific Bell Telecommuting Department. "We soon realized how much 'windshield time' (time wasted behind the wheel commuting) was actually being spent on driving to the office first, then to the client."

The company was naturally pleased to improve service to clients, but there have been other benefits as well. For one thing, moving the work home has resulted in closing three offices with savings on space leases totaling $40,000 annually. There were no deliberate plans to close the first office; all the employees went home and there simply was no one left to mind the store. Two other offices then closed down and several more are expected to close soon.

But the biggest advantage to the program, according to Crawford, is flexibility for everyone concerned—for the company, for the employees, and for the clients. Increased flexibility has meant many jobs have been redefined with a new look at what they are, what they should accomplish, and how.

The program is working so well that Pac Bell's account executives have been looking at telecommuting as a possible solution to clients' problems. Pointing to themselves as a prime example is often the best way to sell the idea. "To some, however, the very word 'telecommuting' sounds foreign. To them, we point out that their own salespeople have been doing it for years. Telecommuting is just a new word to describe it. When they realize that, it doesn't seem like such a weird idea after all."

This may all sound unrealistically positive, but when asked about disadvantages, Crawford said she couldn't think of any. "Maybe it's because everyone in the program volunteered," she said. "They knew their jobs, their managers knew them, and they knew from the advance planning what to expect. No one has voiced a problem and no one has left the program.

If there is a problem, she added, it would be not enough people. "More bodies in more homes around the state would be good for us," she laughs, "We are very, very pleased with the success of our telecommuting program and the enthusiasm with which it has been received. It has already been established that telecommuting works for IT professionals. Now we have proved it is possible for all fields."

PEAT, MARWICK, MITCHELL & COMPANY
New York

Throughout its 100 offices nationwide, this major accounting firm has provided its field auditors with Macs in order to increase productivity. The auditors are now able to work for several days without actually returning to the office.

Like most major accounting firms, this one also has a "stable" of on-call accountants that handle assignments on a freelance basis during peak periods. These independent accountants are mostly former employees or are highly recommended by current employees.

J.C. PENNEY COMPANY, INC.
New York

Telemarketers take catalog orders in Milwaukee, Columbus, Sacramento, Richmond, Buffalo Grove (Illinois), and Atlanta, where the company catalog distribution centers are located. This program has increased from about 18 home workers in 1981 to over 400 today, making it one of the largest and most technologically advanced telecommuting programs in the country. PCs connected to the company via the Internet are supplied, along with two phone lines—one for data and one for voice contact with the customer. Supervisors visit home-based workers to make sure the home work space is adequate. They expect a minimum of 35 square feet of workspace that is isolated from family activities (noise).

Home-based workers are paid the same as in-house workers. In order to qualify to participate in the telecommuting program, a worker must have worked in a Penney's phone center for at least a year. The program is expected to grow even more, since it will save the company a lot of money by not having to build new facilities.

PRIME COMPUTER, INC.
Massachusetts

At any given time, about 100 of Prime's 12,000 employees are working at home on company provided computers. Most are in the customer service area, but others are in management and marketing. To take advantage of the telecommuting alternative, employees must first demonstrate the need.

PUBLIC SERVICE COMPANY OF NEW MEXICO
New Mexico

Working at home is an option offered to permanent employees who need to. PCs are provided as necessary.

QWEST
Colorado

Nearly 6,000 engineers, writers, computer programmers, and their supervisors work at home. Telecommuting has become a fully accepted way of working at Qwest because it has proven to be very economical for the company. Equipment is supplied as necessary. Home workers are represented on the project planning team by The Communications Workers of America. Employee status remains unchanged.

REDMOND
Washington

Redmond's telecommuting program began as an effort to ease traffic congestion. So far there are only a few dozen telecommuters, but any city employee can apply for the option.

SIGNAL CORPORATION
Virginia

Programmers and systems developers are based in Pax River, Maryland, but telecommuting is an option.

SNET
Connecticut

SNET (Southern New England Telecommunications, Inc.) has over 100 telecommuters in several job categories.

SOUTHERN CALIFORNIA ASSOCIATION OF GOVERNMENTS
California

SCAG started its telecommuting program in 1992 with 20 staff members, including accountants, legal staff members, planners and writers. The purpose of the program is to find a way to reduce work-related driving in Southern California by 12% by the year 2000. This project was one of several being conducted under the umbrella of the Central City Association. During the initial project, the home workers kept a log of transportation charges, telecommunications usage and utilities usage. Each was periodically interviewed to determine the best methods for expanding the program. Workers have their choice of part-time or full-time telecommuting. There is no change in salary, benefits, or employee status for anyone who chooses to work at home.

SOUTHERN NEW ENGLAND TELEPHONE
Connecticut

Working at home is an option open to all Southern New England Telephone employees. If the option is needed for any reason, working at home will be permitted as long as the job can be done at home.

STATE OF SOUTH DAKOTA
South Dakota

Working at home is facilitated on a statewide level by several electronic networks and PCs that are provided to all professional personnel in all state agencies. Working at home is considered informal, but is clearly acceptable; especially since it is donated time.

SUN MICROSYSTEMS COMPUTER CORPORATION
California

About 200 employees telecommute on a regular basis, but up to 4,000 are registered to do so at their discretion.

TANDEM COMPUTERS INCORPORATED
California

Most of Tandem's 200 telecommuters are software developers and technical writers.

3COM CORPORATION
California

3Com started experimenting with telecommuting in 1993. Today, there are about 85 employees in a wide variety of jobs who regularly work at home.

TRAVELER'S LIFE INSURANCE
Connecticut

Resident claims operations adjusters are provided with laptop computers so they don't have to return to the office from the field to finish work. Data processors are also provided with laptops, e-mail, formal training in telecommuting procedures, and a telecommuting handbook. Telecommuting is a formal program for established DP employees only.

TRAVELING SOFTWARE
Washington

Traveling Software started a telecommuting program as part of an effort to reduce long commuting times and enhance productivity. There are about 60 programmers, sales staff, and public relations staff involved.

UNION MUTUAL LIFE INSURANCE COMPANY
Maine

Union Mutual's "Flex-Program" is an option offered to employees as needed. Examples of need include, but are not limited to pregnancy or temporary disability. "Currently, the program is driven solely by managers/employees' interests. After expressing a desire to work at home, employees must demonstrate a legitimate need for an alternative work arrangement to their managers."

UNITED PRESS INTERNATIONAL
Washington, DC

Most of UPI's news bureaus are small operations scattered around the country and abroad. It only makes sense to allow the news correspondents and sales reps to work from home if they choose. Since home-based correspondents and reps are regular salaried employees of UPI, normal hiring procedures and requirements apply.

UNITED SERVICES AUTOMOBILE ASSOCIATION
Texas

Programmers for this insurance company are provided with PCs, both for after-hours work and also on a project-by-project basis.

UNIVERSITY OF WISCONSIN HOSPITAL AND CLINIC
Wisconsin

Medical transcriptionists handle physicians' notes for 50 clinics. To qualify for working at home, employees must first gain experience by spending six months in the office doing the same work that will be done at home. Work is to completed on 24- to 48-hour turn-around schedule; same as for in-house workers.

Equipment is provided. Home-based workers are regular employees with salaries and benefits identical to that of in-house workers. Performance is measured by characters typed (home workers are found to be 40-50% more productive than in-house workers). Home workers are represented by Local 2412 of the Wisconsin State Employees' Union. "There is an interest here in expanding the program. We can add one home worker for every one-and-a-half in-house workers."

US GENERAL SERVICES ADMINISTRATION
Washington, DC

The federal government's telecommuting program is called Flexiplace and is sponsored by the President's Council on Management Improvement. Almost 3,000 employees now participate regularly.

WENDY'S INTERNATIONAL, INC.
Ohio

A couple dozen employees in a wide variety of administrative positions work at home as needed. Wendy's has supported telecommuting for a number of years and now provides laptop computers to those who need them at home.

WEYERHAUSER COMPANY
Washington

Marketing personnel can work out of their homes full-time. In-house employees in Washington have the option to work at home part-time on an informal basis. The option is usually used on a project-by-project basis. Weyerhauser has a very flexible time policy in general. The work-at-home option is most common among systems developers, technical professionals, and sales personnel in the Research and Development and Data Processing departments.

LEARNING AT HOME
TO WORK AT HOME

Although there are plenty of opportunities listed in this book for people with limited skills, you have probably noticed many that do require education or skills you don't possess. Of course, additional skills generally bring additional pay, so the incentive to learn new things is strong.

The same reasons you have for wanting to stay home to work probably affect your ability to leave home to go to classes. How do you attend classes 35 miles away after working all day? And even if you were able to find childcare during the day, can you also find it in the evening?For these reasons, home study courses have become more popular than ever before.

Home study, also known as distance learning, involves enrolling in an educational institution that offers lessons specially prepared for self-directed study. The lessons are delivered, completed, and returned by mail one at a time or over the Internet. Each lesson is corrected, graded, and returned to the student by a qualified instructor who provides a personalized student-teacher relationship.

Generally, home study courses include only what you need to know and can be completed in a much shorter time period than traditional classroom instruction. With home study, you don't have to stick to somebody else's schedule. You don't have to give up your job, your time, leave home, or lose income. As in a home-based job, you work at your own pace with the school coming to you instead of you going to the school.

In the past, home study involved books and binders, audiotapes and videos. Those materials are still used (except DVDs have replaced the outmoded formats), but today the majority of home study courses are available over the Internet. In some cases, that is the only way you can get the course. The Internet has proven to be an excellent way to get education and training. In fact, all colleges and universities in the United States offer courses, either with or without credit, online. Now you can get anything from a high school diploma to a PhD online. And the degrees are every bit as valid as those earned by students who attended "real" classes on campus.

Listed in this section are dozens of home study schools. Except where noted, all of them are fully accredited by the Distance Education and Training Council (formerly the National Home Study Council), the nationally recognized accrediting association for distance learning since 1927. Although there are hundreds more such institutions, the ones presented here have been selected because they offer instruction that could help you take advantage of opportunities listed in this book.

———ACCOUNTING/BOOKKEEPING———

Allied Schools
22952 Alcalde Drive, Laguna Hills, CA 92653
www.alliedschools.com

DeVry University
One Tower Lane, Oakbrook Terrace, IL 60181
www.devry.edu.
*Accredited by The Higher Learning Commission (www.ncahlc.org)

Educational Correspondence Training School, LLC
3520 West 26th Street, Erie, PA 16506
www.ectschool.com

Griggs University, Home Study International
12501 Old Columbia Pike, Silver Spring, MD 20914
www.hsi.edu

Penn Foster Career School
P.O. Box 1900, Scranton, PA 18501
www.pennfoster.edu

Thomas Edison State College
> 101 W. State St., Trenton, NJ 08608
> www.tesc.edu
> *Accredited through Middle States Commission on Higher
> Education (www.msche.org)

University of Phoenix
> www.phoenix.edu
> *Accredited by The Higher Learning Commission (www.ncahlc.org)

US Career Institute
> 2001 Lowe Street, Fort Collins, CO 80525
> www.uscareerinstitute.com

——ART, FINE AND COMMERCIAL——

Art Instruction Schools
> 3309 Broadway Street NE, Minneapolis, MN 55413
> www.artinstructionschools.edu

Artist Career Training
> 2013 Kiva Road, Santa Fe, NM 87505
> www.artistcareertraining.com
> *Not accredited by DETC

Penn Foster Career School
> P.O. Box 1900, Scranton, PA 18501
> www.pennfoster.edu

——DATA ENTRY——

Thomas Edison State College
> 101 W. State St., Trenton, NJ 08608
> www.tesc.edu
> *Accredited through Middle States Commission on Higher
> Education (www.msche.org)

———ELECTRONICS———

Cleveland Institute of Electronics
> 1776 E. 17th, Cleveland, OH 44114
> www.cie-wc.edu

Grantham College of Engineering
> 34641 Grantham College Road, Slidell, LA 70469
> www.grantham.edu

Penn Foster Career School
> P.O. Box 1900, Scranton, PA 18501
> www.pennfoster.edu

———GRAPHIC DESIGN———

Penn Foster Career School
> P.O. Box 1900, Scranton, PA 18501
> www.pennfoster.edu

Sessions Online School of Design
> www.sessions.edu

———INCOME TAX———

Ashworth University, Professional Career Development Institute
> 430 Technology Parkway, Norcross, GA 30092
> www.ashworthuniversity.edu

National Tax Training School
> 67 Ramapo Valley Rd. Suite 102, Mahwah, NJ 07430
> www.nattax.com

Thomas Edison State College
> 101 W. State St., Trenton, NJ 08608
> www.tesc.edu
> *Accredited through Middle States Commission on Higher Education (www.msche.org)

─────INFORMATION TECHNOLOGY─────

DeVry University
>One Tower Lane, Oakbrook Terrace, IL 60181
>www.devry.edu
>*Accredited by The Higher Learning Commission (www.ncahlc.org)

Educational Correspondence Training School, LLC
>3520 West 26th Street, Erie, PA 16506
>www.ectschool.com
>*Accredited by the International Association of Continuing
>Education Training (www.iacet.org)

Grantham College of Engineering
>34641 Grantham College Road, Slidell, LA 70469
>www.grantham.edu

PC Age IT Institute
>1259 Route 46 East, Building 4C, Parsippany, NJ 07054
>www.pcage.com
>*Not accredited by DETC

Penn Foster Career School
>P.O. Box 1900, Scranton, PA 18501
>www.pennfoster.edu

─────JOURNALISM/ADVERTISING─────

Penn Foster Career School
>P.O. Box 1900, Scranton, PA 18501
>www.pennfoster.edu

─────LANGUAGES, FOREIGN─────

Berlitz International
>40 West 51st St., New York, NY 10020
>www.berlitz.com

Griggs University, Home Study International
12501 Old Columbia Pike, Silver Spring, MD 20914
www.hsi.edu

——LEGAL TRANSCRIPTION——

US Career Institute
2001 Lowe Street, Fort Collins, CO 80525
www.uscareerinstitute.co

——MEDICAL BILLING/——
MEDICAL CODING

Allied Schools
22952 Alcalde Drive, Laguna Hills, CA 92653
www.alliedschools.com

Blackstone Career Institute
P.O. Box 3717, Allentown, PA 18106
www.blackstone.edu

Meditec.Com
190 S Fort Lane Ste. 5 Layton, UT 84041
www.meditec.com
*Not accredited by DETC

National Electronic Billers
2226-A Westborough Blvd., #504, South San Francisco, CA 94080
www.nebazone.com
*Not accredited by DETC

Penn Foster Career School
P.O. Box 1900, Scranton, PA 18501
www.pennfoster.edu

Thomas Edison State College
>101 W. State St., Trenton, NJ 08608
>www.tesc.edu
>*Accredited through Middle States Commission on Higher Education (www.msche.org)

US Career Institute
>2001 Lowe Street, Fort Collins, CO 80525
>www.uscareerinstitute.com

———MEDICAL TRANSCRIPTION———

Allied Schools
>22952 Alcalde Drive, Laguna Hills, CA 92653
>www.alliedschools.com

At-Home Professions
>2001 Lowe St., Fort Collins, CO 80525
>www.at-homeprofessions.com

Blackstone Institute
>P.O. Box 3717, Allentown, PA 18106
>www.blackstone.edu

Meditec.Com
>190 S Fort Lane Ste. 5 Layton, UT 84041
>www.meditec.com
>*Not accredited by DETC

MTEC, Inc.
>3634 West Market Street, Suite 103, Fairlawn, OH 44333
>www.mtecinc.com
>*Approved by the Ohio State Board of Colleges and Careers (http://scr.ohio.gov)

Penn Foster Career School
>P.O. Box 1900, Scranton, PA 18501
>www.pennfoster.edu.

Thomas Edison State College
101 W. State St., Trenton, NJ 08608
www.tesc.edu
*Accredited through Middle States Commission on Higher Education (www.msche.org)

———PHOTOGRAPHY———

New York Institute of Photography
211 East 43rd Street, Suite 2402, New York, New York 10017
www.nyip.com

Penn Foster Career School
P.O. Box 1900, Scranton, PA 18501
www.pennfoster.edu

———ADMINISTRATIVE ASSISTANT———

Allied Schools
22952 Alcalde Drive, Laguna Hills, CA 92653
www.alliedschools.com

Penn Foster Career School
P.O. Box 1900, Scranton, PA 18501
www.pennfoster.edu

———TECHNICAL WRITING———

Barnes & Noble University
www.barnesandnobleuniversity.com

University of Washington
4311 11th Avenue Northeast, Seattle, WA 98105
www.outreach.washington.edu

———WEB SITE DESIGN/WEBMASTER———

DeVry University

One Tower Lane, Oakbrook Terrace, IL 60181

www.devry.edu

*Accredited by The Higher Learning Commission (www.ncahlc.org)

Thomas Edison State College

101 W. State St., Trenton, NJ 08608

www.tesc.edu

*Accredited through Middle States Commission on Higher Education (www.msche.org)

GETTING A HOME-BASED JOB, STEP-BY-STEP

The first step in getting the home-based job of your choice is to define exactly what it is you want. You should ask yourself what kind of a commitment you are willing to make. Are you looking for a long-term career or just a short-term job? Do you need to support yourself or do you just need some extra income? Do you want to work in the same industry where you've always worked or try something new?

A wide range of occupations is covered in this book. Do you see something you like? If not, back up and give some thought to the type of jobs that can be done at home. While opportunities for home work span a wide spectrum of employment possibilities, not all work can effectively be moved home.

First of all, home work is work, which can be easily measured. Why? Because you and your employer need to know what to expect, such as when the work will begin and when it will be completed. If you are paid a piece rate, which is very common, this factor is crucial. Besides that, your employer wants to know that she's getting her money's worth. Along these same lines, the work should require minimal supervision after initial training.

It is also important to know whether there are physical barriers to doing a particular type of work at home. Work that requires minimal space and no large and/or expensive equipment is ideal. In some cases, the type of equipment and the amount of space used for home work is still restricted by local zoning ordinances.

Where The Work Is

In general, home-based work tends to be available at very large corporations and at very small companies. Mid-sized firms often lack the management expertise available at large companies and may be less willing to take risks than small companies. There are many exceptions to this, however, especially among companies that originally started using home-based workers.

Information-intensive industries such as the banking industry, the insurance industry, and the computer software industry are prime candidates for home work because so much of their work is done via computer and telephone.

All types of sales organizations have traditionally been open to working at home. Real estate, publishing, insurance, pharmaceuticals, apparel, cosmetics, and printing are just a few of the businesses that typically use home-based representatives.

Home businesses are often forced by zoning ordinances to use other home-based workers or else move out of their original home base. Such businesses may need administrative assistants, sales reps, bookkeepers, assemblers, shipping clerks, artists, copywriters, public relations consultants, programmers, lawyers, and accountants.

Any rapidly growing company may also be a good bet. Whenever a company suddenly outgrows its available space, the option of having additional workers provide their own space can be very appealing. Besides, if the growth were temporary, the money spent on additional facilities would be wasted. It is normally far cheaper for a company to pay for extra phone lines, computers, or other equipment for employee's homes than to build new office space.

Moving Your Work Home

Now that you have zeroed in on the job you would like to have at home, you have two options. You can either start from scratch and find a new job starting at home, or you can move your present (or future) job from its current location to your home.

Large corporations are most likely to accept the latter option. There are presently several hundred major corporations in the US that have home-based workers on the payroll. As a rule, however, they don't allow new hires to work at home right from the start. They want to develop confidence in their employees before allowing them to take their work home. You'll find many of these companies listed in the chapter on Telecommuting and Other Employment Options along with advice on how to get started telecommuting at your company.

Starting From Scratch

If you're presently not working and need to find a job you can do at home right from the start, there is a good chance the type of work you're looking for is secondary to your need to be at home.

The first thing you should do is examine your skills and match them up with possible job types. If you don't see anything here that you're already trained for, consider what you would like to learn. Many jobs offer training at a central location or right in your home via the Internet.

Preparing a Résumé

It's time to prepare a résumé that stresses skills needed to work at home. In other words, you should emphasize anything that demonstrates your ability to work well without supervision. Because your employer won't see you very often (or ever, in some cases), your reliability is extremely important. For every job you apply for, you should write a cover letter openly stressing your desire and ability to work efficiently and effectively at home.

There are basically two kinds of résumés—chronological and functional. Both include identifying information, work history, and educational background. Neither is necessarily better than the other, but generally speaking, employers prefer the chronological style because its format is quick and easy to read.

The chronological résumé simply lists your work history according to dates, starting with the most recent and working backwards. Educational background is handled in the same way.

The functional résumé presents essentially the same information, but in a different order. The purpose of this type of résumé is to emphasize your skills. Instead of starting with dates, you head each descriptive paragraph with a job title.

Regardless of the style of résumé you choose, the following rules apply:
- Include only information that is directly relevant to the job for which you are applying. While it is great to have many skills and accomplishments, employers are only interested in what you can offer them in particular.
- Limit your résumé to two pages, one page if at all possible. A 10-page résumé may look impressive, but what employer has time to read it? It will be easier to keep your résumé brief if you carefully follow the rule above.
- Present a professional image. Your résumé should be typed. Leave sufficient margins and double space between paragraphs. Proofread

191

carefully. Grammatical errors and typos could cost you a highly desirable job. You can find some great résumé templates on the Internet—just fill in the blanks and you're good to go.

The Cover Letter

A cover letter is a personalized letter stating your interest in a job in clear, concise terms. You should indicate which job you are applying for and point out a few good reasons why you should be considered. There is no need to repeat any of the information included in the résumé.

Letter of Interest

In some cases an employer is more interested in your aptitude and enthusiasm than in your background. This is often the situation when a training course will be provided, or for "people jobs" such as sales, customer service, and market research positions. The basic requirement here is an ability to relate to people and communicate effectively. How do you prove that ability with a résumé? You can't, really, so you use a letter of interest.

A letter of interest is similar to a cover letter except that you (briefly) describe any background or personality traits that are applicable to the position and then request an application or an interview, or both.

Phone Interviews

Prospective home-based workers are often interviewed over the phone; many are hired without ever meeting their new employers.

After sending in an application, you can normally expect to be called within a week or two if you are going to be considered for an opening in the near future. Of course, you won't know exactly when to expect the call, but you should be prepared right from the start.

- Find out as much as you can about the company ahead of time. Then, make a list of questions you want to ask about the job. Keep the list and a copy of your application near the phone. Don't forget to keep a pen or pencil and paper handy, too.
- Try to use a phone in a quiet part of the house where you will not be interrupted.
- Listen carefully, take your time and answer all questions in a clear, steady voice. Don't mumble. Speak with confidence and honesty.

- Be polite and friendly, but not "chummy."
- Be enthusiastic even if you're not sure you want the job. You can always change your mind later.
- Be prepared to give references if asked.

Most important, you want to present yourself as the right candidate for the job. Ask yourself one question: "Why should this company hire me?" This is, after all, what they are calling to find out.

Don't Expect Too Much

Looking for a job that you can do from home is essentially no different, and definitely no easier, than looking for a job in a "traditional" work place. You cannot assume that because an employer uses home-based workers, that somehow means the employer is desperate for help and getting the job is going to be easy. On the contrary, employers often offer the work-at-home option as an incentive in order to have a larger pool of applicants to choose from. A single small ad in a local newspaper mentioning a job that can be done at home typically elicits hundreds of responses. That means competition, and lots of it, for you. It's up to you, and you alone, to convince any prospective employer that you're a cut above the rest and that you will handle the job professionally with a minimal amount of supervision.

Most home-based worker employers never advertise at all (like most of the ones in this book). They don't need to because the jobs are so sought after, word-of-mouth alone often creates a waiting list of eager applicants. If you should apply to any of these firms and don't receive a reply, understand that they don't have the manpower or the time to do so and your name has been placed on file for possible future openings. Rather than sit around waiting for a response that may not come for quite a while, your time would be better spent seeking out new opportunities in your field that nobody else knows about yet.

In Answer To Your Questions...

1. How are the listings in the book obtained?

Compiling a list of opportunities as diverse as those in this book requires constant research. The listings actually come from many different sources including government agencies, industry associations, trade directories, advertisements, and telephone surveys of certain types of businesses. Of course, some companies write in asking to be listed, but most of the time it's not that easy.

2. How do I know these listings are legitimate opportunities?

There are thousands more work-at-home opportunities than are listed in this book, and yet *The Work-at-Home Sourcebook* is still the most extensive listing of real work-at-home jobs and business opportunities available. To the best of our knowledge, there have been no reports of deceptive practices among the employers listed—and this is after 20 years of publication!Each listing has been verified, and those firms, which write in asking to be listed, are screened with special care. If there is any question as to the legitimacy of the offer, an interview with at least one worker is required before listing the company.

3. What if I don't find what I'm looking for in my area?

The majority of the listings in the job bank that can be done either within a large region or anywhere in the country (or world). And, most of the business opportunities can likewise be operated from wherever you are. But if you still want to pursue a particular job type in a town where there is none listed in this book, you need only follow the instructions found at the beginning of *The Work-at-Home* Job Bank. Do *not* contact an employer that can only hire local residents if you don't live in the same area. You will only be wasting your time and theirs.

4. Is it okay to call a prospective employer?

Unless there is a telephone number published with the listing, the answer is definitely no. Most employers simply don't have the time to talk to anyone who might have questions or be somewhat interested in their company. If you call before you are invited to, you will only alienate a potential employer.

5. Is it better to send a letter of interest or a résumé?

That depends. If an employer has a preference, it will be stated in the listing. Most of the time, a letter of interest is more welcome because of its brevity. A résumé is best in the case of professions requiring a high level of education and experience.

6. What should I do when I don't get a reply to my letter of interest or résumé?

If you don't get a response within a few weeks, you have to assume that there is no interest or no openings. In either case, you shouldn't sit around waiting for that to change. Look for opportunities elsewhere. Finding the work-at-home job you want takes time and diligence.

7. Will I have to pay money to work for any of these companies?

Just as a general rule, you should always be wary of any employer that requires money to work for them. (This does not pertain to business opportunities, which almost always involve an investment.)There are exceptions, however. Positions in sales often require a deposit for a sales kit to get started. All of the listings in this book that require money up-front will refund your money if you change your mind and return the kit in reusable condition. Never pay money to a company if you don't know exactly what the job is and what you are getting for your money.

8. How do you handle complaints about listings?

Fortunately, this is a rare problem. Readers' complaints are usually about a company that has moved, changed its policy toward working-at-home, or simply hasn't responded. Sometimes, an employer will become swamped with applications and ask to be removed from the listings. These requests are always complied with at the first available opportunity.

9. Can I work for more than one company?

Since most work-at-home job opportunities are for independent contractors, it is your right (and obligation according to the I.R.S.) to seek out multiple sources of income. Most employers know that you will need to do this and understand if there is an occasional conflict. If the position or business will require full-time participation, the company will tell you before you begin.

10. Are there any shortcuts to find the listings I want in the book?

Much thought has gone into the organization of this book. It is not always easy to categorize an opportunity. The lines between job opportunities and business opportunities, for instance, are not always clear. Likewise, it is not always easy to decide in what grouping a particular type of opportunity should be placed. For these reasons, and so that you will not miss out on anything, you should take the time to browse through the entire book. If you know exactly what you're looking for, though, you can save a lot of time by looking first at the Table of Contents. There you will see the layout of the book and find the general categories broken down into major sections.

OPPORTUNITIES
IN THE ARTS

Artists of all kinds have been working at home since the beginning of time. An artist is a special breed of worker, with a need for freedom that may be stronger than the need for security. To be able to work when the flash of inspiration strikes is important to the artist; not being forced to work when there is no inspiration is equally important.

Included in the following pages are freelance opportunities for graphic artists, illustrators, designers, calligraphers, photographers, writers, and editors. To get work in any artistic field, the primary requirement is proof of talent, skill, and dependability. Some prospective employers may require evidence of previous publication; others are on the lookout for new talent and will take a look at samples.

Graphic art is a growing field that has traditionally accepted the work-at-home option. Currently, about 80% of all graphic artists work in their own studios as independent contractors. They design, by hand or computer, the visuals for commercials, brochures, corporate reports, books, record covers, posters, logos, packaging, Web sites, and more. Their major clients are ad agencies, publishers, broadcast companies, textile manufacturers, Web hosts, and printers.

Illustrators and calligraphers may find that work is more sporadic. Illustrators often work for publishers, but both illustrators and calligraphers will find the most opportunities among ad agencies and greeting card publishers. Both of these are huge industries. Photographers, writers, and poets will also find this to be fertile ground for home-based work.

The biggest field for photographers is still advertising. Agencies large and small are in constant need of professional photographers who can deliver high quality work according to the concept developed by the agency. Rarely will an agency use an inexperienced photographer; the business is too fast-paced to risk losing time on a photographer who may not work out. A freelance photographer looking for any kind of work should be prepared with a professional portfolio of his/her best work, tear sheets of previously published photos if possible, a résumé, business cards, and samples that can be left on file.

3DTOUR

www.3DTour.com

Positions: This is a virtual tour company providing national coverage and personalized service to clients. The company needs more digital photographers to join its network of over 200 photographers for various 360-degree virtual tour and other digital photography projects.

Requirements: Must have your own digital camera. Send your contact info, qualifications, and coverage area (within one hour drive)

Provisions: Training provided for those without virtual tour experience. A job list will be supplied each week and will allow you to set the photo shoots around your schedule.

ADELE'S II, INC.

17300 Ventura Blvd., Encino, CA 91316

Positions: This producer of high quality personalized giftware uses freelance artists for product design.

Requirements: Submit résumé along with photographs of work samples.

AMBROSIA SOFTWARE

P.O. Box 23140, Rochester, NY 14692

Positions: Ambrosia is a software development firm that works with freelance artists to make their products visually appealing and to add a professional touch. Talented digital artists capable of working on creative projects ranging from interface design to game animation to stunning title graphics are encouraged to apply.

Requirements: Send an electronic sample of your work. Enclose a cover letter with complete contact information. If your portfolio is available online, you may indicate this in your cover letter. The firm keeps a database of freelance artists and their particular specialties, as there is always a project waiting in the wings for artistic collaboration.

AMCAL

2500 Bisso Lane #500, Concord, CA 94520

Positions: Artists and writers for greeting cards and fine art calendars. Themes include country, nostalgia, Christmas, and many others that fall within the fine art categories.

Requirements: Artists send samples in 5" x 7" size along with SASE. Writers send samples of verses. No humor or long poetry. Most commonly purchased are friendship and birthday messages. It's best to check out company's style first before submitting.

Provisions: Pays royalties.

Sent 8/5/15

AMERICAN GREETING CORPORATION

1 American Rd., Cleveland, OH 44102

Positions: Artists, writers, and photographers. Company makes cards, wrapping paper, posters, calendars, stationary, and post cards. Work is on a freelance basis; some is assigned, some is bought.

Requirements: Must send for submission forms first, then send samples of work with letter of interest. If appropriate, ask to arrange for a personal interview to show portfolio.

AMERICAN INSTITUTE OF PHYSICS

2 Huntington Quad #1NO1, Melville, NY 11747

Positions: Scientific publisher seeks copy editors and proofreaders.

Requirements: Bachelor's degree required. Good knowledge of English a must. Experience a plus. Send résumé and salary history.

Provisions: Provides training.

APPINGO

333 Moody Street, Suite 201, Waltham, MA 02453

www.appingo.com

Positions: The Appingo community is a team of talented authors, artists, editors, designers, and producers. Anyone with experience in these areas is encouraged to apply.

Requirements: Send your résumé along with a cover letter indicating your rate and availability. Proofreaders, copy editors, and page formatters will be given a skills test.

AQUENT

www.aquent.com/careers

Positions: This is a placement agency that specializes in placing creative workers including copywriters, technical writers, photographers, and artists. It is a little different than most agencies in that here the workers are the ones who are represented and "sold."

Requirements: Technically, you can live anywhere in the US but you will need to come into an office for an interview and to show your portfolio. Start by going online and filling out the online application.
Provisions: Pays top rates.

ARGONAUT PRESS
504 S. 2nd St., Fairfield, IA 52556
Positions: Photographers. Company produces postcards with contemporary themes.
Requirements: Submit transparencies along with résumé. A guideline sheet is available upon request.
Provisions: Pays for photos outright or in royalties.

ARGOSY PUBLISHING
www.argosypublishing.com
Positions: Argosy Publishing is a development house that creates and produces educational content for K–12 publishers with large projects that need to be written according to strict guidelines on tight deadlines. Argosy's science, math, and reading managing editors use both in-house and freelance talent to create a team of writers and editors for each project. Accepts applications for writers and editors who specialize in writing student and teacher edition content for elementary, middle, and high school textbooks that support students who are learning English.
Requirements: Must have a professional background that includes teaching and writing for ELL/ESL/interventions students. Need strong writing, communication, and organizational skills.
Provisions: Starting salary commensurate with experience and skills.

B5MEDIA
www.b5media.com
Positions: B5media is a global new media network covering a wide variety of topics in entertainment, technology, beauty, health, music, travel, sports, business, and lifestyles. It publishes content written by people from all over the world. Their blogs attract a large, loyal audiences for companies looking to build major brand appeal.
Requirements: Must be a knowledgeable blogger who is willing to make a commitment of time to write several posts per week, as well as promoting the blog through networking with other bloggers, social bookmarking, business message boards, and other interaction. Check the Web site to see which channels have openings. Knowledge of WordPress is desired. E-mail your

application, specifying which blog you are applying for. Include links to writing samples, a list of 5 posts titles that you think display the depth of your knowledge on the topic, and explain why you are the ideal choice. **Provisions:** This is a paid freelance position.

BCC, INC.

25 Van Zant St., Suite No. 13, Norwalk, CT 06855
www.BCCResearch.com

Positions: Freelancers writers for market research assignments. This is a US-based international publisher who hires seasoned writers/market researchers who are capable of preparing technical/economic market research reports discussing components of any one of these industries: biotechnology, healthcare, chemicals, technical ceramics, glasses, polymers and advanced materials, electronics, electronic materials, energy, flame retardancy, membranes/separations, packaging, waste, water, and air treatment, food/beverage, banking, telecommunications, and many other allied industries. **Requirements:** In addition to having a broad knowledge of your chosen industry and good economic/market research skills, you must be able to meet deadlines and adhere to format requirements supplied by the publisher. You will find an author guide, report template and sample full-length report all downloadable at http://buscom.com/guide. A Bachelor's degree is the minimum requirement. Applicants should e-mail a copy of their résumé and indicate the industries/technical areas of greatest interest. If there is a potential match, a detailed application procedure guide will be e-mailed. **Provisions:** Compensation includes an advance against royalties and expense reimbursement.

BEAUTYWAY

555 S Blackbird Roost St., Flagstaff, AZ 86001

Positions: Photographers. Company produces postcards, calendars, and posters. Interested mostly in scenics and animals. **Requirements:** Submit any size transparencies. Guidelines are available; include SASE with request. Prefers to work with previously published photographers. **Provisions:** Pays one-time fee for each photo used.

BENTLEY HOUSE

1410 Lesnick Lane #J, Art Sources Department
Walnut Creek, CA 94596

Positions: Bentley House is a major national publisher of art selling to major accounts, print shops, and distributors at the rate of 100,000 per month. New high-caliber artists are being sought. Preferred subject matter includes anything of interest to "Middle America"; nostalgia, country, scapes, local folk arts, people, animals, etc. Can be any medium: oils, watercolor, acrylics, etc. Original art will be reproduced for mass sale.

Requirements: No prior publishing is required. Bentley House is most interested in long-term working relationships. To be considered, send slides (only) of your work plus a cover letter to introduce yourself. Be sure to number your slides and keep a file of them at home for later reference. Bentley House requires no investment of any kind and suggests strongly that any artist who is approached by a buyer of any kind asking for money up front, *beware*.

Provisions: Reproduced prints sell in the $15 to $60 range. Different arrangements are worked out with different artists; buys outright, on commission, and other. A new line is introduced every four to five months.

BIRDS & BLOOMS
5400 South 60th Street, Greendale, WI 53129
www.birdsandblooms.com

Positions: Freelance photography throughout the United States. The company uses photos of backyard flowers, gardens, senior citizens, landscapes/scenics, rural, travel, agriculture and birds, for a bimonthly magazine.

Requirements: Query with résumé of credits and stock photo list. Send unsolicited photos by mail for consideration and the company will keep samples on file. Be sure to include SASE.

BOOK EDITING ASSOCIATES
www.book-editing.com

Positions: Freelance fiction editors (mainstream and genre, esp. sci-fi) perform both developmental editing and copyediting.

Requirements: Applicants will receive several short editing tests (developmental editing and copyediting). Failed tests will not be marked and returned. Must have 5+ years of fiction editing experience with a history of edited books that have been subsequently published by subsidy/royalty publishing houses (not self-published). Must have time available to accept regular job offers. Submit résumé as Word or RTF attachment. Your résumé or e-mail must contain a list of books edited for published authors (excluding self-published).

BRADFORD EXCHANGE, Attn: Licensing and Artists Relations, 9333 N. Milwaukee, Chicago, IL 60714.

Positions: Bradford is a manufacturer of collectible plates, ornaments, music boxes, and figurines. Freelance professional artists, designers, and illustrators design landscapes and portraits that will be reproduced on the items.

Requirements: For consideration by the art review committee, send one of the following as reference to your work: digital documents of artwork on a CD, printed color references, or a duplicate set of 10 to 20 35mm slides. Include a résumé and any additional information about your work and experience. Do not send original artwork or items that are one-of-a-kind.

BUCKBOARD ANTIQUES ~~Crosstitch?~~

5025 Brettshire Way, Oklahoma City, OK 73107

Positions: Folk art and other traditional country crafts like rag dolls and quilted items will be considered.

Requirements: Send photos and prices you want along with an SASE.

THE CALIFORNIA INSTITUTE OF INTEGRAL STUDIES

1453 Mission Street, San Francisco CA 94103

http://ciis.edu

Positions: Dissertation editors work from home throughout the United States. This is on a part-time, ad-hoc, basis with a quick turnaround when the work is assigned. The editors review dissertations for correct format, style, and citation methods according to CIIS dissertation guidelines.

Requirements: Demonstrated extensive editing experience for academic publications for at least 3 years. Need expertise with at least one of the following formats: APA, MLA, Chicago, and/or American Anthropological Association. Must provide the names of 2 professional references and authors of the recent dissertations that you edited. Send those references along with a brief résumé listing relevant experience, cover letter, and a list of PhD and/or PsyD dissertations edited.

Provisions: Contracts pay fixed rate of $25/hour.

CAMARES COMMUNICATIONS, INC.

3 Wing Drive, Suite 200, Cedar Knolls, NJ 07927

www.camares.com

Positions: Freelance high tech marketing copy writers work from their home offices in Canada. This is a full-service advertising agency serving the high tech business-to-business marketplace with services that include research, planning, marketing, advertising and pubic relations.

Requirements: Requires superior writing skills, 4-5 years experience writing for companies in the high-tech B2B market, and knowledge of the hardware, software, telecom, and/or instrumentation market space. Must be able to write excellent white papers, Web content, and case studies. Must have fully equipped home office including high-speed Internet access and cell phone accessibility. Forward résumé, work samples, and hourly rates.

CARE2.COM
www.care2.com

Positions: Bloggers needed for a variety of subject categories.

Requirements: Must be knowledgeable, insightful, and passionate about your subject, have excellent writing skills, and be able to use WordPress or similar content management tool. Apply online.

Provisions: Pays per post, dependent on experience, with potential bonuses for high traffic and comment posts.

CARLTON CARDS
1 American Rd., Cleveland, OH 44144

Sent 8/5/15

Positions: This is a division of American Greetings. Artists, writers, and photographers design cards and calendars.

Requirements: Artists should submit sketches; photographers submit color transparencies. Send sample portfolio with return postage included. Writers should submit ideas on 3x5 index cards. Be sure name and address is on the back of each card submitted.

Provisions: Payment depends on individual situation. Sometimes ideas are purchased outright, sometimes work is assigned and paid for by the project. New talent is actively solicited.

CHESAPEAKE BAY MAGAZINE
1819 Bay Ridge Ave., Suite 200, Annapolis, MD 21403

Positions: Freelance writers and photographers.

Requirements: Any material about the Chesapeake region will be considered. Photographers submit color photos only. Writers can submit either proposal or complete manuscript.

Provisions: Pays on acceptance.

CMP PUBLICATIONS
3 Park Ave. # 30, New York, NY 10016

Positions: Editors, associate editors, reporters, and writers are all outfitted with wireless laptops in order to transmit material from the field. Freelance stringers are hired to cover business news from all over the country.

Requirements: Hard news reporting experience a must. Must feel comfortable going to top industrial companies looking for stories and information. Apply with résumé and previously published clips.

Provisions: Payment varies. Some reporters are salaried, some are paid by individual contract. Phone charges are reimbursed.

COMSTOCK CARDS, INC.
600 S. Rock Blvd., Suite 15, Reno, NV 89502

Positions: Photographers, artists, and writers are used to design outrageously funny stationery and novelty items.

Requirements: Submit color transparencies, cartoon drawings, or brief verses with strong, but short lead.

Provisions: Pays $50 for each assignment. Will consider royalty arrangement.

CONJUECTURE CORPORATION
www.conjecture.com

Positions: Freelance editors for Web content. A small group of writers is assigned to each editor. The editor is expected to edit the short articles (typically 400 to 600 words) that they submit, insert basic HTML coding, and provide direction on their writing, as needed.

Requirements: Must commit at least 10 hours of work a week, although that number can vary based on how much content the assigned group of writers produce. There is, however, enough work for significantly more hours per week, if desired. You will have to edit daily or, at the very least, every other day. E-mail résumé and cover letter to apply.

Provisions: You can choose your hours and work from anywhere you have an Internet connection. Pays per article edited. The hourly rate generally works out to be about $15 an hour. Some of the more experienced editors, who have effectively coached their assigned writers, approach $20 an hour. Pays twice a month, either by check or PayPal. This is an independent contractor position and is available to US citizens only.

CRAIG COMMUNICATIONS
444 Silver Lane, Oceanside, NY 11572

Positions: Graphic art.

Requirements: Experience required in marketing graphics, advertising and printing. Also, strong desktop publishing skills required. Local residents only, send résumé.

CUP OF COMFORT

P.O. Box 863, Eugene, OR 97440

Positions: Freelance writer of creative nonfiction.

Requirements: Experience is a plus, but it is not required. For guidelines, send SASE or go to www.cupofcomfort.com.

DISPLAY CONNECTION, INC.

131 W Commercial Ave., Moonachie, NJ 07074

Positions: Freelance artists. Company manufacturers advertising display fixtures.

Requirements: Must have experience working in the advertising field and, in particular, with display fixtures. Submit work samples or photos of work and résumés. Prefers local artists.

Provisions: Pays by the project.

DRAGON PENCIL

www.dragonpencil.com/employment.htm

Positions: Illustrators for children's books, specifically picture books, covers, coloring books, and line art.

Requirements: Send an e-mail to opportunity@dragonpencil.com with attached jpg samples of your work. In your e-mail please include your rate per illustration. Must live in the Savannah, GA, area.

DYALOGUE

www.dyalogues.com

Positions: Dyalogues is a site that allows bloggers to have 2-way conversations on arts/entertainment, politics, and technology. They need beta users who can provide valuable feedback.

Requirements: Anyone can do this. Visit Web site for details.

Provisions: Each completed dyalogue earns each participant $10 (payable by PayPal).

ECARDICA

www.eCardica.com

Positions: eCardia is a custom online greeting card company that employs people in remote offices worldwide. During peak holiday periods, the number of staff members can more than double. Employment opportunities include artists, designers, animators, cartoonists, poetry writers, storyboard writers, freelancers, sales associates, and professional marketers.

Requirements: Forward your résumé, portfolio (if applicable), availability, location, and salary requirements to employment@eCardica.com.

EDITFAST

Kanagawa, Japan

www.editfast.com

Positions: Editors, writers, indexers, copy editors, and proofreaders telecommute from all over the world for this company. Projects include novel manuscripts, Web pages, scientific journal articles, technical documents, magazine articles, and computer documentation.

Requirements: Must be reliable with professional experience and qualifications. To be considered as a potential EditFast freelancer, you must first register online.

Provisions: Projects are paid by the word on a project to project basis.

ENESCO IMPORTS CORPORATION

Attn: Ms. Karen George, Art Department,

1 Enesco Plaza, Elk Grove Village, IL 60007

Positions: Enesco provides freelance opportunities in their art department for artists, designers, and sample makers for their giftware line.

Requirements: Artists and designers must have exceptional creativity and the work samples to prove it. Sample makers must have all necessary tools to produce samples from artists' renderings. Must be local resident. To inquire, write to the address above. Absolutely no phone calls will be accepted!

Provisions: Artwork is often bought outright. Others are paid by the project or by the hour.

EVERETT STUDIOS, INC.

5 N Greenwich Rd., Armonk, NY 10504

Positions: Graphic artists and freelance photographers and videographers.

Requirements: Need experienced people who have worked in production, lab, or studio end of the business. Local residents only. Send résumé.

FABJOB.COM

www.fabjob.com

Positions: Writing career guides on a contract basis. Prefers full-time, but will consider part-time.

Requirements: Experience required. For full requirements and application instructions, visit Web site.

Provisions: Pay is $1,500 per career guide.

FREEDOM GREETING CARD COMPANY
774 American Dr., Bensalem, PA 19020

Positions: Writers and artists. Writers sell verses outright. Artists work on assignment only.

Requirements: Samples of work, letter of interest, and SASE required for either type of work.

FUZE
www.ifuze.com

Positions: Fuze is a Web development firm specializing in strategic communications projects including Web sites, interactive sales presentations and product demonstrations, e-mail marketing systems, and on- and off-line advertising and collateral. The company hires both full- and part-time, as well as contract and freelance staff depending on project needs.

Requirements: Check Web site for current opportunities, requirements, and application instructions.

Provisions: Offers competitive compensation and benefit packages.

GERBIG, SNELL, & WEISHEIMER
500 Olde Worthington Rd., Westerville, OH 43082

Positions: This is a large independent global healthcare advertising agency that uses freelance illustrators and photographers to produce advertising materials.

Requirements: Works only with local experienced people. Submit résumé, tear sheets, and business card.

HARCOURT BRACE & CO.
525 B St., #1900, San Diego, CA 92101

Positions: Freelance writing assignments are available from this major business publisher. Artists also work on assignment.

Requirements: Only very experienced writers will be considered. Apply with résumé and writing samples along with letter of interest. Artists should send samples of work along with letter of interest and bio describing in detail background experience.

HERFF JONES
226 Public St., Providence, RI 02905

Positions: Herff Jones, Inc. is an Indianapolis-based manufacturer of motivational and recognition products with 17 production facilities throughout the US and Canada. Freelance illustrators and designers are used to design medals, trophies, and class rings.

Requirements: Several years of experience is required. Submit résumé and samples.

Provisions: Pays by the project.

HUBPAGES

http://hubpages.com

Positions: HubPages is a leading online publishing community that allows writers to share in revenue and make a little extra money. It is always open to new writers who can write topical content about the things that they enjoy.

Requirements: Must be familiar with Web 2.0 tools such as YouTube and Flickr. Blogging experience is a huge plus. Apply by going to HubPages.com/info/problogger.

Provisions: The amount of money that you can make depends upon the quality and amount of content that you publish. HubPages has hundreds of writers who make $25-$50/month and over a hundred writers making anywhere from $100-$1,000+, so there is definitely opportunity to make some substantial revenue.

IKON OFFICE SOLUTIONS

70 Valley Stream Parkway, Malvern, PA 19355

Positions: Content writers to produce business training kits. Topics covered are career advancement, sales achievement, time and productivity enhancement, entrepreneurial development, and small business opportunities.

Requirements: Send contact information and area of interest.

Provisions: Pays flat fee per project.

INTERCONTINENTAL GREETINGS, LTD.

176 Madison Ave., New York, NY 10016

Positions: Freelance artists for greeting cards, gift-wrap, calendars, posters, and stationery. Prefers very graphic designs with some cartoon-style illustrations.

Requirements: Works only with professionals. Send résumé, work samples, and include SASE.

Provisions: Generally pays royalties.

KERSTEN STUDIOS

P.O. Box 1765, Scottsdale, AZ 85252

Positions: Writers and artists for greeting cards. All cards are humorous and seasonal; Christmas, Thanksgiving, Halloween, Mother's Day, Father's Day, Graduation, Easter, Valentine's Day, and St. Patrick's Day.

Requirements: Writers submit batches of short verses for consideration. Artists send sketches or photocopies of finished originals.

LILLIAN VERNON CORPORATION
543 Main Street, New Rochelle, NY 10801

Positions: Freelance artists. Lillian Vernon is one of those rare "kitchen table" success stories. The company is one of the most successful of all direct mail catalog marketers. Products include all kinds of paper products, textiles, house wares, Christmas decor, etc. Freelance artists design and illustrate on assignment only.

Requirements: Only New York metropolitan area artists are accepted. Only uses artists with previous experience. Send letter of interest with tear sheets or samples that can be kept on file.

Provisions: Pays flat fee.

LOMA
2300 Windy Ridge Parkway, #600, Atlanta, GA 30339

Positions: Writers for curriculum and text development and achievement tests. This entails writing and editing at the university level on topics such as insurance, finance, and business.

Requirements: Excellent research skills, the ability to write technical material. Education in insurance, finance, business, or law preferred. Professional experience or degree preferred but not required. Limited travel is required. Samples are required along with a series of rigorous interviews.

Provisions: Pays salary and benefits. Offers flexible hours and the opportunity to telecommute after training period.

MERION PUBLICATIONS, INC.
2900 Horizon Dr., King of Prussia, PA 19406

Positions: Freelance staff writers for newspaper read by health professionals.

Requirements: Must live in the area. Need experience and résumé with samples.

Provisions: Story leads are provided for features.

METRO CREATIVE GRAPHICS
519 8th Ave., New York, NY 10005

Positions: Freelance illustrators. Metro is a clip art dealer that works with dozens of artists.

Requirements: Must apply with résumé and request personal interview to show portfolio of professional work samples. Prefers New York artists, but will consider anyone with real talent.

Provisions: Pay worked out on an individual basis.

MY ESSAY

www.myessay.com

Positions: My Essay is an online review service that critiques college admissions essays. They do not write or re-write essays (that would be unethical). Flexible, part-time, freelance opportunities exist for experienced proofreaders and editors familiar with the application process.
Requirements: Send cover letter and résumé to contact@myessay.com.
Provisions: Pays per essay review.

NEUTRON INTERACTIVE

www.neutroninteractive.com

Positions: Neutron Interactive is a company that creates effective solutions to increase the profitability and performance of post secondary education marketing campaigns. Experienced Web copywriters are needed to write for several of the company's properties.
Requirements: Experience in editorial as well as ad copy is ideal. The preferred candidate has advanced research and writing skills and a solid understanding of basic SEO principles such as the semantic Web and identifying keyword targeting. Must be able to create original and creative Web copy for several different career and education topics at a quick and efficient pace. Some research is required, but most articles can be written in 30-60 minutes.
Provisions: This is a contract position. Pays per article in most cases. Can work from anywhere.

NOBLEWORKS

123 Grand St., Hoboken, NJ 07030

Positions: This company has been called the "Marx Brothers" of the greeting card industry. They purchase photos and some illustration. It is important that you study this company's line first before submitting anything.
Requirements: Send letter of interest first.
Provisions: Pays royalties.

NU-ART, INC.

6247 W. 74th St., Chicago, IL 60638

Positions: Writers and artists for greeting cards, wedding invitations and accessories, and boxed stationery. Cards are for Christmas only.
Requirements: Writers submit verse along with design ideas for total concept. Artists submit color roughs or finished art.

Sent · 8/6/15

OATMEAL STUDIOS
Box 138, Rochester, VT 05767

Positions: Writers and illustrators for greeting card design.

Requirements: The first step for both positions is to send for Oatmeal's guidelines and current market list. Include SASE with your request. Then send several samples with a letter of interest. Or, to get a better idea of what this company is looking for, visit: www.oatmealstudios.com/Writer'sGuides/WG-Pg.htm.

Provisions: Writers are paid for each idea that is accepted. Pay for artists depends on the situation. 90% of Oatmeal's work is done by freelancers.

PARTY DIGEST
www.partydigest.com

Positions: Local correspondents. This is a good opportunity for someone who has tons of energy, a pleasing personality, likes to attend events, and can take pictures (must have your own digital camera).

Requirements: Must be able to cover soirées and e-mail the coverage on a weekly basis to the editorial team, which will then e-mail the coverage to subscribers. Contact editorial@partydigest.com and include any background information you feel is relevant.

PHILLIPS PUBLISHING, INC.
7811 Montrose Road, Potomac, MD 20854

Positions: This newsletter publisher uses up to 10 freelance writers.

Requirements: Must have the necessary expertise to write on high technology topics for business clients. Prefers local residents.

Provisions: Equipment such as PCs and fax machines are provided as needed.

PORTAL PUBLICATIONS
100 Smith Ranch Rd # 210, San Rafael, CA 94903

Positions: Freelance writers. Company produces greeting cards especially for young adult working women.

Requirements: Study the line first and send for market guidelines. Then submit verses on index cards in small batches with SASE.

RED FARM STUDIO

sent 8/4/15

1135 Roosevelt Ave., Pawtucket, RI 02861

Positions: Writers and artists. Company produces greeting cards, gift wrap, and note papers. Artwork used is mostly watercolor.

Requirements: Send for a current market list; include a business size SASE. Then send letter of interest with work samples.
Provisions: Writers are paid by the line. Artists' pay varies depending on the situation.

RENAISSANCE GREETING CARDS
10 Renaissance Way, Sanford, ME 04073
Positions: Writers and artists for all occasion and Christmas cards.
Requirements: Writers send verse ideas; especially likes humorous verse. Include ideas for design. Artists send samples of full color work in batches of a dozen; include résumé. Prefers bright cartoons. Guidelines are available. Be sure to include SASE with your request.

SAMS PUBLISHING
www.samspublishing.com
Positions: Technical editors/reviewers with technical expertise in an existing or emerging development tool, application, or programming environment.
Requirements: Review the guidelines on the Web site for more information and instructions.
Provisions: Can live anywhere in the US.

SAN FRANCISCO BAY GUARDIAN
135 Mississippi St., San Francisco, CA 94107
Positions: Freelance writers produce over half of the contents of this alternative news weekly.
Requirements: Only previously published Bay Area writers will be considered. Especially interested in investigative reporters. Send query with clips of previously published work.

SMALL BIZ COMMUNITY
www.smallbizcommunity.com
Positions: Freelance writers are assigned press releases, media submissions, and placement follow-ups on a national level.
Requirements: Need not have extensive previous publicity experience, but must have a strong work ethic, solid writing abilities, and good speaking skills. No set hours are required, and we will work around family obligations. Work-at-home-moms, emerging business owners, and students are encouraged to apply. Visit Web site and e-mail résumé.

ST. MARTIN'S PRESS
175 Fifth Ave., #1500, New York, NY 10010

Positions: Freelance copy editors.

Requirements: Must be computer literate and experienced. New York residents only.

Provisions: Apply by sending résumé to the managing editor, trade division.

SUITE 101.COM
www.suite101.com

Positions: Part-time opportunities to write articles and surf the Net in a family topic area that you are knowledgeable about and have a passion for. Suite 101 is a community based best-of-Web guide seeking contributing editors to cover a variety of topics ranging from computers to sports to politics. Different levels of participation are available.

Requirements: Good writing skills and Web knowledge. No HTML required. All work is submitted via simple to use online forms.

TALK ABOUT DEBT
www.talkaboutdebt.co.uk

Positions: Finance/money bloggers regularly contribute to this debt help community with insightful blog thoughts on debt and money management.

Requirements: E-mail your name and contact details with your blog URL to matt@talkaboutdebt.co.uk.

Provisions: Accepts 10 posts a month from guest bloggers and pays $50 for each post. There are additional opportunities to generate revenue by writing about topics that are spotlighted.

TODAY.COM
www.today.com

Positions: The Today.com blog network features writers of every skill level and from all walks of life, each with their own unique voice. VIP Bloggers share that point of view with others by creating original content on their own personalized blog while at the same time interacting with readers through comments made to the blog posts.

Requirements: In order to qualify for a paid blog at Today.com you must be 18 years of age or older, have access to a reliable computer and the Internet, be fluent in English, and be passionate about the topic you choose. Apply (register) online.

Provisions: New VIP bloggers are guaranteed $1 per original 100+ word post per day. You also get $2 per thousand unique page views, so the more traffic you get, the more you get paid. Set your own hours and work from anywhere you choose. Each VIP Blog will be reviewed monthly for originality, productivity, and popularity. And payment may be adjusted at that time.

TOUR THIS PLACE
www.tourthisplace.com

Positions: This company provides virtual tours and photography to the real estate industry. Individual freelance photographers take the photographs, stitch them into panoramic images, and upload the panoramas and other still photographs to tourthisplace.com.

Requirements: Must have digital camera equipment (or willingness to purchase camera equipment) that meets tourthisplace.com specifications (see Web site). Also need computer with Internet access, basic photography skills (professional skills not required), reliable transportation with proof of insurance, good communication and customer service skills, and be 18 or older.

Provisions: Contract photographers are paid on a per job basis. This is not a full-time job.

TRINITY REAL ESTATE SOLUTIONS
15303 Dallas Parkway, Suite 510, Addison, TX 75001
www.trinityinspection.com

Positions: Part-time positions for photographers to take digital pictures of houses in your local area for the real estate industry.

Requirements: Must have a digital camera and Internet access. Must be able to take 3 digital photos of each property or properties as requested,(front and both sides of the home), and return them via e-mail same day.

TURNROTH SIGN COMPANY
1207 E Rock Falls Rd, Rock Falls, IL 61071

Positions: Freelance artists design billboards and other kinds of signs on assignment.

Requirements: Submit letter of interest with sketches or finished work samples. Include SASE with all correspondence.

Provisions: Pays flat rates for each project.

UC BERKELEY EXTENSION
http://learn.berkeley.edu/jobs

Positions: Course developers and online instructors work from home via the Internet for UC Berkeley Extension Online.

Requirements: Applicants must possess at minimum a master's degree, and for some courses, a doctorate. Computer skills and a strong knowledge of the Internet are required. Experience with online education is preferred.

Provisions: There are numerous positions available. For complete information on openings, requirements, and compensation, visit online.

VECTOR ART

117 Madison Circle, Horseheads NY 14845

www.vectorart.com

Positions: Vector Art publishes high quality original, monochromatic artwork for the sign, engraving, tattoo, CAD, and routing industry worldwide. The art department is always open to viewing the work of new artists for licensing and publication.

Requirements: To be considered, send electronic samples in ai, eps, or jpeg format to the Art Director.

VICTORY PRODUCTIONS

www.victoryprd.com

Positions: This graphic arts and corporate communications firm maintains a select database of highly experienced editorial and publishing professionals. Many projects require a team of freelance specialists that may include writers, editors, proofreaders, designers, compositors, photographers, and illustrators.

Requirements: Check Web site for current project needs and requirements. Submit cover letter, résumé, and design sample to recruitment@victoryprd.com

VIDEO HOME TOURS

1350 East Touhy Avenue, Suite 110W, Des Plaines, IL 60018

www.vht.com

Positions: VHT provides service to the real estate industry in 65 major US metropolitan cities. They have a nationwide network of photographers and videographers and are always looking for more quality, professional people with photography knowledge and a passion for real estate.

Requirements: Excellent customer service and organizational skills are essential. E-mail résumé to hr@vht.com.

WARNER PRESS, INC.

1201 E. 5th St., Anderson, IN 46012

Positions: Writers and artists for work on greeting cards, calendars, posters, postcards, and plaques. Artists work on assignment. Writers are freelance.

Requirements: Before applying, write for current market list and guidelines. Include SASE. Be sure to study company's style before sending samples. Talented new artists are especially sought.
Provisions: Pay varies.

WCITIES

340 Brannan St., San Francisco, CA 94103

Positions: Writers with photographic skills to review restaurants and other social establishments for this online global publishing company. Assignments are currently available in Canada. Take a look at the Web site to get a good idea of what's needed and the style of presentation: www.wcities.com.
Requirements: Send résumé and cover letter.

WEBMD

669 River Drive, Center 2, Elmwood Park, NJ 07407

www.webmd.com

Positions: Freelance healthcare copywriters work via the Internet for this major consumer health information Web site.
Requirements: Experience is required. Must be able to write creative, effective healthcare (preferably pharmaceutical) copy with little or no supervisory rewrite. Must have experience in writing for the Web, plus healthcare agency experience. Reply with letter and résumé. Copy samples will be requested.
Provisions: Salary, up to $75 per hour.

WORDS4NERDS

1464 Edgeware Road, Victoria, BC, Canada V8T 2J4

www.words4nerds.com

Positions: Freelance technical writer. This is not a full-time or payroll position, but an as-needed contract arrangement only. For US or Canadian writers.
Requirements: Must have minimum of two years' professional experience in tech writing, exceptional spelling and grammar skills, ability to proof and edit your own work, 100% reliability in meeting deadlines, ability to code clean HTML and CSS by hand, and strong knowledge of Word (styles, macros, templates, indices, etc.), FrameMaker, and Acrobat. Qualified applicants should visit Web site, then e-mail a brief outline of your experience and skills, and a link to your online portfolio—do *not* send attachments.

OPPORTUNITIES
IN COMPUTERS

This section includes any situation that specifically requires a computer to get the job done. This doesn't necessarily mean that you must own your own equipment, though it typically does. In some cases, companies provide PCs and the necessary software, but those rare instances are indicated in the listings. On the other hand, a developer or Web designer not only needs to own a computer, but often several different computers.

By nature, technical jobs such as you will find here are often the highest paying positions for home-based workers. In order to compete for these opportunities, you do need to know your stuff. Fortunately, the learning curve has diminished with time and getting training and experience is not nearly as difficult as it was just a few short years ago. There are classes available at most community college, vocational schools, and on the Internet. If you want to do computer-based office work, but lack the necessary skills or need to brush up on the latest software, you can get paid while you learn by signing on with a temporary help agency. Kelly Services and Manpower, to name just two, have excellent training programs—including cross-training on different systems—available to anyone who is on the roster and available for work.

The field for developers has opened up considerably since the last edition of this book. There are all kinds of work available, but the bulk of it is in Web-based applications and e-commerce. In this global marketplace, there is also a lot of translation to be done. Programmers today can work for companies all over the world. The key to getting work as a programmer is to continue learning about languages, compilers, and systems design. Employers like programmers who are enthusiastic about what the company is doing, pay attention to deadlines, document their work properly, and submit clean programs.

Graphic artists are in demand, too. Up until recently, graphic art was mostly about print media. Today, it is more common for a graphic artist to need a certain level of computer savvy including some coding skills. These jobs generally involve making software applications and Web sites appear visually appealing and are vital to making these things "user-friendly."

While the jobs mentioned above require a considerable amount of formal education and references, there is still plenty of opportunity for the self-trained computer geek. Web mastering is now considered a tedious job, lacking in the creativity that most developers and designers crave. Just about anyone with a couple of Web sites to show and a working knowledge of HTML, frames, and Dreamweaver can land a job as a Web master. There are even tutorials on the Internet that can teach you these skills in a weekend.

For those who are willing to help the rest of us understand what's gone wrong with our laptops and what to do about it, there are numerous new opportunities in technical support. In some cases, this is a job that can be accomplished online and/or over the phone. In other cases, face-to-face service is required. The job and your schedule will still be flexible, but you'll need to get out of the office and go make some house calls.

ABILITY GROUP
1255 New Hampshire Ave. NW #112, Washington, DC 20036
Positions: Word processing specializing in transcription of medical, legal, and verbatim tapes. Occasional assignments are mostly overflow.
Requirements: Must be local resident. Word processing equipment is required. Any major word processing software is okay as long as it is PC so that it can be converted. Experienced professionals only.

ACT 1 TECHNICAL
111 Pine Street Suite 915, San Francisco, CA 94111
Positions: This is a personnel placement company with various assignments that come up. FileNet developers for high tech consulting company.
Requirements: Must have at least two years experience developing imaging Web-based applications. Working experience with Visual Basic, Visual C++, and Oracle a must.
Provisions: Pays very competitive salary.

ADVANCED AUTOMATION ASSOCIATES
900 Middlesex Turnpike, Billerica, MA 01821
Positions: About nine home-based keyboarders input data for this data management service.

ALLIED WEB
www.awwg.net

Positions: Allied Web Wholesalers Group (AWWG) is a systems consulting firm that helps clients design and implement Web-based systems. Consultants are needed to help with Web application and e-commerce system design and implementation, Web hosting, Web content design, and database/infrastructure design.

Requirements: Apply online.

Provisions: Offers competitive hourly wages for 1099 consultants and currently offers medical benefits through NASE. For single parents or multi-taskers, flex-work-from-home hours, and liberal leave are provided as needed.

ALLTEL PUBLISHING
50 Executive Parkway, Hudson, OH 44236

Positions: Distributed systems/LAN professionals. ALLTEL provides information-based solutions to financial, telecommunications and mortgage clients in over 47 countries worldwide. These services include information technology outsourcing, call center solutions, and more.

Requirements: Requires college degree or equivalent experience as well as five years experience in the implementation, support, and design of Local Area Networks (LANs) or microcomputer-based systems or three years experience in a management position in a related technical field. Experience in both LAN and WAN environments strongly preferred. Submit résumé with your salary requirements.

ALPHA PRESENTATIONS
5405 Alton Parkway, Irvine, CA 92714

Positions: Typesetting for this commercial printer.

Requirements: Must have Mac computer with Quark Express and Pagemaker for advanced graphic layouts, design and typesetting. Prepare for quick turnover. Local residents mail résumé.

AMERICAN EXPRESS BANK, LTD.
American Express Plaza, New York, NY 10004

Positions: Word processors.

Requirements: Must be local, physically handicapped and disabled. Job requires transcription skills.

Provisions: Complete training and equipment package are provided. Telephone lines link the home work station to company headquarters on Wall Street. A company supervisor can dictate into the system from anywhere;

likewise a home worker is able to access the system any time 24 hours a day to transcribe the dictation. The finished product in hard copy form is then sent back to headquarters electronically. All activity is identified and monitored through the Control Center. "Project Homebound" currently has ten full-time regular employees of American Express.

ARISE

3450 Lakeside Drive, Suite 620, Miramar, FL 33027
www.arise.com

Positions: Arise provides technical support service for cutting edge Fortune 500 companies. Its technical support reps work online from home on a part-time basis handling handle phone, Web chat, and e-mail requests.

Requirements: Must obtain certification.

Provisions: Arise typically pays a service fee to its reps that is based on per call, per minute, or per hour rates. You choose when and how often you provide service with flexible scheduling options that allow you to divide your time into increments as few as 30 minutes. You will have access to the scheduling tools so that your service shift selections can be made from home.

ART & LOGIC

Box 56465, Sherman Oaks, CA 91413

Positions: This is an office-free software services company that develops commercial-quality applications, middleware, drivers, and components. Programmers work entirely online from their own home offices.

Requirements: Experience with C++, Windows, and Mac OS. Applicants will take a programming test online at www.artlogic.com/careers.

Provisions: Art & Logic developers can work from anywhere in North America. "We are aggressively looking for the best software developers in North America. If you have exceptional skills with any of the relevant skills, languages, and platforms, we invite you to submit the application form."

ARTIZEN, INC.

990 Industrial Rd., San Carlos, CA 94070
www.artizen.com

Positions: Programmers for software consulting firm. Artizen maintains a staffing division with a pool of 100,000 qualified professionals that are placed with clients nationwide.

Requirements: Minimum three years experience with relevant languages and platforms such as Java. Job starts in office. Send résumé.

ARTWORX SOFTWARE COMPANY

6017 Pine Ridge Road #280, Naples, FL 34119

Positions: Artworx is a company that develops video games. Programmers are contracted to do conversions from other computers to major brand computers.

Requirements: Résumé, work samples, and references required.

Provisions: Pays by the job.

ASK DR. TECH

www.askdrtech.com

Positions: Ask Dr. Tech is a 24/7 online technical support service.

Requirements: If you are an independent IT consultant, apply online.

AT-HOME PROFESSIONS

2001 Lowe Street, Fort Collins, CO 80525

www.at-homeprofessions.edu

(800) 359-3455

Positions: At-Home Professions is a unique institution established in 1981. It is accredited by the Distance Education and Training Council (DETC) in Washington, DC. At-Home Professions offers accredited training in Professional Medical Transcription. The school's training methods utilize at-home study and can be completed at the student's own pace.

Requirements: Applicants must be a high school graduate, hold a GED, or pass an admissions test. Tuition can be paid as-you-go with no interest. The school is approved for military education benefits as well as SLM Financing.

Provisions: In addition to providing quality training programs and course materials, this organization also includes great follow-up services. At-Home Professions provides their graduates with personal counseling in job-search techniques as well as continuing on-the-job support.

BI-TECH ENTERPRISES, INC.

140 Raynor Avenue, Ronkonkoma, NY 11779

www.bi-tech.net

Positions: Contract programmers write communications and database software according to company specifications for PCs. Custom Web developers also needed.

Requirements: Must be local resident. Extensive experience required. Submit résumé and references.

Provisions: Pays by the project.

BLUE CROSS/BLUE SHIELD OF SOUTH CAROLINA
Columbia, SC 29219

Positions: Local data entry operators for coding health claims. Full-time, 8-hour days. Openings are offered first to in-house employees, who are preferred for their company experience, but will also hire from outside applicants. Prefers to train in-house for 6 to 12 months if possible. Currently it has over 100 workers.

Requirements: Must live in the area.

Provisions: Pays by the line on computer. Training and equipment (including computer and modem) is provided. Home workers are considered part-timers and receive virtually no benefits; employer/employee relations are excellent, however, and the program is considered by all parties concerned to be very successful. Inquires are welcome, but you should expect to be put on a waiting list.

BOYD PRINTING COMPANY, INC.
49 Sheridan Avenue, Albany, NY 12210
www.boydprinting.com

Positions: Typesetting input operators.

Requirements: Must be local resident. Experienced operators with own equipment only.

Provisions: Pays by the word.

BUREAU OF OFFICE SERVICES, INC.
361 S. Frontage Road, Ste 125, Burr Ridge, IL 60521

Positions: Home-based workers do transcription and word processing for both general and medical work.

Requirements: Must have PC and be experienced. Local residents only.

Provisions: Company furnishes all supplies, transcribers, and computer equipment may be rented. Telecommunications has replaced almost all need for pickups and deliveries, but when necessary it is done by company messengers. All home workers are employees (not independent contractors) who are paid by production but who also receive benefits.

BUSINESS COMMUNICATIONS COMPANY, INC.
25 Van Zant St., Suite 2A, Norwalk, CT 06855

Positions: A publisher of technical/economic evaluations of advanced technologies, market forecasts, and industry newsletters, is seeking seasoned writers who are capable of preparing self-contained technical/economic market research reports discussing select components of any of these industries: biotechnology, chemicals, healthcare, banking, advanced materials, electronics, energy, flame retardancy, food/beverage, Internet, telecommunications, membranes/separations, plastics, packaging, waste, water, and air treatment, and allied industries.

Requirements: In addition to having a broad knowledge of their chosen industry, the successful applicant must be able to meet publication deadlines and adhere to finished copy format requirements, which are supplied by the publisher. Minimum requirements for these contract assignments are a Bachelor's degree in a relevant field. Applicants should send a résumé, list of publications, and a brief cover letter identifying the industries/technical areas of greatest interest.

BUSINESS GRAPHICS
3314 Vassar Dr. NE, Albuquerque, NM 87107

Positions: Typesetting input operators.

Requirements: Must be local resident. Experience and computer required.

BUYSELLWEBSITE
www.buysellweb site.com

Positions: BuySellWeb site is actively hiring database designers with at least one year of experience.

Requirements: Applicants need to have database skills in a Windows Vista environment. Contact with a résumé and examples of your work.

Provisions: The position telecommutes and is available to Canadian and US residents only. Bi-weekly paychecks and flexible hours.

CAL-BAY SYSTEMS, INC.
3070 Kerner Boulevard, Suite B, San Rafael, CA 94901
www.calbay.com

Positions: Software engineers for engineering firm specializing in PC-based process automation. Projects cross a broad range of industries and therefore, offer a lot of creative interest. Each project can last anywhere from 3 months to 3 years.

Requirements: Must prefer to work in a changing, dynamic environment and be flexible and eager to work in different areas. Technically, requires coding experience plus in-depth understanding of hard and systems integration. An engineering degree and at least four years experience working with automation software and/or hardware is required. Apply with résumé.

Provisions: You will be provided with cutting edge PC and cell phone. Pays competitive salary and provides profit sharing and full benefits package.

CAPITAL DATA

P.O. Box 2244, Palm Harbor, FL 34682

Positions: Openings for programmers and tech writers to work from home.
Requirements: Must live in Georgia, Florida, or the Carolinas. Must have development and maintenance programming experience. Need the ability to work independently. Manufacturing or distribution background a major plus. Send résumé.
Provisions: Excellent salary with full benefits package.

CARLISLE COMMUNICATIONS

4242 Chavenelle, Dubuque, IA 52002

Positions: Typesetting input operators.
Requirements: Must live in Dubuque in order to pick up and deliver manuscripts and disks. Must be excellent typist with high rate of accuracy.
Provisions: Training and equipment provided. Pays by the character.

CIRCLE GRAPHICS, INC.

8835 Columbia 100 Parkway, Columbia, MD 21045

Positions: Typesetting input operators. Company has 12 operators on call.
Requirements: Must be local resident in order to pick up and deliver work. Computer required; any brand okay.
Provisions: Pays by the character. Will train for company code.

CLARITY CONSULTANTS

1901 South Bascom Ave., Pruneyard Towers, Suite 1300,
Campbell, CA 95008
www.clarity.consultants.com

Positions: Technical writers for online and printed customer documentation for complex Internet telephony products.
Requirements: College degree or equivalent experience, minimum 3 years technical writing in commercial software development, experience in telecommunications or database technical writing, and skills using HTML, Adobe FrameMaker, and ForeHelp. Must be familiar with Windows and UNIX environments. Must live in or around the Silicon Valley.

COGHILL COMPOSITION COMPANY

7640 Whitepine Rd., Richmond, VA 23224

Positions: Typesetting input operators. Company handles all types of commercial typesetting jobs.

Requirements: Must own PC and have high-speed Internet capabilities. Local residents only.

Provisions: Pays by the character.

COMPUTER ASSISTANT
www.computerassistant.com

Positions: Online computer support.

Requirements: Visit the Web site to register your availability, contact information, rate, skills, and the type of work you want. The company will match your skills and availability with the needs of clients and call you or send you e-mail alerts on qualifying jobs that become available in your area.

COMPUTER SOLUTIONS
814 Arion Parkway, Suite 101, San Antonio, TX 78216

Positions: Software engineers for development including object-oriented systems, three-tier architectures, and Web technologies.

Requirements: BS in computer science, engineering or equivalent work experience. Need minimum of one year of Java development experience for productions systems plus two to three years total software engineering, programming experience.

Provisions: Salary, full benefits, and bonuses.

COMPUTEREASE
6460 Harrison Ave., Cincinnati, OH 45247

Positions: Programmers develop software for the construction industry.

Requirements: Positions are in the Cincinnati area. Requires experience with relevant languages. Send résumé.

CONCURRENT TECHNOLOGIES
150 Allen Road, Liberty Corner, NJ 07938

Positions: Web site designers, illustrators, and graphic artists.

Requirements: Requires strong marketing background with Web experience. Strong illustration and 3-D experience a must. HTML, DHTML, CSS, XML, XSL familiarity a plus. Will be responsible for site designs including site theme, color theme, page layout, navigation, image creation, scanning, animation, streaming video, and billboards. Must have some programming knowledge.

Provisions: Offers full-time or part-time contracts. Provides paid training and technical support when needed.

CORPIMAGES.NET

131 11th. Street, SE, Suite B, Washington, DC 20003
www.corpimages.net

Positions: Web site designers and freelance Web site programmers, preferably Pearl/CGI, or C, C++.

Requirements: Supervision and final approval of work will be done at company headquarters, but work can be performed from anywhere in the world you may be. Visit Web site to submit résumé. Please include any programming work you may have done in the past when submitting résumé.

Provisions: Pays hourly rate per CGI program based on certain criteria. "We are constantly looking for self-motivated, creative individuals anywhere in the world."

CRM GRIOT

www.crmgriot.com

Positions: This company needs independent incorporated CRM consultants located throughout the US and EMEA to provide tier 3 and tier 4 (technical and/or functional) CRM implementation support to CRM professionals worldwide.

Requirements: Must have an understanding of technical architectures including RDBMS, client-server, package systems implementation, mobile computing, thin client architecture, Internet technologies, sales, service, and marketing business processes, and call centers. Prior CRM, ERP, consulting experiences a must. May live anywhere in the world, but must speak, read, and write proficient American English at least as a second language. Calls are routed based on language preferences.

CROSS-CURRICULAR CONNECTIONS

www.crosscurricular.com

Positions: Software testers work part-time from home for this virtual educational services company.

Requirements: Must have minimum two years of QA software testing experience including Web-based applications. Prior experience designing software testing strategies and familiarity with Macromedia Flash are strongly preferred. Must be thorough, flexible, have great attention to detail, and be able to work unsupervised from home. Need to have hardware for testing, including both Mac and PC. Familiarity with ASP.net, editorial skills, and Quality Assurance are a plus.

DIGNUS
>8354 Six Forks Road Suite 201, Raleigh, NC 27615
>www.dignus.com

Positions: Software developers.
Requirements: Experience with IBM mainframe, OS/390, and C and/or C++. BS in computer science is also required. Local programmers preferred. Send résumé.
Provisions: Pays competitive salary.

DS SEWING, INC.
>P.O. Box 8983, New Haven, CT 06532
>www.ds-sewing.com

Positions: Internet Web designers, programmers, and graphic artists.
Requirements: Programmers must know HTML, XML, some PERL, some CGI, VB 6, some SQL 7, MS Access, and have network admin skills. Graphic artist must know Adobe Photoshop. Digital photography knowledge is a plus. Must know and use HTML without using an editor. Extensive site design and graphics experience is required. Telecommuters must live in the area.

DUARTE DESIGN, INC.
>161 E. Evelyn Ave, Mountain View, CA 94041
>www.duarte.com

Positions: Duarte Design has a broad network of contractors who help build Web-based marketing programs for businesses. "We are always looking for creative people to join our studio."
Requirements: Must be highly skilled in PhotoShop, Illustrator, PowerPoint, Flash, Director, HTML, etc. and portfolio of your work to show. Submit résumé with cover letter and samples, via e-mail to WeWantYou@duarte.com.

DYNAX RESOURCES, INC.
>6800 Jericho Turnpike #240W, Syosset, NY 11791
>www.dynax.com

Positions: MVS Systems programmers.
Requirements: Must have own PC. CICS, DB2, VTAM experience a plus. Send résumé.
Provisions: Work any hours. Pays $35 to $40 per hour.

ECHO MANAGEMENT GROUP

P.O. Box 2150, 15 Washington Street, Conway, NH 03818

www.echoman.com

Positions: This national software company specializes in the medical and social service markets. They need software engineers to help develop new Windows applications using Delphi and SQL databases.

Requirements: Need experience with Java, HTML, Java Script, and SQL. Apply online.

Provisions: Pays salary commensurate with experience plus benefits.

ECTONE, INC.

11 Great Oaks Blvd, San Jose, CA 95119

Positions: Software engineers.

Requirements: Minimum five years experience with Java technologies. Must have proven proficiency writing JDBC and servlets and developing server-side applications. Must understand WebLogic, e-commerce security, XML, EDI, and nTier applications. Apply with résumé.

ELITE SOFTWARE DEVELOPMENT, INC.

2700 Arrington Road College Station, TX 77845

www.elitesoft.com

Positions: Contract programmers for program components such as algorithms.

Requirements: Prefers programmers who properly test their work and are capable of writing their own documentation.

Provisions: Generally pays by the hour, total sum not to exceed predetermined amount.

FEDERATION OF THE HANDICAPPED

Automated Office Services, 52 Duane St. #26, New York, NY 10011

Positions: Automated Office Systems is the newest of the Federation's programs for homebound disabled workers. It is similar to the typing/transcription department, except that all workers use computers and telecommunications equipment to perform the work.

Requirements: All positions require evaluation through lengthy interviews and personal counseling. All workers must live in New York City.

Provisions: Automated Office Services provides training in word processing procedures. Computers, telecommunication equipment and a phone-in dictation system are provided. All positions pay piece rates. Disability insurance counseling is provided.

FIRST BEAT MEDIA
www.firstbeatmedia.com

Positions: First Beat Media is a domain acquisition, online entertainment media company that targets premier industry domains and develops them into strong portals by attracting mass amounts of traffic and creating a brand that clients can trust. To do this, the company uses programmers, creative Web designers, writers, SEO specialists, link developers, and innovative analysts.

Requirements: Visit Web site for specific requirements and online application.

FUSION GAMES
www.fusiongames.com

Positions: Digital Fusion, Inc. is a developer of computer games and entertainment software.

Requirements: Primarily looks for freelance and contract programmers, 3D and 2D artists. Network and system programmers must be familiar with DirectX and Windows (though Mac programmers will be considered), 'C'and 'C'++, (Lingo considered), game logic, and interface programming. 3D artists must be experienced with modeling, texturing, and animating using Maya, 3D Max, Light Wave, etc. 2D artists need to be very comfortable with Photoshop, Illustrator, and page layout types of programs.

Provisions: Hours and work location are flexible (dependent on project-specific demands). Pay is competitive by project or task.

GATEWAY TECHNICAL SERVICES
36 Chesterfield Ct., Monkton, MD 21111

Positions: Software development.

Requirements: Need solid experience in software development for PC applications. Send résumé describing language capabilities.

GENERATION Z
P.O. Box 820372, Fort Worth, TX 76182
www.generationz.com

Positions: Internet developer. This would be an R&D software systems engineer with experience working with leading edge technologies as well as existing Web technologies.

Requirements: Advanced degree in computer science, engineering or information systems OR 3-4 years equivalent experience in advanced engineering. Advanced skills in UNIX, NT, ODS SQL, and relational databases. Apply by e-mailing your résumé to development@generationz.com.

THE HIVE

www.thehive.com

Positions: The Hive is an organization of developers and engineers working on the next generation of consumer and business applications. It is a virtual organization where people can log in from their homes, a nearby office, one of the company's global office locations, or wherever there is an Internet connection. Team members work with many different technologies on a daily basis such as MySQL, clustering, CSS, JavaScript, etc.

Requirements: Check Web site for current openings and corresponding requirements.

Provisions: Open salary arrangements.

IISTEK CORP

2645 Executive Park Dr., Suite 509, Weston, FL 33331

http://iistek.com

Positions: Search engine optimization specialists. The positions will require the ability to analyze keywords, manage reporting software, customer service, and research new techniques.

Requirements: Must have some Web development experience and extensive experience with the Internet. At least 2+ year's experience required, optimizing Web pages for Google, Yahoo, and MSN with success. A complete understanding of search engine trends and search engine algorithms is a must. The ideal candidate has experience with WordTracker online keyword analysis, WebPosition Gold rank reporting, GRSEO optimization software, and WebTrends traffic analyzer.

Provisions: Can live anywhere. Apply online.

IMAGE WORKS

P.O. Box 3184, Vernon, CT 06066

www.imagesites.com

Positions: Graphic designer. ImageWorks, employs full-time artists and designers, and needs freelance artists from time to time as well.

Requirements: Knowledge of Adobe or Macromedia product line a definite plus, but not entirely necessary. "Show us something persuasive."

Provisions: Can live anywhere in US.

IMPRESSIONS, INC.

2016 Winnebago St., Madison, WI 53704

Positions: Typesetting input operators for book typography.

Requirements: Local residents only. Excellent keyboarding skills are required. Must own computer equipment.
Provisions: Hours are flexible. Pays by the character.

INTELLISTREAM TECHNOLOGIES, INC.
801 West Street, Wilmington, DE 19801
www.intellistream.com

Positions: Network engineers, software developers, and database application developers.
Requirements: Visit online for complete information.
Provisions: Can live anywhere in the US.

INTRACORP
1601 Chestnut St., Philadelphia, PA 19102
www.intracorp.com

Positions: Intracorp develops software for the healthcare management industry. This is a large and well-established company with multiple opportunities for programmers.
Requirements: Minimum two years experience required in any of the following: Oracle Database, Oracle Financials, C++ and C, DEC/VAX VMS, Rdb, RMS, CDD, DEC C, SQL Module, DIBOL, COBOL, and BASIC. Know of UNIX Shell, relational databases, 4GL's, Powerbuilder, object-oriented design and development, Windows NT, and Internet technologies a plus. Apply with résumé.
Provisions: Telecommuting is available to local professionals. Offers professional development/technology training opportunities, competitive salary, and full benefits.

ISC CONSULTANTS, INC.
14 East 4th St., Suite 602, New York, NY 10012
www.isc.com

Positions: ISC, an award-winning Internet and call center consulting firm, seeks freelance graphic designers, producers, and HTML jockeys. The company develops Web sites that people use to perform work. People use ISC systems to: select and buy products online, define and display reports, easily retrieve answers from databases, and transact with other online users.
Requirements: Applicants should have the ability to present complex information clearly and to create "intuitive" easy-to-use visual interfaces. Expertise with HTM editors, Photoshop, Freehand, and Delabelizer is relevant.

JDM INTERACTIVE

www.jdm.com

Positions: HTML designers.

Requirements: Must be fluent in HTML frames, CSS, and JavaScript. Experience with ASP also a plus. E-mail résumé to jobs@jdm.com.

LABMENTORS

www.labmentors

Positions: MSCE mentors. LabMentors provides guided online labs for Web-based training in real-time lab environment over the Internet. Participants can log on anywhere, anytime to gain hands-on experience and advice in the study of Linux, Windows2000, NT, Cisco, or Novell training programs/certification tracks. Programming and database labs will be available soon.

Requirements: Requires very good communication skills (typing is essential), fast and reliable Internet connection, and commitment to work hours (essential).

Provisions: Can live anywhere in US.

LAYKIN

Los Angeles, CA

www.laykin.com

Positions: HTML coders and Web applications copywriters.

Requirements: Experience maintaining multiple mid-sized sites plus skills with Java and PERL. Must understand graphics interfaces and cross platform functions. Apply online at www.laykin.com/lc/lc.htm.

Provisions: Telecommute with full benefits.

LETTER PERFECT WORD PROCESSING CENTER

4205 Menlo Drive, Baltimore, MD 21215

Positions: Company operates a mailing center and publishes three newsletters for businesses in mail-order. About a dozen home-based word processors and data entry operators work mostly on mailing lists and the company's two monthly newsletters.

Requirements: Must be Baltimore resident. Must own PC and have experience using it. Word Perfect software is preferred. Typing speed of 100 to 110 wpm is average among workers here.

Provisions: Will train on Nutshell software. Pays piece rates, which run much higher than in-house rates.

LIFT, INC.

P.O. Box 4264, Warren, NJ 07059

Positions: Lift, Inc., is a nonprofit organization that trains and places physically disabled people as home-based computer programmers for corporate employers. In the past 14 years, program participants have been placed with over 70 major corporations.

Requirements: Applicants must have a severe but stable disability, such as MS or impaired limbs. Pilot programs for blind and deaf workers are underway, too. Standard aptitude tests are applied to find traits as motivation, drive, self-control, and an aptitude for computer programming. Occasionally the candidate already has some training, but prior training is not necessary for entry into the program. Each candidate is trained to specifically meet the needs of the corporate client using whatever language and equipment the employer chooses. Most candidates are trained in systems programming and business applications.

Provisions: Upon completion of training, the programmer will work under contract with Lift for one year. The salary is comparable to that of any other entry-level programmer, with medical and life insurance provided. After the year is up, the corporate employer then has the option of employing the programmer directly. The placement record has been exceptional. Lift operates in most states now and plans to include all 50. Qualified persons are encouraged to apply from any urban location. (All workers are required to go into the employer's office at least once a week and most corporations are located in densely populated areas.)

MACARTHUR ASSOCIATES

500 Fifth Ave, Suite 305, New York, NY 10110

Positions: Software developers.

Requirements: Must have strong experience working with SQL. Must be able to go into the Trenton office at least once a week.

Provisions: Pays salary starting at $75,000 plus full benefits.

MARYLAND STATE GOVERNMENT

Office of Personnel Services & Benefits, 301 W. Preston St., Baltimore, MD 21201

Positions: Information Technology positions working on finance, health, assessments and taxation, public safety insurance, the environment, retirement, agriculture, the treasury, and other applications. Applications are continuously accepted for: Computer Information Services Specialist I, II;

Computer Network Specialist Trainee, I II; DP Programmer Analyst Trainee, I, II; Lead/Advanced.

Requirements: On résumé, list any computer programming languages in which you have expertise.

Provisions: In certain cases sign-on bonuses or tuition reimbursements may be offered.

MAVERICK PUBLICATIONS

P.O. Box 5007, Bend, OR 9770

www.mavbooks.com

Positions: Keyboarding and proofreading. This is a small book-producing company, established in 1968 that uses cottage labor where economics make it advantageous. An optical character reader is used to transfer manuscripts to magnetic disks. Computerized photo typesetting allows corrections to be made on the computer.

Requirements: Must be local resident.

MINDBUILDER

Northbrook, IL

mindbuilder.com

Positions: MindBuilder develops and produces multimedia presentations and training materials for Fortune 500 corporations.

Requirements: Talented computer professionals should be self-directed and Internet-ready. Currently needs hardcore Visual Basic 5 developers with minimum two years experience. Need absolute knowledge of Microsoft Access and Oracle. Also coding projects available for C++, HTML, CGI, Perl, or Java. Any Web development experience is a big plus. Apply online to imageek@mindbuilder.com.

Provisions: Pays competitive salaries plus full benefits.

MINNESOTA DEPARTMENT OF HUMAN RESOURCES

444 Lafayette Rd., St. Paul, MN 55155

Positions: Programmers and systems analysts. The Department has two very large IBM mainframe applications written in Natural using ADABAS as the dbms.

Requirements: Minimum of two years programming experience required. Need experience with Natural and ADABAS, or with other 3rd or 4th GLs. Apply with résumé.

NATIONAL READING STYLES INSTITUTE
P.O. Box 737, Syosset, NY 11791
www.nrsi.com
Positions: Desktop publishing and typesetting.
Requirements: Educational publisher has overflow work only for professionals experienced with Ventura. Local residents only send résumé.

NORTHWESTERN UNIVERSITY
720 University Place, Evanston, IL 60208
Positions: Maintaining database.
Requirements: Must be local resident with experience and equipment. Must obtain home worker certificate from Illinois Department of Labor.

NPD
900 West Shore Road, Port Washington, NY 11050
www.npd.com
Positions: NPD is one of the largest market research firms in the country. They have begun to employ home-based data entry operators to process batches of source documents. The operators are divided into groups of 20 each, with a supervisor for each group. Supervisors are also home-based and are treated the same as in-house data entry supervisors with salaries, benefits, etc. They are provided with PCs for their homes, but do not do data entry work.
Requirements: Good typing skills are necessary. Must be local resident. Must attend quarterly meetings. Must pick up and deliver work about every three days.
Provisions: PCs and all necessary supplies are provided. Training is provided in NPD office for one to two weeks. Work is part-time, therefore, only sick leave and vacation benefits (prorated) are provided; no insurance benefits. Pays piece rates equal to that of in-house workers. Applications are accepted, but there is a waiting list.

ON WORLD, INC.
San Diego, CA
www.onworld.com
Positions: Engineers, market analysts and Web researchers.
Requirements: Visit www.onworld.com/html/theTeam.htm.
Provisions: Can live anywhere in the world.

OPSOL INTEGRATORS, INC.

Opsol Business Park, 1566 La Pradera Dr., Campbell, CA 95008
www.opsol.com

Positions: Web designers for visualizing and developing Web clients to interface with back-end servers.

Requirements: Minimum 1 year experience using HTML and Java. Work samples will be required. Telecommuting is allowed part-time only so only local applicants will be considered. Visit Web site for current openings and apply online.

Provisions: Pays hourly rated based on experience.

ORUS INFORMATION SERVICES

3012 Huron St., Ste 300, Denver, CO 80202

Positions: Programmers for long and short-term contracts.

Requirements: Generally requires at least 5 years of programming experience working on NT platform with Visual Basic, ASP, HTML, Oracle, and XML. Will consider college graduates with the right background.

Provisions: Pays competitive salary and benefits.

PACVIEW INC.

Santa Clara, CA
www.pacview.com

Positions: Java developers.

Requirements: Must be skilled in Java, Servlets, JSP, Struts framework, Hibernate, Tag Libraries and have experience with Oracle or other relational databases. Need knowledge of NT, UNIX, Web Servers, Apache/Tomcat, WebLogic, and iPlanet/Netscape. US applicants only.

Provisions: Pays excellent salary and comprehensive benefits.

PORT CITY PRESS, INC.

1323 Greenwood Rd., Pikesville, MD 21208

Positions: Typesetting input operators for book typography.

Requirements: Local residents only. Experience and equipment required.

Provisions: Pays by the character.

PRATT SYSTEMS

P.O. Box 12405, La Jolla, CA 92039
www.prattsystems.com

Positions: Flash designers for company that provides Web design, Internet marketing, Web hosting, technology projects, and computer security to business clients.

Requirements: Experience using Flash, Photoshop, and Dreamweaver. Page layout skills needed. Send résumé with work samples.
Provisions: Can live anywhere in the United States. Pays $15 per hour.

PROSITES, INC.
32209 Camino Caliari, Temecula, CA 92592
www.prosites.com

Positions: Part-time and full-time designers for Web sites, print advertisements and other graphic design works.
Requirements: Must be capable of compelling work. Expertise in Dreamweaver, Flash, Fireworks, and Photoshop is a major plus. Visit www.prosites.com/careers.htm for more information on application process.

PUBLISHERS CLEARING HOUSE
382 Channel Dr., Port Washington, NY 11050

Positions: Data entry operators work on PCs at home entering names and addresses and other data for mailing lists.
Requirements: Local residents only. Experience, speed, and accuracy are required.
Provisions: Pays piece rates. There is currently a waiting list of 6-9 months because the turnover is so low among the home-based workers.

QUEUE, INC.
1 Control Dr., Shelton, CT 06484

Positions: Contract programmers for writing educational software for Macintosh and/or PCs. Freelance programmers also do conversions and programming to company specifications.
Requirements: Local people are definitely preferred. Apply with résumé and references or work samples. Quality of work is very important.
Provisions: Pays by the job or royalty. Inquiries are welcome.

REMINGTON INTERNATIONAL
10900 Wilshire Blvd., Suite 550, Los Angeles, CA 90024

Positions: Applications software developers for major online mortgage lender.
Requirements: Must possess strong skills in VB, SQL, COM, DCOM, and working on Windows 3-tier architect on NT platform. Prefers local residents.
Provisions: Pays competitive salary and offers excellent benefits package.

RENT A CODER

www.rentacoder.com

Positions: Rent a Coder lets techies locate and bid on coding projects and questions from around the world.

Requirements: Visit the Web site to register (free), then you will receive e-mails as new bid requests come in.

Provisions: Rent a Coder handles payment collection based on your agreed-upon fees. It charges a 15% fee on the profit from the work and questions.

RIGHT ON PROGRAMS

778 New York Ave., Huntington, NY 11743

Positions: Contract software developers. Company produces educational programs for PC and Mac. Also accepts freelance submissions.

Requirements: Must be highly qualified. Submit résumé and references.

ROXBURY PUBLISHING COMPANY

P.O. Box 491044, Los Angeles, CA 90049

www.roxbury.net

Positions: Freelance home-based typesetters are used by this textbook publisher.

Requirements: Must have typesetting equipment (not PC; this is not embedding, this is actual typesetting). Los Angeles residents only. Minimum of five years experience. Send résumé and indicate equipment type.

Provisions: Pay method varies. Inquiries welcome from qualified people, but there is a waiting list.

SPEAK WITH A GEEK

1275 W. Washington Street, Tempe, AZ 85281

www.speakwithageek.com

Positions: Speak With A Geek provides 24/7 online tech support for hardware, software, networking, and peripherals to businesses of all sizes as well as individuals.

Requirements: Must have technical expertise in any or all of the above mentioned areas. Send résumé.

SPHERION

475 Sansome Street, Suite 800, San Francisco, CA 94111

www.spherion.com

Positions: This is an agency that outsources Web masters, Web designers, technical writers, and quality assurance testers.

Requirements: Minimum five years experience is required in each job area.

Apply with résumé and references.

Provisions: Offers competitive salaries and great benefits including profit sharing and 401K.

SPSS, INC.

233 S Wacker Dr. Fl 11, Chicago, IL 60611

Positions: Contract programmers and technical writers. Programmers do conversions of business graphics software. Technical writers are used for documentation and promotional materials.

Requirements: Programmers must have experience with mainframe or super-minis. Applicants for both positions must send résumé and previous work samples.

STANDARD DATA-PREP

6 Dubon Ct., Farmingdale, NY 11735

Positions: Data entry operations.

Requirements: Good skills, experience required. Local residents only. Send résumé.

Provisions: Home workers are full-time employees with 37½ hour work week, benefits, vacations, holiday pay, and 401K.

SWORDSMITH

P.O. Box 242, Pomfret, CT 06258

www.swordsmith.com

Positions: Freelance coders work from their own homes on their own computers, adding the edits and typesetting codes to authors' disks for everything from romances to college textbooks.

Requirements: Applicants must have a strong eye for detail, a love of books and reading, and strong word-processing skills. Typing skills are a plus.

Provisions: Coders may work full- or part-time, and are paid by the job, not by the hour (experienced coders average about $15 per hour, but this varies from job to job). Coders must live within easy driving distance of Swordsmith to pick up and drop off manuscripts, and must be able to train at Swordsmith for a week. "Many of our coders are mothers with small children at home."

TIG FIRST SOURCE

2211 Norfolk, Suite 510, Houston, TX 77098

www.tigfirstsource.com

Positions: Software developers for GUI programming on NT platform.

Requirements: Minimum three years experience working with VC++ plus

MFC and development on NT platform. Educational requirements will be waived only if proven experience is sufficient. Experience with Com, Dcom, and ActiveX is preferred, but will train in those areas if necessary. Only local residents need apply.

Provisions: Pays competitive salary plus benefits.

UNIMATRIX INTERNATIONAL

2101 East Main St., Richmond, VA 23223

www.unimatrix.com

Positions: This is a large computer and Internet company with a wide array of products and services including hardware, software, networking, consulting, repair, Web design and hosting, e-commerce, publishing, etc. There are many positions available for IT professionals including: HTML designers, graphic artists, Shockwave and Flash editors, programmers (CGI, Perl, Java), and e-commerce specialists.

Requirements: Specific experience is not required though the appropriate skills are. The company is mostly looking for qualified individuals who are highly motivated. Apply by sending cover letter and résumé to careers@unimatrix.com.

Provisions: Pays excellent hourly rates. Can live anywhere.

USER TESTING

2672 Bayshore Parkway, Mountain View, CA 94043

www.usertesting.com

Positions: Testers review Web sites using the company's software to record a video of what's happening on the screen—mouse movements, clicks, and keystrokes—and the tester's spoken comments while on the Web site. There are only four questions to answer and reviews take about 10 minutes to complete.

Requirements: Need a Windows computer and fast Internet connection. You can record your voice with a microphone or by telephone. Fill out a one-page form with your demographic information (gender, computer experience). Assignments are based on demographic matches. The form is on the Web site.

Provisions: Pays $10 per view, paid with PayPal.

V-STAFFING

9 Woodcreek Road, Brookfield, CT 06804

www.v-staffing.com

Positions: E-mail optimization and search engine optimization.

Requirements: Must be experienced with meta tags, title tags, keywords,

submission to all major search engines, and search engine optimization. If you are qualified, send your résumé, four references, and times and days you would be available for a phone interview.
Provisions: Pays $10-13 per hour, every two weeks.

VIRTUO GROUP

www.virtuogroup.com
Positions: Oracle implementation consultants.
Requirements: Must be able to install/configure ATG patches, migrate OID users, plan for high availability for OID, and test strategy for SSO and Portal. Must live in the US and willing to travel to Alberta, Canada in two-week segments to provide Oracle implementation expertise. Travel expenses will be reimbursed. Must have excellent English written and verbal skills. An understanding of the French language is desirable—although not required.
Provisions: Virtuo Group offers W-2 and 1099 opportunities. Medical/health benefits are available for W-2 employees.

VISDA ENTERPRISES, INC.

7509 Madison Avenue, Suite 114, Citrus Heights, CA 95610
Positions: Hardware engineers working with OEM solutions for high-speed networking, digital broadcasting, and data storage.
Requirements: Minimum six years experience in directly related work. Must be specifically skilled with RAID Controller, BSCS/BSEE, and hardware architecture and implementation.
Provisions: Offers full-time positions starting at $100,000 plus impressive benefits.

WAVERLY PRESS, INC.

351 West Camden Street, Baltimore, MD 21201
Positions: Waverly Press has been using home keyers for over 15 years to embed code for typesetting medical and scientific publications. This is a high volume operation typesetting over 250,000 pages a year.
Requirements: Applicants must type fast and very accurately. "Some are surprised at the level of skill required for this work. This is not just a typing job." Must live in the area. Also has a pool of proofreaders; must be able to read at a certain rate (about 27,000 characters per hour while simultaneously checking for errors in the copy. A test is given upon application).
Provisions: Initial training is conducted in the plant for six weeks. Workers are then supplied with PC, furniture, miscellaneous office supplies, and "an endless supply of manuscripts." Pay is dependent upon accuracy with three

different rates: low, medium, and high. "Two thirds of our keyers are in the high range." Pays by the keystroke with the complexity taken into consideration; the computer is programmed to measure the work. Piecework with no benefits except a pension plan is available to those with over 1,000 hours a year. Daily van service is available to those who need it.

WEB-ERECTORS

www.web-erectors.com

Positions: Graphic designers and Web designers perform freelance work. Copywriters occasionally needed.

Requirements: Graphic designers must be proficient with Quark and Photoshop (Illustrator a plus). Work involves designing direct mail brochures. Web designers must be proficient with Dreamweaver and Flash. Must have access to Mac. Send résumé, 2-3 nonreturnable samples, and description of experience in graphic design/desktop production.

J. WESTON WALCH

Box 658, Portland, ME 04104

Positions: Company publishes educational courseware. Freelance programmers can submit finished program with documentation for consideration. Contract programmers are also used for conversions and modifications.

Requirements: Freelancers should send only proposal. Contract programmers should submit résumé, work samples, and complete information describing particular expertise.

JOHN WILEY & SONS, INC.

605 3rd Ave., New York, NY 10158

Positions: Contract programmers and technical writers. Company produces technical applications software for the engineering and scientific fields. Various types of work are contracted out to programmers, including conversions, testing, debugging, and some original development. Technical writers do documentation work.

Requirements: Must own and have thorough knowledge of Mac and PC machines. Send résumé, work samples, and references.

Provisions: Payment methods vary according to the situation.

YORK GRAPHICS SERVICES, INC.

3650 West Market Street, York, PA 17404

Positions: Typesetting input operators and proofreaders for book typography.

Requirements: Local residents only. Operators must have good typing skills. Proofreaders must be detail-oriented and have excellent English skills. **Provisions:** All home workers are independent contractors and should understand that there are no guarantees of work assignments. All available work is overflow.

OPPORTUNITIES IN MISCELLANEOUS

What do knitters, notaries, guitar transcribers, jurors, note writers, recruiters, concierges, and lawyers have in common? Absolutely nothing—except they can all find work at home if they choose. As the work-at-home trend continues to grow, more and more types of jobs are opening up to people who never before thought they could ever enjoy the benefits of working at home. This chapter includes an assortment of home-based opportunities that never existed before, most of which defy classification and simply don't fit in any of the other chapters. Some are brand new, like online concierge services. Others, like recruiting—one of the top five fastest growing industries in the United States—are simply changing how business is done. Take a look. You'll be surprised by what you can do to earn a living at home these days.

ADMISSION CONSULTANTS, INC.

333 Maple Avenue East #700, Vienna, VA 22180

www.admissionconsultants.com

Positions: College admission consultants.

Requirements: Must possess strong interpersonal skills, excellent oral and written communication, ability to stay flexible and work well under tight deadlines in a fast-paced environment, in-depth admissions committee experience, and Internet access. Apply online.

Provisions: Competitive pay, comprehensive training, flexible work schedule, and the ability to work at home. You will have the option of a part-time or full-time position. Part-time employees also have the potential to move to a full-time position.

AMERICAN GLOVE CO., INC.
98 Alpine St., Lyerly, GA 30730
Positions: Home manufacture of work gloves. There are currently 34 home workers.
Requirements: Must be local resident and be skilled.

ANALOG ONE
P.O. Box 1016, Freeland, WA 98249
Positions: This is a virtual engineering firm.
Requirements: Must be experienced analog engineer or bench technicians. To apply for a position, submit your résumé and the position for which you are applying to the attention of Human Resources.
Provisions: Offers competitive salary and benefits package.

ARIA COMMUNICATIONS
717 West St. Germain Street, St. Cloud, MN 56301
Positions: This is a handwritten direct mail service that relies on a team of writers who work at home. The work is as simple as writing a note inside a card for nonprofit organizations.
Requirements: Must have legible cursive handwriting and an eye for detail. Must be able to complete 20 hours of training on-site before moving work home. Must be available to work 16-20 hours a week. Must be local resident because work is picked up and dropped off daily. Send letter of interest in your own handwriting to the HR department.
Provisions: Pay is based on the amount of work completed. Provides paid on-site training, 401(k), and numerous corporate supplemental benefits.

BARRY MANUFACTURING COMPANY, INC.
15 Bubier St., Lynn, MA 01901
Positions: Stitching and hand assembly of infant and children's shoe parts.
Requirements: Experience is required. Must be local resident.
Provisions: Some of the work requires machinery, which is supplied by the employer. Pays piece rates equal to minimum wage, which is the same in-house workers are paid for the same work.

BEADNIKS
www.junkyjewelry.com/beadniks.htm
Positions: Beaders and jewelry makers.
Requirements: No experience is necessary, company will train. You do not

need to buy any kits!

Provisions: Average pay is $12 per hour depending on design and materials. Only US residents, over 18 years of age will be considered. Apply online.

BERLIN GLOVES CO.

150 W. Franklin, P.O. Box 230, Berlin, WI 54923

Positions: Home stitchers manufacture gloves and other leather clothing and accessories. Currently there are 18 home workers.

Requirements: Must be local resident and be skilled.

BLUEBERRY WOOLENS

P.O. Box 326, Embden, ME 04958

Positions: Blueberry Woolens is a rural Maine cottage industry employing knitters and seamstresses who work in their homes up and down the Kennebec and Sandy Rivers. Many of the company's designs reflect traditional and classic Scandinavian Tyrolean folk motifs while others are of contemporary origin. Hand-loomed sweaters are made of the finest yarns available using 100% pure wool, which is grown and spun primarily in Maine, or 100% cotton. This is an established and growing company with close to $1 million in annual sales. Currently has a pool of 60 knitters.

Requirements: Enrollment in company's training classes and submission of acceptable samples is required. Must own a knitting machine or purchase one from the company. Must be local in order to pick up and deliver supplies and finished sweaters.

Provisions: Pays per finished sweater. Hours can be full-time or part-time. Workers are independent contractors. Inquiries are welcome as company continues to grow.

CASTLE BRANCH

www.castlebranch.com

Positions: Castle Branch helps businesses make safe and informed decisions by providing employment, business, and tenant screening, as well as drug testing and investigative services. These services are provided by home-based screeners.

Requirements: Experience is a must. Excellent communication skills required. Apply online.

CDS SIGNING SERVICES

www.cdssigning.com

Positions: CDS Signing Services has been serving the lending community since 1998. The company specializes in locating and scheduling mobile notaries nationwide. Prospective online mobile notaries can take advantage of the opportunity by registering online (free).

Requirements: To become part of CDS signing team, simply create a notary profile through the online application and fax your W-9 Form to CDS. Once CDS receives your application and completed W-9 Form you will able to receive signing assignments in your area.

CHA CHA

www.chacha.com

Positions: ChaCha guides answer questions from individuals on a vast range of topics.

Requirements: Must be 18+ years old, fluent in English, and have a US mailing address. You will need a high-speed Internet connection in order to connect to ChaCha systems. Successful guides love researching online and have excellent writing skills. You should have a computer with a minimum of 512MB of RAM-1GB is ideal. Currently, guides are required to use Firefox (a free Web browser) and Flash. Operating Systems must be Windows, Mac, or Linux. Sign up online.

Provisions: Guides are paid on a per-transaction basis, which currently works out to an average of $3 to $9 per hour, though many top guides earn more than that.

CHERRY LANE MUSIC COMPANY

www.cherrylane.com

Positions: Cherry Lane Music was launched in the early 1960s in an apartment overlooking the Cherry Lane Theatre in New York City. It has since evolved into a music publishing house with a staff of 80, plus offices in offices in Los Angeles, Beijing, England, France, Holland, and Canada. Freelance opportunities are available for pop/rock guitar transcribers, piano arrangers, educational music authors (particularly for drums, bass, and acoustic guitar), and editors (particularly for piano and guitar, all styles).

Requirements: Previous writing and editorial experience preferred. Attention to detail and ability to follow music and text style sheets a must. US residents only please. Send a blank e-mail with the subject line "Application Information" to edprintjobs@cherrylane.com and a message will be sent to you with details.

CHICAGO KNITTING MILLS
3344 West Montrose Ave., Chicago, IL 60618
Positions: Home-based sewing of emblems onto outerwear. Currently there are no openings available.
Requirements: Must be local resident and be skilled. Must obtain a home workers certificate from Illinois Department of Labor.

CHIPITA ACCESSORIES
110 E. 7th St., Walsenburg, CO 81089
Positions: Between 75 and 250 home workers handcraft jewelry using beads, stones, semi-precious stones, silver, crystal, and gold. The number of home workers fluctuates with the time of year, number of orders, and number of available workers in this rural area in southern Colorado. Walsenburg is, like most rural areas, economically depressed, but has a history of handcrafts of all kinds created by local artisans. Chipita started by producing and selling one kind of beaded earrings and grew from there. Home workers here are completely independent, having total control over their hours, how often and when they work, etc. The company will sell kits to workers, will show and attempt to sell from new sample designs for workers, or will buy outright as much jewelry as a worker can produce as long as it meets quality standards. A worker can work part-time or full-time, with the opportunity to earn a regular income.
Requirements: Must be a local resident. Contact the company with letter of interest.

CLICK A CLOSE
www.clicknclose.net
Positions: Legal settlement service uses virtual assistants to manage files during the settlement process through an online system that's available to attorneys 24/7.
Requirements: Complete the online application.

CONCIERGE AT LARGE, INC.
404 Camino Del Rio S, Suite 6011, San Diego, CA 92108
Positions: The Concierge At Large network is a pool of seasoned concierge professionals, many of whom are current or former hotel concierges from around the world. The company is always looking for regional experts who are available to work via the Internet, fax, or telephone assisting to fulfill client requests on an as-needed basis.
Requirements: A minimum of one year concierge experience and references

are required. No phone calls will be accepted. Send résumé to the HR department.
Provisions: Generous compensation provided.

COUNSEL ON CALL
www.counseloncall.com

Positions: Counsel On Call is a fastest-growing law firm with a new way to practice law. With six offices (and more opening soon) and hundreds of working Counsel On Call attorneys from coast to coast, the firm is able to provide litigation support teams, career counseling, and many other services in a wide variety of fields and on hundreds of projects.

Requirements: Counsel On Call's attorneys—who have years of quality experience—work individually, in teams, on-site or remotely. Apply online.

Provisions: Counsel On Call attorneys have earned the ability to control when, where, and how they work—whether it's 10 or 70 hours per week.

COUNTRY CURTAINS, INC.
705 Pleasant St., Lee, MA 01238

Positions: Sewing trim on basic curtains. Currently has about 31 home workers.

Requirements: Need sewing machine. Must be local resident.

Provisions: Pick up and delivery provided. Pays piece rates equal to minimum wage.

CRAZOO
www.crazoo.com

Positions: Individuals get paid for posting on forums.

Requirements: Must speak English. Register online (free) to get started.

Provisions: Crazoo pays users $0.03 per new thread, $0.02 per post and $0.002 per referral post. A referral post is each post someone you referred makes. The minimum payout is currently $10, paid by PayPal or check. Paypal payouts are free, but there is a $2 handling fee for checks in North America and $3 for international users.

CYBEREDIT
2000 Lenox Drive, Third Floor, Lawrenceville, NJ 08648
www.cyberedit.com

Positions: Freelance essay editors and résumé writers. Essay editors provide tips on topic selection, rework clumsy sentences, reorganize rambling text, and proofread final essays. Jobs are sent and received via e-mail. Résumé writers help write and edit résumés and cover letters using existing résumés and cover letters plus additional information (if available).

Requirements: Essay editors must be highly educated. Résumé writers should have a strong marketing and/or technical writing background and experience editing and writing résumés and cover letters. Past experience writing marketing and/or advertising copy is a plus. Submit résumé on the Web site.

Provisions: Pay for both positions is based on the project, but the effective per job hourly rate for the essay editors ranges between $15-$25 per hour and $20-$35 an hour for résumé writers.

DAINTY MAID WAITRESS APRONS COMPANY
12 North St., Fitchburg, MA 10420

Positions: Sewing waitress aprons.

Requirements: Must be local resident and own sewing machine. Experience is required.

Provisions: Material is supplied. Pays piece rates. Company only has two home-based employees; opportunities are extremely limited.

DRG TEXAS
Product Development Department, 103 North Pearl Street, Big Sandy, TX 75755

Positions: Sewers, crochet, and needlework specialists.

Requirements: Must be expert in cross-stitch, crochet, and plastic canvas needlecraft mediums. Must have proven stitching ability and be committed to completing assignments on deadline. This is not for hobbyists; only serious professionals need apply. Apply with contact information, letter of interest, description of abilities and stitching experience. Include good photos of work samples.

EEG RECRUITING
P.O. Box 803338, Chicago, IL 60680
www.eegrecruiting.com

Positions: EEG Recruiting has been in recruiting business for over 30 years, originally established to serve the electrical engineering market. It currently uses home-based technical recruiters living all over the country.

Requirements: Must have prior sales, telephone or recruiting experience and have the discipline to work virtually. You will also need intermediate computer skills. Apply on the Web site.

Provisions: Income for EEG recruiters is as high as $200,000 based on commissions as high as 75% of fees ranging up to $45,000. Company offers performance draws, weekly incentives, vacation incentives, management support, and just-in-time training. Also provides state-of-the-art software tools, resources, and information to shorten the recruitment cycle. There are tele-video conferences every Monday morning designed to collaborate, show off stats, and participate in forums and group learning sessions.

EJURY

3609-B West Pioneer Parkway, Arlington, TX 76013

Positions: eJury conducts online mock juries and focus groups to help attorneys determine case value, develop case themes, find the facts to emphasize, and learn "public" attitudes. The results are a tangible, persuasive tool used to promote settlement or prepare for trial. At eJury, each case is tried to a minimum of 50 people.

Requirements: Qualifications for service as an eJuror are much the same as the requirements for actual jury service in the United States: must be at least 18 years of age, a US citizen, be of sound mind and good moral character, able to read and write, never been convicted of a felony, and not be under indictment or other legal accusation of misdemeanor theft or felony theft or any felony charge. Sign up on the Web site.

Provisions: eJury is open to residents in all 50 states. The number of cases available for participation will vary greatly depending on location. Jurors living in major metropolitan areas receive more cases for participation than jurors living in rural areas. For each verdict rendered, eJurors are paid $5-$10 depending on the length of the case (the average is 35 minutes). Payment is made via PayPal.

ERIC ANTHONY CREATIONS

291 Live Oaks Boulevard, Casselberry, FL 32707

Positions: Making wooden frames.

Requirements: Area residents only. Send letter of interest for more information.

FORUM BOOSTING

www.forumboosting.com

Positions: Skilled people are needed for Web site content writing, SEO, and/or paid forum posting.

Requirements: Submit a brief résumé through the company's Web site. No experience is required, but you should point out any skills that you think would make you a valuable addition to the team. You will receive a briefing in the field you are willing to apply for.

Provisions: Pays competitive rates.

FRENCH CREEK SHEEP & WOOL COMPANY, INC.

600 Pine Swamp Rd., Elverson, PA 19520

Positions: Knitting sweaters on hand-operated machines. Currently has about 40 workers. Most of this company's apparel is designed and manufactured as it has been for over 30 years.

Requirements: Must be local resident in order to pick up and deliver supplies and finished sweaters.

Provisions: Some training, specific to the work here, is provided. Pays production rate, which is "well above minimum wage."

ESTELLE GRACER, INC.

950 West Hatcher Rd., Phoenix, AZ 85021

Positions: Knitting and crocheting jackets and sweaters. Work has previously been done by hand only, but company is now going into machine knitting. Currently has about 20 home workers; that number fluctuates up to 200. "Inquiries are always welcome."

Requirements: Must be experienced. Phoenix residents only.

Provisions: Specific training is provided. Home workers are full employees. Pays for production.

FLANNERY AND ANGELI

5156 W. Locust, Fresno, CA 93722

Positions: Seamstresses make aprons for this designer apron company.

Requirements: Quality seamstresses only. Need to know how to make a self-bias trim and welt pockets. Company is based in Fresno, California, so you must live in the central valley.

Provisions: Pays per piece. Part-time contract work only.

HAUSERNET

www.hausernet.com

Positions: The company uses "mailing decoys" to provide various promotion tracking and marketing intelligence services for major national firms. For example, some sample merchandise may be sent to check on delivery of customer orders or mailing lists need to be protected against misuse. The decoy agents simply have to mark the date received on each special piece as it comes in, enter it on the company Web site, and save the mailings for a period of time.

Requirements: Due to very high interest, most areas are covered. To find out if coverage is needed in your area, go to the Web site and enter your zip code on the inquiry page. If there is an opening, follow the instructions.

Provisions: Participants are credited for each valid item accurately reported. Any mailing costs are reimbursed. There may be extra potential opportunities. From time to time some participants get to keep test shipments of merchandise or get free copies of magazines.

HEALTHCARE RECRUITERS INTERNATIONAL
5220 Spring Valley Road, Suite 40, Dallas, TX 75254
Positions: Recruiters for the healthcare industry.
Requirements: Prefers individuals with experience recruiting for medical companies, medical facilities, and others within the medical community, but will consider any high energy, articulate self-starter. Complete the personal data profile and forward it to one of the HealthCare Recruiters International offices nearest you (see Web site).
Provisions: Offers commission driven compensation packages that allow you to earn income based on your efforts and skills.

HR ADVICE
P.O. Box 313, Mountain Lakes, NJ 07046
Positions: Human Resources professionals provide answers to HR questions via computer or phone.
Requirements: Must have at least 10 years experience, a functional HR specialty, the ability to network into company systems, and the ability to work on an independent basis under strict deadlines (within two hours of receiving questions). Register for employment on the company Web site.
Provisions: Pays per response.

INDIAN JEWELERS SUPPLY
2105 San Mateo Blvd. NE, Albuquerque, NM 87110
Positions: Jewelry making. There are currently seven home workers.
Requirements: Must be local resident.

INFORMATION TECHNOLOGIES
www.inft.net
Positions: This is one of the largest collectors and compilers of public records such as tax liens, and bankruptcies in the country. They specialize in collecting information on financially distressed individuals and companies. Services are provided by home-based court abstractors/data collectors in various regions around the nation.
Requirements: You qualify if you are currently collecting tax lien or judgment information from any region. Fill out the company's employment form online.

Provisions: All work is conducted electronically. This is an independent contractor position and the pay is based on the quantity of records collected.

IRES

www.iresinc.com

Positions: This executive recruiting firm needs executive recruiters, staffing consultants, healthcare recruiters, science/chemistry recruiters, and personnel research assistants.

Requirements: Requires an above-average personality coupled with a high level of ambition/motivation and good persuasion skills. Prefers people with experience in business sales, management (any area), personnel/human resources, brokerage/financial planning or insurance sales, retail, hospitality, or any other industry experience requiring excellent "people skills." Go to Web site for instructions on how to apply.

JELLYBEAN SERVICES

www.jellybeanservices.com

Positions: This company offers a variety of business services including lead generation, courthouse research, mock juries, telemarketing, appointment setting, recruiting, Web design, and more.

Requirements: Applications are accepted (online) for any type of position, but you can visit the Web site to learn what and where current openings exist. Some positions require certain skills and experience; others do not.

Provisions: Most positions pay twice a month, on the 10th and 25th. Mock jury payments are paid out the day that you serve directly by the client.

JURY INSIGHTS

http://juryinsights.com

Positions: This firm assists attorneys with their cases through mock jury research. There are several types of mock jury projects, including online projects, that vary in terms of the time spent as well as the compensation.

Requirements: Visit the Web site and fill out the online application.

JURYTEST NETWORKS

28 State Street, Suite 1100, Boston, Massachusetts 02109
www.jurytest.com

Positions: This firm performs mock trials online using home-based mock jurors. The summons comes in the form of an e-mail, the juror reviews the lawyer's case, and then provides feedback through an online questionnaire, voice recording, or chatroom deliberations.

Requirements: Register to be a juror online.

Provisions: Pays by the case. You will know how much you will be paid ahead of time and can choose to accept or decline the case. Payments will likely range from between $5 per case to $50 per case for more complicated and involved cases. Payment is provided via PayPal or written check.

JUST ANSWER
www.justanswer.com

Positions: Topic experts are paid to answer questions, offer advice, and generally share valuable experience to businesses and individuals.

Requirements: Apply online. Note that only about 10% of candidates are accepted so fill out your résumé with care.

Provisions: You can choose to work as little or as much as you want. Some experts supplement their income while others work here for their primary income. Experts earn 25% of what a customer is offering for an answer and above average experts earn 50%. Payment is made via PayPal.

K-C PRODUCTS
1600 East 6th Street, Los Angeles, CA 90023

Positions: Sewing vinyl travel bags, garment bags, mattress covers, and appliance covers.Up to 16 home workers are employed.

Requirements: Need ordinary sewing machine. Must live nearby.

Provisions: Pays piece rates.

KNOW BRAINERS
www.knowbrainers.com

Positions: Home-based experts answer questions from individuals in a wide range of subject areas including entertainment, history, science, pet care, parenting, automotive, home contracting, computer help, health, and law.

Requirements: To become an approved expert and qualify to receive payments, become an active member of the community by asking and answering the free questions. Once you do so, send an e-mail to experts at knowbrainers.com to express interest in the approved expert program. Include your KnowBrainers username and relevant information about your professional/academic/personal background.

LEISURE ARTS, INC.
5701 Ranch Rd., Little Rock, AR 72212

Positions: Knitting of outerwear. Currently there are 177 home workers.

Requirements: Must be local resident with experience.

LIVING EARTH CRAFTS

600 E. Todd Rd., Santa Rosa, CA 95407

Positions: Production of several types of crafts. Most work consists of sewing bags, vinyl pieces, sheets, blankets and pad covers.

Requirements: Must own sewing machine. Must live in Santa Rosa. Experience is required.

Provisions: Materials are supplied. Workers are considered regular employees with medical and dental insurance, paid holidays and sick leave. Pays piece rates. Applications are kept on file indefinitely.

MECHANICAL TURKS

www.mturk.com

Positions: Home-based people complete Human Intelligence Tasks (HITs). There are currently over 16,000 HITS available to choose from. All you do is accept the HIT and follow the instructions. When you're done, submit your work.

Requirements: Anyone, anywhere can do this. Register online.

Provisions: After the requester approves your work, money is deposited into your Amazon Payments account.

MIA GYZANDER DESIGN

5427 W. Pico Blvd., Suite 204, Los Angeles, CA 90019
www.miagyzander.com

Positions: Pattern makers, sample makers, cutters, and seamstresses for costume construction and also for the fashion division. This is a fast-moving and creative costume and fashion company.

Requirements: Must be experienced. Local residents only.

Provisions: Part-time and/or full-time on contract basis. Compensation is about $12-$15 an hour depending on how fast you work.

MOUNTAIN LADIES & EWE, INC.

Box 391 Route 7, Manchester Village, VT 05254

Positions: Knitters make ski hats and sweaters. Products are sold both retail and wholesale. Currently has 25 permanent home workers.

Requirements: Prefers workers that live within a 60-mile radius of Manchester Village. Must own knitting machine. Pick up and delivery of supplies and finished work is required of each knitter.

Provisions: Specific training is provided. All supplies are provided. Pays production rates, but workers are considered regular employees and receive basic benefits provided by law. Inquiries are welcome from qualified applicants.

MOYER PARALEGAL SERVICES

245 Portage Trail Extension West, Unit 2, Cuyahoga Falls, OH 44223

Positions: This paralegal service provides virtual support services for attorneys including mobile notary services.

Requirements: Apply online.

NATIONAL BACKGROUND SCREENING

P.O. Box 744 Lancaster, OH 43130

www.nationalbackgroundscreening.com

Positions: Applications are accepted from independently contracted court researchers and verifiers in most states. Court researchers regularly conduct felony and misdemeanor criminal and on occasion, civil judgment and lien searches. Verifiers conduct employment, educational and professional reference verifications.

Requirements: Researchers and verifiers must successfully complete the online questionnaire designed to test knowledge and experience in public record research, judicial process and/or interview skills. Researchers must be able to physically visit the courthouse in the assigned county and conduct an "on-site" search.

Provisions: Fees are negotiable based upon volume and paid bi-weekly.

OFFICE DETAILS

www.officedetails.com

Positions: Office Details is always accepting applications from self-motivated individuals seeking to work as independent contractors in the virtual assistance and concierge industry. All work is completed via the Internet, e-mail, fax, phone, and other forms of virtual communication.

Requirements: A minimum of five years of proven experience as an administrative or concierge professional is required. Candidates who are experienced virtual assistants or freelancers will be given priority consideration. Required skills include superior attention to detail, organization, excellent verbal and writing skills, and proficiency in Microsoft and Adobe software applications. Must have your own fully equipped office. E-mail résumé to contractor@officedetails.com.

OPUZZ VOICE

www.opuzzvoice.com

Positions: This firm connects clients to more than 300 voice-over professionals all over the world. Everything is done virtually (online) from auditioning to delivering completed recording projects.

Requirements: Anyone can try this—it's open to anyone from anywhere in the world. Simply sign up online and submit your auditions for customers from around the globe.

Provisions: Set your own rates.

PIONEER STAFFING

www.pioneerstaffing.com

Positions: This staffing firm specializes in the restaurant industry. They hire contract recruiters, on-call virtual assistants, and researchers.

Requirements: In order to be considered for employment at Pioneer, your home office must be properly configured and meet certain home office requirements. Check the Web site. Register on the Web site to submit your résumé and you will receive e-mail updates as openings become available.

Provisions: Offers competitive pay and a wide array of employee benefits.

PROBATE.COM

2435 South Ridgewood Avenue, South Daytona, FL 32119

www.probate.com

Positions: This legal firm hires researchers from all over the country to visit courts to check probate cases in which the heirs or their addresses are unknown.

Requirements: No experience necessary. Visit the Web site and fill out the employment form.

Provisions: Pays a finder's fee based upon a percent of net recovery. Also provides supportive material if needed such as brochures, forms, Rolodex cards, and genealogical charts.

RECRUIT ZONE

www.recruitzone.com

Positions: Recruit scouts act as regional consultants for their local high school athletes and coaches.

Requirements: Former athletes and coaches, sales and marketing professionals, or anyone who just loves high school sports is encouraged to explore this unique sports career. Visit the Web site and fill out the scout application online.

Provisions: Offers both full-time or part-time positions, as well as an attractive compensation plan.

RESEARCH PARTICIPANTS INSTITUTE
P.O. Box 541086, Dallas, TX 75354

www.researchparticipants.com

Positions: This firm conducts research projects that pay home-based participants to review presentations and provide opinions through online questionnaires and other measurement instruments.

Requirements: Register online (free). All you need is a computer with a Web browser and access to the Internet. You will be contacted via the e-mail address you register with when you are selected to participate in online projects. Once assigned to a project, you may complete it when it's most convenient for you, as long as your work is complete by the project deadline. Project length(s) can vary from 15 minutes to 2 hours. Anyone over the age of 18 and eligible to work in the United States can participate.

Provisions: All projects that you complete in a given month are paid at the end of that month.

RUTH HORNBEIN SWEATERS
8804 19th Avenue Apt 2, Brooklyn, NY 11214

Positions: Knitting of outerwear. Currently there are only 5 home workers.

Requirements: Must be local resident.

SIGNING SOURCE, INC.
www.signingsource.com

Positions: This is a nationwide signing service that is constantly looking for trained notaries in the mortgage industry who are ready to start immediately.

Requirements: If you have experience or have worked in the real estate market and understand the signing requirements of loan documents then this company can provide work for you. If you are able to receive fax and e-mail docs, let them know as that could increase your business. They will provide whatever software you might need to fulfill a closing on time. Go to the Web site and download the application, fill it out, and fax it to the company.

SOUTHERN GLOVE MFG. CO., INC.
749 AC Little Dr., Newton, NC 28658

Positions: Stitching of gloves. This company has been in business since 1945.

Requirements: Must be local resident.

SUNLARK RESEARCH

www.sunlarkresearch.com

Positions: Sunlark Research provides court research and data collection services to the legal community. They have many types of court researchers gathering various information from the public records available. The information gathered is generally very basic such as names and addresses, which is then entered into database or spreadsheet software, depending on the needs of the client. The amount of work available in a given county depends largely on the population base and growth and mobility of the area. Very small counties (i.e. 10,000 people) may have only one hour of work per month while a very large county (over 1,000,000 population) could keep a fast-working researcher busy for 30-40 hours per week and could even need to be done by a team.

Requirements: Fill out the online application. You can also check the Web site for locations that are currently in need, but they will accept an application from anywhere.

Provisions: Pay is per record with a potential for a raise in just 30-45 days.

TRIAL JURIES

www.trialjuries.com

Positions: This company hires people for online focus groups that realistically assess the strengths and weaknesses of a lawyer's case prior to going to trial.

Requirements: Anyone can participate. By simply signing up online, you will be eligible to receive assignments and be a part of the "virtual juries" that review cases submitted by participating law firms.

Provisions: Your work to review the attorneys' case submissions and answer their questions should take about an hour. In most cases, you'll earn $30. For more complex cases, you'll be paid more. Payments are made via PayPal within a few days of your completion of your work on each case.

UNIQUE ONE

P.O. Box 744, 2 Bayview Street, Camden, ME 04843

Positions: Knitting of sweaters using both wool and cotton yarn for retail shop. Currently has 9 home workers.

Requirements: Must be experienced and be a local resident.

Provisions: Training is provided. If home worker doesn't own a knitting machine, Unique 1 will lease one. Pays piece rates. "Camden is tourist town, so the summer is the best time for us, especially for custom orders."

UNITED DATA NETWORK

98 Anastasia Drive, Carriere, MS 39426

Positions: United Data Network hires court researchers nationwide. A court researcher visits courthouses in their particular area to research and compile data from public records. The research does not require in-depth research. Most is basic data collection of information found on the first two pages of the document itself. Most positions are part-time and on a independent contractor status.

Requirements: Experience is preferred, but not necessary since the company will provide training. You do need to be available to visit the courthouses, have Internet access, be computer literate, have typing skills of at least 35 words a minute, and have programs necessary to access Excel, Word, and PDF documents. Visit the Web site to see which areas are currently hiring and to download an application.

VITAL SIGNING

www.vitalsigning.com/notary.html

Positions: Vital Signing is a nationwide signing service serving the real estate loan market in all 50 states.

Requirements: Visit the Web site and click on your state to learn what the requirements are in your state.

VT AUDIT

www.vtaudit.com

Positions: If you have experience in processing payroll or you have worked with bills of lading in shipping and receiving, you can join this company's team of home-based auditors. Training is provided via Webcast to create workers compensation and/or general liability audits for property and casualty insurance clients nationwide.

Requirements: To be considered for employment, you must have a professional environment at your home, a land line, high-speed Internet via Cable or DSL, and the ability to call a Kansas City, MO telephone number without incurring a monthly bill that is unmanageable for you to cover. Especially need people in Kentucky, Michigan, Illinois, Nevada, Ohio, Massachusetts, Wisconsin, and Colorado. E-mail your résumé to hr@callcenteroptions.com.

WEB TRACER

www.webtracer.com

Positions: WebTracer is an international search firm specializing in the business of locating the current address, telephone number and place of employment of missing debtors.

Requirements: Must have at least one year of experience as a professional skip tracer to be considered for this home-based career opportunity. Go to the Web site to download the application.

WRITE ON RESULTS

10 North Wisner Street, Suite A, Frederick, MD 21701

www.writeonresults.com

Positions: Write On Results is looking for responsible individuals with neat handwriting to assist them with their handwritten direct-mail projects.

Requirements: Must live within a 30-minute drive or less from the office in Frederick, MD, so that you can pick up and drop off materials. Visit the Web site and fill out the application form. You will be contacted with details (only if you live in the area).

Provisions: You can work from home, set your own schedule, and earn extra money.

ZAP JURY

www.zapjury.com

Positions: This firm hires online jurors to deliberate on actual cases and advise lawyers about them. A lawyer for one side or the other, and sometimes lawyers for both sides, will post a case summary on a special Zap Jury Webpage and ask for reactions to the case. Online jurors are sent a list of the new cases as they are posted and there is a page that shows all the open ones. You pick one that interests you or, if none does, you wait until an interesting one comes along. (Sometimes the most interesting thing about a case is the fee for doing it.) After you read the summary, you answer questions posted by the lawyers and submit the answers and any comments you have. There is no obligation to evaluate any cases. How often you do is entirely up to you.

Requirements: Sign up online.

Provisions: Lawyers post the fees they're willing to pay with cases so you know what you'll get before you take the case. Zap Jury only takes 10% of that fee. There are ways to increase your income; see Web site for a complete explanation.

ZAUDER BROTHERS, INC.

10 Henry St., Freeport, NY 11520

Positions: Handwork involved in the manufacture of wigs, toupes, and theatrical makeup. Up to eight home workers are employed here.

Requirements: Must have specific experience with this kind of work. Must be local resident.

OPPORTUNITIES
IN OFFICE SUPPORT POSITIONS

"Desk jobs" are among the fastest growing categories of home-based opportunities. Just about any kind of job that is performed in an office setting can just as easily be done at home. The availability of inexpensive office equipment combined with various phone service options makes it easier now than ever before.

Some companies hire home office workers directly, but many times they are hired through service bureaus. For instance, insurance policies have been typed by home workers for many years. But the insurance companies have nothing to do with the hiring of home typists. Instead, the insurance companies contract with policy processing service bureaus. The service bureaus are responsible for all phases of the policy processing and do all the hiring and training.

Service bureaus are popping up everywhere in the medical transcribing field. Medical transcription is the top of the line of word processing. Not only is it the most financially rewarding of all keyboarding jobs, it is an industry that continues to grow at break neck speed and there are more openings for jobs than most employers can fill. For that reason, working at home is an accepted form of workstyle. Most service bureaus will allow you to work anywhere in the world as long as you are capable of doing the work.

The job of medical transcription involves typing doctors' reports and correspondence from recordings, which are usually accessed via the Internet with a WAV player. Employers often require several years of experience and test applicants to ensure they have a thorough knowledge of medical terminology. To get the necessary background, there are courses available through community college, private vocational schools, and on the Internet. A complete course generally takes from three to six months. But even then, you will need some practice in order to keep up with the 24-hour turnaround time required by most companies. One good way to gain some experience is to sign up with one or more temporary employment agencies. Explain what you're trying to do and ask to be assigned to any medical office jobs that come up.

Foreign language translation is included in this section because so much of the work requires office skills such as word processing, proofreading, typesetting, and transcribing. Again, this is a field handled almost entirely by service bureaus. Most translators work at home and many work for service bureaus located in another state or even another country.

Translation is not a job for amateurs. It requires a high level of proficiency in a foreign language and some bureaus will only hire native language translators. It is also necessary to have special expertise in a given field in order to be able to work with the lingo peculiar to that field. For instance, if you are a translator specializing in the legal field, you would need an understanding of legal terminology not only in English, but in the foreign language as well.

There is a new kind of service bureau that has blossomed since the last edition—the virtual staffing agency. Companies such as Team DoubleClick are able to provide office support services of all kinds, from office administration to business writing, to clients worldwide. They draw from a database of hundreds of workers that will never leave home and never meet the client they're working for. They even get paid online.

A STAT TRANSCRIPTION
5967 Hensel Rd., Port Orange, FL 32127

Positions: Acute care medical transcribers and editors work full-time on hospital transcription.

Requirements: Requires four years experience as a transcriptionist. Need demonstrated ability to transcribe all providers (ESL, accents, fast dictators included). Must be dependable and detail oriented. All shifts are needed including third shift. Must have computer system with Win98, Win2000 Professional, Win ME or Win NT, and Word for Window 95 version 7.0 or Word for Windows 98 version 8.0 or Word 2000. Company utilizes Dictaphone ExText and ExVoice plus TransNet. Must have high-speed Internet access, either cable modem or DSL.

Provisions: Compensation is dependent upon experience and individual contract. Send résumé. Live anywhere nationwide.

ABELSON LEGAL SEARCH
1700 Market Street, Philadelphia, PA 19103
www.abelsonlegalsearch.com

Positions: This is a placement agency serving the legal field. Occasionally has positions that allow for working from home.

Requirements: Must be qualified, experienced, and live in the Philadelphia area. Should have good computer system.
Provisions: Check Web site for opportunities and more information.

ABS MEDICAL TRANSCRIPTION SERVICES
Suite 301 - 2275 Atkins Avenue, Port Coquitlam, BC, Canada V3C 1Y5
www.absmed.com
Positions: Medical transcriptionists work at home throughout Canada.
Requirements: Must be qualified MT with typing speed of 60 wpm or better, at least 2 to 3 years of hospital/radiology experience, and experience in one of the following: General surgery, orthopedics, oncology, cardiology, neurology, or gynecology. Need to have high-speed Internet, MS Word 2000, FTP software, WAV pedal and headphones, and medical dictionaries. Positions *only* open to Canadian residents.

ACCU-DOC
32 Pin Oak Road, Skillman, NJ 08558
www.accu-doc.net
Positions: Medical transcriptionists work from home nationwide. Work is mostly for doctors' offices.
Requirements: Minimum ten years working experience as a transcriptionist. You will need MS Word and FTP software.
Provisions: Starting pay is .08 per 65 characters including spaces.

ACCURAPID TRANSLATION SERVICES, INC.
806 Main St., Poughkeepsie, NY 12603
Positions: Technical translators in all languages. Company specializes in business, engineering and scientific documents.
Requirements: Thorough knowledge of foreign language and English is required. Must also have experience in one of the three specialties. For translators outside the area, a computer and modem is required. Submit résumé, noting areas of technical expertise and type of computer and telecommunications equipment.
Provisions: Pays by the word on most contracts.

ACCUPRO SERVICES
20449 Red Bird St., Spring Hill, KS 66083
Positions: Medical transcriptionists work full-time from home throughout the United States and Canada.
Requirements: Minimum two years experience of hospital transcription in

any specialty. Experience specifically doing hospital discharges and ops for all specialties. You will need a WAV pedal, high-speed Internet access, and FTP software.

Provisions: Company supplies transcription software (MPWord).

ACCU-SCRIPT TRANSCRIPTION SERVICES, INC.
540 N. Lapeer Rd. #394, Lake Orion, Michigan 48362

Requirements: Must have at least 5 years of experience as a transcriptionist in acute care. Must have full library of reference books including the AHDI Book of Style. Submit résumé that includes a list of of platform/transcription systems that you have worked on as well as the areas where you have the most working experience. Need computer with Windows 2000 or higher and Microsoft Word 2000 or higher (transcription platform provided).

Provisions: Pays competitive line rates. Full or part-time. Positions open nationwide.

ACCUSTAT, INC.
W12006 Emer Road, Humbird, Wisconsin 54746

Positions: Hospital transcriptionists work at home nationwide. Work is primarily ER dictation.

Requirements: Minimum three years as a transcriptionist. Must be able to maintain a minimum of 98% accuracy. Need to have Word 98 or higher plus HIPAA compliant computer firewall. Must have high-speed or cable modem.

Provisions: Company provides Lanier NextWAV Player on a "rental basis" for qualified candidates. Pays 10 cents per 62 character line including spaces plus incentive and holiday bonus pay. Transcriptionists here can decide when and how much they will be available to work

ACCUTRAN
3480 N. CR 1100 W., Royal Center, IN 46978
www.accutran.net

Positions: Medical transcriptionists work part-time at home nationwide.

Requirements: Minimum two years experience as a transcriptionist. Need MS Word FTP software, WAV pedal, and e-mail.

Provisions: Pays per 65 character line with spaces.

ACCUTRANZ MEDICAL TRANSCRIPTION SERVICES, INC.
4494 Southside Blvd, Jacksonville, FL 32216

Positions: Medical transcriptionists work from home nationwide doing hospital transcription in all specialties. Full-time acute care MTs transcribe

H&Ps, discharge summaries, consultations, and operative reports.

Requirements: Minimum five years experience as a transcriptionist. Need WP5.1/Corel or Word-based software plus high-speed Internet access.

Provisions: Competitive gross-line rate in WP51 with volume incentive bonuses available.

ACCUWRITE WORD PROCESSING SERVICE
63124 Alderton Rd., Flushing, NY 11374

Positions: Medical transcription, legal transcription, and word processing.

Requirements: Medical transcription requires accuracy and experience as well as the ability to understand different accents. Requires an PC with Word Perfect and micro/standard transcribing machine. Legal transcription requires experience with depositions and hearings. Word processing is for manuscripts such as books and technical articles, mailing lists and personalized letters. Must have strong Word Perfect experience and skill in addition to own equipment. Must be from surrounding area to get to the office for pick-up and drop-off. Send résumé.

ACTION TRANSLATION & INTERPRETATION BUREAU
7825 W. 101St., Palos Hills, IL 60465

Positions: Foreign language translators work in all languages and subjects.

Requirements: Thorough knowledge of both foreign language and English is required. Some particular area of expertise is also necessary. Residents in Northern Illinois only. Submit résumé and references.

ADEPT WORD MANAGEMENT
P.O. Box 710438, Houston, TX 77271

Positions: Legal and medical transcription. All specialties available.

Requirements: Must have experience or have completed the SUM program. Knowledge of Word Perfect required. Local residents only.

Provisions: Pays by the line.

AD-EX WORLDWIDE
1733 Woodside Rd., # 115, Redwood City, CA 94061

Positions: Translators and some technical writers for translation of technical, sales, and legal documents, as well as literature, into any major language, or from other language into English. Word processors and typesetters also used, but only those with foreign language expertise. Work is sent via the US mail, Federal Express, or electronically.

Requirements: Only experienced, skilled professionals will be considered. Must be versed in one or more industrial, scientific, technical, military, or bio-med fields. Knowledge of foreign language is secondary, but must be thorough. Need word processor. Send résumé and work sample.

Provisions: Payment methods vary. 90% of staff works at home. Average 10 to 40 workers a day.

ADVANCE LANGUAGE STUDIOS
500 N Michigan Ave., #538, Chicago, IL 60610

Positions: Translators and typesetters with foreign language expertise work in all languages and subjects.

Requirements: Experienced local translators only. Submit résumé and references.

ALDERSON REPORTING
1111 14th St. NW, Suite 400, Washington, DC 20005

Positions: Scopist proofreaders (legal transcribers) working from audiotape cassettes to written transcripts.

Requirements: Must type 80 wpm minimum or 15 pages per hour. Need excellent vocabulary and spelling skills in variety of industries, including legal, educational, medical, and government. Solid PC skills, attention to detail, accuracy, and ability to meet deadlines required. Experience preferred. Local residents send résumé.

Provisions: Part-time or full-time hours available with flexible day or evening shifts.

ALL PURPOSE TYPING SERVICE
1550 McDonald Ave. #202, Brooklyn, NY 11230

Positions: Word processing on Word Perfect module (not character set) in Russian, Hebrew, and Arabic. Work is on reports, theses, etc.

Requirements: Must know database Paradox. Experience and skill required. Send résumé.

Provisions: Offers sizable contracts (over 100 pages).

ALL TYPE, INC.
2202 Route 130, North Brunswick, NJ 08902
www.alltype.net

Positions: Medical transcriptionists work from home nationwide doing work for hospitals, clinics, and doctors' offices.

Requirements: Minimum four years experience required. Must have high-

speed Internet access. Visit Web site and fill out online application.
Provisions: Pays $40,000+ per year plus comprehensive benefits package for the full-time employees. Equipment is provided along with 24/7 technical support. Training is provided remotely and in NJ office with hourly training fee plus travel. Benefits include: direct deposit for paychecks, health insurance, dental coverage and prescription plan, accrued paid time off annually, continuing education financial assistance, funding for CMTs to maintain their certification, and 401(k) savings plan.

ALLIED INTERPRETING & TRANSLATING SERVICE
320 N. Alta Vista Blvd., Los Angeles, CA 90036
Positions: Foreign language translation of legal and medical documents. All languages.
Requirements: Certification required. Los Angeles residents only. Apply with résumé.

ALL-LANGUAGE SERVICES, INC.
77 W 55th St., New York, NY 10017
Positions: Translators handle legal, technical, financial, medical, and engineering documents.
Requirements: Prefers native language translators. Prefers New York residents because some projects require coming into headquarters. Résumé and references required.
Provisions: Pay methods vary according to assignment.

AMERICAN TRANSCRIPTION SOLUTIONS, INC.
4400 140th Avenue North, Suite 100, Clearwater, Florida 33762
Positions: Medical transcriptionists with at least 3 years experience work from home nationwide. Clinic transcription needed most, but the company does many types of transcription.
Requirements: Need Windows XP or later, Microsoft Word 2000 or later, and ATSI Platform. Must be comfortable with ESL dialects. Testing is required. Visit testing site at http://atsi.mttest.com.
Provisions: All transcriptionists start out as independent contractors, but may elect employee status after 90 days. At that point, generous benefits are offered to full-time employees including medical/dental, paid time off, and direct deposit.

AQUARICON

1925 Eastlake Ave E, Apt 205, Seattle WA 98102
http://aquaricon.com

Positions: Data entry. Job involves purchasing used books (using company money) at thrift stores and book sales, enter data about the books into database, and ship them to buyers daily. Everything is paid for, no investment is required.

Requirements: Live in any large city. Need computer, printer and Internet connection. Data entry speed and accuracy test will be given. Must be available 20 hours per week during weekdays. Must purchase at least 150 books per week.

Provisions: You are paid a fee of $1 for each book purchased, and 50 cents for each book shipped, as an independent contractor. This translates into approximately $15 to $20 per hour depending on your data entry and organizational skills. No need to report to an office, all work is done at home or in stores. Visit Web site for more information.

ATHENS REGIONAL HEALTH SERVICES

1199 Price Ave., Athens, GA 30606

Positions: Medical transcriptionists.

Requirements: Must have high school diploma or GED and typing speed of at least 65 wpm. Medical terminology helpful. Need some knowledge of word processing and dictating equipment. Send résumé.

Provisions: Several shifts available, including Saturdays.

AT-HOME PROFESSIONS

2001 Lowe Street, Fort Collins, CO 80525
www.at-homeprofessions.edu
(800) 359-3455

Positions: At-Home Professions is a unique institution established in 1981. It is accredited by the Distance Education and Training Council (DETC) in Washington, DC. At Home Professions offers accredited training in Professional Medical Transcription. The school's training methods utilize at-home study and can be completed at the student's own pace.

Requirements: Applicants must be a high school graduate, hold a GED, or pass an admissions test. Tuition can be paid as-you-go with no interest. The school is approved for military education benefits as well as SLM Financing.

Provisions: In addition to providing quality training programs and course materials, this organization also includes great follow-up services. At-Home Professions provides their graduates with personal counseling in job search techniques as well as continuing on-the-job support.

Close up: At-Home Professions

As you look through this chapter, it's obvious there is a great need for medical transcriptionists. You'll also notice the job requires knowledge and skill.

So how do you take advantage of such a large, growing opportunity? One option is by learning at home with At-Home Professions. The home study course was designed by people experienced in the field and can be completed in about four to six months. The school is accredited by the Distance Education and Training Council in Washington, DC. Graduates of At-Home Professions boasts about the quality of education as well as the success in gaining employment. Graduates obtain lifetime access to the Graduate Services Department that assists with résumé preparation, interview skills, and job search strategies. However many graduates say they never required assistance because once the skills are in place, getting the work is easy.

Two years ago, Joanie Radtke decided she wanted to have a career where she could work from home and make money. With two small children at home, she knew she needed to find something that would be rewarding while providing a flexible work schedule. Knowing she had already invested time and money in a previous college degree and was unable to find work in her field, she was cautious about making the same mistake twice.

She had heard about medical transcriptionists working from home but thought "working from home and getting paid a decent salary sounded just too good to be true." She was a busy stay-at-home wife and mother who needed to fit training around her other priorities.

After hearing a commercial on the radio advertising At-Home Professions' distance-learning program, Joanie knew it was a sign that she needed to attend the free one-hour information session near her home. She was excited about what she heard at the seminar and thought "It sounded great!" She took all of the information home and reviewed the course materials, as well as researched potential salary and career demand for medical transcriptionists. It met all of her requirements and she enrolled a month later. Joanie felt the course more than prepared her to succeed as a medical transcriptionist. It was "well laid out and was so interesting, it really kept my attention."

Shortly before graduation, Joanie was offered a position with a local medical clinic. Today she is living her dream and working from home. "I love the fact that I am making a great contribution to my family's income and am able to stay home and raise my children at the same time. I love this job!"

AXION DATA SERVICES

800 Bursca Dr., Suite 804, Bridgeville, PA 15017

www.axiondata.com/employreq.htm

Positions: Company uses home-based data entry contractors to provide a wide range of data entry and data enhancement services to business clients.

Requirements: Must be competent PC user with high-speed Internet access. Refer to Web site for detailed requirements.

Provisions: Pays on a per-piece basis. Each project is different, varying in complexity. For some projects, the amount of data to be entered is small and people are able to input anywhere from 2-4 forms per minute. Compensation for these projects ranges from 4-8 cents per form. Other projects are complex, requiring 30-60 minutes per document, with compensation ranging from $5-9 per document. All contractors working on the same project are paid the same per-piece rate. Pays every 2 weeks.

BERLITZ TRANSLATION SERVICE

180 Montgomery Street, #1580, San Francisco, CA 94104

Positions: Berlitz is a huge translation bureau with offices all over the country and in 23 foreign countries as well. Freelance translators in all languages work in all subject areas.

Requirements: Thorough knowledge of foreign language and English required. Only experienced translators are considered. Can live anywhere, but for those not near a Berlitz office, a computer and modem are required. Make note of equipment type on résumé.

Provisions: Pays by the word.

BLESSING HOSPITAL

1005 Broadway, Quincy, IL 62301

Positions: Medical transcribers.

Requirements: Minimum three years experience required. Must have own equipment. Local residents only may apply.

BLUE RIDGE TEA AND HERB LTD.

26 Woodhull St., Brooklyn, NY 11231

Positions: Stuffing envelopes.

Requirements: Need intelligent (common-sense) people to stuff envelopes of different classifications for shows and conventions. Must report daily. Vehicle necessary for loading of boxes.

BON TEMPS

15 Maiden Lane, New York, NY 10038

www.bontempsny.com

Positions: This is a temporary placement agency that occasionally places home-based word processors, paralegals, proofreaders, and other clerical support workers in the legal industry. Serves New York City and the surrounding area. Visit the Web site to check current needs.

CAPTION COLORADO

www.captioncolorado.com

Positions: Caption Colorado, which has been one of the largest providers of real-time captioning in the US since 1991, now employs over 100 stenocaptioners across the country to handle the captioning of local news for over 100 television stations in 25 major cities. Also provides captioning for sporting events, large stadium events, satellite conferences, internet broadcasting, stock quarterly reporting, and churches. Several types of position are available: full-time and part-time, morning and evening, and weekend and weekday. Captioners work into full-time positions as work becomes available. Starting part-time is mandatory for new real-time captioners. Time is needed to refine skills and to reduce the error rate to 1% or less before acquiring more work.

Requirements: See Web site for detailed requirements and to obtain application.

Provisions: Pays competitive rates plus a benefits package including health, dental, vision, disability, life, flexible dependent and spending accounts, and 401k.

CARONDELET HEALTH NETWORK, ST. MARY'S HOSPITAL

1601 W. St. Mary's Road, Tucson, AZ 85745

Positions: Medical transcription.

Requirements: Must live in Tucson area. Apply in person.

Provisions: Full-time and part-time opportunities exist for both highly trained transcribers and entry level applicants with desires to get into the health care field on the ground floor. For the latter, there is training available (this is highly unusual). Income potential up to $40,000 per year.

CENTRAL DATA PROCESSING

603 Twinridge Lane, Richmond, VA 23235

Positions: Data entry for permanent part-time.

Requirements: PC operators must be able to enter data on a tight time

schedule (24-48 hours turn-around). Must be able to give 25-35 hours per week, be responsible for 4 to 5 hours per day unsupervised, and be able to do weekend work. Keyboarding speed must be a minimum of 60 wpm. Need home phone, car and flexibility to pick up and take work home (10 - 11:30 a.m., 2 to 5 times per week). Must live within 20 to 25 minutes of office.
Provisions: Pays $8 per hour. Will train in office, so no experience is necessary. PC is furnished or you can use your own.

CERTIFIED TRANSLATION BUREAU, INC.
2778 E. Gage Ave., Huntington Park, CA 90255
Positions: Foreign language translators for all subjects.
Requirements: Experienced translators only; any language. Apply with résumé and references.

CHILDREN'S HOSPITAL
4800 Sand Point Way NE, Seattle, WA 98105
Positions: Medical transcription of dictated medical and surgical reports from all specialty clinics and hospital service for the permanent hospital medical record.
Requirements: Must have multi-specialty hospital transcription experience, and advanced, highly accurate, and rapid typing skills. Excellent knowledge of spelling, grammar, and medical terminology, as well as a good working knowledge of Word Perfect, MS Word, and the use of electronic communications are required. A high level of attention to detail is also necessary. Local, qualified applicants should send résumé and cover letter.

CHRONICLE TRANSCRIPTS, INC.
815 West Avenue J, Lancaster, CA 93534
www.CTiMed.com
Positions: Medical transcriptionist needed nationwide.
Requirements: Minimum five years experience as a transcriptionist.
Provisions: Full-time positions available. Competitive pay based on 65 cpl including spaces. Health and PTO benefits for full-time employees. Pay is by direct deposit. Submit online application at www.ctimed.com/careers/careerapp.aspx.

CLAIM NET, INC.
9 Corporate Park, Irvine, CA 92606
Positions: Claim Net is a temporary employment agency specializing in placing medical claims personnel since 1983.

Requirements: Two years minimum experience processing medicals is required. Local residents submit résumé.

Provisions: Full-time and part-time positions available.

CLERICAL PLUS
97 Blueberry Ln., Shelton, CT 06484

Positions: Data entry, word processing, and transcription.

Requirements: Must own PC and have and be adept at WordPerfect, Word, MultiMate, and MSWord.Transcription work is usually medical. For that, you will need a micro tape transcriber and experience. Must be local resident. Submit résumé.

CLICKNWORK
http://clicknwork.com

Positions: This is a homesourcing service bureau that's been around since 2000. Outsources home-based analysts, researchers, information specialists, and generalists—phone interviewers, writers, trendspotters, mystery shoppers, data entry specialists, translators, and more. Especially interested in recruiting ready-to-work teams and their managers.

Requirements: Must be highly experienced and proficient in your field. Turnover is understandably low, but you are encouraged to "register" by submitting a résumé online anyway. This is ad hoc work so projects will be sporatic.

Provisions: Pays via PayPal.

COMMONWEALTH TRANSCRIPTION SYSTEMS
P.O. Box 592, Saybrook, CT 06475

Positions: Transcriptionists/typists. Work types assigned by skill level.

Requirements: Need minimum 2 years transcription experience and excellent computer skills. Send résumé.

Provisions: Flexible schedules and competitive earning potential.

COMPUTER SECRETARY
300 W. Peachtree NW, Suite 11H, Atlanta, GA 30308

Positions: Word processing, legal and medical transcription.

Requirements: Must own PC or Mac with Word Perfect and Lotus 1,2,3. Experience and good skills required. Local residents send résumé.

CONTINENTAL TRANSLATION SERVICE, INC.

501 5th Ave. # 1400, New York, NY 10017

Positions: Freelance translators handle technical manuals, legal documentation, marketing projects, and medical transcription in most foreign languages.

Requirements: Thorough knowledge of foreign language and English required. Must have expertise in one of the areas mentioned above. Submit résumé. Prefers New York residents.

Provisions: Pay methods vary.

CORLESS & ASSOCIATES

1904 West Cass Street, Tampa FL 33606

www.corlessassociates.com

Positions: Attorneys in State and Federal litigation fields deal with disputes over construction law, personal injury, insurance coverage, mold, and products liability. Work in virtual office environment.

Requirements: Three to five years experience preferred, with scientific and medical background a plus. Tampa residents only.

COSMOPOLITAN TRANSLATION BUREAU, INC.

53 W. Jackson Blvd., Suite 1260, Chicago, IL 60604

Positions: Cosmopolitan is a very old translation bureau that handles all languages and subjects.

Requirements: Native translators are preferred, but will consider translators with absolute knowledge of a foreign language and good English skills. Must have a particular area of expertise for the terminology of that field (such as legal or medical). Chicago translators only. Submit résumé and references.

CPR TECHNOLOGIES TRANSCRIPTION SERVICE

25129 The Old Road #303, Stevenson Ranch, CA 91381

Positions: Medical transcription.

Requirements: Prefers local residents. Must have minimum 2 years recent acute care experience with ESL doctors expeirence. Send résumé as an attached MSWord document or as formatted e-mail text to: employment@cpr-tech.com. Pre-employment screening tests are required.

Provisions: Provides an MT-friendly software interface and 24-hour technical support. Offers competitive salaries with room for growth, shift differential pay for the weekends, payroll direct deposit, and colleague referral bonuses. Each MT is assigned to one hospital account, so they have the opportunity to grow and learn the dictators on the account. "CPR Technologies is always looking for dedicated, dependable transcriptionists to join our team."

CPS MEDTEXT
58 Sprucewood Dr., Levittown, NY 11756

Positions: Medical transcribers.

Requirements: Must be a well-seasoned pro with own equipment. Local residents only mail résumé.

DEVENTURE HEALTH PARTNERS
Offices in Ohio and California

www.deventure.biz

Positions: Highly skilled medical transcriptionists and voice recognition editors work nationwide. The company handles all kinds of medical transcription so any specialty is welcome.

Requirements: Applicants must have Windows XP and Word 2000 (or greater), minimum of 512 MB of RAM, and 9 pin foot pedal. Apply online.

Provisions: Offers very competitive line rates and a comprehensive benefits package to full-time employees including 6 paid holidays, 2 weeks of PTO, paid training, production incentives, annual bonuses, health, dental, optical, life, short-term and long-term disability insurance, and company sponsored 401k plan. Additional benefits include a bi-weekly payroll with direct deposit offered, support staff available 24/7, and a high volume of work.

DION DATA SOLUTIONS
3775 EP True Pkwy. Suite 281, West Des Moines, IA 50265

www.diondatasolutions.net/opportunities.htm

Positions: This is a full service data management service bureau with a home-based staff.

Requirements: Must type at least 60 wpm with accuracy and possess excellent verbal and written communication skills. You will need computer skills including Internet, e-mail, e-mail attachments, downloading and uploading files, etc. Your home office must be equipped with a PC (desktop) and stable Internet connection. Applications are accepted via e-mail only: ddsapps@diondatasolutions.com

Provisions: All training and programs provided at no cost.

DLM BUSINESS SOLUTIONS
12138 Central Ave., Mitchellville, MD 20721

Positions: This virtual assistant company handles word processing, desktop publishing, résumé service, writing/editing, Web design/hosting, Internet research, and event planning.

Requirements: Experience is required. Must have your own computer equipment and proper home office setup. E-mail dlmbus@onebox.com for application.

277

DOMENICHELLI BUSINESS SERVICES

302 Ventura Street, Ludlow, MA 01056

www.moderndayscribe.com

Positions: Hires medical, legal, and general transcriptions nationwide. All work is done via virtual network.

Requirements: High school education, two years of transcription experience, and strong virtual communications skills. Must be able to complete (transcribe and self-proof) a minimum of one hour of audio daily. Only candidates with proficiency in MSWord and whose home offices are equipped with Start-Stop or WAV pedal digital transcription systems *and* standard-size tape transcribers will be considered. FTP capabilities are also required. Forward résumé and/or visit Web site.

DTS AMERICA, INC.

750 Old Hickory Blvd, Nashville, TN 37201

Positions: Medical transcription and proofreading.

Requirements: Only local applicants with a minimum of three years experience as transcriptionists will be considered. Send résumé.

DWH OFFICE SERVICES

101 Brightside Ave., Pikesville, MD 21208

Positions: Word processors and transcribers.

Requirements: Must own PC with Word Perfect plus standard and micro transcribing equipment. Skills and experienced required. Only local residents will be considered. Mail résumé.

EASTERN MAIL & DATA PROCESSING, INC.

3253 Route 112, Medford, NY 11763

Positions: Data entry.

Requirements: Must have production-quality work. Need PC with adequate hard drive. Must be highly qualified and test for 10,000 keystrokes with alpha and numeric experience. Local residents only send résumé.

Provisions: Company provides software and training for three days only. Turnaround time for finished work will be between 24 and 72 hours.

EASTERN CONNECTICUT HEALTH NETWORK, INC.

71 Haynes St., Manchester, CT 06040

Positions: Medical transcription.

Requirements: Previous medical transcription experienced required. Strong knowledge of anatomy, physiology, and medical terminology required. CMT preferred. Area residents only send résumé.

Provisions: Various full-time and part-time shifts available. Offers salary with benefits package.

EDiX CORPORATION
4445 Eastgate Mall, San Diego, CA 92121

Positions: Medical transcription.

Requirements: Minimum three years acute care hospital transcription experience required. Also need a commitment to quality work and an extensive medical terminology background. Apply with résumé.

Provisions: Pays competitive salary and excellent benefits.

ELMHURST MEMORIAL HEALTHCARE
855 N. Church Rd., Elmhurst, IL 60126

Positions: Full and part-time medical transcribers.

Requirements: Experience is required and specific experience working in radiology is preferred. Local applicants only send résumé.

Provisions: To work at home, you must be qualified to work without supervision.

EMPLOYEE BENEFIT SERVICES, INC.
6235 Morrison Boulevard, Charlotte, NC 28211

Positions: Claims processors.

Requirements: Experience is preferred, but not required. Send résumé and salary requirements. Local residents only.

ETRANSPLUS
2525 Perimeter Place Drive, Nashville, Tennessee 37214
www.etransplus.com

Positions: Transcriptionists with any specialty are welcome to apply, but hospital transcriptionists are especially needed. Can live anywhere.

Requirements: Requires 2 years experience.

Provisions: Pays $500 sign-on bonus to full-time MTs. Offers flexible schedules, steady accounts, highly competitive wages paid bi-monthly, 24/7 technical support, production based bonuses, medical coverage (Blue Cross/Blue Shield), vision and dental coverage, Rx, life and AD7D long term disability, 9 PTO Days per year, and direct deposit.

EVERETT CLINIC

3901 Hoyt Avenue, Everett, WA 98201

Positions: Medical transcription.

Requirements: Minimum two years experience in a multi-specialty or hospital environment required. Local residents send résumé.

Provisions: Offers 40 hours per week, flexible shifts, telecommuting, with daily tape pickup at main campus in Everett.

EXCELLENCE TRANSLATION SERVICE

P.O. Box 5863, Presidio of Monterey, Monterey, CA 93940

Positions: Foreign language translators for general and technical documentation. All languages.

Requirements: Thorough knowledge of foreign language and English required. Can live anywhere in California. Submit résumé and references.

EXECUTIVE OFFICE SERVICES

120 Bannon Ave., Buchanan, NY 10511

Positions: Word processors, data entry, and medical transcribers.

Requirements: Need PC with Word Perfect for word processing, plus database for data entry and for medical transcription, a micro/standard transcribing machine. Skills and experience is required for any position. Must be local resident. Send résumé.

EXPEDICT

www.expedict.co.uk/workfaq.php

Positions: Home-based typists and audio transcribers work all over the world so that the company can provide a 24/7 service to clients.

Requirements: PC and high-speed Internet. Apply online.

FEDERATION OF THE HANDICAPPED

52 Duane St. #26, New York, NY 10014

Positions: The Federation operates the Home Employment Program (HEP) for homebound disabled workers only. Within HEP there is a typing/transcription department.

Requirements: All positions here require evaluation through lengthy interviews and personal counseling. All workers must live in New York City.

Provisions: The workshop provides training plus any extra help necessary to overcome any unusual problems an individual might have. Pick up and delivery of supplies and finished work is provided regularly. Necessary equipment is provided. Pays piece rates. Disability insurance counseling is provided.

FUTURENET TECHNOLOGIES CORP.
222 E. Huntington Dr., #208, Monrovia, CA 91016
www.futurenet-tech.com
Positions: Medical transcriptionists and medical editors.
Requirements: Requires 5 years experience. FutureNet software provided. PC with Windows 98 or better required. Send résumé via snail mail ONLY.
Provisions: Flexible scheduling. Can live anywhere. Pays competitive line rate and generous bonus program.

GARRETT TRANSCRIPTION SERVICE
8460 Rippled Creek Court, Springfield, VA 22153
Positions: Medical transcription.
Requirements: Experienced transcribers only with expertise on Word Perfect. Springfield residents only. Send résumé.

GLOBAL LANGUAGE SERVICES
2027 Las Lunas, Pasadena, CA 91107
Positions: Foreign language translators of general and technical documents. All languages.
Requirements: Prefers native language translators, but will consider certified translators. Some special area of expertise is required. Submit résumé.

GLOBESPAN MEDICAL, INC.
16870 West Bernardo Dr. Suite 400, San Diego, CA 92127
www.globespanmedical.com
Positions: Highly skilled medical transcriptionists and editors work nationwide using voice recognition.
Requirements: Minimum 5 years experience as transcriptionist. Must be US resident. Transcription testing is required as part of the application process. High-speed DSL or cable Internet services only, wav player (Express Scribe, etc), foot pedal, and Microsoft Word are required. Company provides DocShuttle software (DocShuttle experience is a plus). FTP experience is also a plus. E-mail résumé (visit Web site for instructions).
Provisions: Full-time and part-time positions available for all shifts (company works 24/7). Pays $0.04 cpl. Payments will be made by direct deposit.

GUARD INSURANCE GROUP
16 South River St., Wilkes-Barre, PA 18703
Positions: Claims representative for Worker's Compensation carrier. Job entails performing investigations, gathering information and handling litigation files.

Requirements: Minimum 4 years experience working on Worker's Compensation claims in the state of Pennsylvania specifically. Local, qualified applicants send résumé and cover letter.
Provisions: Pays salary plus full benefits.

HART SYSTEMS, INC.

60 Plant Ave., Hauppauge, NY
Positions: Data entry.
Requirements: Must be local for daily drop-off. Call for interview.
Provisions: Training program provided.

SPHERIS ECHART

21670 Ridgetop Cir. # 100, Sterling, VA 20164
Positions: Spheris eChart is a national medical transcription company.
Requirements: Minimum three years medical transcription experience. Apply with résumé.
Provisions: Pays excellent salary with full benefits.

HIGHLAND PARK HOSPITAL

718 Glenview Ave., Highland, IL 60035
Positions: Medical transcribers. This is a new and small operation and opportunities are limited.
Requirements: Minimum three years experience required. Must have proper equipment. Local residents only.

HIRECHECK

805 Executive Center Drive West, Suite 300, St. Petersburg, FL 33702
www.hirecheck.com
Positions: Background checkers for employment screening service. These are non-criminal searches. Job involves calling past employers, maintaining paperwork and documentation, data entry, and processing of information.
Requirements: Requires previous customer service experience, typing speed of 45 wpm, computer and Internet skills, and above average telephone skills. You will also need to have a total of three separate phone lines, a computer, high-speed Internet access, a fax machine, and a telephone with voice mail. Must be able to perform 20 searches a day. Applicants will need to come to the St. Petersburg office for one week of unpaid training.
Provisions: Pays $2.50 for each completed search.

JOHN HANCOCK MUTUAL LIFE INSURANCE CO.

P.O. Box 111 Boston, MA 92117

Positions: Underwriting.

Requirements: Qualifications include nursing/medical background, minimum two years underwriting experience, ability to meet high productivity standards, with superior communication, organizational, and analytical skills, attention to detail, flexibility, motivation, and ability to adapt to dynamic environment. Proficiency in computer software is essential. Send résumé.

ILLINOIS HOSPITAL JOINT VENTURES

1151 Warrenville, Naperville, IL 60601

Positions: Medical transcribers.

Requirements: Must be local resident. Extensive experience is required. Must own necessary equipment.

Provisions: Pays piece rates.

IMEDX

P.O. Box 1153, South Point, OH 45680

www.imedx.com

Positions: Medical transcriptionists and QA editors work nationwide at home as independent contractors.

Requirements: Minimum 5 years as a transcriptionist in any specialty. Get online application at www.imedx.mttest.com

Provisions: Software provided. Pay based upon abilities. Pays by the line.

INLINGUA TRANSLATION SERVICE

8950 Villa La Jolla Dr., #2110, La Jolla, CA 92037

Positions: Inlingua is a major translation bureau with more than 200 offices all over the world. Freelance translators handle legal, business, and medical documentation in all languages.

Requirements: A thorough knowledge of foreign language and English is required. Submit résumé and note special areas of expertise.

Provisions: Pays by the word.

INTERNATIONAL LANGUAGE & COMMUNICATIONS CENTERS, INC.

79 W. Monroe, Suite 1310, Chicago, IL 60603

Positions: Freelance translators handle business documents.

Requirements: Must be expert in a foreign language and English.

Experience working with business documents is required. Requires translators with own computers. Must live in the Chicago area. Submit résumé and references.

INTERNATIONAL TRANSLATION BUREAU
125 West 4th, Los Angeles, CA 90013

Positions: Foreign language translators for general documentation. All major languages.

Requirements: Experienced translators only. Prefers to work with Los Angeles area residents. Submit résumé and references.

INTREP SALES PARTNERS
P.O. Box 75, Franklin Park, NJ 08823

Positions: Company offers virtual services including appointment setting, lead generation, list acquisition, script development, administrative support, and database management.

Requirements: If you have experience in any of the above-mentioned areas, send résumé.

KAISER PERMANENTE MEDICAL GROUP
27400 Hesperian Blvd., Hayward, CA 94545

Positions: Financial analysts.

Requirements: College degree in business administration, economics, health care administration, operations research, or public health administration. An MBA would be ideal. Minimum four years experience as a financial analyst with at least one year in health care. Strong skills in the Microsoft Office environment is necessary and mainframe programming experience is preferred. Bay area residents only send résumé.

Provisions: Pays salary plus excellent benefits.

KELLER'S MEDICAL TRANSCRIPTION SERVICE
6475 Camden Ave # 102A, San Jose, CA 95120

Positions: Medical transcription.

Requirements: Clinic or hospital experience required. Local applicants send résumé.

Provisions: Flexible scheduling.

KEY FOR CASH
www.keyforcash.com

Positions: Data entry.

Requirements: Must be at least 18 years old live in one of the continental 48 states, and legally be able to work in the United States. Requires a computer, Internet connection, and JavaScript-enabled Web browser. Go to the Web site and sign up (free). Note that there is a waiting list.

Provisions: Can live (and work) anywhere in the lower 48. You can work as much or as little as you want, at whatever time of day you want. Pay is based on how much you do. There is a waiting list here, so it may take a few months to actually get work.

LAKE REGIONAL HEALTH SYSTEM
5816 Highway 54, Osage Beach, MO 65065

Positions: Medical transcribers for not-for-profit healthcare institution.

Requirements: Typing speed of at least 60 wpm, transcription experience using medical in large medical setting, thorough knowledge of medical terminology, and good communication and organizational skill. Must have word processing and dictation equipment. Local transcribers send résumé.

Provisions: You can work at home after completing in-house training.

LANGUAGES UNLIMITED
11250 Roger Bacon Dr., Reston, VA 20190

Positions: Freelance translators work in all languages on documentation for international businesses.

Requirements: Must be very experienced in foreign language translation and in working with business documents such as patents, taxes, or finance. Submit résumé and references.

LEAPLAW
Velawcity Inc., 20B Milliston Road, Suite 169,
Millis, MA 02054
www.leaplaw.com

Positions: Independent home-based attorneys work in litigation, corporate, real estate, tax, environmental, employment, and immigration areas. Company is an emerging "knowledge service provider" to the legal industry, located in Metro Southwest Massachusetts. Visit Web site for more information.

LIBRARY OF CONGRESS
National Library Service for the Blind and Physically Handicapped, Washington, DC 20542

Positions: Homebound disabled proofreaders in the Braille Development Section.

Provisions: A training program is available to teach blind people to proofread Braille materials. A certificate is awarded upon completion of the program. Work is farmed out to homebound workers from the Library's production department on a piece rate basis. Number of participants varies.

LEGAL AID OF AMERICA, INC.
www.legalaidofamerica.com

Positions: Paralegals work at home nationwide in major market areas. Work is part-time.

Requirements: Must be familiar with Family Law and/or Bankruptcy (Chapter 7). Litigation and research. A minimum of 3 years experience required in divorce, custody, child support, small claims, and/or expungements and responses. Must have access to legal forms and/or software to prepare documentation. Need fax machine, e-mail address, and Internet access. If interested, please forward a cover letter, résumé, and a sample of previous legal documentation that you have prepared through Web site.

Provisions: Pays $15 per hour.

MD-IT
http://md-it.com/employment.htm

Positions: Company is always interested in qualified, US-based medical transcriptionists with experience in both general and specialty medicine.

Requirements: A minimum of 2 or more years of experience is required. Full-time positions require a minimum 1,000 to 1,200 lines per day. Must be able to work in multiple specialty areas. Need thorough knowledge and practice of AHDI Book of Style. Windows XP or Vista, MS Word 2003 or higher, Internet Explorer 6 or 7, high-speed Internet (no dial-up), up-to-date antivirus software, Express Scribe, medical spell-checker, and text-expansion software. Go to the Web site to complete the online application process. Transcription testing is required as part of the application process. US applicants only—no companies.

Provisions: Full-time positions available nationwide. Offers progressive pay, paid training, semi-monthly direct deposit of paychecks, and full benefit package that includes PTO and holiday pay. Pay is per dictated minute with rate dependent on experience and testing.

MECHANICAL SECRETARY
10816 72nd Ave., Flushing, NY 11375

Positions: Word processors and transcribers. Work covers several areas: medical, legal, insurance, advertising and general business. Currently has 15 home workers and there is a very long waiting list.

Requirements: Must have good skills and own approved equipment; PC with Word Perfect for word processing plus a Dictaphone for transcribing. Experience is required. Send résumé. Must be resident of Manhattan, Brooklyn, or Queens.
Provisions: Pick up and delivery of supplies and finished work is provided. Pays production rates. Full-time work only.

MEDCOMP, INC.
206 N Washington St. # B17, Alexandria, VA 22303
Positions: Medical transcription.
Requirements: Must own computer, printer and phone line for call-in. Medical transcription experience required. Local residents send résumé.
Provisions: Part-time hours available for work-at-home positions.

MEDICAL TRANSCRIPTION SERVICE
4450 Belden Village St., NW #506, Canton, OH 44718
Positions: Medical transcription.
Requirements: Equipment and experience required. Local residents only send résumé.

MEDIFAX, INC.
10003 South Roberts Road Palos Hills, IL 60465
Positions: Medical transcription for emergency department, individual physicians, and hospitals.
Requirements: Looking only for high quality workers in the local area.
Apply online: http://medifax.net/employ1.htm.
Provisions: Pays good rates and offers bonuses. Career advancement opportunities including 3 levels for MTs, trainers, supervisors, and quality assurance specialists are available. Provides comprehensive benefits package for full-time employees including life, dental, and medical coverage.

MED-TECH RESOURCE, INC.
2252 NW Pkwy SE # D, Marietta, GA 30067
Positions: Medical transcription. Active hiring is ongoing for all shifts and work types and for full-time and part-time employees plus those interested in working as independent contractors.
Requirements: Experience required. See other requirements and apply online at www.med-tech.net/requirements.htm.
Provisions: Work from home after training on company's system. Offers full benefits package.

MED/TEXT TRANSCRIPTION
5116 99th St., SW, Mukilteo, WA 98275
Positions: Medical transcription.
Requirements: Two years multi-specialty experience required. Local residents send résumé.
Provisions: Full-time, flexible hours available.

MEDQUIST, INC.
www.medquist.com
Positions: Medical transcribers for all work types, including hospital overflow work; discharge summaries and operative reports. Currently has over 6,000 home workers and 90 offices nationwide, including Los Angeles, San Francisco, Sacramento, Denver, and Chicago. For job opportunities near you, check the Medquist Web site: www.medquist.com.
Requirements: Acute care experience is required. A test in medical terminology is given to all applicants.
Provisions: Online training is available. Choice of part-time or full-time hours is available. Equipment is provided on a rental basis if necessary. Pays production rates that vary depending on the part of the country where you're located. Inquiries are always welcome from qualified transcribers. "MedQuist is always looking for talented individuals to join our team. Our career opportunities include professional, transcription, coding, and support positions."

MEDSCRIBE
3325 Hendricks Ave., Jacksonville, FL 32207
Positions: Nationwide medical transcribing specializing in emergency departments.
Requirements: There is an online screening test and application at www.med-scribe.com. Minimum weekly commitment of 6000 lines*, 1 line = 65 characters incl. spaces, excluding headers and footers. *This is based on a daily commitment with at least 20% of weekly budget being transcribed on Saturday or Sunday.
Provisions: Can work anywhere in the continental United States. Pays competitive line rates, offers weekly line commitments, and premium pay for weekends and holidays. Also provides for continuing education. Schedules can be flexible.

MED-TYPE

SunMark Professional Bldg.,
417 Welshwood Dr., Suite 206, Nashville, TN 37210
www.medical-transcription-company.com

Positions: Medical transcribers for individual, group multi-specialty practices, and hospitals.

Requirements: Experience and proof of quality work is essential. Must be local resident.

MEDWARE

2250 Lucien Way # 305, Maitland, FL 32751

Positions: Medical transcription.

Requirements: Experience in emergency room transcription preferred. Minimum six months to one year of experience in transcription required. Commitment to quality work a must. CMT desired. Must be available for weekend work.

Apply online: www.medwaremt.com/contactus.html.

Provisions: Full and part-time positions available with multiple scheduling options available. Full benefits package offered to remote workers.

METROPOLITAN RESEARCH ASSOCIATES, LLC

305 Madison Avenue, Suite 1240, New York, NY 10165

Positions: Clinical scientists and researchers for supporting clinical trials for the pharmaceutical, biotech, and medical device industries. Jobs entail reviewing clinical trail protocols and providing summary reports with professional recommendations.

Requirements: A complete understanding of the entire clinical research process is first and foremost. Education and several relevant years of experience are required.

Provisions: These are long-term contract positions. Telecommuting is allowed, but only to local residents.

MODERN SECRETARIAL SERVICE

1122 S. Robertson Blvd., #10, Los Angeles, CA 90035

Positions: Word processors. Company specializes in insurance policy typing, but does all types of legal and general work. "We're always looking for good people."

Requirements: Must have good equipment and skills. Test will be given. Los Angeles residents only.

MOUNTAIN WEST PROCESSING

P.O. Box 2044, Missoula, MT 59806

Positions: This company provides coding, audio transcription, and competitive research services to financial institutions, corporations, online businesses, and nonprofit organizations throughout the US. Projects includeinterviews, conversations/statements, manuscripts/books, faxes, audio broadcasts, reports, conferences/seminars/teleseminars, speeches, etc.

Requirements: Must be experienced typist, proficient with MS Word (or Word Perfect if it's a legal position). Need to have or be willing to obtain a digital foot pedal. Must be independent contractor residing in the US. All legal transcription work requires US citizenship. Otherwise, US residency and the right to work here is sufficient. Visit www.mountainwestprocessing.com/page5.html for specific requirements and application instructions.

Provisions: Pay per audio minutes is determined by how many minutes of voice audio you transcribe. For example, .35/audio min = $21/audio hr. If you had 60 min of audio, you would receive $21 regardless of how long it took you to do it.

MRECORD

4900 Waters Edge Dr. Ste 275, Raleigh, North Carolina 27606
www.mrecord.com

Positions: Medical transcriptionists, editors, and QA/auditors.

Requirements: Minimum 1 year of experience as a doctor office transcriptionist. Must have Windows 98 or newer, high-speed Internet, and USB foot pedal (Infinity pedal not compatible). Résumés can be uploaded on testing site,. http://careers.mrecord.com/transcribers_job_application.aspx

Provisions: Pay based upon experience and quality of work. Nationwide positions available.

MULBERRY STUDIO, INC.

52 John F. Kennedy St., Harvard Square, Cambridge, MA 02138

Positions: This is an international, full service transcription company that's been around since 1974. Also offers a full word processing, data entry and proofreading service. Workers have the choice of working on-site or at home. Those who work at home are considered freelancers.

Requirements: Need a typing speed of 75 wpm, excellent grammar and language skills, experience in transcription and word processing, and a minimum of two years experience. Go to www.mulberrystudio.com/jobs.htm for application instructions.

Provisions: Pays competitive rates.

NATION'S CARELINK
5701 Shingle Creek Pkwy #400, Minneapolis, MN 55430

Positions: Administrative assistants for nationwide health assessment company. Job entails conducting health interviews with clients who have applied for insurance. The work is done at home on a PC and on the phone during a 5-hour work shift. Work is performed primarily in the evening.
Requirements: Send résumé with salary requirements.
Provisions: Training is provided. Weekly hours are 30+.

NATIONWIDE INSURANCE
One Nationwide Plaza, Columbus, OH 43215

Positions: In-home care representatives. This is a full-time job that involves traveling around the service area inspecting property inspections and dealing with small business commercial customers.
Requirements: College degree preferred. Must have a solid knowledge of construction standards and regulations, home building material and contents, and standard homeowner insurance coverages. Must complete specified Home Care core curriculum on claims, loss control, and basic insurance principles. Minimum two years experience is required. Must meet physical requirements. Send résumé.

NET TRANSCRIPTS
www.nettranscripts.com

Positions: Company provides Web-based transcription services to criminal justice and law enforcement agencies. Hires individuals who can transcribe audio content of criminal investigations, internal affairs, and patrol reports.
Requirements: You must have prior experience transcribing for a law enforcement agency (police department, sheriff's department, etc.), type 80+ WPM, have excellent grammar, outstanding accuracy and proofreading skills, have experience with MS Word, and must demonstrate strong computer literacy. A full criminal background check is required. Particularly interested in bilingual individuals with Spanish as their first language. Apply online.

NETWORK REPORTING
www.networkreporting.com

Positions: Transcription of depositions.
Requirements: Must live in the Detroit metro area. Requires accurate typing speed of 75 wpm plus computer and Word Perfect experience. Will consider training right candidates.
Provisions: Full-time positions. Comprehensive training and equipment provided. Earnings directly related to the quality and quantity of work.

NEWSBANK, INC.

58 Pine Street, New Canaan, CT 06840

Positions: About 20 indexers and proofreaders produce current affairs references from their home offices. The work is part-time; each works from 20 to 25 hours per week.

Requirements: Must be local in order to pick up and drop off work twice a week and attend meetings.

Provisions: There is a three-month training period in-house for learning the company's indexing methods and how to use a personal computer. All equipment is provided.

NORTH AMERICAN CO. FOR LIFE & HEALTH INSURANCE

525 W Van Buren St, Chicago, IL 60607

Positions: General office work.

Requirements: Must be local resident with office experience. Must obtain home worker certificate from Illinois Department of Labor.

NORTHERN ILLINOIS MEDICAL CENTER

4201 Medical Center Drive, McHenry, IL 60601

Positions: Medical transcription.

Requirements: Must be local resident with experience and equipment. Must obtain home worker certificate from Illinois Department of Labor.

NORWEGIAN CRUISE LINE

7665 Northwest 19th Street, Miami, FL 33126

Positions: Vacation planners.

Requirements: Must have high school diploma or equivalent, excellent communication skills, minimum 1 year experience in customer service or sales, scheduling flexibility, PC skills, and travel or e-commerce sales experience is preferred.

Provisions: Training is provided in Broward County, FL. Great travel perks, benefits, salary, and bonuses.

OMNILINGUA, INC.

306 6th Avenue Southeast, Cedar Rapids, IA 52401

Positions: Native-speaking translators for work in many different fields. All languages are eligible.

Requirements: Expertise in any area of business is necessary.

Provisions: Can live anywhere. Pay methods vary. Inquiries are welcome from qualified translators.

ONSITE

www.onss.com

Positions: Company provides electronic litigation support to the legal industry. Data entry and document coding is done remotely by home-based workers. Work can be done 24/7 subject to coding project availability.

Requirements: Must have high-speed Internet access, computer with 17" monitor, an e-mail account, and a printer. Previous legal knowledge preferred.

Provisions: Compensation is based on the number of documents that are accurately completed on a per document basis. Pays once a month.

ORACLE TRANSCRIPTION, INC.

4007-B Norbeck Rd., Rockville, MD 20853

Positions: Medical transcriptionists.

Requirements: Hires only the best MTs available. Requires a minimum 3 years of experience, with 3 to 5 years experience in medical records preferred. Must also have excellent medical terminology knowledge in a variety of medical specialties, knowledge of current drugs, excellent grammar and punctuation skills, an ability to meet tight turnarounds, and accuracy rate of 98%.

Apply online: www.oracleti.com.

Provisions: Offers full-time (5,000 lines per week) or part-time (3,500 lines per week). Training is provided in your home over the phone.

OSI TRANSCRIPTION

6140 Central Church Road, Douglasville, GA 30135

www.ositranscription.com

Positions: Medical transcriptionists work as home-based employees nationwide. Any specialty welcome, but clinic experience especially needed.

Requirements: Minimum 2 years as a transcriptionist. high-speed Internet access is required. Apply online.

Provisions: Pays competitive line rates and offers annual raises. Offers full benefits including health, dental, vision, life, PTO, celebratory days, holiday differential pay, CMT sign-on bonus, 401K with employee match, and job advancement opportunities. This is one of the rare employers that offers health insurance to part-time employees. Computers available to qualified candidates.

OUTSOURCING LAW

Bierce & Kenerson, 400 Madison Avenue, 14th Floor,
New York, NY 10017

www.outsourcing-law.com

Positions: This is a US national network of outsourcing attorneys, experienced in managed services contracting, strategic alliances, joint ventures, teaming agreements and similar corporate transactions.

Requirements: Must have at least 10 years of experience in corporate and technology law, with at least 5 years of experience in outsourcing transactions. Can live anywhere in US, but particularly interested in candidates in Washington, DC, Boston, Chicago, Denver, St. Louis, Seattle and Florida. Visit Web site for more information.

Provisions: Up to $250,000 per year.

PALM COAST DATA
11 Commerce Boulevard, Palm Coast, FL 32164

Positions: Data entry keyers work from home on PCs linked directly to Palm Coast Data by telephone line. The work consists of inputting customer information, like names and addresses, or revisiting information already in the database, such as a customer's change of address. All home keyers are independent contractors.

Requirements: Must have a personal computer and Internet connection. If the Internet connection is dial-up, then two separate phone lines will be necessary. Prefers workers who live near one of the two offices (Palm Coast, Florida, or Louisville, Colorado).

Provisions: Pays piece rate.

THE PEAK ORGANIZATION, INC.
25 West 31st Street, Penthouse, New York, NY 10001
www.peakorg.com

Positions: This is a professional staffing agency that occasionally places home-based paralegals in the New York area. Visit the Web site for more information and to see current opportunities.

THE PERMANENTE MEDICAL GROUP, INC.
3801 Howe Street, Oakland, CA 94611

Positions: Financial analysts and consultants for the largest medical group in Northern California. Responsibilities include supporting budget allocation decisions, providing analytical support to management in the financial department, and providing stats.

Requirements: Must have a degree in business administration, economics, health care administration, operations research or public health administration. A Master's degree is preferred. Minimum four years experience is required, preferably in the health care field. Must be comfortable working with Microsoft Office. Programming experience would be ideal.

Provisions: Telecommuting is available to the right candidates. Excellent salary and benefits.

PETERS SHORTHAND REPORTING CORPORATION
3336 Bradshaw Rd., Sacramento, CA 95827
Positions: Court reporting and transcribing.
Requirements: Must be local resident. Some travel is required. Experience is necessary.
Provisions: Pays hourly, plus piece rates, plus expenses.

PHILBRICK TRANSCRIPTIONS, INC.
59 Carmel Hill Road North, Bethlehem, CT 06751
www.philbricktranscription.com
Positions: Medical transcriptionists work at home nationwide as independent contractors.
Requirements: Minimum 5 years as a transcriptionist. Apply online.
Provisions: Pays competitive rates. Steady work. Paid bi-weekly via direct deposit.

POMONA VALLEY HOSPITAL MEDICAL CENTER
1798 N. Garey Ave., Pomona, CA 91767
Positions: Hires Level III medical transcribers.
Requirements: Requires experience in the Basic 4 with a minimum of 5 years on the job including 2 to 3 years acute care hospital experience. Must be production oriented and be DSL line qualified. Excellent spelling, grammar and knowledge of medical terminology and anatomy a must. Local residents only please.

PREMIER TRANSCRIPTION
155 Tri County Pkwy # 210, Cincinnati, OH 45246
Positions: Medical transcription.
Requirements: Minimum two years hospital experience required. Local applicants send résumé.
Provisions: Flexible schedule and top pay.

QT MEDICAL SERVICES, INC.
334 East Lake Rd., #308, Palm Harbor, FL 34685
Positions: Medical transcription.
Requirements: Must be highly qualified with at least 3 years of hospital transcription experience. All medical specialties are needed.
Apply online: http://qtmedical.com. Local residents only.

RAPID TRANSCRIPT, INC.

4311 Wilshire Blvd., #209, Los Angeles, CA 90010

Positions: This is a well-established medical transcription company that provides services both locally and nationwide to hospitals, physician groups, and imaging centers. They are always looking for good transcriptionists to work part-time or full-time.

Requirements: Apply online at www.rapidtranscript.com, then complete a 25-minute transcription test. Requires 1 year as a working MT, preferably in acute care. Relies most heavily on test scores for hiring decisions.

Provisions: Pays .07 to .095 cents per 65-character line (includes spaces and enters). Also offers bonuses. This is one of the rare companies that encourages newbies.

R&B STEN-TEL

http://rbsten-tel.com

Positions: Both medical and nonmedical transcriptionists work at home for this national transcription service provider. Nonmedical work is in the areas of legal, insurance, law enforcement, corporate, conference, and education. The company utilizes patented Web-based dictation and transcription equipment to facilitate the transcribing of reports and other important documents and letters.

Requirements: Experience is required. Visit the Web site and apply online.

Provisions: Offers competitive compensation.

ROSE RESNICK LIGHTHOUSE

214 Van Ness Ave., San Francisco, CA 94102

Positions: This agency is the largest of its kind in Northern California, providing services to the blind and visually impaired community since 1902. There is a constant need of certified literary Braille transcribers with knowledge of computer Braille code. The agency supports Braille production using Duxbury and/or MegaDots.

Requirements: If you meet the qualifications mentioned above, send your list of qualifications, rate list, and contact information to Damian Pickering either by mail or e-mail: dpickering@lighthouse-sf.org.

RICHMOND REPORTING

535 Broadhollow Rd., Melville, NY 11747

Positions: Legal transcribers.

Requirements: Need people with law industry background and knowledge of legal depositions. Must be able to do 70 wpm with accuracy and be able to report to the office 2 to 3 times a week to drop off work. Must own or have access to a computer with laser printer and a Stenorette (a Dictaphone machine with a reel-to-reel spool tape, *not* a cassette tape). Stenorette must have a foot pedal. Work is based on individual contracts. Send résumé.

MARION J. ROSLEY SECRETARIAL SERVICES
41 Topland Rd., Hartsdale, NY 10530

Positions: Word processors, all types of transcription (medical, legal, etc.), and graphic art.

Requirements: Need all levels of people for word processing using Macintosh, Word Perfect and Windows. Local residents mail résumés.

SANS CONSULTING SERVICES, INC.
90 John Street, Suite 313, New York, NY 10038

www.sans.com

Positions: This is a technical and legal placement agency that sometimes places home-based paralegals, legal clerks, and legal proofreaders in the New York City area. Visit Web site for more information and to check current openings.

SCRIBES ONLINE
1310 Beulah Rd., Pittsburgh, PA 15235

Positions: Company employs approximately 70 medical language specialists around the country. These are full-time positions for experienced transcriptionists.

Requirements: High productivity and experience with digital dictation systems. Two years of in-patient transcription experience working with a variety of reports and specialties. Prefers in-patient and surgical experience as well as knowledge of productivity enhancement tools. Must have familiarity with home PC, Internet protocols and electronic communications.

Provisions: Pays per line plus incentive bonus. This is a high volume service.

SECRETARY ON CALL
307L Cuernavaca Dr., N., Austin, Texas 78733

Positions: Legal secretaries.

Requirements: Minimum 5 years experience. Apply via e-mail to jobs@secretaryoncall.com.

SELECT TRANSCRIPTION, INC.

544 3rd St., Elk River, MN 55330

Positions: This is a medical transcription company-owned and operated by transcriptionists.

Requirements: Must have a minimum of two years medical transcription experience in either an acute care of clinic setting. Local applicants send résumé.

Provisions: Pays excellent wages plus health benefits are available.

SETON HEALTH

Attn: Human Resources, 1300 Massachusetts Ave., Troy, NY 12180

Positions: Medical transcribers.

Requirements: Experience working in medical records department of hospital is required. Local residents send résumé.

Provisions: Pays good rates. Offers flexible scheduling.

SH3, INC.

5338 Longview Rd., Kansas City, MO 64137

Positions: Freelance translators for this service bureau.

Requirements: Thorough knowledge of French, German, Italian, or Spanish. You must be experienced and able to provide telecommunications, IBM PC (or compatible) disks. Send résumé.

SHERMAN HOSPITAL

934 Center St., Elgin, IL 60120

Positions: Medical transcribing.

Requirements: Must be local resident. Equipment, good skills and a minimum five years experience are required.

SOURCECORP, INC.

43 Inverness Drive East, Englewood, CO 80112

www.srcp.com/sourcecorp

Positions: SOURCECORP is a business process outsourcing and consulting firm that supports information intensive industries such as commercial, financial, government, healthcare, and legal services.

Requirements: Must have a professional home office equipped with up-to-date computer equipment. Accepts résumés from qualified candidates in Colorado, Arizona, Kansas, Tennessee, and California *only*.

Provisions: Pays competitive salaries and offers full benefits package including health and dental insurance, 401(k), paid vacations and holidays, educational reimbursement, and more.

SPEAK-WRITE

P.O. Box 1570, Whitefish, MT 59937

www.speakwrite.com

Positions: Legal and general transcriptionists and word processors work from their home offices throughout the United States and Canada via the Internet.

Requirements: Must have extensive experience word processing using Word 2000. Must be an expert at grammar, including punctuation and have extensive experience at generating documents in proper form. Must be detail-oriented and be able to proofread your own work quickly and accurately. Minimum accurate typing speed of 75 wpm required.

Provisions: Visit Web site for more information.

STAFFCENTRIX

www.staffcentrix.com

Positions: This is a placement agency that finds virtual assistants who perform a variety of administrative and other business tasks from their home for CEOs and other clients. Since 1999, the company has helped over 5,000 people from 65+ countries around the world find their place in the virtual workforce.

Requirements: Depends entirely on the position and company hiring. Visit Web site for current job leads and read details carefully.

STAT TRANSCRIPTION SERVICES

6475 Camden Ave., #210, San Jose, CA 95120

Positions: Medical transcription.

Requirements: Two years experience in radiology. Local applicants send résumé.

Provisions: "STAT Transcription Service is a growing company and is always looking for highly qualified medical transcriptionists to join our MT team."

STEN-TEL

www.sten-tel.com

Positions: Transcriptions work as independent contractors for this provider of secure transcription, dictation, voice processing, document management and videoconferencing products, and services. The company uses their own patented Internet-based transcription, document management and distribution technologies designed for fast-paced medical, legal, law enforcement, insurance, and business environments.

Requirements: Experience is a must. Visit the Web site and apply online.

TALK2TYPE TRANSCRIPTIONS, INC.

14101 Valleyheart Drive, Suite 101, Sherman Oaks, CA 91423
www.talk2type.net

Positions: Transcribers.

Requirements: Minimum typing speed of 85+ words per minute. Especially want people who can work nights. Local residents only.

Provisions: Full and part-time positions available.

TEAM DOUBLE CLICK

W10530 Airport Road, Lodi, WI 53555
www.TeamDoubleClick.com

Positions: Team Double Click is a service bureau that teams up home-based workers with employers. They have a database of over 1000 virtual workers in dozens of job capacities. One of their greatest needs is for administrative assistants, but all kinds of workers are needed to provide help with: mailings, marketing assistance, answering phones, appointment setting, research, Web design, bookkeeping, graphic design, data entry, e-mail processing, customer support, telemarketing, writing, audio editing, data entry, and transcription.

Requirements: Visit the Web site and fill out the online application form. Workers can live anywhere but must have Internet access since all work is assigned and completed online.

Provisions: All workers are independent contractors. Typically pays within one week.

Close up: Team Double Click

There is a new kind of service bureau emerging thanks to the Internet and Web-based technology. It's known as a virtual staffing agency. Team Double Click is one such agency, based in tiny Lodi, Wisconsin. It is owned and operated by Gayle and Jim Buske. A mere year after hanging out their virtual shingle, the company already has over 1,000 virtual workers in their database and over 150 clients around the world.

Team Double Click is able to provide clients as far away as Saudi Arabia with numerous administrative, creative, and/or technical services. Gayle Buske says, "Our virtual assistants can do almost anything that an in-person staff member can do—except filing, of course." Team members are home-based professionals of all kinds including administrative assistants, data entry workers, writers, editors, graphic designers, marketing pros, Web designers, transcribers, telemarketers, and more.

The virtual professionals here are all freelancers. They join the team by filling out an extensive form online that outlines skills and experience. When a client calls looking for help, Team Double Click quickly searches the database and reviews résumés to see who might be a fit. Anyone who is a good candidate is contacted individually to discuss the project. Sometimes projects are unusual and it's difficult to find the right person easily. When that happens, the agency sends out a "group call" via e-mail, asking anyone who is capable and available to reply.

For team members, the agency offers flexibility, marketing, and good pay. For example, the pay for general administrative work is about $18 an hour. Other tasks pay more. Team Double Click gets a 15 percent cut. It's a good deal for freelancers who don't have the time or inclination to market their own services or deal with the headache of billing.

Virtual staffing is still in its infancy and there aren't many companies out there like Team Double Click—yet. But the technology is here and trends follow technology. For example, only two years ago most transcription service bureaus needed home workers to live nearby so that tapes and finished hard copies could be picked up and delivered every day. Now the technology has evolved to the point where all transcription can—and is—being done online. With high-speed Internet connections plus a new type of transcribing machine (WAV), transcribers can live anywhere including the most remote areas.

"At some point we'd like to see virtual help as a universal way of doing business," Gayle says. It's going to take some time to educate potential business clients on the benefits of hiring virtual assistants. But it will happen. Anyone who doesn't believe that should remember that only 15 years ago working at home in any capacity was considered odd. Now it's the accepted norm.

"Lately, we've noticed a trend with the new clients we're adding," says Gayle. "Many are actually hiring us to take work away from bricks-and-mortar assistants. It's not because they're unhappy with them or their work—they're giving it to us because they've learned that hiring virtually is much more convenient and economical for them. I find this so encouraging. Our world is moving that much closer to a new way of working and hiring—virtually! It's our mission to make virtual working and virtual hiring the thing to do."

TELETRANS, INC.

22471 N. 81st Ave., Peoria, AZ 85382

Positions: Company needs medical transcribers in the Phoenix area. This is a fully digitalized service.

Requirements: Minimum three years transcription experience or graduate of medical transcription school and experience with MS Word. Must work on a 48 hour turnaround. To apply, send résumé as an attached MS Word document or as a formatted e-mail text to: employment@teletransinc.com. Put "résumé" on the subject line.

Provisions: Pays competitive line rate.

TERRA NOVA TRANSCRIPTION

100 Elizabeth Avenue, Suite 122, St. John's
NL, Canada A1B 1S1
www.terranovatrans.com

Positions: Medical transcriptionists work from home nationwide (US).

Requirements: Requires three years as a transcriptionist and high-speed Internet connection. Company does many types of transcription so any specialty is welcome to apply. Must be able to adhere to strict deadlines. Applicants must show good judgment in dealing with confidential material and consistently maintain 98% accuracy.

Provisions: This is a full-time employment situation. Pay is based on experience

THOMAS TRANSCRIPTION SERVICES, INC.

P.O. Box 26613, Jacksonville, FL 32226
www.thomastx.com

Positions: Medical transcriptionists are needed nationwide. "We are always looking for qualified medical transcriptionists to join our company."

Requirements: Minimum three years experience. Visit www.thomastx.com/employment.htm for application form.

TIGERFISH

www.tigerfish.com/employment.html

Positions: Transcription of a wide variety of materials, from single subject interviews to focus groups, documentary film footage to corporate research projects, police interrogations to depositions.

Requirements: Must be a quick typist with a good ear for language and a strong sense of written English. Must be a US citizen or legal resident. Must have high-speed Internet access (no dial-up), a telephone number where you regularly can be reached, a Windows-based computer (Macs unfortunately are not compatible with the video timecoding software used), and a copy of Express Scribe transcription software (it's a free program that can be downloaded from the company's Web site. Express Scribe is fine to use for the test and evaluation period, but ultimately if you continue to transcribe with Tigerfish, you will need to purchase a copy of Start Stop's Power Play for Windows Media. Apply online.

TOTAL OFFICE, INC.

1170 Sutherland Ave., Akron, OH 44314

www.totaloffice.cc

Positions: This is a virtual assistant service bureau that specializes in providing account administration and administrative services to financial advisors nationwide.

Requirements: Because you will be a subcontractor, you will need to have your own equipment. Send résumé and you will be contacted when your services are needed. Résumés are kept on file for 6 months.

TRANSCEND SERVICES, INC.

945 E. Paces Ferry Rd., NE #1475, Atlanta, GA 30305

Positions: Medical language transcriptionists.

Requirements: Minimum three years acute care transcription experience in full service hospital or clinic. Must work at least 35 hours per week. Local applicants only please.

Provisions: Supplies PC hardware and software configured to company requirements. Pays production rates exceeding $30k per year plus incentive and production bonuses and benefits.

TRANSCRIPTION SOLUTIONS

97 Washington Ave, Des Moines, IA 50317

Positions: Medical transcription.

Requirements: Must be local and experienced. Send résumé.

TRANSCRIPTION, TECHNOLOGY, AND SUPPORTER

40 Higgins Road, Chichester, NH 03258

www.tts-mt.com

Positions: This is one of the oldest medical transcription companies in New Hampshire. The company now has more than 50 medical transcriptionists and speech recognition editors working remotely across the country. All shifts available.

Requirements: Minimum of three years experience in medical transcription, any specialty. Only US citizens/residents. You will be required to produce a

minimum of 125 lines per hour/text and/or 250 lines per hour/edit. Apply online.
Provisions: Pays competitive rates. Compensation is based on a 65-character line including spaces, headers and footers. Offers continuous work flow, assigned accounts, shift differential, direct deposit with online payroll statements, 26 pay days annually, choice of employee or independent contract status, and employee bonus referral. Full-time employees receive benefits including health, and RX with 50% employee premium paid. Benefits also include 15 paid days off per year, production incentives, and advancement opportunities.

24 HOUR SECRETARY

1004 Reisterstown Road, Pikesville, MD 21208
Positions: Medical and legal transcription.
Requirements: At least three years experience with certificate preferred. Must own PC with Word Perfect and the ability to take all types of tapes. Must be from surrounding area and come to the office to pick up documents. Will work with modem, but still needs to be local. Send résumé.

UPDATE LEGAL

www.updatelegal.com
Posiitons: This is a legal placement agency with offices in San Francisco, Boston, New York, Houston, Newark, and Philadelphia. They place attorneys, paralegals and practice support staff with law firms and corporate legal departments. They occasionally have opportunities that permit part-time work from home.
Requirements: Must be highly qualified and experienced. Visit Web site to check current opportunities.
Provisions: Pays competitive rates.

VERDICTS.COM

www.verdicts.com
Positions: Paralegals work at home in the Eastern and Central United States. This firm publishes jury verdict summaries and uses legal researchers for case summaries. Each case takes about 1 to 2 hours to complete.
Requirements: Must have legal or casualty claims background. Requires a good understanding of the basics of personal injury litigation and the ability to write a coherent story that accurately reflects the essential issues of a specific jury trial. Must have computer with high-speed Internet access.
Provisions: Full-time and part-time hours available. Pays a flat rate of $20 per completed summary plus telephone expenses. Most researchers here complete 500 to 800 case summaries annually.

VERNA MEDICAL TRANSCRIPTIONS
156 Smithwood Avenue, Milpitas, CA 95035

Positions: Medical transcribers for all types of medical records.

Requirements: Experience is necessary. Must own good typewriter and transcribing machine with either standard or micro cassettes. Must be local resident in order to pick up and deliver supplies and finished work.

Provisions: Pays piece rates. Part-time or full-time work is available.

VIDEO MONITORING SERVICE
185 Berry St. #6400, San Francisco, CA 94107

Positions: News monitors for national broadcast news retrieval service.

Requirements: Reliability, attention to detail, and good writing skills required. Need PC with modem. Openings are in Sacramento area. Submit résumé.

VITAC
www.vitac.com/careers.htm

Positions: Realtime captioners, production coordinators, offline captioners, translators, and multi-language quality control editors. These are specialists interested in making a difference in the lives of deaf and hard-of-hearing Americans. They are responsible for transcription and/or placement and timing of stylistically accurate captions for prerecorded television shows airing on all major networks.

Requirements: Visit company Web site for information and application instructions.

WAY WITH WORDS
1916 Pike Place, Suite 9, Seattle, WA 98101
www.waywithwords.com

Positions: This leading transcription and translation company has many major clients all over the world including two national parliaments, several government agencies, universities, courts, national newspapers, and blue-chip corporations. Home workers provide a wide variety of translation and transcription services.

Requirements: Apply online.

WEBMEDX
5901-C Peachtree Dunwoody Road NE, Suite 450, Atlanta, GA 30328
www.webmedx.com

Positions: Medical transcriptionists work at home nationwide. Prefers multispecialty transcriptionists. These are full-time employment positions.

Requirements: Minimum two years experience as a transcriptionist. Go to company Web site to complete our online application and testing process.

Provisions: Provides paid training, 24/7 technical support, user-friendly typing platforms, and computer equipment. Also provides excellent benefits including medical, dental, vision and life insurance, short-term and long-term disability, accidental death and dismemberment, PTO, holiday pay, 401k plan, and competitive pay with production incentives, shift differentials and weekend differentials.

WORD PROCESSING UNLIMITED

6404 Crestwood Rd., Baltimore, MD 21239

Positions: Transcribing, data entry, and desktop publishing.

Requirements: Looking for people with higher skill levels and equipment. Strong Word Perfect, tape transcription, and knowledge of database packages required. For desktop publishing, a familiarity with Mac and a strong background required. Local residents only should send résumés including cover letter and statement of monies required.

WORDMASTERS

1616 S Dean Rd., Orlando, FL 32825

Positions: Straight text typing and chiropractic transcription. Also writing and typing résumés.

Requirements: Must own and have experience on Word Perfect 5.1, Windows, and Lotus. Work on 24-hour turnover. Local residents mail résumé.

WORDNET

30 Nagog Park, P.O. Box 976, Acton, MA 01720

Positions: Professional freelancers translate technical manuals and documentation in and out of all major languages.

Requirements: Must be experienced and skilled both in languages, technical verbiage, and computers. Because translation projects are transmitted electronically all over the world, a computer and modem is required. Send résumé.

WORDSMART

250 5th Ave., Suite 202, New York, NY 10001

Positions: Transcribers.

Requirements: Need only top transcriptionists (70-75 wpm) with WordPerfect and standard cassette equipment. Much of the work is from

phone conversation tapes; familiarity with banking terminology required.
Provisions: Pays $5 per single space page.

WORDTRONICS DIRECT MAIL SERVICE BUREAU
100 Hamilton Ave., White Plains, NY 10601

Positions: Data entry and letter shop services.

Requirements: For data entry, must own PC for creating mailing lists. Must be quick and efficient. Also experienced people stuffing, sealing, and bulk-rate letter shop services. Local residents only mail résumés.

Provisions: Earn $8 to $12 per hour on a per-piece payment.

OPPORTUNITIES
IN SALES

The field of sales has long been a traditional from-home opportunity. Today, most salespeople have offices at home and some even conduct all their business from home.

Sales may be the only true opportunity to earn an executive level income with literally no educational requirements or experience. It is particularly good for women, who often report doubling or tripling their income after leaving other types of jobs. It also allows for a maximum amount of flexibility in terms of time spent and when it is spent.

When does it take to be a good salesperson? Good communications skills are at the top of the list. You must truly enjoy talking to people to make it in sales. You must be careful to listen to them as well. Assertiveness is also important. This does not mean you must be aggressive or go for the "hard sell," but shrinking violets aren't likely to make it in this field. The toughest part of this job is handling rejection. Nobody likes rejection; some people are traumatized by it. But, it goes with the territory. The professional salesperson knows that with each rejection, s/he is one step closer to a successfully closed sale.

Sales is a profession with its own set of rules, just like any other profession. The job basically consists of prospecting for customers, qualifying the prospect to make sure the potential customer is a viable prospect, making the presentation, overcoming objections, closing the sales, and getting referrals. A good company will teach you all you need to know about each of these steps. You can also find classes in salesmanship for both beginners and advanced students at community colleges and adult learning centers.

Many of the opportunities listed in this section have interesting ways of introducing the product. Home parties are especially fun and easy. Many home parties now seem more like classes than sales pitches with hands-on demonstrations in cooking, baking, needlework, and crafts. If you think you might be interested in a particular company, you can check it out first by hosting your own party. You'll not only be able to check out the company first hand, but you'll earn a bonus gift at the same time.

For those who want to be home all the time, telemarketing is the best bet. Telemarketing jobs rarely exceed four hours a day, but the pay can equal a full-time salary for a good communicator. For additional opportunities in telemarketing, look in your local newspaper "help wanted" ads.

ACCU-FIND
196 W Moorestown Rd., Wind Gap, PA 18091
www.accufind.com
Positions: Sales reps are responsible for creating new accounts and servicing established accounts.
Requirements: Must have sales experience, knowledge of Internet is helpful.
Provisions: Offers flexible hours, salary, good commissions plan, and health benefits availability.

ALCAS CUTLERY CORPORATION
1116 East State Street, P.O. Box 810, Olean, NY 14760
www.cutco.com
Positions: Alcas makes cutlery, cookware, and tableware. The products are sold with the aid of mail-order catalogs.
Provisions: Catalogs and other supplies are provided. Pays commission.

ALOETTE COSMETICS, INC.
4900 Highlands Pkwy SE, Smyrna, GA 30082
www.aloette.com
Positions: Direct sales of skin care cosmetics. Contact the franchise owner nearest you to get started: www.aloette.com/careers#1.

AMERICAN BARTER EXCHANGE, INC
20 Broadhollow Rd. # 3011A, Melville, NY 11747
www.barteramerica.com
Positions: Telemarketing.
Requirements: Home-based telemarketers are trained to make appointments for outside salespeople to explain company's barter association and benefits. Must be articulate and capable of dealing with business people. Local residents only.
Provisions: Pays base salary plus commission and phone bill.

APARTMENTSTORES.COM
www.apartmentstores.com

Positions: Telephone sales involving advertising sales to businesses within real estate and relocation industries. ApartmentStores.com is a leading Internet-based real estate company and Web site for finding apartments for rent and moving companies.

Requirements: Must have proven sales experience and computer with broadband (high-speed) Internet access.

Provisions: Can live anywhere in the US.

ARBONNE INTERNATIONAL, INC.
678 E Walnut Brook Dr., Murray, UT 84107
www.arbonne.com

Positions: Direct sales of European cosmetics and skin care products. Reps build customers bases using any direct sales methods that work for them. Sign up online to become an Arbonne independent consultant.

Provisions: Training and ongoing managerial support is provided. Pays commission.

ART & SOUL, INC.
1229 Seitz Dr., Waukesha, WI 53186
www.artandsoulinc.com

Positions: Direct sales of personalized products; watercolor and ink cartoon lithographs, magnets, key/bag tags, note pads, frames and designer t-shirts.

Requirements: Although optional, there is a standard business supply kit available for $100. It contains catalogs, advertising brochures, training booklets, personalizing equipment, etc.

Provisions: Prices, and therefore profits, are set by you.

ARTISTIC IMPRESSIONS, INC.
240 Cortland Ave., Lombard, IL 60148
www.artisticinc.com

Positions: Home party sales of art works.

Provisions: Excellent income with flexible hours—$1000 a month part-time.

Positions: Automobile parts specialist to help non-Volkswagen dealers with inventory. Duties include providing parts expertise, parts management, assistance with merchandising and administration of inventory.

Requirements: Must have thorough knowledge of automotive operations.

Product knowledge of Volkswagen and/or Audi preferred, but not required. Qualified local residents send résumé.

Provisions: Pays great salary plus offers full benefits.

AVON PRODUCTS, INC.

www.avon.com

(800) FOR-AVON

Positions: Avon, which is known for door-to-door sales, doesn't rely solely on this method anymore. Instead, its huge number of reps often use telemarketing methods to arrange home parties and make appointments for exclusive showings.

Requirements: Reps are required to buy samples, hostess thank-you gifts, and necessary paperwork.

Provisions: Pays commission. Management opportunities are available. You can now join the organization online.

BEAUTICONTROL, INC.

2121 Midway Road, Carrollton, TX 75006

www.beauticontrol.com

Positions: BeautiControl primarily markets a cosmetic line that is tied into the "seasonal" method of color coordination. A secondary line of women's apparel is marketed in the same way. In 1985, the company topped $30 million in gross sales. BeautiControl does not use the party plan method of direct sales, but rather focuses on one-on-one sales. This is accomplished through intensive training, personal development, and corporate support of the consultants. A free color analysis is offered to potential customers; this has proven to be the company's most powerful marketing tool.

Requirements: A one-time investment has been reduced to $99. It covers the cost of over $900 worth of products, services, and training.

Provisions: Personal earnings are reported in the company's monthly in-house publication, *Achiever*, and typically range from $12,000 down to $3,700 per month after being in the company for about two years. It is not unusual for new Consultants to earn $100 to $200 per day. There are opportunities to earn trips, diamond jewelry, and a new Mustang convertible.

BEAUTY BY SPECTOR

1 Spector Place, McKeesport, PA 15134

Positions: Sales of hair goods and wigs for men and women.

BIZARRE PROMOTIONS, INC.

18708 Telegraph Rd, # C1, Romulus, MI 48174

Positions: Reselling of promotional products.

Requirements: $25 for start-up kit is rebated with $300 in sales.

Provisions: Offers access to over 500,000 promotional products imprinted with your customers' information.

BLUE ZEBRA USA

25 Pequot Avenue, Suite A, Port Washington, NY 11050

www.bluezebrausa.com

Positions: This is a professional appointment setting company. Team members schedule appointments with businesses.

Requirements: Must be experienced, highly motivated, and professional. Requires five years of business-to-business sales experience and three years of experience cold calling businesses. Visit the Web site and résumé via e-mail.

Provisions: Hours are hours per day for a total of 20-40 hours per week minimum. Pays commission per contract. Advancement opportunities.

BROWN BAG GOURMET GOODIES

http://brownbaggourmet.com

Positions: Direct sales of gourmet coffees, teas, cocoas, cappuccinos, biscotti, cookies, chocolate spoons, and flavored stir sticks.

Provisions: Plenty of company support and a free Web site provided by the company.

BUSINESS EDGE

1040 Avenue of the Americas, 24th Floor, New York, NY 10018

www.business-edge.com

Positions: Telemarketing for Web hosting and design firm.

Requirements: Positions available only in Manhattan and Connecticut.

Provisions: Starting out the job is commission only, but can move up to salary plus commission.

CALL DEPOT

2218 SE 25th Ave., Homestead, FL 33035

Positions: Telemarketing of software in the $1,000 range.

Requirements: Sales experience required.

Provisions: Pays 25% commission.

CASEPOST INC.

101 Pacifica, Irvine, CA 92612

www.casepost.com

Positions: Telemarketers set appointments over the phone for client development specialists to meet with attorneys. Casepoint is a new client development service for the legal profession.

Requirements: Proven record of calling on professionals required.

Provisions: Pay is negotiable.

CHARMELLE, INC.

136 Freelon St., San Francisco, CA 94107

www.charmelle.com

Positions: Selling jewelry for this European-owned company that supplies high-quality European designed costume jewelry at affordable prices to the US market. The collection includes jewelry and accessories for both women and men. Each piece in the collection has been hand-finished and plated with thick gold, rhodium, or silver plating to ensure the highest possible quality. Sells through party plan and direct.

Provisions: Excellent training is provided. Pays commission.

CINTAS CORPORATION

332 Mclaws Cir # 111, Williamsburg, VA 23185

www.cintas.com

Positions: Telemarketing for commercial uniform company.

Requirements: Need exceptional verbal and organizational skills. Apply in person.

Provisions: Set your own schedule, approximately 25 hours per week during school hours. Benefits include medical, dental, retirement, and profit sharing.

CONCEPT NOW COSMETICS

12020 Mora Dr. # 9, Santa Fe Springs, CA 90670

www.conceptnowcosmetics.com

Positions: For 20 years, this company has been selling an extensive line of skin care products primarily though party plan sales. Reps operate through the United States, Mexico, Canada, Puerto Rico, and the Virgin Islands.

Requirements: No start-up fees.

Provisions: No set territories. Training is available and includes tapes, manual, presentation outline and company support. Car allowance is provided along with specified promotions. Pays commission only for reps and override for managers.

COX COMMUNICATIONS CORP
www.coxmedia.com

Positions: Part-time reps.

Requirements: Basic computers skills required along with a PC and Internet access. Prefers someone with experience in public relations or sales.

Provisions: Cox Media has offices in 35 cities. Visit the Web site to find opportunities near you.

COZY PLACES
Attn: Human Resources, 1658 E. Capitol Expressway, Suite 520, San Jose, CA 95121

www.cozyplaces.com

Positions: Telemarketers to promote and sell advertising on Cozyplaces.com, a comprehensive online nationwide directory for Bed and Breakfast inns.

Requirements: Must be experienced telemarketer with 2-3 years direct telesales experience. Must be comfortable with cold calling.

Provisions: Can live anywhere in US.

CREATIVE MEMORIES
3001 Clearwater Road, St. Cloud, MN 56301

www.creativememories.com

Positions: Party-plan sales of books, hobby products, photo albums, and photography products.

CRESTCOM INTERNATIONAL, LTD.
6900 E Belleview Ave., Greenwood Village, CO 80111

www.crestcom.com

Positions: Professional phone marketers book seminars for well-known speaker and management trainer.

Requirements: Local professionals send résumé indicating experience.

Provisions: Work 25 hours per week. Pays base salary plus commission and bonus program.

D. J. ARDORE, INC.
P.O. 188, Mountain Lakes, NJ 07046

www.djardore.com

Positions: Telemarketers set appointments and also handle some data entry. This company produces a restaurant/dining guide. The appointments are for sales reps to meet with restaurants and sell advertising space.

Requirements: Must live within driving distance of company headquarters. Need PC with Internet access. Apply via e-mail with résumé.

Provisions: Pay equals $10-$12 an hour plus bonus incentives.

DESKTOP AUTHOR
P.O. Box 875, Strawberry Hills NSW 2012 Australia
www.catalogstudio.com

Positions: Ad sales. This Australian company is looking for reps anywhere in the United States to sell its inexpensive applications software to businesses of all sizes. Visit Web site for sample demo.

Requirements: Prefers experienced sales reps who have contacts within the advertising and business community.

Provisions: Pays commission only; 30% on every software sale and 20% on the production services. Software sells for $105 and production services is about $500 for typical turnkey production. Go to Web site to apply.

DISCOVERY TOYS, INC.
2530 Arnold Dr., Suite 400, Martinez, CA 94553
www.discoverytoysinc.com

Positions: Discovery Toys was started as a home-based business in 1982. The company markets a line of educationally sound toys and accessories through home parties. Home party demonstrators and their supervisors are all home-based.

Requirements: Send letter of interest.

Provisions: Complete training is provided. Pays commission and override. Can live anywhere. You can now register to work with the organization online.

DONCASTER
581 Rock Road, Rutherfordton, NC 28139
www.doncaster.com

Positions: Doncaster trains women to be fashion consultants, "Selling the art of dressing well." Fashion Consultants present the Doncaster collection in private showing in their own homes four times a year. These fashions are considered to be investment quality and are designed primarily for career women.

Provisions: Training is provided. Pays commission. Management opportunities are available.

DUDLEY PRODUCTS AND PUBLICATIONS

1080 Old Greensboro Rd., Kernersville, NC 27284

www.dudleyq.com

Positions: Direct sales of cosmetics using home parties as primary sales method.
Provisions: Training is provided. Pays commission and override for managers.

EAST COAST DRIVING SCHOOL

475 Wall St., Princeton, NJ 08540

www.eastcoastdrivingschool.com

Positions: Telemarketing.

Requirements: Telephone support needed for evenings and weekends in the Princeton/Trenton area. Script, leads provided.

ELECTRIC MOBILITY CORPORATION

Number 1 Mobility Plaza, Sewell, NJ 08080

Positions: This manufacturer of electric mobility three-wheelers uses a national network of independent reps to demonstrate and sell their products. All reps are home-based, but must travel to demonstrate the products to interested buyers because they are either elderly or handicapped.

Requirements: This is not hard sell; reps must be easy going, caring, efficient and very organized. Apply with résumé.

Provisions: Leads are generated through national advertising and are prequalified by telemarketers before being sent to reps. Territories are assigned by zip codes. Commissions are about $300 per sale.

ELECTROLUX CORP.

5956 Sherry Ln #1500, Dallas, TX 75225

www.electrolux.com

Positions: Direct sales of vacuum cleaners, floor polishers, and attachments.

FASHION TWO TWENTY, INC.

250 Coventry Dr., Painesville, OH 44077

http://fashiontwotwentycosmetics.com

Positions: Direct sales of extensive line of quality cosmetics. Reps start by conducting home parties. After building an established clientele, home parties are usually replaced with prearranged personal consultations.

Requirements: There is usually a $15 fee to cover the cost of the manual and data processing. A new rep must also purchase the standard Show-Case kit. New consultants are expected to submit at least $150 retail orders per month.

Provisions: Pays commission. Management opportunities exist.

FINELLE COSMETICS

480 Lowell St., Andover, MA 01810

www.finelle.com

Positions: Direct sales of cosmetics and skin care products.

FLETCHER CONSOLIDATED, INC.

6475 Perimeter Drive, #114, Dublin, OH 43016

www.fcon.com/appt

Positions: Appointment setter. The job involves contacting schools, churches, youth sports organizations and large employers in specific areas around the country. You will not be asking for money at any point—and you are not really "selling" anything.

Requirements: Must be a good communicator. Experience is a plus but is not required. You will need Internet access and e-mail. You must be willing to work at least 15 hours per week during normal business hours.

Provisions: Training provided. Pays per appointment on a sliding scale - the more appointments you set in a week, the more you are paid for each. Earnings typically amount to $15-$25 per hour and more is possible. Visit Web site for more information and to see what area is open.

FRIENDS LIFE CARE AT HOME, INC.

1777 Sentry Parkway West, 210 Dublin Hall, Blue Bell, PA 19422

Positions: This is a unique Quaker-based long-term care program that needs sales/marketing reps in New Castle County, Delaware and Chester County, Pennsylvania. It is the largest continuing-care-at-home provider in the US.

Requirements: Need minimum of two years experience in sales/marketing to seniors with an understanding of long term care issues, and knowledge of the region. Must have demonstrated ability to work independently. Send résumé and salary history.

THE GOOD NATURE CO., INC.

Oxford, MI

e-mail: info@thegoodnatureco.com

Positions: Party plan sales of lawn and garden ornaments, garden tools and accessories, bird houses and feeders.

Requirements: You must choose one of two business kits; both are affordable.

Provisions: Flexible hours, commission plan with monthly bonuses and other incentives.

GREEN LAKE CHIROPRACTIC

9750 3rd Ave NE #103, Seattle, WA 98103

Positions: Telemarketers.

Requirements: Must be experienced and be local resident.

Provisions: Pays $8 per hour to start plus bonuses. Offers choice of day or evening hours.

GROLIER INCORPORATED

90 Sherman Turnpike, Danbury, CT 06816

Positions: Grolier is best known for publishing *Encyclopedia Americana* and has expanded into other educational publishing (such as the Disney series and *Mr. Light*).

Provisions: Training is provided in one-week classroom sessions. No leads, no territories. Sales are direct and usually accomplished by setting appointments by phone in advance of the presentation. Pays commission (about 23%) to reps plus override to managers. Some expenses such as phone and car are reimbursed on an individual arrangement with management.

GUPTA TECHNOLOGIES

975 Island Drive, Redwood Shores, CA 94065

http://guptaworldwide.com

Positions: Software sales agents sell company's SQLBase database and team developer rapid application development tool directly to end users and resellers.

Requirements: At least three years experience selling software products. Prefer those with contacts that can be converted into sales.

Provisions: Has territories available throughout North America. Pays commission only.

HEALTH ADMINISTRATION SYSTEMS, INC.

10270 Old Columbia Road, Suite 110, Columbia, MD 21046

http://has.com

Positions: Marketing specialists develop sales leads, enhance publicity, and target products and services. The goal is to increase company's local, regional, and national presence.

Requirements: Marketing experience is required. E-mail résumé.

Provisions: Part-time or full-time positions available.

HERBALIFE INTERNATIONAL

6711 Valjean Ave, Van Nuys, CA 91406

www.herbalife.com

Positions: Direct sales of weight control food products.

HOME AND GARDEN PARTY

2938 Brown Rd., Marshall, TX, 75672

www.homeandgardenparty.com

Positions: This is a home-based party plan business featuring home decor items such as hand-turned stoneware pottery, framed prints, terracotta pottery, figurines, brass accessories, etc.

Requirements: There is an initial start-up cost of $150, which covers the cost of a sample kit with a retail value of more than $300. You could recover your total investment in less than two months and the company guarantees a one-year buy-back option if you leave. You are not required to carry inventory.

Provisions: Offers generous commission schedule plus override commissions, sponsor bonuses and possible infinity bonuses.

HOME & GROUNDS

1020, 29th St. NW, Washington, DC 20007

www.homeandgrounds.com

Positions: Telemarketing for this B2B and consumer-based advertising company that focuses on the home improvement, home plans, service contractor, interior design, home furnishings, real estate, art, antiques, nurseries, and landscape markets.

Requirements: Telemarketing experience is preferred but not necessary.

Provisions: Can live anywhere in the US. Pays aggressive commissions and "stock options bonuses." Apply with résumé.

HOME INTERIORS & GIFTS, INC.

1649 W Frankford Rd, Carrollton, TX 75007

www.homeinteriors.com

Positions: Direct sales of pictures, figurines, shelves, foliage, and other home accents. Reps set up exclusive shows that include about 35 pieces of merchandise. After the show, the rep offers individual service and decorating advice to the customers.

Requirements: Reps must order, deliver, and collect. Start-up packages cost $39 and $129.

Provisions: Training is provided in the form of ongoing sales classes, weekly meetings and monthly decorating workshops. The average rep presents about three shows a week and works about 25 hours a week.

IDAHO STATESMAN
1200 N Curtis Rd., Boise, ID 83706

Positions: Independent sales representative for *The Idaho Statesman*. Job entails contacting former subscribers by phone.

Requirements: Must be self-motivated and able to overcome objections. Apply to circulation sales/marketing manager.

Provisions: Offers flexible schedule to suit your availability.

IMS TECHNOLOGY TELESALES
317 La Mesa Avenue, Encinitas, CA 92024

www.telesalesspecialists.com

Positions: B2B telemarketing and prospecting for high technology clients. In addition to calls, job entails mailing follow-up, lead generation, inquiry qualification, database development, list cleaning, product sales, surveys, marketing research.

Requirements: This is a job for professionals only. College graduates only. Requires business-to-business or corporate sales experience or previous high tech experience. You will need a fully equipped home office with PC. You will be required to work a minimum of 15 hours per week on a flexible basis.

Provisions: Part-time or full-time schedule available. Work schedule is flexible, typically 10-35 hours per week. Pays $15 per hour plus commission.

INFINITY INSURANCE COMPANY
P.O. Box 444, Birmingham, AL 35201

Positions: Business development representatives for insurance company.

Requirements: Must be willing to travel daily within your territory. Some overnight travel will also be required. You will need a college degree and two years of successful sales experience. Apply with résumé.

Provisions: Pays salary plus benefits and offers performance incentives, laptop, company vehicle, and a comprehensive training program.

INTREP, INC.
5178 Marks Court, New Albany, OH 43054

www.intrep.com

Positions: Telemarketing for progressive outsourcing company.

Requirements: Must have solid business background and be comfortable communicating at all management levels. Inside sales experience required as well as computer and software knowledge. Must have customer service orientation. You will need a well equipped home office with computer system and broadband Internet access.

Provisions: All geographical areas are open. Apply online.

ITXTEND
5490 McGinnis Village Place, Suite 208, Alpharetta, GA 30005
www.itxtend.com

Positions: Telemarketers for this software development and IT Services company. Company has a strong focus in healthcare.

Requirements: Must be organized and able to make cold calls. Need telemarketing and/or sales experience.

Provisions: Flexible schedule. Pays $10 to $12 depending on experience. Atlanta only.

JAFRA COSMETICS, INC.
P.O. Box 5026, Westlake Village, CA 91359
www.jafra.com

Positions: Jafra makes high quality, "natural" cosmetics and skin care products. Reps sell the products through the party plan and by offering free facials to participants.

Provisions: Pays commission.

THE KIRBY CORPORATION
1920 W. 114 St., Cleveland, OH 44102
www.kirby.com

Positions: Kirby has been selling its vacuum cleaners door-to-door for many years. Now, reps use telemarketing methods to prearrange demonstrations.

Provisions: Some write-in leads are provided. Pays commissions.

KITCHEN-A-FAIR
900 North 400 West Suite #15, North Salt Lake, Utah 84054
www.kitchenafair.com

Positions: Kitchen-A-Fair is a 20-year-old maker of cookware, kitchen accessories, and home decorative items. All products are sold in home demonstrations. There is no ordering, packing, or shipping merchandise and no collection by the consultants.

Provisions: Training is provided. Regional advertising is provided by the company and the resulting inquires are passed along to the area consultants. The initial kit is free. Pays commission to consultants and up to 7% override to managers.

LONGABERGER MARKETING, INC.

1360 E. Main St., Dresden, OH 43821

Positions: Longaberger markets maple wood baskets that are handmade in America. Each basket is signed by the weaver. Longaberger consultants sell the baskets though home parties.

Requirements: The initial investment of $300 covers the cost of sample baskets, catalogs, invitations, a handbook, and enough materials to hold several shows.

Provisions: Training is provided not only for sales techniques but for learning how to best decorate and display the baskets. Pays commissions starting at 25% plus overrides for managers. Three levels of management opportunities exist. Managers are provided with special management award baskets, mailings, meetings, training sessions, incentives, and other awards.

LUCKY HEART COSMETICS, INC.

138 Huling Ave., Memphis, TN 38103

Positions: Lucky Heart is a line of cosmetics for black women. The products are sold direct by independent distributors in any way they choose.

Requirements: A one-time $10 start-up fee is required.

Provisions: Color catalogs, samples and testers are provided. Pays commission plus bonuses. Management opportunities exist.

MACKE WATER SYSTEMS, INC.

190 Shepard Ave. Suite A, P.O. Box 545, Wheeling, IL 60090
www.mackewater.com

Positions: Appointment setters. Macke Water Systems is a national provider of "bottle-less" water coolers, purification systems, and national coffee service. This is business-to-business appointment setting for sales reps in your local area or you can call nationwide, which should increase your earning potential.

Requirements: Minimum two years sales and/or telemarketing experience. Need computer with Internet access and a separate phone line.

Provisions: Leads are provided by logging into the company's online database. Pays per appointment set. Training provided. Can live anywhere.

MARY KAY COSMETICS, INC.

8787 Stemmons Freeway, Dallas, TX 75247

www.marykay.com

Positions: Beauty consultants and sales directors. Mary Kay started this cosmetics empire on her kitchen table in 1963. In 1984 there were 151,615 consultants and 4,500 sales directors producing over $300 million in sales. All of these people worked from their homes.

Requirements: An investment of $100 is required to start.

Provisions: Pays commission up to 12%. Offers incentives such as jewelry, furs, cars and trips through special promotions and contests. Consultants can earn over $30,000 annually, generally averaging over $10 an hour after taxes. Directors average over $100,000 a year. Can live anywhere.

MASON SHOE MANUFACTURING COMPANY

1350 Williams St., Chippewa Falls, WI 54729

www.bamason.com

Positions: Mason is a 35-year-old family business with an extensive line of American made, quality shoes. All shoes are guaranteed for quality and fit and can be easily exchanged or refunded.

Provisions: Reps are provided with catalogs and all necessary supplies. Incentive bonus plans several times a year. Portion of the retail price is taken out by the rep before placing the order with the company.

MATRIX TECHNOLOGY GROUP

120 Wood Avenue South, Suite #300, Iselin, NJ 08830

www.matrixonweb.com

Positions: Lead generation and sales of Internet software for business applications.

Requirements: Must have strong cold calling skills and actually love to close a sale. Some computer experience is necessary. Should be able and willing to make at least 200 calls each day to generate leads. Go to Web site to apply.

Provisions: This is a full-time position that pays well, over $40,000 per year.

MANAGEMENT RECRUITERS OF SACRAMENTO

2316 Bell Executive Lane, Suite 100, Sacramento, CA 95825

www.mrsacramento.com

Positions: Healthcare accounts managers. Job involves selling long-term energy contracts in the national healthcare vertical market.

Requirements: Must have experience dealing with Fortune 1000 level

323

executives and energy departments. Must be free to travel extensively to customer locations and trade shows. College graduates only. Although no energy industry experience is required, you must have at least five years of sales experience in the healthcare field with a proven track record of success.
Provisions: Can work from your home office anywhere in the continental United States.

MELALEUCA, INC.
3910 S. Yellowstone Hwy, Idaho Falls, ID 83402
www.melaleuca.com
Positions: This is a well-established company that has been around since 1985. It offers a line of natural and unique everyday products that are highly effective yet pleasant and safe to have in the home. All products are marketed through a network of sales consultants. Send for information.

THE MEMORY TRAINING INSTITUTE
264 Main St, Portland, CT 06480
Positions: Telemarketers set appointments with upper level management.
Requirements: Must be available weekends only, no weekends. Must enjoy phone work, be a self-starter, have successful telemarketing experience, be able to work without supervision, and be able to produce eight appointments each week.
Provisions: Will train using a proven system. Pays well. Live anywhere in United States.

MIRACLE MAID
8383 158th Ave., NE, Redmond, WA 98052
www.renaware.com
Positions: Miracle Maid cookware is sold through pre-arranged product demonstrations in customers' homes.
Provisions: Training is provided. Pays commission.

MOONWOLF ENTERPRISES
5303 Quintana St., Riverdale, MD 20737
www.moonwolf.net
Positions: Selling Web hosting, design, and other services.
Requirements: Must be motivated and self-starting. Knowledge of technical aspects of the Internet is a definite advantage, but is not required.
Provisions: This is a 100% telecommute position. Pays commission.

NSA, INC.

3926 Willow Lake Blvd, Memphis, TN 38118

www.nsavirtualoffice.com

Positions: Direct sales of natural supplements. NSA offers a proven program for part-time sales opportunities wherein a person can work 8-12 hours per week and earn up to $10,000 a year.

Requirements: New distributors of NSA products must first be sponsored by someone who is already a distributor. If one cannot be located, then the interested person must attend a regional training class. A schedule will be provided upon request.

Provisions: Training is provided. NSA products are sold through a trial use approach. A customer is given the opportunity to try the product for a few days, and then make the decision whether or not to purchase. Because of this method of selling, NSA recommends that distributors have 4-5 units on hand for this purpose. NSA provides a credit line so that the new distributor has no purchase requirements to get started. Pays commission plus bonuses through the company-sponsored rebate program.

NATURE'S SUNSHINE PRODUCTS, INC.

1655 N Main, Spanish Fork, UT 84660

www.naturessunshine.com

Positions: Direct sales of herbs, vitamins, and personal care products.

Requirements: New distributors must attend a one-week training session at company headquarters at their own expense. Reps are trained to sell the products through network marketing.

Provisions: Commissions start at 8% and go up to 30%. Managers receive generous override commissions. Participating managers receive health and dental insurance, new car allowance, and a retirement program. Sales aids and incentive programs are provided to everyone.

NEAR & ASSOCIATES

5955 Carnegie Blvd., Suite 300, Charlotte, NC 28209

www.nearassociates.com

Positions: Sales reps develop new business for this outsourcing firm.

Requirements: Proven track record of at least seven years selling outsourcing services and/or executive placement services.

Provisions: Pays base salary plus commission.

NEO-LIFE DIAMITE INTL
3500 Gateway Blvd., Fremont, CA 94538

www.gnld.com

Positions: Direct sales of household products, vitamins, minerals, and some food products. Multilevel techniques are used.

Requirements: A small investment is required.

Provisions: Pays commission on a sliding scale.

NOEVIR, INC.
1095 S.E. Main St., Irvine, CA 92714

www.noevirusa.com

Positions: Direct sales of cosmetics manufactured by Noevir, all of which are completely natural and herbal. Noevir has over 15,000 operators currently serving the United States. The company is an affiliate of a larger Japanese company, and also has an office in Canada. Noevir is a wholly owned subsidiary of Noevir, Co., Ltd., the second largest direct selling company in Japan.

Requirements: The initial investment in Noevir is $30 for registration in addition to the purchase of one starter kit. These kits contain products, training information, and samples for the new operator. The kits (choice of two) are $150. There is also a third option, which is a "build-your-own" kit. The minimum purchase for this kit is $50.

Provisions: Noevir offers a generous compensation package in addition to very high quality products.

OFFSHORE DATA ENTRY, a subsidiary of High Tech Exports, Gujarat
India

www.offshoredataentry.com

Positions: This company has openings for highly skilled marketing consultants to sell marketing data entry services to businesses. This is a global company with opportunities to work anywhere in the world—USA, Canada, Europe, Australia, etc.

Requirements: Minimum 4-5 years of marketing and 1-2 years of experience in data entry field. Must be IT savvy.

Provisions: Pays very high commissions. Can choose to work on exclusive or non-exclusive basis. Visit Web site, then e-mail résumé.

KENNETH OLSON & ASSOCIATES
399 Main St., Los Altos, CA 94022

Positions: Telemarketers for B2B insurance sales.

Requirements: Must be local resident. Prefers experience in B2B dealings.
Provisions: Specific training is provided. Leads are also provided. No high pressure selling involved. Part-time hours only. Pays salary plus "substantial" commission.

ORIFLAME INTERNATIONAL

P.O. Box 977, Waxhaw, NC 28173

www.oriflame.com

Positions: Direct sales reps for European cosmetics line. Oriflame International is a high-quality cosmetic line that has gained a reputation for being "the largest, most prestigious direct sales company in Europe." Company has been expanding throughout the US for about 10 years. Advisors are trained as skin consultants. Business does not usually consist of door-to-door or party style sales. More often, advisors act as make-up artists and customers come to their home offices by appointment only. Opportunity also for part-time sales leadership positions. Significant "ground floor" opportunity for Group Directors.
Provisions: Complete training is provided. Commissions are reportedly the highest in the US for a direct sales company.

OUR WEDDING VENDORS

www.ourweddingvendors.com

Positions: Regional sales of online advertising for wedding services.
Requirements: Minimum three years experience in online ad sales. Must have excellent communications and phone skills. Will need a home office with phone, voice mail, fax, computer, e-mail and Internet access.
Provisions: Can live anywhere in the US to apply, but must live within the region assigned. Check the Web site to see which regions are currently available. Industry and sales training is provided. Pays commission.

PAMPERED CHEF

350 South Rohlwing Road, Addison, IL 60101

www.pamperedchef.com

Positions: Hosting home parties called Kitchen Shows, where you'll demonstrate how Pampered Chef products can be used to easily and quickly prepare gourmet meals.
Provisions: Pays commission. There is plenty of room for advancement into management positions. This company offers a lot of support, particularly for working mothers.

PARTYLITE GIFTS

59 Armstrong Rd. #A, Plymouth, MA 02360

www.partylite.com

Positions: Home party sales of decorative accessories and giftware for the home.
Provisions: Pays commission plus bonuses. Management opportunities available.

PETRA FASHIONS, INC.

35 Cherry Hill Drive, Danvers, MA 01923

Positions: Direct sales of lingerie and sleepwear. All items are under $30. Petra consultants demonstrate the lingerie collection in private home parties. Consultants test show guests' "romance ratings" and offer fashion advice on garment style and fit. They do not collect money, take inventory, or make deliveries. Petra accepts Mastercard and VISA and all show orders are shipped C.O.D. by UPS directly to the party hostess.
Requirements: No investment or experience is necessary. Petra offers a free starter kit of sample garments and paperwork that is valued at more than $500. There are no quotas or sales territories.
Provisions: Petra provides free training, hostess incentives, profit per show in excess of $75, advancement opportunities, overrides, awards, and recognition.

POLA, U.S.A., INC.

251 East Victoria Avenue, Carson, CA 90746

www.pola.com

Positions: Home party sales of cosmetics.
Requirements: A start-up kit requires an investment.
Provisions: Pays commission.

POWERGY, INC.

111 Chestnut St., Providence, RI 02903

http://powergy.com

Positions: Sales reps for power quality/energy conservation device.
Requirements: There is a refundable $75 deposit required for a sales kit.

PRIMERICA

391 Gamble Oak Ct., Millersville, MD 21108

www.primerica.com

Positions: Auto and home insurance sales for top national company.
Provisions: Regional center does all paper work and service.

PRINCESS HOUSE, INC.
470 Myles Standish Blvd., Taunton, MA 02780

www.princesshouse.com

Positions: Home party sales of crystal products.

Provisions: Pays commission plus override for managers. Training is provided.

PROCARD INTERNATIONAL
6709 West 119th Street, #501, Overland Park, KS 66209

www.procardinternational.com

Positions: Marketing associates. Company represents over 300,000 dentists, doctors, and attorneys, over 1/2 of all hospitals, 83% of all pharmacies, and over 10,000 vision centers nationwide. Job involves activating accounts for people who have already requested dental, vision, prescription drug, and legal services.

Requirements: No sales experience is necessary for this job.

Provisions: Permanent or part-time positions available. Can live anywhere. Free leads provided.

QUALITY LOGIC
5401 Tech Circle, Moorpark, CA 93021

www.qualitylogic.com

Positions: Account managers for high tech sales to large enterprise accounts

Requirements: Must have at least seven years experience selling software business solutions above the $500,000 price point. College graduates only. Proven ability to telecommute without supervision. No travel is required.

Provisions: Full-time positions only. Can be anywhere in the US.

QUICK PRACTICE
500 N Broadway, Ste 256, Jericho, NY 11753

www.quickpractice.com

Positions: Sales of medical software. Home telemarketers give away this company's product for free to qualified healthcare professionals.

Requirements: Previous telemarketing experience required. Internet a plus. Send résumé.

Provisions: Pays $4.50 per qualified lead, plus 5% commission on sales that close from your leads. Average sale is $1200.

REGAL WARE, INC.

1675 Reigle Dr., Kewaskum, WI 53040

www.regalware.com

Positions: Direct sales of cookware, usually through home parties.

Provisions: Training is provided. Pays commission.

RELIV DISTRIBUTORS

136 Chesterfield Ind. Blvd., Chesterfield, MO 63005

www.relivonline.com

Positions: Nutritional products that combine the ingredients from science and nature in targeted, well balanced, easy to use formulas.

Provisions: Weekly local meetings and training sessions, national conference calls, 24-hour story call lines, conferences, and simple-to-use sales tools.

REXAIR, INC.

P.O. Box 3610, 3221 W Big Beaver Rd # 200, Troy, MI 48007

www.rainbowsystem.com

Positions: Direct sales of Rainbow vacuum cleaners, AquaMate, and related products.

R3X.NET, INC.

709 West Huron St., Ann Arbor, MI 48103

www.r3x.net

Positions: This company is in the business of very high level business consulting. Executive sales professionals here call on high level decision makers and corporate CEOs. Only those with this kind of experience will be considered.

Requirements: Must have a proven track record of exceeding quotas. Only the most qualified will be hired. Hours will average 35 to 40 per week.

Provisions: Those who qualify receive a free computer and high-speed Internet access. The income potential here is huge, but it will be well earned. This is not an opportunity for amateurs. For complete information on this opportunity, visit the company Web site.

SALADMASTER, INC.

912 113th St., Arlington, TX 76011

www.saladmaster.com

Positions: Home party sales of cookware and tableware.

Provisions: Training is available. Pays commission plus bonus plan.

SAN FRANCISCO CHRONICLE
Circulation Department, 925 Mission, San Francisco, CA 94103
Positions: Telemarketers sell subscriptions. Work is part-time.
Requirements: Some previous telemarketing experience is required.
Provisions: Can live anywhere in Northern California. Training is provided. Some leads are supplied. Pays commission and bonuses.

SCHOOL CALENDAR
1135 W. Morris Blvd., Morristown, TN 37813
www.morrcom.com
Positions: Account executives sell advertising space. Company is a 30-year-old publishing firm.
Requirements: Must be bondable.
Provisions: A protected territory is assigned. Training and accounts are provided. Pays commission and bonuses.

SECURE COMMUNICATION, INC.
150 W 28th St, New York, NY 10003
Positions: This company, Ergotron SCI, offers computer solutions and flat pane monitors to the hospital, manufacturing, and financial markets. They seek computer-literate individuals capable of operating independently to introduce hot new products to major organizations.
Requirements: Need experience calling Fortune 1000 companies and hospitals.
Provisions: Training, excellent compensation, and benefits are offered along with telecommuting option.

SHAKLEE CORPORATON
Shaklee Terraces, 444 Market Street #3600, San Francisco, CA 94111
www.shaklee.com
Positions: Shaklee's line of products includes "natural" cosmetics, health care products, household products, and now some services as well. All of Shaklee's products are sold by independent distributors.
Requirements: Distributors must stock inventory in all basic products, which does require a cash investment.
Provisions: Pays commission.

SILHOUETTE MARKETING
27350 SW 95th Ave., Wilsonville, OR 97070
Positions: This merchandise demonstration service needs schedulers and field managers in major West Coast cities.

Requirements: Schedulers need to be experienced, able to manage people, possess organizational skills, and be able to work flexible hours from home. Field managers also need to be available to work flexible hours, have a car, and be able to interview and hire reliable people. Send résumé.

SKYLIGHT TRAINING AND PUBLISHING, INC.

2626 S. Clearbrook Dr., Arlington Heights, IL 60005

Positions: SkyLight is the educational training and publishing division of Simon & Schuster. They need national accounts reps to sell to school personnel.

Requirements: Must have a Bachelor's degree (Master's degree preferred); excellent verbal and written communication skills; computer skills in word processing, database, presentation software; and a commitment to service. Sales experience should be in maintaining and managing territories, developing new leads through cold calling, and group presentations. Teaching or administrative experience in a school setting is important. Apply with résumé and include salary requirements.

SMITH MARKETING GROUP

1608 West Campbell Avenue, #196, Campbell, CA 95008

www.smithmarketinggroup.com

Positions: This is a full-service marketing and public relations agency offering part-time, full-time, temporary, and long-term sales positions in business development.

Requirements: Must be a business development professional capable of identifying new prospects and generating new business for the firm. Would prefer those with experience doing business development for marketing, communications, graphic design, public relations, or temporary staffing agency. Send résumé or apply online.

Provisions: Set your own flexible schedule. Pays commission only.

SOUTHERN LIVING AT HOME

P.O. Box 830951, Birmingham, AL 35283

www.southernlivingathome.com

Positions: Selling products that mirror the lifestyle found in Southern Living magazine through home parties.

Requirements: Purchase of a basic starter kit for $199. The kit has approximately a $500 value in product and business supplies, all the supplies needed to begin, catalogs, order forms, a Consultant Handbook with video, etc.

SPINS

118 2nd Street, 3rd Floor, San Francisco, CA 94105

www.spins.com

Positions: Regional sales and account management. Company provides marketing information to the natural products industry. This is a rapidly expanding market with many new opportunities.

Requirements: Requires the highest level of interpersonal and selling skills, strong analytical skills, and a technical aptitude. Prefers applicants with two or more years of experience in sales and also working with syndicated data. College graduates only. Knowledge or a keen interest in natural products. Must be proficient in the use of Windows, MS Office, and Excel.

Provisions: Provides competitive salary and bonus package with full benefits and stock options. Submit résumé via e-mail.

STAMPIN' UP!

12907 S 3600 W, Riverton, UT 84065

www.stampinup.com

Positions: Innovative products for creative stamping ideas, offering the latest in designs and techniques as well as hundreds of stamps and accessories. All products are sold via direct sales.

STORYTIME FELTS

www.funfelts.com

Positions: Direct sales of educational products based on storytelling.

Requirements: Must purchase a starter kit. A complete kit costs $100, but there is a "mini-supply kit" for only $30.

Provisions: Pays from 20% to 35% profits, plus additional bonuses. There are also plenty of marketing tools available to help you.

SUCCESS MOTIVATION INSTITUTE, INC.

P.O. Box 2508, Waco, TX 76702

www.success-motivation.com

Positions: SMI is the world leader in personal and professional development. Their products help businesses and sales organizations improve results.

Requirements: Must fill out application and be accepted by the company. $100 for a sales kit is the only cost.

Provisions: Sales training kit includes a cassette tape, full-color visual, two videotapes, starter supply of forms, and a "Success Guide."

SUMMIT VIEWS

540 N. Santa Cruz Ave #260, Los Gatos, CA 95030

www.summitviews.com

Positions: Independent sales reps follow-up on sales of products to natural food stores and hotels. The product is a densified wood firelog that is environmentally friendly, called Goodwood.

Requirements: Requires flexibility, great phone abilities, sense of humor, and interest in both the environment.

Provisions: Flexible part-time (10-20 hours per week). Pays hourly plus commission.

SUNLAND INTERNATIONAL

6280-P San Ignacio Avenue, San Jose, CA 95119

www.sunland-intl.com

Positions: Telemarketing sales reps for a leading supplier of DVD and CD drives, recordable media, external storage products, digital video recording peripherals, and software.

Requirements: Strong phone and customer services skills required.

Provisions: Part-time and full-time positions available. Can live anywhere.

SVI AMERICA CORPORATION

15800 John J Delaney Dr., Charlotte, NC 28210

Positions: Sales reps for the metro New York/New Jersey and New England territories.

Requirements: At least five years experience selling services to businesses. Need to be computer literate, have excellent multi-tasking and time management skills, and be able to set up and work in a telecommuting environment with little direct supervision.

TALENT WORLD MAGAZINE

38 West 32nd St. #805, New York, NY 10001

www.talentworld.biz

Positions: Part-time telemarketers for ad space sales.

Requirements: Must live in Manhattan. Prefers those with proven phone sales. Ad sales experience a plus. Inexperienced may apply.

Provisions: Leads provided. Salary dependent on experience, plus commission. Training provided.

TASTEFULLY SIMPLE
1920 Turning Leaf Lane SW, Alexandria, MN 56308
www.tastefullysimple.com
Positions: Tastefully Simple offers gourmet quality food that takes only minutes to prepare. Consultants market over 30 upscale, convenience-driven gourmet foods through taste testing parties by providing recipes, meal ideas, and entertaining suggestions.

THOMSON POLK DIRECTORIES
4709 Golf Rd. #600, Skokie, IL 60076
www.citydirectory.com
Positions: Thomson Polk has been the leading publisher of city directories since 1870. They are looking for sales reps and account executives to market city and statewide directories and other sales lead products to business in their local areas.
Requirements: Must have two years of college with marketing education, business-to-business sales experience, and strong communication skills.
Provisions: Pays base salary starting the mid-$20,000 range plus unlimited bonus potential.

TIME-LIFE BOOKS
8280 Willow Oaks Corporate Dr., Fairfax, VA 22031
www.timelife.com
Positions: Direct sales of educational publications.

TRI-CHEM, INC.
681 Main Street #24, Belleville, NJ 07109
www.tri-chem.com
Positions: Tri-Chem has manufactured craft products since 1948 and the complete line is now sold in more than 40 countries around the world. The leading product in their line is a liquid embroidery paint. Reps conduct craft classes to show potential customers how to use the products.
Requirements: To become a Tri-Chem instructor, you must host an introductory class, book at least four more classes for your first two weeks, and pay a small registration fee.
Provisions: Training is provided. Pays commission starting at 25% and going up to 50% with volume. Tri-Chem offers new instructors a consultant kit worth up to $260 and bonus coupons for free products worth up to $234. Bonus programs provide additional earnings, vacation trips plus special seminars and conventions to enhance training. Management opportunities are available.

TUPPERWARE HOME PARTIES

P.O. Box 2353, Orlando, FL 32802

http://order.tupperware.com

Positions: Direct sales of plastic food storage containers, cookware, and children's toys.

TYNDALE HOUSE PUBLISHERS, INC.

351 Executive Dr., Carol Stream, IL 60188

www.tyndale.com

Positions: Home-based telemarketers.

Requirements: Must be local resident. Experience required.

UNION TRIBUNE

4069 30th Street, Suite 9, San Diego, CA 92104

Positions: Telemarketers sell subscriptions.

Requirements: Must live in the San Diego area. Self-discipline is important.

Provisions: Training is provided. Some leads are supplied. Pays commission plus bonus.

USA TODAY

1000 Wilson Blvd., Circulation Dept., Arlington, VA 22234

Positions: Telemarketers solicit subscriptions. Work is distributed to home workers on a local basis only through USA Today's distributors. Distributors can be found in the phone book, or you can contact the main office to locate the distributor in your area.

USBORNE BOOKS AT HOME

P.O. Box 470663, Tulsa, OK 74147

www.ubah.com

Positions: Usborne's award-winning children's books have been sold worldwide since 1973. The books are all four-color, lavishly illustrated, information-packed books that children love to read. There is a wide range of subjects covering hobbies, science, nature guides, and more. Beginning in 1981, Usborne books have been successfully sold through home parties in Australia, Hong Kong, Singapore, England, and now the United States. The home business division sells over 600 Usborne titles with new publications being announced semi-annually. It also offers four methods of selling: home parties, fundraisers, book fairs, and direct sales. Usborne Books at Home is also a member of the Direct Selling Association.

Provisions: No experience necessary, training materials provided, no territories, no inventory to maintain, and no collections or product delivery. The investment of $70 or $160 includes all training materials, supplies and the base kit or mini-kit of Usborne books. The start-up kit includes training materials and supplies for only $25.

VITA CRAFT CORPORATION
11100 West 58 Street, Shawnee, KS 66203
www.vitacraft.com
Positions: Home party sales of cookware, china, crystal, tableware, and cutlery.
Provisions: Pays commission and bonuses. Training is provided.

WATER RESOURCES INTERNATIONAL, INC.
2800 East Chambers St., Phoenix, AZ 85040
Positions: Direct sales of water conditioning and purification systems.

WATKINS INCORPORATED
P.O. Box 5570, Winona, MN 55987
www.watkinsonline.com
Positions: Watkins is a well-established company that uses independent reps to sell its extensive line of household goods including food, health products, and cleaning items.
Requirements: A small start-up investment is required.
Provisions: Pays commission.

WCNET
www.wcnet.org
Positions: Appointment setters to set qualified appointments for sales managers. This is B2B calling during normal business hours.
Requirements: Must be self-motivated and have experience in sales or telemarketing. Visit Web site and apply via e-mail.
Provisions: Pays weekly and reimburses cost of phone.

WEDDING SOLUTIONS
6347 Caminito Tenedor, San Diego, CA 92120
www.weddingsolutions.com
Positions: Regional advertising sales managers for the largest publisher of wedding planning books in US.
Requirements: Must be seasoned sales professional with three to five years of experience selling online and/or print advertising. Must have proven advertising

sales experience and closing ability, excellent writing, intermediate to advanced computer skills, Internet experience, communication and interpersonal skills.
Provisions: Offers $50,000 to $120,000 salary. Provides comprehensive sales support include all online marketing material; Web-based CRM software, targeted leads in assigned territories, company 800 number, personal voicemail, and e-mail. There are over 50 territories in US; visit Web site to see which are open.

WELCOME WAGON

Welcome Wagon Bldg., 145 Court Ave., Memphis, TN 38103
www.welcomewagon.com

Positions: Welcome Wagon is a personalized advertising service. Individuals in all areas work from home to represent local businesses in the homes of brides-to-be, new parents, and newcomers.
Requirements: Outgoing personality, articulate, past-business or community experience. Car is a necessity.
Provisions: Training is provided. Flexible scheduling, part-time or full-time. Pays commission.

THE WEST BEND CO.

Premiere Cookware Division, 400 Washington St., West Bend, WI 53095
www.westbend.com

Positions: Direct sales of cookware and electrical appliances. The company started in 1911 and has been a member of the Direct Selling Association since 1927. West Bend has a deep respect for the direct selling industry because of the success of their other company, Tupperware.
Provisions: Training is provided through the use of Zig Ziglar training programs. In addition to commission, reps earn bonuses and can advance to management.

WORKSHOPS OF GERALD E. HENN

3672 Silliman St., New Waterford, OH 44445

Positions: This is a party-plan direct selling company that markets 19th century decorative products. They manufacture the products in Ohio and take great pride in their quality. The company has nearly tripled in size during the past few years and currently has over 2,000 independent contractors that work out of their homes as our sales representatives. Over 90% are working part-time and nearly 100% are female.
Provisions: New people start at a commission rate of 25% and ship products directly to the hostess.

WORLD BOOK, INC.

510 Merchandise Mart Plaza, Chicago, IL 60654

Positions: World Book, the encyclopedia publisher, sells its products through the use of direct sales reps.

Provisions: Training is provided. Some leads are provided. Pays commission. Sales kit costs $55. Management opportunities are available

X-RITE, INC

4300 44th St SE, Grand Rapids, MI 49512

www.xrite.com

Positions: Graphic art sales for this developer and manufacturer of instrument and software for color measurement and control. The products are sold into the graphic design, digital imaging, photographic, medical, plastics, and paints and coatings industries, among others. Positions are in the Boston area and reps will solicit orders in the Northeast territory.

Requirements: Need five years minimum professional selling experience in the graphic arts industry. Need proven organizational skills, BA/BS in graphic arts, motivation to work at home, and a willingness to travel overnight 25-50%.

Provisions: Offers competitive compensation, benefits including sales incentives, stock purchase, tuition reimbursement, and retirement plan.

YELLOW FREIGHT SYSTEMS, INC.

2627 State Road, Bensalem, PA 19020

Positions: Account sales for Yellow Freight, the largest LTL carrier in the United States.

Requirements: This opportunity is in Philadelphia. Must have college degree and 3-5 years sales executive experience in a service industry. Related industry experience is a plus.

Provisions: Pays competitive base salary plus incentives and a full range of flexible benefits.

ZONDERVAN BOOK OF LIFE

P.O. Box 6130, Grand Rapids, MI 49506

www.zondervan.com

Positions: The Book of Life is a set of books based on the parables of the Bible. The company was established in 1923 and has always used direct salespeople to market the product.

Requirements: A refundable $20 deposit is required.

Provisions: The deposit buys a sales kit, which includes all necessary training materials. Pays commission on a sliding scale, which increases with volume. Cash bonuses and promotions are available. Also available are credit union membership, company-paid insurance, and a deferred retirement compensation plan.

OPPORTUNITIES
WORKING WITH PEOPLE

In this section you will find a lot of jobs that have one basic requirement in common—the ability to work well with people. Both at-home and from-home jobs are included. Such jobs include telephone surveying, customer service, fundraising, recruiting, and staffing coordination—among many others.

Telephone surveying involves calling consumers to ask specific questions about their buying habits, or more weighty questions of social significance. The names and numbers are supplied and the surveyor is paid for each call. The work is not usually steady; it tends to come and go. This can be good for someone who cannot make a permanent commitment. If you want steady surveying work you should sign up with several companies in order to ensure back-to-back assignments.

Customer service is a profession that is finally coming into its own. American companies are starting to realize the importance of listening to their customers and trying to satisfy their needs. A customer service representative is basically a problem-solver. The job requires an ability to listen and record customers' comments accurately. Today, some of the country's biggest and best-known corporations have call centers staffed entirely by home-based workers scattered around the nation. And there are also customer service bureaus that hire hundreds of home-based customer service reps that handle the calls for even more major corporations. Getting these jobs is fairly simple, too. Applications, interviews, training, and even getting paid—it's all done online!

Fundraising can also be an easy job. It doesn't pay as well as surveying, usually only minimum wage plus a small bonus for bringing in so much in donations. It is, however, very easy work to get and it can be good experience leading to more sophisticated and higher paying phone work.

Staffing coordination is a fairly new opportunity for home workers. This work is found most often in the burgeoning healthcare field. Agencies are used to fill the staffing needs of hospitals, nursing homes, and outpatients. Calls come in day and night, but most agencies don't keep their doors open 24 hours a day. After 5 p.m. on weekdays and on weekends, calls are forwarded to a staffing coordinator's home. It is the coordinator's job to dispatch nurses and home health care workers, as they are needed during those hours. Most coordinators have pagers, so they need not be completely homebound.

Field surveying is a job that is custom made for someone with an outgoing personality. The word "field" indicates that most of the work is done outside—which may mean in a mall, at a movie theatre, or door-to-door. The surveyor collects answers to survey questions in the field and then returns home to fill out the paperwork. It is perfect for the person that needs the flexibility that working from home offers, but who doesn't want to be stuck inside all the time. Field surveyors work for market research firms and opinion pollers.

1-800-FLOWERS.COM
1-800-flowers.com

Positions: 1-800-FLOWERS.COM operates a global call center staffed with customer service agents who work from work. The home-based agents are serve as the first contact customers have with the company. They complete transactions in real time, working simultaneously with multiple software applications. Most are considered temporary workers since this tends to be a seasonal business.

Requirements: Must be a resident and live in Florida, New Mexico, New York, Ohio, Oklahoma, Texas, or Virginia. Must be highly PC literate and have your own PC with a reliable high-speed Internet connection. The ability to type 35 words per minute is essential. Prior call center experience is strongly preferred. Strong written and verbal communication skills as well as fundamental math skills are required. Availability must be very flexible as the workload is dependent upon the number of customers who are placing orders. Apply online.

Provisions: Pays competitive hourly rate plus generous bonus.

AAA CHICAGO
975 Meridian Lake Drive, Aurora, IL 60504

Positions: Independent travel agents work from home booking leisure travel.
Requirements: Must have a minimum 3 years experience, GRS/CRS knowledge, and a current leisure travel client base. This is for independent travel agents in Chicagoland and Northern Indiana only.

Provisions: Unlimited earning potential, ability to make your own hours, exclusive AAA savings with vendors, and ability to book your clients with reputable and secure companies that only AAA can provide.

A BRIGGS PASSPORT & VISA EXPEDITORS

1054 31st St NW Suite 270, Washington, DC 20007

www.abriggs.com

Positions: Answering customer calls on Friday nights and weekends, total of about 150 calls.

Requirements: Must have constant Internet connection and have separate phone line. Need voicemail system to pick up calls that come in while you are talking to customers. You must be within local calling range of Washington, DC.

Provisions: Training provided in Georgetown office for two or three days, and the job begins when you are trained and can take calls at home. The pay is $100 per weekend. You must work every weekend.

ACCOLADE SUPPORT CALL CENTER

www.accoladesupport.com/techjob.html

Positions: Full and part-time agents work as PC desktop support agents. All home-based workers are independent contractors.

Requirements: Must be able to provide desktop troubleshooting, resolve Internet connectivity issues, and support software applications. In addition, you will need a US-based home telephone number (land lines only, no cell phones or VOIP phones), a corded telephone set with a headset (no cordless phones), a PC with Windows XP or Vista, your PC wired to a cable modem, DSL modem, or broadband connection (no wireless connections), and a quiet environment where you can take calls without being disrupted or callers hearing any noise or sounds in the background. Apply through the Web site.

Provisions: $8.25 to $10 per hour.

ACD DIRECT

P.O. Box 1526, Layton, UT 84041

www.acddirect.com

Positions: Home-based call center agents take inbound and place outbound calls to customers.

Requirements: Call center experience (preferably work at home) is a *must.* Requires a high quality computer with high-speed Internet service, dedicated phone line, and dedicated office with a door. You will be required to complete all initial training before taking calls and complete ongoing/recurrent training. Apply through the Web site.

AIS MARKET RESEARCH

1320 E Shaw Ave.#100, Fresno, CA 93704

www.aismarketres.com

Positions: Field surveyors in the San Joaquin Valley.

Requirements: Must be resident of either Fresno or Modesto. Market research or similar experience required. Send for application.

Provisions: Work is part-time and sporadic. Pays by the survey.

ALL STAR PERSONNEL, INC.

21625 Chagrin Blvd., Beachwood, OH 44122

www.a1jobs.com

Positions: Recruiters identify and source applicants, phone screen, and interview candidates by analyzing qualifications and matching hiring criteria.

Requirements: Three years of non-exempt and exempt level recruiting and hiring required. Work is full-time. Local area residents send résumé.

ALPINE ACCESS

1120 Lincoln St #1400, Denver, CO 80203

www.alpineaccess.com

Positions: Alpine Access is a call center company that provides customer service solutions using home-based employees. About 300 home-based customer service representatives currently handle inbound calls for a variety of companies including J. Crew and 1-800-Flowers. There is some data entry involved in the work.

Requirements: Must be able to work 20 hours a week on a regular schedule. All applications are processed online. If you pass the initial screening, you will be interviewed over the phone.

Provisions: Pays $8-$14 an hour. Paid on-the-job training.

AMERICAN RED CROSS

2700 Wilshire Blvd., Los Angeles, CA 90057

Positions: Telephone recruiters locate potential blood donors.

Requirements: Two years telemarketing experience required. Must be available Sunday through Thursday. Excellent communications skills necessary. Los Angeles residents only. Send résumé.

Provisions: Pays hourly rate.

AMERICAN THRIFT STORE

401 W. Jefferson Blvd., Dallas, TX 75208

Positions: Telemarketers call for donations.

Requirements: Local residents only.

AMVETS

2840 Lafayette Rd., Indianapolis, IN 46203

Positions: Fundraisers call for donations of clothing and household articles.

Requirements: Must live in Indianapolis.

Provisions: Pays hourly wage plus bonus plan.

ARISE VIRTUAL SOLUTIONS

3450 Lakeside Drive, Suite 620, Miramar, FL 33027

www.arise.com

Positions: Matches work-from-home agents with open positions in sales, technical support and customer service. Arise contracts with its clients to provide certain levels of service, which are mirrored by Arise's contracts with the Virtual Services Corporations (home workers). Arise typically pays a service fee to its Virtual Services Corporations that are based on per call, per minute, or per hour rates. Service opportunities in the sales arena also offer sales-related incentives and rewards.

Requirements: Must be available to work a minimum 15 hours per week. Must invest in your own certification courses and equipment. Must incorporate.

Provisions: You choose when and how often you provide service with flexible scheduling options that allow you to divide your time into increments as few as 30 minutes. Arise provides you with access to the scheduling tools so that your service shift selections can be made from home. Admissions process takes as little as 7 days.

ARO Outsourcing

3100 Broadway, Suite 100, Kansas City, MO 64111

www.callcenteroptions.com/careers.asp

Positions: ARO is a contact center for some of the nation's leading corporations based on a work at home business model. Call agents train at home and work at home 100% of the time.

Requirements: You will be answering inbound and outbound calls. To qualify for this position you must have extensive customer service background and skills. You must be able to type efficiently and accurately. There is no cold calling or telemarketing within the position.

Provisions: The company hires in the states and geographic locations based upon clients' needs at any given time. If they are currently not hiring in your specific area, they will keep your detailed information on file, and contact you via e-mail when something is available in your area. Apply through the Web site.

ARTHRITIS FOUNDATION

657 Mission St. # 603, San Francisco, CA 94109

www.arthritis.org

Positions: Telephone recruiters find volunteers to go door-to-door for donations. This program repeats every fall and spring for about two months each time.

Requirements: Must live in the Bay area. Experience is not required, but the director says this work is very difficult and may not be suitable for newcomers. Must be available to work (call) during the evening hours of 6:00-9:30 p.m.

Provisions: Pays per recruitment.

ATC HEALTHCARE SERVICES, INC.

5151 E Broadway Blvd Suite 530, Tucson, AZ 85712

www.atchealthcare.us

Positions: Weekend staffing coordinator for temporary agency.

Requirements: Must be local, organized, and people-oriented. Strong organizational skills also needed. Phone skills are a must.

AURALOG

3710 E. University Drive, Suite #1, Phoenix, AZ 85034

www.auralog.com

Positions: This distance learning company has two kinds of home-based jobs: online tutors and customer service representatives. Both are part-time positions with four-hour shifts around the clock. Customer service reps customers' questions about Auralog 's tools, their training program, and any technical problems they may encountered. Online tutors teach and lead telephone conversations with learners.

Requirements: Online tutors, your native language is English and Spanish is required. Customer service reps need excellent writing skills, a good knowledge in Windows (any version), and a familiarity with text chat tools such as MSN Messenger or Yahoo Messenger. Experience in after-sales service or call center would be a plus. All home-based workers must reside in Georgia, Pennsylvania, Maryland, Virginia, North Carolina, New Hampshire, or Arizona. PC and Internet connection is required. Apply online

Provisions: Pays customer service reps up to $9 an hour. Pays online tutors up to $15 an hour.

BECKER & ASSOCIATES

www.becker-assoc.com/jobs/job_opening_marketing_assis.html

Positions: Professional marketing assistants.

Requirements: Apply through Web site.

Provisions: Typical pay range is $10 to $15 per hour with some of their clients offering bonuses on top of the hourly pay.

BRAIN FUSE

www.brainfuse.com

Positions: Online math, reading, and science tutoring for students in grades 3–12. This is flexible part-time work that can be done online from anywhere.

Requirements: Must be certified teacher. Apply online.

Provisions: Pays $10 an hour. Pick your own schedule.

CALIFORNIA COUNCIL FOR THE BLIND

3919 W Magnolia Blvd., Burbank, CA 91505

Positions: Fundraisers telephone for donations of household discards.

Requirements: Must be resident of greater Los Angeles area. Good phone manner necessary.

Provisions: Pays hourly plus bonus plan.

CAMBRIDGE HOME HEALTHCARE

61322 Southgate Rd #2, Cambridge, OH 44256

Positions: On call staffing for nursing agency.

Requirements: Need to be available evenings and weekends. Local applicants send résumé.

CANADIAN DIABETES ASSOCIATION

National Life Building, 400-522 University Ave, Toronto
ON, Canada M5G 2R5
www.diabetes.ca

Positions: Recruiting people in the St Margaret's Bay, Prospect, Herring Cove, Timberlea and the Hammonds Plains areas to canvas for door to door campaign.

Requirements: Must live in Halifax, Nova Scotia. Must have excellent organizational and communication skills.

Provisions: This is part-time work paying $7 an hour.

CAREMORE IN-HOME SERVICE
189 Lakeview Commons #100, Gibbsboro, NJ 08026
Positions: On-call coordinator.
Requirements: RN with maturity, good judgment, problem solving and ability to work effectively with full-time RN care managers. Local applicants send résumé.

CAREONE, INC., a division of Ascend One
8930 Stanford Blvd., Columbia, MD 21045
Positions: CareOne provides a variety of products and services to help consumers better manage their finances. The company has a national virtual customer care team who work at home offering customer service by responding to the inbound calls from existing customers.
Requirements: Minimum 2 years of customer service experience including some recent contact center telephone customer service experience preferred. Must have professional home office environment with PC, high-speed Internet connection, and dedicated phone line (land line only). Need to attend five to six weeks of training in Pittsburgh and be able to work a schedule that includes evenings (such as M-F, 1 p.m. to 10 p.m) or Saturdays (such as M,T,W,F, and Saturday, 9 a.m. to 6 p.m.).
Provisions: Offers a competitive salary ($25,000-$30,000 starting base) and comprehensive benefits package.

CAR-LENE RESEARCH
2127 Northbrook Ct., Northbrook, IL 60062
Positions: Field surveyors and telephone interviewers for market research assignments.
Requirements: Must live in Deerfield, IL; Pomona, CA; Santa Fe Springs, CA; Northbrook, IL; Hanover, MA; Dallas, TX; or Richardson, TX. Market research experience is required.
Provisions: Pays by the survey.

CATALINA IN-HOME SERVICES
1602 E. Fort Lowell Rd., Tucson, AZ 85719
Positions: On-call scheduler for evenings.
Requirements: Scheduling experience required. Must be computer proficient and be willing to make long-term commitment. Local applicants send résumé.

CERTIFIED MARKETING SERVICES, INC.

7 Hudson St., Kinderhook, NY 12106

Positions: Market research surveys are conducted nationwide by independent, part-time field workers.

Requirements: Must be over 18 years of age. No experience is required, but good organization and communication skills are helpful. Write for information.

Provisions: Hourly wage, travel expenses, and reimbursables.

CONNECTICUT CHILDREN'S MEDICAL CENTER

282 Washington St., Hartford, CT 06106

Positions: Nursing for RN's Pediatric Advice Line. Provide telephone triage, communications to providers, and data entry.

Requirements: Experience in ED, pedi ambulatory, pedi critical care, or pedi homecare required. Need Connecticut RN license, strong communication skills, schedule flexibility, and ability to make autonomous decisions and be accountable. Local professionals send résumé.

Provisions: Pays competitive salary plus benefits.

CONSUMER OPINION SEARCH, INC.

10403 Clayton Rd., St. Louis, MO 63131

Positions: Field surveyors.

Requirements: St. Louis residents only. Good communication skills required.

Provisions: Pays by the survey.

CONVERGYS

www.convergys.com

Positions: Hires home-based agents to serve as customer service, technical assistance or sales agents for clients. Company currently has over 75,000 employees in 70 countries (not all are home-based).

Requirements: A home office environment that is quiet and free from distraction, a PC that meets the requirements of the Home Agent platform (you can test your PC during the on-line application process), high-speed Internet access, USB headset with a built-in digital signal processor, telephone with a mute button to be utilized during training, team meetings, and individual coaching and technical support sessions. Must complete and submit application online.

Provisions: Paid training is provided in your home. Convergys Home Agents can select from applicable benefits that include paid time off, paid training, company holidays, 401(k) plan, employee stock purchase plan, life insurance, medical coverage, dental coverage, vision coverage, and more.

COVERED BRIDGE GIRL SCOUT COUNCIL
1100 Girl Scout Lane, Terre Haute, IN 47807
Positions: Membership specialists to expand membership within assigned communities.
Requirements: Prefers Bachelor's degree. Must be willing to work flexible hours. Send cover letter, résumé, and salary requirements.
Provisions: This is a 100% telecommute position.

CUSTOM HOME FOOD SERVICE
2070 Attic Parkway NW, Kennesaw, GA 30152
Positions: Telemarketing (no sales).
Requirements: Work at home in the Marietta area.
Provisions: Pays salary plus bonus.

DAVIS MARKET RESEARCH SERVICES, INC.
23801 Calabasas Rd., Calabasas, CA 91302
Positions: Field surveyors.
Requirements: Local residents only. Experience working with the public required.

DEVON CONSULTING
950 W. Valley Road, Suite 2602, Wayne, PA 19087
www.devonconsulting.com
Positions: Technical recruiting. Duties include querying the company database and the Internet for qualified candidates, phone screening, interviewing, administering tech check skill testing, reference checking, attending job fairs and other strategic recruiting events, and various administrative duties.
Requirements: Must live near company headquarters. Ideal candidates should have excellent verbal communication skills, computer knowledge and the ability to handle multiple tasks. Minimum three years IT recruiting experience required. You will be required to come in to the company office occasionally. Send résumé.
Provisions: Offers flexible schedule and advancement opportunities.

DISABLED AMERICAN VETERANS
273 E. 800 South, Salt Lake City, UT 84111
Positions: Telemarketers use the phone to ask for donations of household articles.
Requirements: No experience required. Must live in Salt Lake City.
Provisions: Pays minimum hourly wage plus bonus plan.

DISABLED AMERICAN VETERANS OF COLORADO
8799 North Washington, Denver, CO 80229

Positions: Fundraisers call for donations of household discards to be sold through thrift stores.

Requirements: Denver residents only. Must have good phone voice and self-discipline.

Provisions: Training provided. Pays small hourly wage plus bonus plan.

DOCUMENT DO-IT-YOURSELF
www.document-do-it-yourself-service.com

Positions: Remote customer service reps provide quality support through e-mail, phone, and chat. They handle support and service tickets, answer common questions, and do basic data entry and logging. Working from home is encouraged.

Requirements: Need great phone voice and people skills, typing speed of 50 wpm or more, and minimum two years of desk customer service experience. Spanish is a big plus. Send résumé to: management@Document-Do-It-Yourself-Service.com

EDEN STAFFING
420 Lexington Ave., # 2100, New York, NY 10016

Positions: Dispatchers for large staffing company. Work entails dispatching temporary workers and acting as liaison with clients.

Requirements: Must be articulate and quick thinking. Experience is preferred, but not required. Local residents only send résumé. Must available for midnight to 8 a.m. shift.

EDUCATE ONLINE
www.educate-online.com

Positions: Online teachers provide live instruction (personalized reading and math programs) for students in grades K-12 facilitated exclusively via the Internet. Cutting edge technology allows students to talk and interact with teachers in a real-time online classroom. This is a part-time opportunity that's ideal for at-home parents, retired teachers, or teachers who are not able to travel to a traditional classroom setting.

Requirements: Must have the ability to teach both reading and math in one of the following subject combinations: reading and math (Grades 3 - 8) or math (Grades 3 - 8) and algebra. Must have at least two years of classroom teaching experience in an academic setting and have a current or former teaching certification from a US state. Substitute and emergency 30-day teaching certifications are not accepted. Must have at least a Bachelor's degree and be able to successfully pass a background check process including FBI fingerprinting. Must be available to work at least 10 hours a week. Eight of the 10 hours must be worked Monday through Friday between the hours of 5 and 9 p.m. during peak season (October through February). Must have a reliable Microsoft based PC to use for work purposes that meets specific technical requirements (see Web site for details). Bilingual candidates especially needed. **Provisions:** Offers paid training, flexible scheduling, $10 an hour, and a part-time employee benefits package including medical and dental coverage as well as a 401(k) retirement savings plan.

EDUCATIONAL PARTNERS ASSOCIATION
www.epa-cpr.com
Positions: Phone survey clerk (no sales).
Requirements: Must be a resident of Ottawa, Ontario. Must be fluent in English. Computer skills are a plus. Knowledge of e-mail required.
Provisions: This is off-hours part-time employment. Pays $10 hourly for 12 to 30 hours per week.

EL CAMINO MEMORIAL PARK
5600 Carol Canyon Rd., San Diego, CA 92121
Positions: Telemarketers conduct surveys over the phone.
Requirements: Experience dealing with the public. Must live in San Diego.
Provisions: Training is provided. Pays salary plus bonus.

ELECTRONIC SEARCH, INC
5105 Tollview Dr., # 245, Rolling Meadows, IL 60008
Positions: Research recruiters, assistants, account executives, national account managers, and résumé processors. Work entails name and résumé sourcing, research, profiling, and Internet job posting.
Requirements: Must be motivated, organized, have excellent communication skills, and have a good home office setup.
Provisions: Full-time and part-time openings available. Training provided.

ETR TECHNOLOGY CENTER
180 Oser Avenue, Suite 400, Hauppauge, NY 11788
www.etrtechcenter.com
Positions: Pharmaceutical staffing and recruiting.
Requirements: Knowledge of the pharmaceutical marketplace. Experience in pharmaceutical staffing with a proven track record. Must live in the New

Jersey/New York area. Visit Web site and apply via e-mail.

Provisions: Provides excellent compensation package.

FACTS 'N FIGURES

14550 Chase St., #78B, Panorama City, CA 91402

Positions: Market research and public opinion surveys are conducted by field surveyors and telephone interviewers.

Requirements: Must be resident of greater Los Angeles. Interviewing experience is required.

Provisions: Pays by the survey.

FUTURO INFANTIL HISPANO

2227 E Garvey Ave., N, West Covina, CA 91791

Positions: Foster agency needs bilingual English/Spanish social workers for counseling or social psychology in the Pomona and Huntington Park areas.

Requirements: Must have MSW, MFCC, or Master degree in child counseling, child psychology, or development.

Provisions: Offers salary plus excellent benefits plus telecommuting option.

GALLUP POLL

Attn: Field Dept, 47 Hulfish Street, 100 Palmer Square, Suite 200, P.O. Box 310, Princeton, NJ 08542

Positions: Market researchers for field research. Across the country, there are 360 sampling areas. Market researchers conduct surveys in the field (usually door-to-door), returning home only to do the "paperwork." There are almost 2,000 of these home-based researchers around the US. This work is permanent part-time. It is conducted during weekends, approximately 1 - 2 weekends per month.

Requirements: No experience required and no age restriction for persons over 18. You need only to be able to read well, talk with people and have a dependable car. Send work experience, address and phone number with letter of interest.

Provisions: An applicant must complete sample work which is tested and graded before job begins. After a person is accepted as an interviewer, Gallup's techniques are self-taught using an Interviewer's Manual and by communicating with the Field Administrator in the Princeton Office. All workers are independent contractors and are expected to meet minimum quotas. Pays an hourly wage plus expenses. "We're always looking for responsible people, especially permanent part-timers."

GAVEL & GOWN SOFTWARE, INC.
184 Pearl St., Suite 304, Toronto, ON, Canada M5H 1L5
Positions: This software manufacturer specializes in case management applications for the legal community with a market that encompasses all of North America. IT professionals wanting to become authorized resellers or certified consultants should forward résumé.

GENERATION Z
www.generationz.com
Positions: Recruiting IT professionals for this Internet development firm.
Requirements: Strong technical knowledge of recruiting. Familiarity with technologies such as OS, protocols, connectivity, various software applications, certifications and programming languages. Computer or technology degree or equivalent experience is required as well as a minimum three years in sales and management. E-mail your résumé to development@generationz.com.
Provisions: Salary is over $100,000.

GOOD SAMARITAN COMMUNITY HEALTHCARE
407 14th Ave., SE, Puyallup, WA 98371
Positions: Medical professionals perform night telephone triage from 5 p.m. to 8 a.m. with some home visitations possible.
Requirements: Local professionals send résumé.
Provisions: Pays salary plus full benefits.

HARVEY RESEARCH ORGANIZATION, INC.
600 Perinton Hills Office Park, Fairport, NY 14450
Positions: Interviewers to work as independent contractors on continuing assignments. Work is available in all major cities. There are 50 to 100 interviewers in each sampling area. Most interviews are conducted in the field.
Requirements: Experience is necessary. Write a letter of interest. You will be sent an application, then a sample survey to complete before being hired permanently.
Provisions: Pays by the survey.

HAYES MARKETING RESEARCH
7840 El Cajon Blvd., Suite 400, La Mesa, CA 92041
Positions: Field surveyors and telephone interviewers for market research.
Requirements: Local area residents only. Experience required.
Provisions: Pays by the survey.

HIGHLINE COMMUNITY HOSPITAL
13030 Military Rd S, Tukwila, WA 98168

Positions: On-call nursing, home infusion. Triage and respond to all calls making scheduled and unscheduled visits.

Requirements: Home care/infusion experience preferred. Local RNs submit résumé.

HIRERIGHT, INC.
2100 Main Street Suite 400, Irvine, CA 92614

www.hireright.com

Positions: Telephone researchers. This is a B2B Internet company that is currently focused on delivering pre-employment screening services that help employers rapidly hire the right person the first time. They now have over 3,800 researchers. The system is Internet-based.

Requirements: Must be energetic and enthusiastic phone researchers who can quickly and accurately complete employment and education verifications for company's clients. The ideal candidate should have experience working within a call center environment, processing high volume software-based transactions. Excellent written and verbal communications are essential. Must be familiar with e-commerce and the Internet and be comfortable with technology.

Provisions: This is a full-time job paying $10 to $12 per hour.

HOSPICE OF SAN FRANCISCO
225 30th, San Francisco, CA 94121

Positions: Staffing coordinator for non-office hours.

Requirements: Experience in medical staffing required. Must live in San Francisco. Good phone manner important. Knowledge of medical terminology preferred.

Provisions: Pays hourly rates.

H/P TECHNOLOGIES, INC.
4545 N. 36th St. Suite 114, Phoenix, AZ 85018

www.hptechnologies.com

Positions: Technical recruiters within the healthcare industry.

Requirements: Must be ambitious and possess industry experience, strong sales background and recruiting experience. Also need to have excellent computer, Internet searching, and technology skills.

Provisions: No cap on commissions. Recruiters here earn up to $100,000 per year.

HUMAN RESOURCES PROFESSIONAL GROUP (HRPG)

P.O. Box 231276, Encinitas, CA 92033

www.hrpg.com

Positions: Recruiting in the San Diego area for HR consulting firm serving small and mid-sized businesses. Company provides recruitment and staffing, audits and compliance, employee relations, training, on-site HR management and special projects.

Requirements: Must have minimum of two years recruiting experience, particularly in the areas of IT, biotech, medical device, pharmaceutical, and sales. Must be able and willing to travel all over SD County, have the ability to work on-site or from home, including access to the Internet.

Provisions: Positions are hourly and hours and assignments are flexible. Visit Web site and apply via e-mail with "Recruiter" in the subject line.

ILLINOIS AMVETS

4711 W. 137th St., Crestwood, IL 60445

Positions: Fundraisers phone for donations of household articles.

Requirements: There are 10 locations in Illinois; you must reside in one of them. No experience necessary outside of good speaking ability.

Provisions: Part-time hours are flexible. Pays commission for every pick-up; averages about $7.50 an hour.

INSIGNIA SOLUTIONS

51 Columbia, Aliso Viejo, CA 92656

Positions: Technical support and customer service agents work at home for this 20-year old mobile and wireless device management company.

Requirements: Must have customer service experience and technical knowledge of mobile devices. Send résumé.

INTEGRITY STAFFING

30042 Mission Blvd., Suite 121-238, Hayward, CA 94544

www.integritystaffing.org

Positions: Recruiting entry level to executive level positions such as office administration, management, sales, marketing, accounting, healthcare, or IT. Duties will include searching and recruiting quality candidates through use of Internet recruiting, cold calling, and referrals; interviewing candidates via telephone and in person interviews as necessary; performing reference checks; and participating in review meetings with supervisor. Must have a fully functional home office.

Provisions: The salary is commission based.

INTERIM HEALTHCARE
1601 Sawgrass Corporate Parkway, Sunrise, FL 33323
Positions: This franchised agency (previously known as Medical Personnel Pool) is a nursing staff placement agency with office coast to coast. In some areas where "satellite offices" operate in outlying area, home-based staffing coordinators are used to take incoming calls and dispatch nurses to work assignments. In some offices, this is done only at night and on weekends.
Requirements: Some phone experience is preferred. Staffing experience is also preferred, but not necessary. Must be self-directed. Write to find the office nearest to you or look it up in your local phone book.

ISPEAKUSPEAK
Plaza Cordon, 1, Madrid, Spain 28005
www.ispeakuspeak.com
Positions: Online ESL telephone teacher.
Requirements: No previous ESL experience is required as complete training is included. Must be a native English speaker, be IT literate, have computer with digital connection to Internet, and have land line. ESL Studies or other educational field studies (completed or in progress) is appreciated but not necessary. Business experience working in non-related ESL fields is appreciated but not necessary. After submitting résumé, the successful candidates will receive an initial screening telephone interview of 20 minutes. Selected candidates will then be given access codes to the ISUS platform to watch training tutorials on method and materials. A practice student will be assigned to the teacher and a 2nd interview will be conducted using a role-play interview method. If the candidate performs well in this role-play interview, the next step is a final induction session on materials and methodology. A final 30-minute test class will be assigned as the last step in the process. Having completed this test, the candidate will receive an ISUS tutor certificate and can come on board as a member of staff. The entire process can be conducted over the space of 5 days, requiring a maximum of 15 hours of the candidate's time.
Provisions: Rates of pay are very competitive and quoted according to your country of residence and local currency. Teachers are hired as freelance workers and are paid for the number of hours they do on a monthly basis. Candidates can live anywhere in the world. Teachers can normally teach up to 25-30 hours a week, Monday to Friday although teachers can work as little or as much as they want. As students are scattered across time zones, teachers enjoy a maximum level of flexibility as the ISUS Coordination Department (responsible for assigning students to tutors) has a wide range of timetables to choose from. Most teachers prefer to work in blocks of 2-4 hours.

J. LODGE
13130 Westlinks Terrace, Ste 5, Fort Myers, FL 33913
www.jlodge.com

Positions: Call analysts work at home for this call center in permanent, part-time careers. Work consists of listening to pre-recorded phone calls from clients and evaluating the performance of the agent and comments of the customer. The analysis is entered onto an online scorecard along with coaching comments focused on helping the agent improve their customer service skills.

Requirements: The J.Lodge model employee is on SSDI due to a physical disability. The minimum work and education experience requirements vary from one contract to another, but usually require a college degree and previous supervisory experience. Need a PC (specifications will be forwarded to you during the interview process) and a cable-speed Internet connection. The work demands a quiet work space so that you can concentrate on each call without distraction. You will also participate in various conference calls with other team members on a regular basis so you will need a telephone at your work station. The entire interview and training process is conducted remotely with you in your home office. The company is always accepting applications. Apply at employment@jlodge.com.

J&R FIELD SERVICES, INC.
747 Caldwell Ave., North Woodmere, NY 11581

Positions: Field surveyors.

Requirements: Market research experience is required. Must be local resident.

JACKSON ASSOCIATES
1140 Hammond Dr., N.E. #H, Atlanta, GA 30328

Positions: Field and telephone interviewers for market research surveys.

Requirements: Experience required. Must be local resident.

Provisions: Pays by the survey.

JOE COCHRAN AGENCY
1032 Huffman St., Fort Wayne, IN 46808

Positions: Appointment setters for insurance agency. Calls are made to select clients; no cold calls.

Requirements: Local residents only.

JOHNS HOPKINS HEALTH CARE, LCC

Human Resources, 6704 Curtis Court, Glen Burnie, MD 21060

Positions: Specialty care coordinator for intensive care coordination and case management.

Requirements: Bachelor's degree in nursing with Master's preferred. Must be licensed as RN in Maryland and have 7 years of nursing experience including case management for at least 2 years. Although this job is home-based, you will be traveling locally much of the time. Local qualified nurses, send résumé and cover letter.

Provisions: Offers generous salary and benefits.

KC DISTANCE LEARNING

650 NE Holladay, Suite 1400, Portland, OR 97232

www.kcdistancelearning.com

Positions: KC Distance Learning (KCDL) is a leading provider of distance learning programs for middle school and high school students including core, foreign language, honors, and AP courses. Courses are delivered to students across the US, in both online and correspondence formats. Home-based teachersreview and edit high school curriculum for several areas. Projects include reviewing and updating content and labs as needed, as well as aligning to state standards.

Requirements: Need 1-2 years of classroom experience. Must have 20 hours a week available. Apply online.

Provisions: Pays $18 an hour.

KELLY SERVICES, INC.

Positions: Staffing coordinators. Kelly relies on home-based staffing coordinators to take calls and dispatch temporary personnel during the night as a service to clients who operate on 24-hour shift rotations.

Requirements: Some experience in personnel placement is required. Write to locate the office nearest or find it in the phone book, then apply directly to that office.

Provisions: Positions are considered part-time only. Pays flat salary.

KENDA SYSTEMS, INC.

One Stiles Road, Salem, NH 03079

www.kenda.com

Positions: Technical recruiters with good connections and experience with successful IT placements.

Requirements: Proven record of success. Visit Web site, then e-mail résumé.
Provisions: Payment is 100% commission.

THE KIDNEY FOUNDATION

Positions: Fundraising on a local level. Work involves calling for donations of household items.
Provisions: Training provided. Pays hourly wage plus bonuses. The Kidney Foundation has branch offices in every city. Call the one nearest you for more information.

KINSHIP

3210 Oliver Ave N, Minneapolis, MN 55412

Positions: Local coordinators recruit and train volunteer mentors for youth.
Requirements: BA in social work or psychology required. Need reliable vehicle, experience with MS Word, knowledge of Dakota Co. Vol Management, public speaking, and experience with youth. Send résumé.
Provisions: Offers flexible hours working from home. Pay includes benefits.

LIVEOPS

www.liveops.com

Positions: Liveops is one of the largest virtual call centers in the world with over 20,000 home agents. Customer service calls for a variety of major corporations are routed through this center—all answered by people who work from home. As independent contractors, agents are paid for the business services they provide to LiveOps. Typically, agent services include handling order calls or support calls for LiveOps clients.
Requirements: Must apply online and complete the company's certification process.
Provisions: Once accepted into the LiveOps network, agents use the LiveOps online scheduling system to commit to providing services, in half-hour increments, at times of their choosing. Agents can also choose to work at any time while uncommitted. While LiveOps independent agents handle calls around-the-clock, 24/7/365, demand for agents varies by half-hour block. In most cases, Agents invoice LiveOps per minute of talk time. Each program will have a unique rate per minute. In addition, many clients provide additional selling incentives for certain products or services. These incentives can dramatically increase Agent revenue as Agents become more confident in their ability to sell the products and services.

LOS ANGELES MARKETING RESEARCH ASSOCIATES
5712 Lankershim Blvd., North Hollywood, CA 91601
Positions: Field interviewers.
Requirements: Interviewing experience required.
Provisions: Pays by the survey.

LOUIS HARRIS AND ASSOCIATES
111 Fifth Ave., New York, NY 10020
Positions: Market researchers and opinion surveyors are needed in the field.
Requirements: No experience is necessary. Louis Harris has several hundred sampling areas and it is necessary to live in one of them. Write and ask for an application, which will be kept on file. When something comes up, you will be called. If you are ready for work, you will receive your instructions over the phone. How you complete the assignment from there is up to you.
Provisions: Pays by the survey, about $15 to $50+ per survey.

LUANNE GLAZER ASSOCIATES, INC.
596 Glenbrook Rd. #10, Stamford, CT 06902
Positions: Field surveyors and telephone interviewers for market research.
Requirements: Must be local resident. Excellent communication skills and ability to follow directions explicitly required.
Provisions: Training is provided. Pays by the survey.

MARY LUCAS MARKET RESEARCH
4101 Rider Trl N #100, Earth City, MO 63045
Positions: Field surveyors and telephone interviewers.
Requirements: Market research experience is required. Must be resident of greater St. Louis area.

MAXIM HEALTHCARE SERVICES
2250 N. Druid Hills Rd., NE, Atlanta, GA 30329
Positions: Medical on-call coordinator for after hours and weekends.
Requirements: Prior staffing experience is necessary. Local applicants send résumé.

MEDLINK OF OHIO
20600 Chagrin Blvd., Beachwood, OH 44122
Positions: Homecare and staffing agency has need for part-time and weekend staffing coordinator to work from home with pager to respond and schedule service for clients.
Requirements: Local applicants send résumé.

MY BABY SHOWER FAVORS

c/o Customer Service Jobs,
230 N Maple Ave, Suite 136, Marlton, NJ 08053

Positions: Customer service and order management.

Requirements: Must live near the company headquarters in Marlton, NJ. Major responsibilities and requirements include good communication skills, creative problem solving abilities, multi-tasking abilities, strong computer literacy and familiarity with MS Word, Excel, Internet Explorer, HTML, and general computer skills. Dreamweaver and FTP knowledge a plus. Download an application at www.mybabyshowerfavors.com/jobopenings.htm and mail the completed application to the address above.

Provisions: This is a salaried position, not hourly. Pay depends upon experience.

NATIONAL ANALYSTS

1835 Market St., Philadelphia, PA 19103

Positions: Opinion surveys are conducted in the field.

Requirements: Must live in one of the sampling areas. Experience is preferred.

Provisions: Training is provided. Pays by the survey.

NATIONAL OPINION RESEARCH CENTER

Social Science Research Center of the University of Chicago
6030 South Ellis Avenue, Chicago, IL 60637

Positions: Interviewers for long-term social science research projects. This nonprofit organization is the oldest research center in the country, founded in 1941. Research contracts come from government agencies and other institutional clients generally to study behavioral changes in specified areas of the population. There are 100 "area probability centers," plus studies are conducted in other locations specifically requested by the clients. All workers are considered part-time, temporary independent contractors though projects often last up to 14 months. Most work is done face-to-face, some is done over the phone. Currently has over 700 interviewers and is actively seeking more, particularly in metropolitan areas.

Requirements: Must be available a minimum of 20 hours a week; some work 40 hours a week. Need to be people-oriented, independent, outgoing, somewhat aggressive, able to follow instructions precisely and pay attention to details. Send letter of interest.

Provisions: Training is provided; general training takes about a day and a half in the office. Project briefings are a combination of written materials and oral instructions over the phone. Pays minimum wage plus expenses. Pay goes up with experience or with particular qualifications that may be hard to find. Annual increases are based on performance.

Close up: NORC

Founded in 1941, NORC is the oldest survey research organization established for non-commercial purposes. NORC is a not-for-profit organization affiliated with the University of Chicago.

Survey research is the collection of accurate, unbiased information from a carefully chosen sample of individuals.

Some organizations do opinion polls, asking people to rate the performance of public officials, for example. Others do market research, asking about such things as the products people use. NORC does social science research, asking about people's attitudes and behavior in areas of social concern, such as education, housing, employment (and unemployment), and health care.

NORC's clients include the American Cancer Society, Harvard University, the Rockefeller Foundation, the US Dept. of Labor, and the Social Security Administration to name just a few. Nowhere will you find higher standards of quality in research of this kind.

To date, NORC has conducted more than 1,200 surveys. This may not sound like a lot considering the thousands that are conducted for companies like Gallup. Unlike Gallup, though, NORC surveys are "longitudinal," meaning the same people are surveyed over long periods of time. Over 1,000 part-time NORC interviewers are located in cities, towns, and rural areas throughout the United States. Many, but not all, are home-based. Each assignment is on a temporary, per-project basis. The average project lasts about 6 months. All interviewers must be available to work at least 20 hours a week and 40-hour weeks are common.

About half of the people work for NORC have been with the company for more than five years. That's an outstanding record in an industry where rapid employee turnover is the norm. Nevertheless, NORC is constantly seeking more qualified interviewers—especially in hard-to-staff metropolitan areas such as New York, Chicago, Los Angeles, and Miami.

Field Director Miriam Clarke says, "We look for someone who is people-oriented, outgoing, and somewhat aggressive. Someone who does not like to be tied to a desk is a good candidate actually. Being able to follow instructions precisely is important, too."

An hour and a half of general training is provided at a central location. After that, project briefings are handled by mail, e-mail, and phone.

The pay range depends upon where you live and your experience. Any particular qualifications, such as foreign languages, pay extra. Pay raises come once a year and are based on performance. Employees are encouraged to take on additional responsibilities that will put them in line for management opportunities. But that doesn't mean giving up the benefits of working at home. NORC managers are just as likely to be home-based as the surveyors they supervise.

NATIONAL REMEMBER OUR TROOPS CAMPAIGN
> www.nrotc.org

Positions: In-home fund-raisers are needed in all 50 states.
Requirements: Experience is not a requirement.
Provisions: This is a real full-time W2 employer/employee job that still allows you to work 100% at home. $40-$60,000 per year is realistic.

NATIONAL TELECOMMUTING INSTITUTE, INC.
> www.nticentral.org
> 11 Arlington Street, Boston, MA 02116

Positions: NTI matches people with disabilities to customer service (primarily), technical assistant and transcriptionist jobs. Equipped with voice and computer connections, NTI employees have provided service for customers of organizations and companies such as the Internal Revenue Service and AAA Roadside Assistance.
Requirements: If you're disabled and want to work at home, check the list of current openings on the Web site. If you don't find one this time, fill out an application so they can contact you about jobs posted in the future.
Provisions: The number of positions and the compensation levels for each job vary. Wages are typically $8-15 per hour.

NEW
> www.newcorp.com

Positions: Customer care representatives answer customer questions and resolve issues relating to claims, warranties, and servicing products.
Requirements: Need previous customer service, retail, or call center experience (1 year). Must be able tocomplete a structured training program (3 – 4 weeks). Need a basic aptitude for electronics, basic PC skills including good familiarity with a Windows environment, and a typing speed of at least 30 wpm. Apply online.

NITEO SERVICES, INC.

P.O. Box 11053, Champaign, IL 61826

www.niteoservices.com

Positions: Customer care firm utilizes a remote staffing business model that enables them to provide staff with substantially more experience and expertise than traditional teleservices firms. The company's support teams provide customer and technical support via e-mail, instant messaging, and the telephone. "We are seeking support representatives and managers with good writing and customer service skills."

Requirements: Begin application process online.

Provisions: Offers competitive rates and provides exceptional flexibility to telecommuting workers. Work full-time or part-time at home. Set work hours that are convenient to your lifestyle.

NORWEGIAN CRUISE LINE

7665 Northwest 19th Street, Miami, FL 33126

Positions: Vacation planners (reservations agents) for major cruise line.

Requirements: A high school diploma or equivalent is required. Also required are good English communication skills, a minimum of one year of customer service or sales experience, PC skills, and the flexibility to work a variety of shifts. Send résumé.

OLSTEN HEALTH CARE SERVICES

Positions: Staffing coordinators. Olsten now has over 300 offices nationwide in its health care services division. Each office has a minimum of two home-based staffing coordinators job sharing on a seven-days-on, seven-days-off routine. The job consists of taking calls during the day, at night, and on weekends to dispatch appropriate personnel for hospital and home health care positions.

Requirements: Some staffing experience or medical background is required. Write to locate the office nearest you, then apply directly to that office.

Provisions: Pays weekly salary plus placement bonuses.

ONEIL RESEARCH

412 E. Southern Avenue, Tempe, AZ 85282

www.oneilresearch.com/employment.htm

Positions: Survey takers, researchers, and managers.

Requirements: Apply online.

OPINION RESEARCH CORPORATION
600 College Road East, Princeton, NJ 08540

Positions: Opinion surveyors conduct interviews in the field in New Jersey only.
Requirements: Ability to communicate effectively with people is a must. Send letter of interest.
Provisions: Pays by the survey.

ORION INTERNATIONAL CONSULTING
400 Regency Forest Drive, Cary, NC 27518
www.orioninternational.com

Positions: As a recruiter/e-cruiter, you place qualified, newly separated US military technicians and veterans in various careers with this company's clients nationwide.
Requirements: Ability to use the Internet and in-depth knowledge of military life. A minimum of three years of recruiting experience with a retained search firm is required. You will also need strong skills in communications with candidates and clients, résumé writing, interview preparation, and networking. Send résumé.
Provisions: Pays $40,000 to $60,000 per year plus outstanding benefits including medical, dental, disability, profit sharing, and 401K.

OVERFLOW USA
445 Broadhollow Rd., Suite 419, Melville, NY 11747
www.overflowusa.com/jobs.html

Positions: Independent virtual call center agents are paid on a per call basis.
Requirements: Must demonstrate an aptitude for interpersonal communication and possess a basic knowledge of operating a personal computer. Apply online.
Provisions: The Company is looking for mature individuals who desire to work from home and who are computer-literate to serve as "Independent Virtual Call Center Agents." Independent Agents will earn an appropriate fee for each call answered. The rate per call will vary depending on the client handled. It is anticipated that the current call rate will be between $1.40 and $1.70. Additionally, there may be incentives and bonuses available to an agent for educating customers on related products and services of the business they are representing. Additionally, there may be incentives and bonuses available. This is a self-employment opportunity to earn up to $40,000.

PREVENT BLINDNESS OKLAHOMA

4545 N.W. 16th St., Oklahoma City, OK 73127

Positions: Fundraisers.

Requirements: Must have home phone available for use 15 hours per week, evenings. Local residents only.

Provisions: Pays $10 per hour plus bonus.

PROSELECT

P.O. Box 72613, Marietta, GA 30007

www.proselectonline.com.

Positions: IT executive recruiters work with Account Managers in staffing existing job openings.

Requirements: Must be experienced in locating and screening of IT personnel.

Provisions: Telecommuting and flexible working hours.

PRO STAFF

www.prostaff.com

Positions: Executive recruiters. Pro Staff is one of the largest privately owned staffing companies in the country.

Requirements: Qualified individuals will have a strong background in client sourcing and development in addition to recruiting of executives and other high level professionals. Strong presentation and negotiation skills are a must. Bachelors degree is preferred. Must have at least five years recruiting experience. Proficiency in MS Office is necessary. Only the most highly qualified candidates will be given home office consideration.

Provisions: The company has regional offices across the country. Visit the Web site and click on the region you're interested in for more information.

PURPLE HEART SERVICE FOUNDATION

Positions: Part-time telemarketers solicit for donations.

Requirements: Must work well with the public. Personal interview will be required. Look for the office nearest you in your local phone book and contact that office directly.

Provisions: Hours are flexible. Pays commission of $10+ an hour.

QUEST DIAGNOSTICS

https://careers-ext.questcareersite.com

Positions: Tele-interviewers work part-time from home completing insurance applications via telephone.

Requirements: The work from home position would require working from the Lee's Summit office for 6-8 weeks. Need DSL/Cable Internet connection and home telephone line with local Kansas City area number. Apply online.

READYNURSE STAFFING SERVICES
2602 Highlands Blvd. North, Palm Harbor, FL 34684
www.readynurse.com
Positions: On-call staffing coordinator to handle phone calls after office hours.
Requirements: Staffing experience helpful. Customer service and phone skills required.
Provisions: Part-time hours.

REALTY EXECUTIVES OF DENVER
7901 E Belleview Ave, Englewood, CO 80111
Positions: Appointment setter for real estate company. (No sales.)
Requirements: Must be local resident with good phone skills.
Provisions: Pays salary plus bonus.

REMY CORPORATION
1637 Wazee Street, 2nd Floor, Denver, CO 80202
www.remycorp.com
Positions: IT recruiters.
Requiremetns: Must have minimum three years of success in technical recruiting or staffing. Record must be verifiable. Local Denver residents preferred, but not necessary if qualified.
Provisions: Pays base salary plus commission totaling well into the six figures.

RESEARCH TRIANGLE INSTITUTE
Hanes Building, Research Triangle Park, Raleigh, NC 27601
Positions: Interviewers for opinion research surveys conducted primarily in the field. Research Triangle is a nonprofit social research organization operating nationwide.
Requirements: Good communication skills needed. Send letter of interest.
Provisions: Pays hourly rate in some areas, pays by the survey in others. Training is provided.

RESOURCE SPECTRUM
P.O. Box 2195, Grapevine, TX 76099
www.spectrumm.com
Positions: Recruiters. Resource Spectrum is a multi-million dollar staffing firm serving companies throughout the world. Must live in one of the major markets.

Requirements: Experience recruiting in the IT, legal biotech, accounting, financial, civil engineering, environmental engineering, construction, executive, marketing, or healthcare fields.

Provisions: All recruiters work and start on commission only with no base salary.

ROBERTE VERIFICATIONS

www.roberteverifications.com

Positions: Phone surveyors and mystery shoppers.

Requirements: Must be fluent in English, but French is an advantage. Must live in Ottawa area. Experience in retail customer service required. Must have computer with Windows. High school graduates only. Visit Web site for more information.

Provisions: Pays $10 per hour plus some benefits. This is very part-time work, on call.

THE ROPER ORGANIZATION

566 Boston Post Road., Mamaroneck, NY 10543

Positions: Opinion surveyors conduct research within sampling areas around the country. All research is conducted in the field.

Requirements: No opinion surveying experience is necessary, but experience involving some kind of public contact is preferred. Write and ask for name and address of nearest field supervisor.

RUTH GOLDER INTERVIEWING SERVICE

1804 Jaybee Rd., Wilmington, DE 19803

Positions: Field interviewers for market research.

Requirements: Interviewing experience required. Must live in Chester or Delaware County, Pennsylvania, or Salem County, New Jersey.

S.A.I. STAFFING

Grosse Pointe Woods, MI 48236

www.saistaffing.com

Positions: Personnel placement for professional and technical staffing firm.

Requirements: Must be knowledgeable and experienced recruiter (minimum five years). Applicants will go through a reference and security check. Need to live within driving distance of headquarters.

Provisions: Pays excellent commissions.

SALES CONSULTANTS OF BLOOMINGTON, INC.
707 N. East St., Suite 4, Bloomington, IL 61701
www.scbloomington.com

Positions: This is a global search and recruiting firm with over 1,100 offices worldwide. Recruiters work at home.

Requirements: Must have sales experience, industry knowledge, and communication skills. College degree required. Previous recruiting experience is preferred but not required. You must be within driving distance of the Bloomington/Normal area. Must be PC literate and have virtual home office capabilities.

Provisions: Provides comprehensive training. Offers flexible hours and aggressive commission plan. Average earnings for full-time recruiters after one full year is $70,000.

SELECT COMFORT CORPORATION
6105 Trenton Ln N., Minneapolis, MN 55442
www.selectcomfort.com

Positions: Scheduling coordinator, customer service. This position includes working with customer 100% on the phone.

Requirements: Must be high school graduate (or GED), have excellent customer service and communication skills, have Windows computer experience including MS Word and Excel, and be a good problem solver with attention to detail and accuracy. Must live in Chicago. Some experience in scheduling, routing and customer service definitely preferred.

Provisions: Pays $11 to $13 per hour.

SERVICE 800
2190 West Wayzata Blvd., Minneapolis, MN 55356
http://hq.service800.com/repapplication.asp

Positions: Conduct interviews with customers who have recently had a service experience.

Requirements: Must be able to articulate well verbally and in written form. Previous customer service experience, computer knowledge, and telephone skills are mandatory. Apply online.

Provisions: This company operates in the US and also in England. See Web site for additional information.

SETKA, INC.
3223 Crow Canyon Road, Suite 250, San Ramon, CA 94583
www.setka.com

Positions: Technical recruiters/account managers.

Requirements: Experience in IT or professional staffing. Local residents only.
Provisions: Pays excellent commission. Offers long term opportunities to work either full-time or part-time.

SMYTH FIVENSON COMPANY
8513 Irvington Avenue, Bethesda, MD 20817
www.smythfivenson.com

Positions: Recruiters.
Requirements: Must have broad experience in human resources.
Provisions: Looking for part-time workers especially.

SOFTPATH SYSTEM
1945 Cliff Valley Way NE, Suite 312, Atlanta, GA 30329
www.softpath.net

Positions: IT recruiters recruit, interview, refer, place, and support qualified candidates.
Requirements: Must live in the metropolitan area of Washington DC Degree preferred but not required, but must have a minimum of two years experience in staffing industry OR three years in sales and/or in a technical arena with proven track record. Local market experience would be ideal.
Provisions: This is a full-time position.

SOFTWARE TESTING SERVICES, INC.
620 Cranbury Road Suite 202, East Brunswick, NJ 08816
www.stsv.com

Positions: Technical recruiting in the East Brunswick, NJ area. The company is an established provider of quality assurance and software testing services to Fortune 1000 companies in the NY tri-state area.
Requirements: Must have minimum 2-3 years of technical recruiting, consulting, telecommunications experience.
Provisions: Pays base salary of $40-$45K plus commissions.

STAFFING AT HOME, INC.
P.O. Box 50832, Pasadena, CA 91115
www.staffingathome.com

Positions: This service bureau specializes in home-based customer service, inbound and outbound telemarketing, order processing, and technical support.
Requirements: Must apply online. You will need a PC, fax (optional), printer, DSL or cable modem, and noise reducing headset. There is a one-time $5 application processing fee.
Provisions: The company expects to hire 10,000 more home-based workers.

One client alone is going to require 1,000-2,000 customer service agents to be hired over the next 6 months.

STRATEGIC RESOURCE PARTNERS, INC.

111 N. Sepulveda Blvd Suite 250, Manhattan Beach, CA 90266
www.strategicrp.com

Positions: IT recruiters.

Requirements: Bachelor's degree and at least three years successful IT recruiting experience. Local residents only.

Provisions: Pays $25 per hour.

STUDY WEB

www.plato.com/about-us/careers.aspx

Positions: Hires home-based people with expertise and/or knowledge in various fields to assist with home work online.

Requirements: Apply online.

Provisions: Offers competitive wages and an excellent benefit package that features medical and dental insurance; flexible spending programs; paid-time off (PTO), and holiday pay; 401(k) retirement savings plan; stock purchase plan; tuition reimbursement; and more.

SUMMIT HEALTH CARE

1850 Lee Road, Winter Park, FL 32789

Positions: Medical staffing coordinator.

Requirements: Prior staffing experience is required. Must be detail oriented, flexible, and self-motivated. Good communication skills a must. Local residents submit résumé.

Provisions: Top pay. After-hours work only.

SYLVAN LEARNING CENTER

Littleton, CO
(888) EDUCATE

Positions: Flex agents (a.k.a. educational consultants) for Sylvan's national call center, working at home on the phone.

Requirements: Must have 3+ years of customer sales or customer service experience and at least an associate's degree. Must be available for inhouse training.

Provisions: Offers total annual compensation of $44-60,000, three weeks vacation to start, medical insurance, 401(k), and advancement opportunities.

TELETECH
www.hirepoint.com/athome/index.html

Positions: Customer service reps, technical support, and back office support such as transcribing and order processing.

Requirements: Need PC that meet specific requirements, high-speed Internet service (Cable or DSL, no satellite or dial-up), analog land line telephone (not mobile, cellular, VoIP or cordless), and a home location where you can commit to work uninterrupted by others and one that is free from background noise such as family members, appliances, traffic, pets, TV/music, etc. Complete online application and you will be contacted for a phone interview.

Provisions: Pays hourly rates based on type of work being done. Also provides performance-related bonuses and paid interactive training.

TEMPOSITIONS
Home Health Care Division, 140 Geary St #4, San Francisco, CA 94104

Positions: Staffing coordinator for evenings and weekends.

Requirements: Experience in medical staffing required. Must live in San Francisco.

Provisions: This is part-time work only.

THE THOR GROUP
3601 Aviation Blvd. Suite 3900, Manhattan Beach, CA 90266
www.thorgroup.com

Positions: Recruiters.

Requirements: Minimum two years recruiting experience. To see what areas are open, visit Web site.

Provisions: Pays $60k-$150k per year. Telecommuting is offered only after training is completed.

TIME ANSWERING
877 Jefferson Ave., St. Paul, MN 55102

Positions: Customer service for 24-year old inbound telemessaging center.

Requirements: Local residents write to request interview.

Provisions: Full-time shifts for both day and evening schedules available. Pays good monthly salary plus full benefits including medical, dental, retirement, and vacation.

U-HAUL
Arizona

Positions: Agents work from home in limited geographic areas, answering incoming calls from customers in need of emergency road service. After gathering detailed information, you will dispatch calls to the appropriate shop or service providers who will assist the customer. The emergency road service/customer service department is open 24/7. Scheduling is based on call volume.

Requirements: Must have good customer service communication skills, clear speaking voice, and pre-installed Windows Vista, Windows XP or Service Pack Two operating system. Need PC knowledge and a reliable cable or DSL broadband Internet connection. Must purchase your own multimedia USB headset with a noise-canceling microphone (very inexpensive on eBay). Complete application at www.uhaulhr.com/waps/prescreen.aspx.

Provisions: Offers paid training, flexible work scheduling, and part-time positions. Pays $7 an hour.

UNIQUE COMPUTER INC.

27-08, 42nd Road, Long Island City, New York 11101
www.uciny.com

Positions: Technical recruiters in New York and Washington DC.
Requirements: Minimum four years experience as technical recruiter.
Provisions: Pays excellent commissions. Visit Web site and apply via e-mail.

UNITED CEREBRAL PALSY

1217 Alhambra Blvd., Sacramento, CA 95816

Positions: Fundraising by phone. Job consists of calling for donations of household discards for about four hours a day.
Requirements: Must live in Sacramento.
Provisions: Pays hourly wage plus bonus plan.

UNITED CEREBRAL PALSY

29498 Mission Blvd., Hayward, CA 94544

Positions: Fundraising by phone.
Requirements: Bay area residents only.
Provisions: Pays hourly rate plus bonus and vacation.

VALIDATED RESPONSE

www.validatedresponse.com

Positions: Customer service agents.
Requirements: Must have professional and articulate phone voice, strong interpersonal skills, and PC with high-speed Internet access via hardwire connection (no wireless).
Provisions: The convenience of working from home and setting your own hours. Offers flexible schedules, generous compensation plan, and bonus programs and incentives.

VETERANS' REHABILITATION CENTER
9201 Pacific Avenue, Tacoma, WA 98444

Positions: Fundraisers phone for donations of household items, clothing, etc.
Requirements: Must come to Tacoma for short training session. (Can live in Seattle.)
Provisions: Paid training is provided. Pays guaranteed hourly wage. Inquiries are welcome.

VIRTUSERVE
www.virtuserve.com

Positions: A North American-based virtual call center that hires home agents for various services, such as telemarketing, help desk support, and survey research. By hiring home agents, VirtuServe can provide major corporate clients prices competitive with offshore rates, thereby keeping jobs here in the US. This is commonly known as "homesourcing." Home agents conduct surveys, provide help desk services, set appointments, and handle inbound customer service.
Requirements: First apply online. If accepted, you will need broadband data connection to the Internet with a minimum upload speed of 128kps (high-speed cable, not DSL), dedicated work computer, a noise-canceling headset, dedicated sound proof or quiet office or workspace, good phone skills and friendly attitude, and the ability to define work schedule and be available during those stated work hours. Canadian applicants must meet requirements set by Canadian and or Provincial government to work as an Independent contractor.
Provisions: Positions open to US and Canadian citizens.

VIPDESK
324 North Fairfax Street, Alexandria VA 22314

www.vipdesk.com

Positions: Home-based concierge and customer service agents are hired to work with various companies. VIPdesk hires thousands of home agents to provide their corporate clients (and a total customer base of 20 million) with these services.
Requirements: Must apply online and attend a training class in one of the US cities where they are located.

VISITING NURSE ASSOCIATION
101 West Chestnut Street, Louisville, KY 40202

Positions: Medical staffing coordinator.
Requirements: Medical background with staff/schedule experience required. Local applicants send résumé.

WEST CORPORATION

11808 Miracle Hills Dr., Omaha, NE 68154

www.west.com

Positions: This is a major customer service outsourcing provider that finds customer service agents based out of their homes for a variety of industries, including pharmaceutical, retail and hospitality. Depending on the project, you may be obtaining, entering, and verifying customer information, answering questions, resolving issues, explaining sales features, or offering additional products or services, all while providing exceptional customer service.

Requirements: An online application process followed by Web-based training.

Provisions: Hourly wage paid while training. Option to take advantage of medical and dental related benefits from an outside provider. West-At-Home offers schedules based on either per minute rate, per call OR guaranteed hourly rate. If total earnings (whether via per minute, per call or guaranteed hourly rate) are less than minimum wage, employee compensation will be trued up to meet their local minimum wage requirements (our employees will always earn the greater of the two pay scales). West-At-Home employees are paid on a biweekly basis and direct deposit and/or pay card options are available immediately. The company places thousands of home workers all over the country with Fortune 1000 companies. Visit the Web site to find current opportunities and review requirements (such as what kind of computer you might need).

WORKING SOLUTIONS

1820 Preston Park Blvd., Suite 2000, Plano, TX 75093

www.workingsol.com/home.htm

Positions: Hiring for various phone jobs, such as taking hotel reservations, product orders, and more.

Requirements: Prefers highly educated and trained professionals who have great communication and multi-lingual skills with knowledge of specific products and industries so they can ramp up quickly to meet specific client needs. Fill out application on the Web site.

XACT TELESOLUTIONS

www.xactservices.com/company/careers

Positions: Employs a staff of over 200 home-based customer service agents who take calls in a fast-paced, customer-driven environment.

Requirements: Bilingual a plus. Computer and high-speed Internet connection required. Apply on the Web site.

~ *Index* ~

Alphabetical

1-800-FLOWERS.COM................................342
3Com Corporation 177
3DTour..197
10 TIL 2..21
24 Hour Secretary................................304
A Briggs Passport & Visa Expeditors.................343
A Card-In-The-Yard 84
A Stat Transcription 264
AAA Chicago.................................342-343
Abelson Legal Search 264-265
Ability Group..218
Accolade Support Call Center.............343
Accounting/bookkeeping schools...........181-182
Accu-Doc 265
Accu-Find...309
Accu-Rate...21
Accu-Script Transcription Services, Inc. 266
Accupro Services............................265-266
Accurapid Translation Services, Inc. 265
Accustat, Inc...266
Accutrak Inventory Specialists 21-22
Accutran 266
Accutranz Medical Transcription Services, Inc.......
....266-267
Accuwrite Word Processing Service 267
ACD Direct...343
Act 1 Technical 218
Action International 22
Action Translation & Interpretation Bureau....267
Actor's Garage 95
Ad-Ex Worldwide 267-268
Adamczyk, Jo....................................26-27
ADC Telecommunications, Inc. 154
Adele's II, Inc. 197
Adept Word Management 267
Administrative assistant schools 187
Admission Consultants, Inc. 244
Advanced Automation Associates 218
Advance Language Studios...................268
Aegin Place..84
Aetna Life & Casualty 154
Air Brook Limousine 22
Air Products & Chemicals, Inc..............155
Airbag Technology, Inc. 11
AIS Market Research............................344
AIS Media, Inc..68
Alcas Cutlery Corporation 309
Alderson Reporting 268
All-Language Services, Inc....................269
All Purpose Typing Service...................268
All Star Personnel, Inc. 344
All Type, Inc. 268-269
Allabout Honeymoons 121
Allergan, Inc. 155
Allied Interpreting & Translating Service 269
Allied Schools.........................181, 185-187
Allied Web 219
Allstate Insurance Company 155

Alltel Publishing 219
Aloette Cosmetics 124, 309
Alpha Presentations 219
Alpine Access.......................................344
Alternative Board..............................22-23
Ambrosia Software 197
Amcal 197-198
American Barter Exchange, Inc............309
American Crafts Gallery 135
American Elite Homes, Inc. 76
American Entertainment Distributors 109-110
American Express Bank, Ltd.........219-220
American Express Travel Related Services
    Company, Inc....................................155
American Glove Co. Inc.........................245
American Greeting Corporation 198
American Institute..................................23
American Institute of Physics 198
American Institutes For Research 155
American Leak Detection 56
American Mobile Sound 124
American Red Cross 344
American Thrift Store 344
American Transcription Solutions, Inc. 269
Amerispec Home Inspection Service 76
Ameritech Corporation 155
AMF Bowling Products Group, Inc.......156
Amsoil, Inc...11
Amtrak 156
Amvets...345
Analog One 245
Anasazi, Inc..156
Andrews Glass Company, Inc. 156
Anne Menaker Gordon & Co. 135-136
Apartmentstores.com 310
Appearance Plus, Inc..............................11
Appingo 198
The Apple Tree 136
Apollo Group, Inc. 156
Apple Computer, Inc. 156
Aquaricon 270
Aquent 198-199
Arbonne International, Inc. 310
Archadeck...40
Argonaut Press 199
Argosy Publishing 199
Aria Communications 245
Arise 220
Arise Virtual Solutions 345
Arizona, Department of Administration 157
ARO Outsourcing..................................345
Art & Logic 220
Art & Soul, Inc......................................310
Art Instruction Schools 182
Arthritis Foundation 346
Artique, Inc. 136
Artisans Gallery 136
Artist Career Training 182

Artistic Impressions, Inc..................310-311
Artists' Parlor 137
Artizen, Inc. 220-221
Artworx Software Company 221
Arthur Andersen & Company 157
Arthur D. Little, Inc. 157
Arts & Artisans, Ltd. 137
Artworks Park City.............................137
Ashworth University, Professional Career
    Development Institute 183
Ask Dr. Tech 221
AT&T 157
At-Heel Learning Centers 104
At-Home Professions...............23, 186, 270-271
ATC Healthcare Services, Inc. 346
Athens Regional Health Services............270
Auralog 346
Aussie Pet Mobile 104
Auto Appraisal Network 12
Automotive services........................10-18
Autoplus Window Stickers 12
Avante Window Fashions 41
Avita, Inc...137
Avon Products, Inc. 311
Axion Data Services 272
B5Media 199-200
Baltimore Evening Sun 157
Banctec 157
Bankers Trust Company.........................158
Banks, Bentley & Cross 24
Barbara Schwartz Accessories 137
Bark Busters 105
Barnes & Noble University 187
Barry Manufacturing Company, Inc. 245
Bathcrest 42
Batterymarch Financial Management Company
   158
BCC, Inc..200
Bearcom Building Services..................57-58
Beadniks.....................................245-246
Beauticontrol, Inc..............................311
Beauty By Spector 311
Beautyway 200
Becker & Associates 347
Bellatlantic 158
Bell Communications 158
Bell South 159
Beneficial Corporation..........................159
Bentley House 200-201
Berlin Gloves Co. 246
Berlitz International 184
Berlitz Translation Service 272
Best Western Hotels International............159
Better Business Bureau 122
Bevinco Bar Systems Ltd. 24
Bi-Tech Enterprises, Inc.........................221
Biltmore Franchise Consulting 24
Bingo Bugle 115-116
Birds & Blooms 201
Birthflowers.Com 41-42
Bizarre Promotions, Inc.........................312
Blackstone Career Institute................185-186
Blessing Hospital 272
Blind Doctors Training Academy 57
Blue Cross/Blue Shield 153, 159, 222
Blue Ridge Tea and Herb Ltd. 272

Blue Zebra USA..................................312
Blueberry Woolens 246
Bon Temps 273
Book Editing Associates 201
Bookminders, Inc. 159
Bookkeeping Express 25
Borg-Warner Chemical Company 160
Boswell, Matt 107-108
Boyd Printing Company, Inc. 222
Bradford Exchange 202
Brain Fuse 347
Brass Smith House.............................138
Bristol-Myers Squibb Company 160
Bronner Manufacturing and Tool Company ..160
Brooklyn Women's Exchange, Inc. 138
Brown Bag Gourmet Goodies................312
Brown Williamson Tobacco Company 160
Buckboard Antiques............................201
Buckley, Bill.....................................117
Business Communications Company, Inc.222-223
Business Edge 312
Business Graphics 223
Business Round Table...........................25
Business services 19-39
Buske, Gayle 300-301
Butler Learning Systems 25
Buylink Corporation 138
BuySellWebsite 223
Cal-Bay Systems, Inc...........................223
California Council For The Blind 347
The California Institute of Integral Studies 202
California State Department of General Services
   160
Call Depot..312
Cambridge Home Healthcare 347
Cambridge Sales 138
Camares Communications, Inc. 202-203
Canadian Diabetes Association 347
Candy Bouquet..................................85
Capital Data 224
Caption Colorado 273
Car-Lene Research..............................348
Care2.com 203
Caremore In-Home Service 348
CareOne, Inc. 348
Carlisle Communications 224
Carlton Cards....................................203
Carnegie Art Center 139
Carondelet Health Network, St. Mary's Hospital ..
   273
Carpet Network 42
Castle Branch 246
Catalina In-Home Services 348
CDS Signing Services...........................247
Ceiltech 58
Central Data Processing...................273-274
CEO Focus 27
Certified Marketing Services, Inc. 349
Certified Translation Bureau, Inc. 274
CFO Today 27-28
Cha Cha 247
Charmelle, Inc....................................313
Chatas Glass Company 161
Chem-Dry Carpet, Drapery and Upholstery
    Cleaning 58
Cherry Lane Music Company 247

Chesapeake Bay Magazine 203
Chicago Knitting Mills 248
Children, services for 95-104
Children's Hospital 274
Children's Technology Workshop.......................95
Chilton Credit Reporting 161
Chipita Accessories...248
Chips Away...12
Christmas Concepts 86
Christmas Décor...86-87
Chronicle Transcripts, Inc. 274
Cigna Corporation...161
Cintas Corporation 313
Circle Graphics, Inc. 224
Citibank..161
Claim Net, Inc. 274-275
Clarity Consultants 224
Clarke, Miriam 363
Clean & Happy Windows 43, 59
Cleaning and maintenance services 55-67
Cleannet USA..59
Clerical Plus 275
Cleveland Institute of Electronics 183
Casepost Inc. 313
Click A Close 248
Clicknwork 275
Client Connection, Inc. 28
(The) Client Touch/Cardsenders 26-27
Clutterbusters 87
CM IT Solutions..68
CMP Publications 203-204
Coffee News USA 115-117
Coghill Composition Company.................224-225
Coldwater Creek Home.....................................139
Collage Gallery 139
Color-Crown Corporation 43
Colorado Department of Personnel 161
Colorado National Bank 162
Comfort Keepers 85
Commission, working on.......................................1
Commonwealth Transcription Systems 275
Companion Connection Senior Care 85
Complete Music, Inc. 124-125
The Compucare Company 162
Compuchild USA 68-69
Computer and Technical Services 67-75
Computer Assistant 225
Computer Explorers 96
Computer Medics of America 69
Computer Secretary 275
Computer Solutions 225
Computer Troubleshooters 69
Computerease 225
Computertots 96
Comstock Cards, Inc...204
Concept Now Cosmetics....................................313
Concerto Networks...70
Concierge At Large, Inc. 248-249
Concrete Technology, Inc.....................................43
Concurrent Technologies 225
Connecticut Children's Medical Center...........349
Conjuecture Corporation 204
Consumer Opinion Search, Inc. 349
Continental Illinois Bank 3
Continental Translation Service, Inc................276

Control Data Corp. 153
Convergys..349
Corless & Associates 276
Corpimages.Net 226
Corvallis Arts Center, Linn-Benton Council For
    The Arts...139
Cosmopolitan Translation Bureau, Inc. 276
Cost Containment Solutions, Inc. 28, 76
Counsel On Call 249
Country Curtains, Inc. 249
Cover letters 192
Covered Bridge Girl Scout Council 350
Coverall Cleaning Concept 59-60
Cox Communications Corp 314
Cozy Places 314
CPR Technologies Transcription Service 276
CPS Medtext 277
Crack Team, The 44
Craig Communications 204
Crawford, Leslie 174-175
Crazoo 249
Create-A-Book, Inc. 117-118
Creative Colors International, Inc. 44
Creative Memories 314
Creative Photo Concepts 110
Crestcom, Int'l, Inc. 28-29, 314
Critter Control, Inc...44-45, 105
CRM Griot 226
Cross-Curricular Connections 226
Cruise Line International Association 122
Cruise Planners...121
Cruiseone 122
Cruises Inc. 122-123
Cup of Comfort..205
Curtis 1000 162
Custom Home Food Service 350
Cyberedit 249-250
Cybertary 29
Dafa Sales 140
Dainty Maid Waitress Aprons Company 250
The Dale Group..60
Data entry schools 182
Data General Corporation 162
Davis Market Research Services, Inc. 350
Davlins 140
Debt Zero 77
Decor & You, Inc..45
Decorated Products Company 162
Decorating Den 45
Delaware Center For The Contemporary Arts140
The Dentist's Choice...125
Denver, City and County 163
Desktop Author 315
Detail Plus 13
Detroit Free Press 163
Deventure Health Partners 277
Devon Consulting 350
DeVry University 181, 184, 188
Digital Equipment Corporation 163
Dignus 227
Dion Data Solutions 277
Disabled American Veterans 350
Disabled American Veterans of Colorado........351
Disability Associates 77
Disciple's Directory, Inc......................................118

Discovery Toys, Inc. 315
Display Connection, Inc. 205
Distance Education and Training Council (DETC)
....23
D. J. Ardore, Inc. 314-315
DLM Business Solutions 277
Document Do-It-Yourself 351
Dr. Glass 60
Dr. Vinyl & Associates, Ltd. 46
Domenichelli Business Services 278
Doncaster 315
Doody Calls...................................104, 106
Dragon Pencil 205
DRG Texas 250
Drama Kids Int'l, Inc. 96-97
Dry Cleaning To-Your-Door 88
DS Sewing, Inc. 227
DTS America, Inc. 278
Duarte Design, Inc. 227
Dudley Products and Publications 316
Dura-Oak Cabinet Refacing Products.......46
DWH Office Services.................................278
Dyalogue 205
Dynax Resources, Inc. 227
E-Backups 70
Eagleshotz 110
Eastern Mail & Data Processing, Inc. 278
Eastern Connecticut Health Network, Inc. ....
....278-279
Eastman Kodak Company 163
eCardia..204
Echo Management Group 228
Ectone, Inc. 228
Eden Staffing...351
Editfast..206
EDiX Corporation.....................................279
Educate Online 351-352
Educational Correspondence Training School, LLC
....181, 184
Educational Partners Association 352
EEG Recruiting 250-251
eJury 251
El Camino Memorial Park 352
Electric Mobility Corporation 316
Electrolux Corp. 316
Electronic schools 183
Electronic Search, Inc 352
Electronic Services Unlimited 164
Elite Software Development, Inc...............228
Eliza J 125
Elmhurst Memorial Healthcare.................279
Empire Business Brokers, Inc......................29
Employee Benefit Services, Inc.................279
Encouragym Active Learning Programs 97
Enesco Imports Corporation 206
Entrees On Trays, Inc. 88
Entrepreneur Magazine 122
Entrepreneur's Source 29-30
Equitable Life Assurance 163-165
Eric Anthony Creations 251
Escrow Overload...1
eShipping 30
Especial Day...140
Etco, Inc. 141
eToys 140-141
ETR Technology Center.......................352-353

eTransplus 279
Everett Clinic 280
Everett Studios, Inc...................................206
Excellence Translation Service 280
Executive Office Services 280
Expedict 280
Expense Reduction Consulting, Inc. 30
Expetec Technology Services 70
eYardsale.com 30
Eziba 141
Fabjob.Com 206
Faces N Cups, Inc 110
Facts 'N Figures.......................................353
Fair Labor Standards Act of 1938 (FLSA) 4-5
Fashion Two Twenty, Inc. 316
Federal Reserve Bank...............................165
Federation of the Handicapped 228, 280
Fetch! Pet Care, Inc..................................106
Fibrenew 13
Fiesta Cartoon Maps................................118
Filtafry 31
Finelle Cosmetics......................................317
First Beat Media 229
First National Bank of Chicago 165
Fitzgerald's 13
Flack, Frank 56
Flannery and Angeli 252
Fleming, David 161
Fletcher Consolidated, Inc. 317
Flexiplace 3
Flexitime 3
Floor Coverings International 46
Foliage Design Systems...............................47
Ft. Collins..165
Forum Boosting 251
Franchise Market Magazine......................122
Franchise Times 122
Franzen Enterprises 141
Freedom Greeting Card Company 207
Freedom of the Workplace bill 4
French Creek Sheep & Wool Company, Inc. 252
Friendly Computers....................................71
Friends Life Care At Home, Inc.................317
Fusion Games 229
Futurenet Technologies Corp....................281
Futuro Infantil Hispano 353
Fuze 207
Galeria El Dorado.....................................141
Gallery of The Sandias 142
Gallery/Shopat Wesleyan Potters 142
Gallup Poll 353
Gannett 166
Garrett Transcription Service....................281
Gateway Technical Services 229
Gavel & Gown Software, Inc. 354
GE Plastics 166
Geeks On Call America 67-68, 71
Geico Direct..166
General Telephone 166
Generation Z 229, 354
Georgia Power 166-167
Gerbig, Snell, & Weisheimer 207
Glas-Weld Systems 14
Glass Mechanix, Inc. 13
Glass Technology, Inc.................................13
Global Language Services 281

Globespan Medical, Inc. 281
The Good Nature Co., Inc. 317
Good Samaritan Community Healthcare 354
Graffitti Graphics 119
Graphic design schools 183
Grantham College of Engineering 183-184
Grassroots Handcrafts 142
Grave Groomers 88-89
Green and Christmas Concepts 31
Green Lake Chiropractic 318
Griggs University, Home Study International ....
....181, 185
Griswold Special Care...............................89
Grocery Lady 89
Grolier Incorporated.................................318
The Growth Coach.....................................32
GTE 167
Guard Insurance Group 281-282
Gumball Gourmet 125-126
Gupta Technologies 318
Gym Rompers 97
Handpiece Express 126
Harcourt Brace & Co. 207
Harrington, Dawn 72-73
Harris Trust and Savings Bank...................167
Hart Systems, Inc....................................282
Hartford Insurance Group 167
Harvey Research Organization, Inc. 354
Hausernet 252-253
Hatch, Orrin...4
Hawkeye's Home Sitters 89
Hayes Handpiece......................................126
Hayes Marketing Research..........................354
Health Administration Systems, Inc. 318
Healthcare Recruiters International 253
Heaven's Best Carpet & Upholstery Cleaning........
....60-61
Herbalife International 319
Herff Jones 207-208
Hewlett Packard Laboratories.....................167
Hi-Tech Industries 14
High Tech Exports, Gujarat.........................326
High Touch High Tech 98
Highland Park Hospital 282
Highline Community Hospital 355
Hirecheck...282
Hireright, Inc. 355
The Hive 230
Ho Math & Chess Learning Centre 98-99
Holt, Rinehart, & Winston 168
Home and Garden Party 319
Home & Grounds......................................319
Home Employment Enterprise Act (HR2815) 4
Home Fixology 47
H.O.M.E., Inc. 142-143
Home Interiors & Gifts, Inc. 319-320
Home Office Deduction...............................7
Home Remedies....................................47-48
Home Staging Resource 77
Home-Study License..................................26
Home Tutoring 100
Home Video Studio, Inc...........................109, 111
Homequity, Inc..168
Homes & Land Publishing Corp. 119
The Homesteader 120
The Hometeam Inspection Service, Inc. 78

Homewatch International, Inc. 90
Honeywell, Inc. 168
Hospice of San Francisco 355
Household International..............................168
Housemaster of America, Inc. 78-79
H/P Technologies, Inc. 355
HR Advice..253
Hubpages...208
Human Resources Professional Group (HRPG) ....
....356
Hunting Lease Network..............................80
Husted Gallery & Art Frames......................143
The H.W. Wilson Company 168
I9 Sports 127
Idaho Statesman 320
Idea Vision 48
Ident-A-Kid Services of America, Inc........111-112
Iistek Corp 230
Ikon Office Solutions 208
Illinois Amvets..356
Illinois Hospital Joint Ventures 283
Image Works 230
Imedx 283
Impressions, Inc. 230-231
IMS Technology Telesales 320
independent contracting 1
Income tax schools 183
Indian Jewelers Supply 253
Industrial Indemnity Insurance 169
Infinity Insurance Company 320
Information Access Company.......................169
Information Technologies 253-254
Information technology schools 184
Inlingua Translation Service........................283
Inneractive Inc..90
Integrity Staffing 356
Intellistream Technologies, Inc. 231
Intercontinental Greetings, Ltd. 208
The Interface Group Ltd. 80
Interim Healthcare 357
International Business Machine (IBM) 168
International Franchise Association 122
International Homes of Cedar, Inc. 80
The International Ladies Garment Workers Union
....5
International Language & Communications
    Centers, Inc...................................283-284
International Mergers and Acquisitions 81
International Translation Bureau 284
Interquest Detection Canines 32
Intracorp 231
Intrep, Inc. 320-321
Intrep Sales Partners 284
Intuit 169
Inxpress 32
Ires 254
ISC Consultants, Inc. 231
Ispeakuspeak..357
Itxtend 321
Jackson Associates 358
Jafra Cosmetics, Inc..................................321
J&R Field Services, Inc...............................358
Jani-King International, Inc. 61
Janitize America, Inc.................................61
Jan-Pro 61-62
J.C. Penney Company, Inc. 175

JDM Interactive 232
Jellybean Services 254
Jet-Black Sealcoating & Repair 48
Jet Propulsion Laboratory 170
J. Lodge 358
J. Marco Galleries 143
Joe Cochran Agency...............................358
John Hancock Mutual Life Insurance Co. 283
Johns Hopkins Health Care, LCC 359
John Wiley & Sons, Inc. 242
Johnston, Joyce 112
Journalism/advertising schools 184
Julie Hall 143
June Wedding, Inc. 91
Jury Insights 254
Jurytest Networks...........................254-255
Just Answer 255
Just the Fax 71-73
J. Weston Walch 242
Kah-Nee-Tah Gallery...............................143
Kaiser Permanente Medical Group 284
KC Distance Learning 359
K-C Products 255
Keller's Medical Transcription Service 284
Kelly Services, Inc. 359
Kenda Systems, Inc. 359-360
Kennedy Brothers Marketplace 144
Kenneth Olson & Associates..........326-327
Kersten Studios 208
Key For Cash 284-285
The Kidney Foundation............................360
Kinderdance International, Inc. 100
Kindermusik International 101
Kinship...360
The Kirby Corporation 321
Kitchen-A-Fair 321-322
Kitchen Solvers..................................48-49
Kitchen Tune-Up, Inc. 49
Know Brainers...255
Kott Koatings...49
Kustom Cards International, Inc. 33
Labmentors..232
Labor laws..4
Lafayette Venetian Blind.........................170
Lake Regional Health System 285
Langenwalter Industries, Inc...............49-50
Languages, foreign, schools....................184
Languages Unlimited...............................285
Lanier Business Products, Inc 170
Lawn Doctor...50
Laykin...232
Le Gourmet Gift Basket, Inc. 127
Leadership Management, Inc. 33
Leaplaw..285
Legal transcription schools.....................185
Legalaid of America, Inc. 286
Leisure Arts, Inc. 255
Lenco Electronic, Inc. 170
Letter of interest 192, 194
Letter Perfect Word Processing Center 232
Library of Congress 285-286
Lift, Inc..233
Lil'Angels..112-113
Lillian Vernon Corporation......................209
Lindal Cedar Homes, Inc. 81

Liquid Resins International 14-15
Little Black Book For Every Busy Woman 33
Little Scientists 101
Liveops 360
Living Earth Crafts...................................256
Locationlube..15
Loma 209
Lon Waltenberger Training Services 54
Longaberger Marketing, Inc. 322
Loose Ends 144
Los Angeles County 170
Los Angeles Marketing Research Associates ....
....361
Louis Harris and Associates 361
Love of Country 144
Luanne Glazer Associates, Inc. 361
Lucky Heart Cosmetics, Inc. 322
Luksa Industries, Inc................................113
MacArthur Associates 233
Macke Water Systems, Inc. 322
Magic Rice, Inc. 127-128
Mahy, Pat 1
Maid Brigade 62
The Maids International.............................62
Maid Services of America 62-63
Maintenance Made Simple 50
Management Recruiters of Sacramento ..323-324
Mansfield Art Center 144
Marine Midland Bank...............................170
Marion J. Rosley Secretarial Services 297
Marks, Don 17-18
Marty Wasserberg & Associates 144-145
Marty Wolf Game Company 128
Mary Kay Cosmetics, Inc. 323
Mary Lucas Market Research...................361
Maryland State Government 233-234
Mason Shoe Manufacturing Company 323
Matco Tools 15
Matrix Technology Group........................323
Maverick Publications 234
Maxim Healthcare Services 361
McDonald Douglas 171
McGruff Safe Kids 101
McLaughlin, Ann....................................4-5
MD-IT 286
MDM International Multi Media 109, 113
Mechanical Secretary 286-287
Mechanical Turks 256
Med-Tech Resource, Inc. 287
Med/Text Transcription 288
Med-Type 289
Medcomp, Inc...287
Medical coding schools 185-186
Medical transcription schools.................186
Medical Transcription Service.................287
Meditec.Com 185-186
Medifax, Inc..287
Medlink of Ohio 361
Medquist, Inc...288
Medscribe...288
Medware...289
Megahertz Corporation 171
Megatrends 56
Melaleuca, Inc. 324
Mellon Bank...171

The Memory Training Institute 324
Merion Publications, Inc. 209
Merrill Lynch 171
Metro Creative Graphics 209
Metropolitan Life Insurance Company 172
Metropolitan Research Associates, LLC 289
Metropolitan Water District of Southern
     California 172
Mia Gyzander Design 256
Micro-Reality Micro-Mile 128
Mike Feinberg Co. 145
Miles Kimball 145
Mindbuilder 234
Mini-Golf, Inc. 128-129
Minnesota Department of Human Resources ......
    234
Miracle Maid 324
Miracle Method 50-51
Mr. Electric 51
Mr. Plant 33-34
Modern Secretarial Service 289
Molly Maid, Inc. 56, 63
Monsanto Agricultural Group 172
Montgomery Ward & Company. Inc. 172
Moonstone Gallery 145
Moonwolf Enterprises 324
Mossy Creek Pottery 145-146
Mountain Ladies & Ewe, Inc. 256
Mountain West Processing 290
Moyer Paralegal Services 257
Mrecord 290
MTEC, Inc. 186
Mulberry Studio, Inc. 290
Multilink Incorporated 172
Murphy, Marianne 79
My Baby Shower Favors 362
My Essay 210
Naisbitt, John 56
Nanny Poppinz 101-102
National Electronic Billers 185
Naperville Fine Art Center & Gallery 146
Nation's Carelink 291
National Analysts 362
National Background Screening 257
National Detail Systems 15-16
National Home Builders Association 56
National Opinion Research Center (NORC) ....
    362-364
National Pro Clean Corporation 64
National Property Inspections 81
National Reading Styles Institute 235
National Remember Our Troops Campaign ..364
National Tax Training School 183
National Telecommuting Institute, Inc. 364
National Tenant Network, Inc. 82
Nationwide Carpet Brokers 51-52
Nationwide Insurance 291
Nature's Sunshine Products, Inc. 325
Near & Associates 325
Neo-Life Diamite Intl 326
Nerd Force 73
Net Transcripts 291
Network Reporting 291
Neutron Interactive 210
New 364
New York Institute of Photography 187

New York Life Insurance Company 172
Newsbank, Inc. 292
Nilles, Jack 161
Niteo Services, Inc. 365
Nobleworks 210
Noevir, Inc. 326
Nortel Networks 172-173
North American Co. For Life & Health Insurance ..
    292
North Carolina National Bank 173
Northern Illinois Medical Center 292
Northfield Arts Guild 146
Northwest Images 146
Northwestern Bell Information Technologies ..173
Northwestern University 235
Norwegian Cruise Line 292, 365
Novica Wholesale 146-147
NPD 235
NSA, Inc. 325
Nu-Art, Inc. 210
Novus 16
Oatmeal Studios 211
Octagon Center For The Arts 147
Office Details 257
Office Support 263-307
Offshore Data Entry 326
Olsten Health Care Services 365
Omegasonics 64
Omnilingua, Inc. 292
On World, Inc. 235
Oneil Research 365
The Online Gift Show 147
Onsite 293
Open2view.Com 113-114
Opinion Research Corporation 366
Opportunities In Computers 217-243
Opsol Integrators, Inc. 236
Opuzz Voice 257-258
Oracle Transcription, Inc. 293
Oriflame International 327
Orion International Consulting 366
Ortho Pharmaceutical Corporation 173
Orus Information Services 236
OSI Transcription 293
Our Wedding Vendors 327
Outdoor Connection 121, 123
Outsourcing Law 293-294
Overflow USA 366
Pacific Bell 153, 173-175
Pacview Inc. 236
Padgett Business Services 34
Palm Beach Specialty Coffee 129
Palm Coast Data 294
Pampered Chef 327
P & L Inflatables, Inc. 129
Paramount Home Beauty 91
Parker Interior Plantscape, Inc. 52
Party Digest 211
Party Personnel 91-92
Partylite Gifts 328
Patty-Cakes International, Inc. 129
PC Age IT Institute 184
The Peak Organization, Inc. 294
Peat, Marwick, Mitchell & Company 175
Pee Wee Workout 102

Penn Foster Career School 181-187
The Permanente Medical Group, Inc. 294-295
Personal services 83-84
Personal Touch Products, Inc. 130
Pet Butler 104, 106-108
Pet Services...104-109
Pet-Tenders 108
Peters Shorthand Reporting Corporation 295
Petra Fashions, Inc. 328
Pets Are Inn 108
Philbrick Transcriptions, Inc. 295
Phillips Publishing, Inc. 211
Phone Interviews 192-193
Photo and video services 109-115
Photography schools 187
Pioneer Staffing 258
Plan Ahead Events...34
PMA Franchise Systems.......................................35
Pola, U.S.A., Inc..328
Pomona Valley Hospital Medical Center.........295
Poopsie's 147
Pop-A-Lock..16-18
Port City Press, Inc. 236
Portal Publications 211
Posigrip 52
The Potter, Etc. 148
Powergy, Inc. 328
Prairie House 148
Pratt Systems 236-237
Pre-Fit Franchises, Inc. 102
Premier Transcription.......................................295
Pressed4time 92
Prevent Blindness Oklahoma 367
Prime Computer, Inc. 176
Primerica...328
Princess House, Inc...329
Prints & Patches 148
Priority Management Systems 35
Pro Staff..367
Probate.com 258
Procard International 329
Professional Carpet Systems 65
Profitable Hobbies 130
Proforma, Inc..36
Project HomeWork..3
Property improvement companies.............40-55
Proselect 367
Prosites, Inc..237
Proventure Business Group, Inc. 82
Public Service Company of New Mexico 176
Publishers Clearing House 237
Publishing services 115-120
Purosystems, Inc. 52-53
Purple Heart Service Foundation 367
Puttin' On The Dog 148
Puzzle Machine 130-131
QT Medical Services, Inc..................................295
Quality Logic 329
Queue, Inc. 237
Quick Practice 329
Quest Diagnostics 367-368
Quietbeauty Mobile Spa 92
The Quilt Racque 149
Qwest..176
R3X.NET, Inc...330

R&B Sten-Tel 296
Rapid Transcript, Inc..296
Radtke, Joanie...271
Readynurse Staffing Services 368
Realty Executives of Denver 368
Regalware, Inc. 330
Richmond Reporting...................................296-297
Real estate and financial services 75-83
Recruit Zone 258
Recruiters Professional Network 36
Red Farm Studio 211-212
Redmond 176
Referral Institute..36
Reliv Distributors 330
Remington International 237
Remote Backup Systems 73
Remy Corporation 368
Renaissance Executive Forums, Inc. 37
Renaissance Greeting Cards 212
Rent A Coder 238
Research Triangle Institute...............................368
Rescuecom 74
Research Participants Institute.........................259
Resource Spectrum 368-369
Résumés 191-192, 194
Rexair, Inc. 330
Right On Programs 238
Roberte Verifications 369
The Roper Organization 369
Rose Resnick Lighthouse 296
Roxbury Publishing Company 238
Ruth Golder Interviewing Service 369
Ruth Hornbein Sweaters...................................259
Safety Matters 93, 102
S.A.I. Staffing 369
SH3, Inc. 298
St. Martin's Press...213
Saladmaster, Inc..330
Salaries 1-2, 190
Sales Consultants of Bloomington, Inc...........370
Sales Opportunities 308-340
Samco 149
Sams Publishing...212
San Francisco Bay Guardian 212
San Francisco Chronicle 331
Sandler Systems 37
Sans Consulting Services, Inc. 297
Sassy South 149
Save It Now! 37
School Calendar..331
Screen Machine 53
Scribes Online 297
Secretary On Call 297
Secure Communication, Inc. 331
Seeking Sitters 93
Select Comfort Corporation 370
Select Transcription, Inc. 298
Service 800...370
Servicemaster 65
Servpro 66
Sessions Online School of Design....................183
Setka, Inc. 370-371
Seton Health 298
Seventeenth Colony House 149
Shaklee Corporation..331

Sherman Hospital 298
Shock PR 38
Show of Hands 150
Sierra Judgment Recovery 82
Signal Corporation 176
Silhouette Marketing 331-332
Sitters Unlimited 93, 102-103
Skylight Training and Publishing, Inc. 332
Small Biz Community.............................212
Smith, Blake 86-87
Smith Marketing Group 332
Smyth Fivenson Company 371
Snap-On Tools 18
SNET 176
Snowe, Olympia 4
Soft-Temps Worldwide............................74
Softpath System....................................371
Software Testing Services, Inc. 371
Sourcecorp, Inc. 298
Southern California Association of
    Governments 177
Southern Glove Mfg. Co., Inc...................259
Southern Living At Home......................332
Southern New England Telephone............177
Space Walk/Inflatable Zoo 131
Speak With A Geek 238
Speak-Write 299
Spectrum Unlimited 120
Spherion..238-239
Spheris eChart 282
Spins 333
Sportslife Enterprises, Inc......................131
Spring-Green Lawn Care 53
SPSS, Inc. 239
Staffcentrix 299
Staffing At Home, Inc. 371-372
Staging Diva......................................82
Stampin' Up!......................................333
Standard Data-Prep 239
Starscapes International 53
Starting a home-based business 191-195
Stat Transcription Services......................299
State of South Dakota 177
Statements Unlimited 150
Steamatic, Inc. 66
Sten-Tel 299
Stephens, Brandon 86-87
Stork News of America, Inc. 131-132
Strategic Resource Partners, Inc. 372
Stretch-N-Grow 103
Study Web 372
Success Motivation Institute, Inc.............333
Summit Health Care 372
Summit Views 334
Sun Microsystems Computer Corporation 177
Sunland International 334
Sunlark Research 260
Super Coups Cooperative Direct Mail 38
Super Mommies Fitness 94
Surface Doctor 53
Susi's Gallery For Children 150
SVI America Corporation 334
Swisher Hygiene 66-67
Swordsmith 239
Sylvan Learning Center.........................372

Systems Forward 16-17
Talent World Magazine 334
Talk2type Transcriptions, Inc. 299
Talk About Debt 213
Tandem Computers Incorporated............177
Tastefully Simple 335
Tattoo A Pet, Inc. 109
Taxes 6
Team Double Click 132, 300-301
Technical writing schools 187
Telecommuting 152-179
Teletech..373
Teletrans, Inc. 302
Temp agencies 217
Tempositions..373
Terra Nova Transcription 302
Thrifty Impressions 74
Thomas Edison State College ..182-183, 186-188
Thomas Transcription Services, Inc. 302
Thomson Polk Directories.......................35
The Thor Group 373
Tig First Source 239-240
Tigerfish...................................302-303
Time Answering 373
Time-Life Books 335
Time Plus, Inc. 38
Today.Com....................................213-214
Top Secret Science Corp. 103-104
Total Accessories 150
Total Nutrition Technology.......................94
Total Office, Inc. 303
Tour This Place 214
Transcend Services, Inc. 303
Transcription Solutions 303
Transcription, Technology, and Supporter............
   303-304
Travel services 121-123
Traveler's Life Insurance 178
Traveling Software 178
Tri-Chem, Inc......................................335
Trial Juries..260
Trinity Real Estate Solutions 214
Tupperware Home Parties 336
Turnroth Sign Company 214
Tyndale House Publishers, Inc. 336
Tyniec, Jack 164-165
U-Haul.......................................373-374
UC Berkeley Extension 214-215
Ultra Bond..18
Unco Industries, Inc. 132
Unimatrix International..........................240
Union Mutual Life Insurance Company.........178
Union Tribune 336
Unique Computer Inc. 374
Unique One 260
United Cerebral Palsy...........................374
United Data Network 261
United Press International 178
United Services Automobile Association 178
University of Phoenix.............................182
University of Washington 187
University of Wisconsin Hospitaland Clinic 179
Update Legal 304
USA Today 336
USA For Healthclaims, Inc. 39

US Career Institute 182, 185-186
US General Services Administration................179
Usborne Books At Home 336-337
Use-What-You-Have Interiors 53
User Testing 240
Vacations 6-7
Validated Response 374
Vector Art 215
Vendx 133
Verdicts.Com 304
Verna Medical Transcriptions 305
Veterans' Rehabilitation Center 375
Victory Productions 215
Video Home Tours 215-216
Video Monitoring Service............................305
Videomasters 114
Village Weavers 150-151
VIPDesk 375
Virtuo Group 241
Virtuserve 375
Visda Enterprises, Inc.................................241
Visiting Angels 94
Visiting Nurse Association 375
The Visual Image, Inc. 109, 114
Vita Craft Corporation 337
Vitac 305
Vital Signing 261
V-Staffing..240-241
VT Audit..261
Warner Press, Inc......................................216
WSI Internet...75
Water Resources International, Inc..................337
Watkins Incorporated.................................337
Waverly Press, Inc......................................241-242
Way With Words 305
WCNET 337
WCities...216
Web-Erectors..242
Web site design/webmaster schools 188

Web Tracer...261-262
WebMd..216
Webmedx 305-306
Wedding Solutions.......................................337-338
Weed Man..54
Welcome Wagon...338
Wendy Gordon Glass Studio, Inc., & Craft Gallery
....151
Wendy's International, Inc..............................179
The West Bend Co. 338
West Corporation 376
Weyerhauser Company 179
Wheelchair Getaways, Inc...........................121, 123
Wholesale Crafts, Inc. 151
Window Gang...67
Wirth Business Credit 39
Woodstock Gallery, Inc. 151
Word Processing Unlimited 306
Wordmasters 306
Wordnet 306
Words4nerds 216
Wordsmart 306-307
Wordtronics Direct Mail Service Bureau 307
Work space 7-9
Workshops of Gerald E. Henn 338
Working Solutions.......................................376
Working with people 341-377
Worldwide Express 39
Write On Results...262
X-Rite, Inc..339
York Graphics Services, Inc.........................242-243
Xact Telesolutions.......................................376
Yellow Freight Systems, Inc...........................339
Yvette Fry 151
Zaio.com 83, 114-115
Zap Jury 262
Zauder Brothers, Inc....................................262
Zondervan Book of Life 339-340
Zoning ordinances 5, 190

State and Country

Alabama

Artisans Gallery 136
Infinity Insurance Company 320
Patty-Cakes International, Inc. 129
Southern Living At Home..............................332

Alaska

Computer Medics of America 69

Arizona

Anasazi, Inc. 156
Apollo Group, Inc. 156
Arizona, Department of Administration 157
ATC Healthcare Services, Inc.........................346
Auralog..346
Beautyway 200
Bell South 159
Best Western Hotels International 159
Biltmore Franchise Consulting 24
Candy Bouquet...85
Carondelet Health Network, St. Mary's Hospital ..
....273

Catalina In-Home Services 348
Fiesta Cartoon Maps....................................118
H/P Technologies, Inc. 355
International Mergers and Acquisitions 81
Kersten Studios 208
Leisure Arts, Inc. 255
Maintenance Made Simple 50
The Potter, Etc. 148
Speak With A Geek 238
Starscapes International 53
Teletrans, Inc..302
U-Haul..373-374
Water Resources International, Inc...................337

California

Act 1 Technical 218
Ad-Ex Worldwide 267-268
Adele's II, Inc. 197
AIS Market Research....................................344
Allergan, Inc. 155
Allied Interpreting & Translating Service 269
Alpha Presentations 219

Amcal 197-198
American Institutes For Research 155
American Leak Detection 56
American Mobile Sound 124
American Red Cross 344
Apple Computer, Inc. 156
Art & Logic 220
Arthritis Foundation 346
Artizen, Inc. 220-221
AT&T 157
Aussie Pet Mobile 104
Auto Appraisal Network 12
Avante Window Fashions 41
Banks, Bentley & Cross 24
Banctec 157
Bentley House 200-201
Berlitz Translation Service 272
Cal-Bay Systems, Inc. 223
California Council For The Blind 347
The California Institute of Integral Studies 202
California State Department of General Services 160
Casepost Inc. 313
Certified Translation Bureau, Inc. 274
Charmelle, Inc. 313
Christmas Concepts 86
Chronicle Transcripts, Inc. 274
Claim Net, Inc. 274-275
Clarity Consultants 224
(The) Client Touch/Cardsenders 26-27
Collage Gallery 139
Concept Now Cosmetics 313
Concerto Networks 70
Concierge At Large, Inc. 248-249
Cozy Places 314
CPR Technologies Transcription Service 276
Cybertary 29
The Dale Group 60
Debt Zero 77
Deventure Health Partners 277
Discovery Toys, Inc. 315
Duarte Design, Inc. 227
Ectone, Inc. 228
EDiX Corporation 279
El Camino Memorial Park 352
eToys 140-141
Excellence Translation Service 280
Facts 'N Figures 353
Fetch! Pet Care, Inc. 106
Fitzgerald's 13
Futurenet Technologies Corp. 281
Futuro Infantil Hispano 353
General Telephone 166
Global Language Services 281
Globespan Medical, Inc. 281
Green and Christmas Concepts 31
GTE 167
Gupta Technologies 318
Handpiece Express 126
Harcourt Brace & Co. 207
Hayes Handpiece 126
Hayes Marketing Research 354
Herbalife International 319
Hewlett Packard Laboratories 167
Hireright, Inc. 355

Home Staging Resource 77
Home Tutoring 100
Hospice of San Francisco 355
Human Resources Professional Group (HRPG) 356
IMS Technology Telesales 320
Industrial Indemnity Insurance 169
Information Access Company 169
Inlingua Translation Service 283
Inneractive Inc. 90
Integrity Staffing 356
The Interface Group Ltd. 80
International Translation Bureau 284
Intuit 169
Jafra Cosmetics, Inc. 321
Jet Propulsion Laboratory 170
K-C Products 255
Kaiser Permanente Medical Group 284
Keller's Medical Transcription Service 284
Kenneth Olson & Associates 326-327
Kott Koatings 49
Langenwalter Industries, Inc. 49-50
Laykin 232
Living Earth Crafts 256
Los Angeles County 170
Los Angeles Marketing Research Associates 361
Management Recruiters of Sacramento 323-324
McDonald Douglas 171
MDM International Multi Media 109, 113
Metropolitan Water District of Southern California 172
Mia Gyzander Design 256
Mr. Plant 33-34
Modern Secretarial Service 289
Moonstone Gallery 145
National Detail Systems 15-16
Neo-Life Diamite Intl 326
Noevir, Inc. 326
Novica Wholesale 146-147
Omegasonics 64
On World, Inc. 235
Opsol Integrators, Inc. 236
Pacific Bell 153, 173-175
Pacview Inc. 236
Paramount Home Beauty 91
The Permanente Medical Group, Inc. 294-295
Personal Touch Products, Inc. 130
Pet-Tenders 108
Peters Shorthand Reporting Corporation 295
Pola, U.S.A., Inc. 328
Pomona Valley Hospital Medical Center 295
Portal Publications 211
Pratt Systems 236-237
Prosites, Inc. 237
Quietbeauty Mobile Spa 92
Rapid Transcript, Inc. 296
Remington International 237
Renaissance Executive Forums, Inc. 37
Rose Resnick Lighthouse 296
San Francisco Bay Guardian 212
San Francisco Chronicle 331
Screen Machine 53
Setka, Inc. 370-371
Shaklee Corporation 331
Sitters Unlimited 93, 102-103
Smith Marketing Group 332

Southern California Association of
   Governments 177
Spectrum Unlimited 120
Spins 333
Staffing At Home, Inc. 371-372
Stat Transcription Services..........................299
Strategic Resource Partners, Inc. 372
Summit Views 334
Sun Microsystems Computer Corporation 177
Sunland International 334
Talk2type Transcriptions, Inc. 299
Tandem Computers Incorporated..............177
Tempositions 373
The Thor Group 373
3Com Corporation 177
Union Tribune 336
United Cerebral Palsy..................................374
User Testing 240
Verna Medical Transcriptions 305
Video Monitoring Service............................305
Visda Enterprises, Inc...................................241
WCities...216
Wedding Solutions.................................337-338

Colorado
10 TIL 2...21
Allabout Honeymoons 121
Alpine Access 344
Alternative Board.......................................22-23
At-Home Professions...................23, 186, 270-271
Bark Busters 105
Cambridge Sales 138
Chipita Accessories......................................248
Client Connection, Inc...................................28
Colorado Department of Personnel 161
Colorado National Bank 162
Create-A-Book, Inc..................................117-118
Crestcom, Int'l, Inc......................................28-29, 314
Denver, City and County 163
Disabled American Veterans of Colorado........351
Disability Associates 77
Dr. Glass 60
Ft. Collins...165
Glass Technology, Inc......................................13
Homewatch International, Inc. 90
Le Gourmet Gift Basket, Inc. 127
Mike Feinberg Co. 145
Miracle Method 50-51
National Pro Clean Corporation 64
Orus Information Services 236
Qwest..176
Realty Executives of Denver 368
Remy Corporation...368
Show of Hands 150
Sourcecorp, Inc...298
Surface Doctor 53
Sylvan Learning Center 372
Ultra Bond...18

Connecticut
Aetna Life & Casualty 154
BCC, Inc..200
Business Communications Company, Inc.222-223
Clerical Plus 275
Commonwealth Transcription Systems 275

Connecticut Children's Medical Center............349
Curtis 1000..162
Decor & You, Inc...45
DS Sewing, Inc..227
Eastern Connecticut Health Network, Inc. 278-279
Entrepreneur's Source 29-30
Gallery/Shop at Wesleyan Potters 142
Grolier Incorporated....................................318
Hartford Insurance Group 167
Homequity, Inc...168
Image Works 230
Little Scientists 101
Luanne Glazer Associates, Inc. 361
The Memory Training Institute....................324
Newsbank, Inc..292
Philbrick Transcriptions, Inc. 295
Queue, Inc...237
SNET 176
Southern New England Telephone................177
Swordsmith 239
Traveler's Life Insurance 178
V-Staffing 240-241

District of Columbia
A Briggs Passport & Visa Expeditors................343
Ability Group..218
Alderson Reporting 268
Amtrak..156
Blue Cross/Blue Shield 153, 159, 222
Corpimages.Net...226
Geico Direct..166
Home & Grounds...319
Leaplaw 285
Library of Congress 285-286
United Press International 178
US General Services Administration................179

Delaware
Delaware Center For The Contemporary Arts 140
Especial Day..140
Grassroots Handcrafts 142
Intellistream Technologies, Inc. 231
Ruth Golder Interviewing Service 369

Florida
A Stat Transcription 264
Accutranz Medical Transcription Services, Inc.......
  266-267
American Entertainment Distributors 109-110
American Institute...23
American Transcription Solutions, Inc. 269
Appearance Plus, Inc......................................11
Arise 220
Arise Virtual Solutions 345
Artworx Software Company 221
Autoplus Window Stickers 12
Call Depot..312
Capital Data 224
Ceiltech 58
CFO Today 27-28
Color-Crown Corporation 43
Concrete Technology, Inc...............................43
Corless & Associates.....................................276
Coverall Cleaning Concept 59-60
Cruise Planners...121

Cruiseone 122
Cruises Inc. 122-123
Eric Anthony Creations 251
Expense Reduction Consulting, Inc. 30
Filtafry 31
Foliage Design Systems...........................47
Hirecheck 282
Home Fixology 47
Homes & Land Publishing Corp. 119
I9 Sports 127
Idea Vision 48
Ident-A-Kid Services of America, Inc....111-112
Iistek Corp 230
Interim Healthcare 357
J. Lodge 358
Kinderdance International, Inc. 100
Magic Rice, Inc. 127-128
Medscribe...288
Medware..289
Norwegian Cruise Line...................292, 365
Palm Beach Specialty Coffee 129
Palm Coast Data....................................294
Plan Ahead Events 34
Posigrip 52
Probate.com 258
Purosystems, Inc. 52-53
QT Medical Services, Inc.......................295
Readynurse Staffing Services 368
Soft-Temps Worldwide.............................74
Stretch-N-Grow 103
Summit Health Care 372
Tattoo A Pet, Inc. 109
Thomas Edison State College ..182-183, 186-188
Tupperware Home Parties 336
Wordmasters...306

Georgia

AIS Media, Inc. 68
Aloette Cosmetics 124, 309
American Glove Co. Inc...........................245
Athens Regional Health Services.........270
Birthflowers.Com...............................41-42
Blind Doctors Training Academy 57
Computer Secretary 275
Computer Troubleshooters 69
Custom Home Food Service 350
Dragon Pencil 205
Eagleshotz 110
Federal Reserve Bank............................165
Floor Coverings International 46
Georgia Power 166-167
Itxtend 321
Jackson Associates 358
Lanier Business Products, Inc 170
Loma 209
Maid Brigade 62
Maid Services of America 62-63
Maxim Healthcare Services 361
Med-Tech Resource, Inc. 287
Nationwide Carpet Brokers 51-52
OSI Transcription 293
Padgett Business Services 34
PMA Franchise Systems............................35
Proselect 367
Puttin' On The Dog 148

Sassy South 149
Sierra Judgment Recovery 82
Softpath System.....................................371
Time Plus, Inc. 38
Total Accessories 150
Transcend Services, Inc.........................303
Webmedx 305-306

Idaho

Coldwater Creek Home, ...139
Gumball Gourmet 125-126
Heaven's Best Carpet & Upholstery Cleaning........
....60-61
Idaho Statesman 320
Melaleuca, Inc. 324
Thrifty Impressions 74
Vendx 133

Illinois

AAA Chicago 342-343
Action Translation & Interpretation Bureau....267
Advance Language Studios.....................268
Allstate Insurance Company 155
Ameritech Corporation 155
Arthur Andersen & Company 157
Artistic Impressions, Inc.................310-311
Arts & Artisans, Ltd................................137
Blessing Hospital 272
Bradford Exchange 202
Car-Lene Research..................................348
Chicago Knitting Mills 248
Cosmopolitan Translation Bureau, Inc. 276
Creative Colors International, Inc. 44
EEG Recruiting.................................250-251
Electronic Search, Inc 352
Elmhurst Memorial Healthcare..............279
Enesco Imports Corporation 206
First National Bank of Chicago 165
Franzen Enterprises 141
Harris Trust and Savings Bank, ...167
Highland Park Hospital 282
Household International..........................168
Illinois Amvets..356
Illinois Hospital Joint Ventures 283
International Language & Communications
                    Centers, Inc...........283-284
Lenco Electronic, Inc. 170
Liquid Resins International 14-15
Macke Water Systems, Inc. 322
Medifax, Inc..287
Mindbuilder...234
Naperville Fine Art Center & Gallery 146
National Opinion Research Center (NORC) ....
....362-364
Niteo Services, Inc.................................365
North American Co. For Life & Health Insurance..
....292
Northern Illinois Medical Center 292
Northwestern University.........................235
Nu-Art, Inc. 210
P & L Inflatables, Inc. 129
Pampered Chef..327
Poopsie's 147
Prairie House 148
Pre-Fit Franchises, Inc. 102
Safety Matters 93, 102

Sales Consultants of Bloomington, Inc. 370
Samco 149
Sherman Hospital 298
Skylight Training and Publishing, Inc. 332
Spring-Green Lawn Care 53
SPSS, Inc. 239
Thomson Polk Directories 35
Turnroth Sign Company 214
Tyndale House Publishers, Inc. 336
Video Home Tours 215-216
Woodstock Gallery, Inc. 151

Indiana
Accutran 266
Amvets 345
CEO Focus 27
Compuchild USA 68-69
Covered Bridge Girl Scout Council 350
Encouragym Active Learning Programs 97
Home Video Studio, Inc. 109, 111
Joe Cochran Agency 358
Lafayette Venetian Blind 170
Save It Now! 37
Warner Press, Inc. 216

Iowa
Argonaut Press 199
Buylink Corporation 138
Carlisle Communications 224
Dion Data Solutions 277
Micro-Reality Micro-Mile 128
Octagon Center For The Arts 147
Omnilingua, Inc. 292
Transcription Solutions 303

Kansas
Accupro Services 265-266
Outdoor Connection 121, 123
Party Personnel 91-92
Procard International 329
Vita Craft Corporation 337

Kentucky
Brown Williamson Tobacco Company 160
Cost Containment Solutions, Inc. 28, 76
Visiting Nurse Association 375
Wheelchair Getaways, Inc. 121, 123

Louisiana
Dura-Oak Cabinet Refacing Products 46
Gym Rompers 97
Pop-A-Lock 16-18

Maine
Blueberry Woolens 246
Coffee News USA 115-117
H.O.M.E., Inc. 142-143
J. Weston Walch 242
Renaissance Greeting Cards 212
Union Mutual Life Insurance Company 178
Unique One 260

Maryland
24 Hour Secretary 304
A Card-In-The-Yard 84
Baltimore Evening Sun 157

CareOne, Inc. 348
Chesapeake Bay Magazine 203
Circle Graphics, Inc. 224
Cleannet USA 59
Clutterbusters 87
Decorating Den 45
DLM Business Solutions 277
DWH Office Services 278
Gateway Technical Services 229
Health Administration Systems, Inc. 318
Johns Hopkins Health Care, LCC 359
Letter Perfect Word Processing Center 232
Maryland State Government 233-234
Moonwolf Enterprises 324
Oracle Transcription, Inc. 293
Phillips Publishing, Inc. 211
Port City Press, Inc. 236
Primerica 328
Sandler Systems 37
Smyth Fivenson Company 371
Waverly Press, Inc. 241-242
Wendy Gordon Glass Studio, Inc., & Craft Gallery
151
Word Processing Unlimited 306
Write On Results 262

Massachusetts
Advanced Automation Associates 218
Appingo 198
Arthur D. Little, Inc. 157
Barry Manufacturing Company, Inc. 245
Batterymarch Financial Management Company
158
Brass Smith House 138
Country Curtains, Inc. 249
Dainty Maid Waitress Aprons Company 250
Decorated Products Company 162
Digital Equipment Corporation 163
Disciple's Directory, Inc. 118
Domenichelli Business Services 278
Eliza J 125
Eziba 141
Finelle Cosmetics 317
The Homesteader 120
John Hancock Mutual Life Insurance Co. 283
Jurytest Networks 254-255
Locationlube 15
Mulberry Studio, Inc. 290
Multilink Incorporated 172
National Telecommuting Institute, Inc. 364
Partylite Gifts 328
Petra Fashions, Inc. 328
Pressed4time 92
Prime Computer, Inc. 176
Princess House, Inc. 329
Proventure Business Group, Inc. 82
Referral Institute 36
Shock PR 38
Super Coups Cooperative Direct Mail 38
Susi's Gallery For Children 150
Top Secret Science Corp. 103-104
Wordnet 306

Michigan
Bizarre Promotions, Inc. 312
Critter Control, Inc. 44-45, 105

Detroit Free Press 163
The Good Nature Co., Inc. 317
Janitize America, Inc. 61
Molly Maid, Inc. 56, 63
R3X.NET, Inc. 330
Rexair, Inc. 330
S.A.I. Staffing 369
X-Rite, Inc 339
Zondervan Book of Life 339-340

Minnesota
ADC Telecommunications, Inc. 154
Aria Communications 245
Creative Memories 314
Davlins 140
Grave Groomers 88-89
Honeywell, Inc. 168
Jet-Black Sealcoating & Repair 48
Kah-Nee-Tah Gallery...........................143
Kinship...360
McGruff Safe Kids 101
Minnesota Department of Human Resources ......
....234
Nation's Carelink 291
Northfield Arts Guild 146
Novus 16
Pets Are Inn 108
Select Comfort Corporation 370
Select Transcription, Inc. 298
Service 800, 370
Tastefully Simple 335
Time Answering 373
Watkins Incorporated..........................337
Wirth Business Credit 39

Mississippi
United Data Network 261

Missouri
ARO Outsourcing................................345
Consumer Opinion Search, Inc. 349
Crack Team, The 44
Dr. Vinyl & Associates, Ltd....................46
E-Backups 70
eShipping 30
Lake Regional Health System 285
Mary Lucas Market Research...............361
Monsanto Agricultural Group..............172
Reliv Distributors 330
SH3, Inc...298
VT Audit...261

Montana
Mountain West Processing....................290
Speak-Write 299

Nebraska
Complete Music, Inc. 124-125
Hunting Lease Network..........................80
The Maids International...........................62
National Property Inspections 81
Northwestern Bell Information Technologies ......
....173
West Corporation 376

New Hampshire
Echo Management Group 228
Kenda Systems, Inc. ....
....359-360
Recruiters Professional Network 36
Transcription, Technology, and Supporter.............
....303-304

New Jersey
Accu-Doc 265
Air Brook Limousine 22
All Type, Inc. 268-269
Andrews Glass Company, Inc................
....156
Artique, Inc. 136
Bell Communications 158
Beneficial Corporation.........................159
Bronner Manufacturing and Tool Company ..160
Camares Communications, Inc. 202-203
Caremore In-Home Service 348
Carpet Network 42
Chatas Glass Company 161
Concurrent Technologies 225
Cyberedit 249-250
D. J. Ardore, Inc. 314-315
Display Connection, Inc. 205
Electric Mobility Corporation 316
Equitable Life Assurance 163-165
Gallup Poll 353
Housemaster of America, Inc. 78-79
HR Advice 253
Intrep Sales Partners 284
Lawn Doctor 50
Lift, Inc...233
Marty Wasserberg & Associates ...144-145
Matrix Technology Group....................323
My Baby Shower Favors 362
Nobleworks 210
Opinion Research Corporation............366
Ortho Pharmaceutical Corporation 173
Parker Interior Plantscape, Inc. 52
Software Testing Services, Inc. 371
Tri-Chem, Inc..335
USA For Healthclaims, Inc. 39
WebMd 216

New Mexico
Aegin Place..84
Business Graphics 223
Gallery of The Sandias 142
Public Service Company of New Mexico 176

Nevada
Action International 22
Comstock Cards, Inc.............................204
The Dentist's Choice 125
Faces N Cups, Inc 110
Friendly Computers...............................71
Glass Mechanix, Inc. 13
Hi-Tech Industries 14
Marty Wolf Game Company 128
Open2view.Com 113-114

New York
Accuwrite Word Processing Service 267

Actor's Garage 95
Alcas Cutlery Corporation 309
All Purpose Typing Service......................268
All-Language Services, Inc......................269
Ambrosia Software 197
American Barter Exchange, Inc...............309
American Express Bank, Ltd..............219-220
American Express Travel Related Services
    Company, Inc. 155
American Greeting Corporation 198
American Institute of Physics 198
AMF Bowling Products Group, Inc. 156
Avita, Inc..137
Bankers Trust Company............................158
Barbara Schwartz Accessories 137
Bi-Tech Enterprises, Inc.............................221
Blue Ridge Tea and Herb Ltd. 272
Blue Zebra USA..312
Bon Temps 273
Boyd Printing Company, Inc. 222
Bristol-Myers Squibb Company 160
Brooklyn Women's Exchange, Inc. 138
Business Edge...312
Certified Marketing Services, Inc. 349
Citibank..161
CMP Publications................................203-204
Companion Connection Senior Care 85
Continental Translation Service, Inc.........276
CPS Medtext...277
Craig Communications 204
Dynax Resources, Inc.................................227
Eastern Mail & Data Processing, Inc. 278
Eastman Kodak Company 163
Eden Staffing...351
Empire Business Brokers, Inc.....................29
ETR Technology Center....................352-353
Everett Studios, Inc....................................206
Executive Office Services 280
Federation of the Handicapped 228, 280
Hart Systems, Inc.......................................282
Harvey Research Organization, Inc. 354
Holt, Rinehart, & Winston 168
Home Remedies......................................47-48
The H.W. Wilson Company 168
International Business Machine (IBM) 168
Intercontinental Greetings, Ltd. 208
ISC Consultants, Inc..................................231
J.C. Penney Company, Inc. 175
J&R Field Services, Inc...............................358
John Wiley & Sons, Inc.............................242
Lillian Vernon Corporation.......................209
Louis Harris and Associates 361
MacArthur Associates 233
Marine Midland Bank................................170
Marion J. Rosley Secretarial Services 297
Mechanical Secretary 286-287
Megahertz Corporation 171
Merrill Lynch 171
Metro Creative Graphics 209
Metropolitan Life Insurance Company 172
Metropolitan Research Associates, LLC 289
National Reading Styles Institute 235
Nerd Force 73
New York Life Insurance Company 172
NPD 235

Outsourcing Law.............................293-294
Overflow USA 366
The Peak Organization, Inc. 294
Peat, Marwick, Mitchell & Company 175
Publishers Clearing House 237
Quick Practice 329
Rescue.com 74
Richmond Reporting.........................296-297
Right On Programs 238
The Roper Organization 369
Ruth Hornbein Sweaters...........................259
St. Martin's Press 213
Secure Communication, Inc. 331
Seton Health 298
Standard Data-Prep 239
Talent World Magazine 334
Unique Computer Inc. 374
Use-What-You-Have Interiors 53
Vector Art 215
Wordsmart 306-307
Wordtronics Direct Mail Service Bureau 307
Yvette Fry 151
Zauder Brothers, Inc.................................262

North Carolina

American Elite Homes, Inc. 76
Dignus 227
Doncaster 315
Dudley Products and Publications 316
Employee Benefit Services, Inc. 279
High Touch High Tech 98
Kindermusik International 101
Mrecord..290
Near & Associates 325
Nortel Networks 172-173
North Carolina National Bank...............173
Oriflame International 327
Orion International Consulting 366
Professional Carpet Systems 65
Research Triangle Institute.......................368
Southern Glove Mfg. Co., Inc...................259
Stork News of America, Inc. 131-132
SVI America Corporation 334
Swisher Hygiene 66-67
Total Nutrition Technology.......................94
Window Gang 67

Ohio

All Star Personnel, Inc. 344
Alltel Publishing 219
American Crafts Gallery 135
Butler Learning Systems 25
Cambridge Home Healthcare...................347
Carlton Cards..203
Comfort Keepers 85
Computerease 225
eYardsale.com 30
Fashion Two Twenty, Inc............................316
Fletcher Consolidated, Inc.........................317
Gerbig, Snell, & Weisheimer 207
Grocery Lady 89
The Growth Coach......................................32
The Hometeam Inspection Service, Inc. 78
Imedx 283
Intrep, Inc. 320-321

J. Marco Galleries 143
June Wedding, Inc. 91
The Kirby Corporation 321
Longaberger Marketing, Inc. 322
Love of Country 144
Matco Tools 15
Medical Transcription Service 287
Medlink of Ohio 361
Moyer Paralegal Services 257
National Background Screening 257
Nationwide Insurance, ...291
Pee Wee Workout 102
Premier Transcription 295
Proforma, Inc. 36
Total Office, Inc. 303
Wendy's International, Inc. 179
Wholesale Crafts, Inc. 151
Workshops of Gerald E. Henn 338

Oklahoma
Buckboard Antiques 201
Prevent Blindness Oklahoma 367
Seeking Sitters 93
Usborne Books At Home 336-337

Oregon
Cup of Comfort 205
Detail Plus 13
Dry Cleaning To-Your-Door 88
Glas-Weld Systems 14
Just the Fax 71-73
KC Distance Learning 359
Loose Ends 144
Maverick Publications 234
Mossy Creek Pottery 145-146
National Tenant Network, Inc. 82
Silhouette Marketing 331-332

Pennsylvania
Abelson Legal Search 264-265
Accu-Find 309
Air Products & Chemicals, Inc. 155
The Apple Tree 136
Axion Data Services 272
Beauty By Spector 311
Bellatlantic 158
Bookminders, Inc. 159
Chips Away 12
Cigna Corporation 161
Devon Consulting 350
Freedom Greeting Card Company 207
French Creek Sheep & Wool Company, Inc. ..252
Friends Life Care At Home, Inc. 317
Griswold Special Care 89
Guard Insurance Group 281-282
Ikon Office Solutions 208
Intracorp 231
Kustom Cards International, Inc. 33
Mellon Bank 171
Merion Publications, Inc. 209
Mini-Golf, Inc. 128-129
National Analysts 362
The Quilt Racque 149
Scribes Online 297
Visiting Angels 94
Yellow Freight Systems, Inc. 339

Rhode Island
Herff Jones 207-208
Powergy, Inc. 328
Red Farm Studio 211-212

South Carolina
Accutrak Inventory Specialists 21-22
Jan-Pro 61-62
Little Black Book For Every Busy Woman 33

South Dakota
Expetec Technology Services 70
Kitchen Tune-Up, Inc. 49
State of South Dakota 177

Tennessee
Amerispec Home Inspection Service 76
At-Heel Learning Centers 104
DTS America, Inc. 278
eTransplus 279
Lil'Angels 112-113
Lucky Heart Cosmetics, Inc. 322
Med-Type 289
NSA, Inc. 325
Remote Backup Systems 73
School Calendar 331
Servicemaster 65
The Visual Image, Inc. 109, 114
Welcome Wagon 338

Texas
Accu-Rate 21
Adept Word Management 267
American Thrift Store 344
Beauticontrol, Inc. 311
Christmas Décor 86-87
CM IT Solutions 68
Computer Explorers 96
Computer Solutions 225
Computertots 96
Dafa Sales 140
DRG Texas 250
eJury 251
Electrolux Corp. 316
Elite Software Development, Inc. 228
Entrees On Trays, Inc. 88
Generation Z 51
Healthcare Recruiters International 253
Home Interiors & Gifts, Inc. 319-320
Interquest Detection Canines 32
Jani-King International, Inc. 61
Leadership Management, Inc. 33
Mary Kay Cosmetics, Inc. 323
Mr. Electric 51
Nanny Poppinz 101-102
Pet Butler 104, 106-108
Research Participants Institute 259
Resource Spectrum 368-369
Saladmaster, Inc. 330
Secretary On Call 297
Servpro 66
Steamatic, Inc. 66
Success Motivation Institute, Inc. 333
Super Mommies Fitness 94
Tig First Source 239-240

Trinity Real Estate Solutions 214
United Services Automobile Association 178
Village Weavers 150-151
Working Solutions...376
Worldwide Express 39

Utah
ACD Direct 343
Arbonne International, Inc. 310
Artworks Park City...137
Bathcrest 42
Bearcom Building Services.............................57-58
Chem-Dry Carpet, Drapery and Upholstery
      Cleaning 58
Disabled American Veterans 350
Inxpress 32
Kitchen-A-Fair 321-322
Nature's Sunshine Products, Inc. 325
Profitable Hobbies 130
Stampin' Up! 333

Vermont
Kennedy Brothers Marketplace 144
Mountain Ladies & Ewe, Inc. 256
Prints & Patches 148

Virginia
Admission Consultants, Inc.................................244
Archadeck...40
Bookkeeping Express 25
Central Data Processing...............................273-274
Cintas Corporation 313
Coghill Composition Company.................224-225
The Compucare Company 162
Doody Calls...104, 106
Drama Kids Int'l, Inc. 96-97
Gannett...166
Garrett Transcription Service............................281
Geeks On Call America 67-68, 71
Languages Unlimited..285
Medcomp, Inc...287
Signal Corporation 176
Spheris eChart 282
Sportslife Enterprises, Inc....................................131
Time-Life Books 335
Unimatrix International...240
Videomasters 114
VIPDesk 375

Washington
Airbag Technology, Inc. 11
Analog One 245
Aquaricon 270
Bingo Bugle 115-116
Carnegie Art Center 139
Children's Hospital 274
Clean & Happy Windows 43, 59
Creative Photo Concepts 110
Everett Clinic 280
Good Samaritan Community Healthcare 354
Green Lake Chiropractic 318
Highline Community Hospital 355
International Homes of Cedar, Inc. 80
Lindal Cedar Homes, Inc......................................81
Lon Waltenberger Training Services 54

Med/Text Transcription 288
Miracle Maid 324
Northwest Images..146
Redmond 176
Space Walk/Inflatable Zoo 131
Traveling Software 178
Veterans' Rehabilitation Center 375
Way With Words 305
Weyerhauser Company 179

West Virginia
Borg-Warner Chemical Company 160
GE Plastics 166

Wisconsin
Accustat, Inc. 266
Amsoil, Inc. 11
Art & Soul, Inc...310
Berlin Gloves Co. 246
Birds & Blooms 201
Impressions, Inc. 230-231
Kitchen Solvers 48-49
Mason Shoe Manufacturing Company 323
Miles Kimball..145
Regalware, Inc. 330
Snap-On Tools 18
Team Double Click 132, 300-301
Unco Industries, Inc. 132
University of Wisconsin Hospital and Clinic ..179

Australia
Desktop Author 315

Canada
Bevinco Bar Systems Ltd. 24
Business Round Table..25
Canadian Diabetes Association 347
Children's Technology Workshop........................95
Fibrenew 13
Gavel & Gown Software, Inc. 354
Graffitti Graphics 119
Hawkeye's Home Sitters 89
Ho Math & Chess Learning Centre 98-99
Luksa Industries, Inc..113
Priority Management Systems 35
Puzzle Machine 130-131
Staging Diva 82
Terra Nova Transcription.....................................302
Weed Man..54
Words4nerds 216
WSI Internet 75
Zaio.com 83, 114-115

India
Offshore Data Entry 326

Japan
Editfast..206

Spain
Ispeakuspeak...357

Puerto Rico
Galeria El Dorado...141